THE ESSENTIAL
WYNDHAM
LEWIS

AN INTRODUCTION TO HIS WORK

Also by Julian Symons

Biography and Autobiography

A. J. A. Symons, His Life and Speculations
Charles Dickens
Thomas Carlyle: The Life and Ideas of a Prophet
Horatio Bottomley
Notes From Another Country
The Tell-Tale Heart: the Life and Works of Edgar Allan Poe

Poetry

Confusions about X
The Second Man
The Object of an Affair

Social and Military History

The General Strike
Buller's Campaign
England's Pride: the Story of the Gordon Relief Expedition

Literature and Criticism

The Thirties: A Dream Revolved
Critical Occasions
Bloody Murder: From the Detective Story to the Crime Novel
Critical Observations
Makers of the New: The Revolution in Literature 1912-1939

and many crime novels

THE ESSENTIAL
WYNDHAM
LEWIS

AN INTRODUCTION TO HIS WORK

EDITED BY
JULIAN SYMONS

ANDRE DEUTSCH

First published in 1989 by
André Deutsch Limited
105-106 Great Russell Street
London WC1B 3LJ

ISBN 0 233 98376 7

Phototypeset by Falcon Graphic Art Ltd.
Wallington, Surrey
Printed in Great Britain by
Ebenezer Baylis and Son Limited, Worcester

For C.J. Fox
most genial of Lewisites

CONTENTS

INTRODUCTION

i The Attitude of Genius

You walked down a white-tiled passage, rather like the entrance to a public lavatory, rang a bell. The man who opened the door was tall and bulky, the face broad and white, the brown eyes mild beneath an artist's big black hat. This was Wyndham Lewis as I saw him in his Notting Hill Gate studio half a century ago, a man in his middle fifties, his movements slow, voice catarrhal and gentle except when touched by enthusiasm or anger, manner polite but enquiring. He agreed readily to co-operate with the production of a special number dealing with his work in the little magazine I ran, and after it had appeared I saw him frequently in the months before the War, less often when he had returned to England from Canada and the United States in the late Forties.

What makes one feel in the presence of genius, rather than of intelligence and ordinary talent? I can vouch for the feeling but not explain it, any more than could the novelist and critic Walter Allen when he said Lewis was one of the two or three geniuses he had met, and discerned a tragic dimension in him missing from Auden; or T.S. Eliot, who said he had never really known Lewis the man, but also called him the most fascinating personality of his time. The testimonials could be multiplied, some of them coming from those who neither liked Lewis nor greatly admired him as writer and visual artist, but still felt themselves in the presence of an extraordinary, perhaps inimical, force when in his company.

Yet the company was agreeable, the reverse of pretentious, genial and not at all forbidding. Feet up, glass of whisky in hand, he would express unbuttoned views about other writers and artists past and present, and encourage one to do the same. Geoffrey Grigson remembered that at their first meeting, in an ABC teashop, Lewis asked across the tea and

1

buns what he knew about Goya, Gogol, Conrad, and whether he admired Virginia Woolf. With me it was Kafka, the pre-Raphaelites, Ruskin and Carlyle. Others could tell the same story, with different names. He had no ordinary small talk, but a great appetite for cultural gossip. Fed bits of such gossip, he would create verbal fantasies about the behaviour of current literary figures often wildly funny, and sometimes so far outside the bounds of their possible behaviour as to have a surreal absurdity. These visions of the impossible were generally too caricatural to be called malicious, and they were not confined to his numerous enemies. Walter Allen was delighted but startled when, meeting Lewis for only the second time, he was asked whether he would like to write a book about his host. Allen played for safety by mentioning other possible candidates. What about Grigson or Symons? Grigson would produce a pastiche, Lewis said, and Symons was just waiting for him to die and would then have a book out about him in no time. Allen was shocked at this attitude towards admirers, but he should not have been. Lewis acknowledged few equals, whether among friends or enemies. He talked as he wrote, from the attitude of genius.

That image of an alien force, a visitor from a planet where the whole conception of life and its proper ordering was different, is the best way to see Wyndham Lewis. Behind the immediate geniality there seemed to be a kind of inner rage, at the conditions of life, the nature of society, the dullness of other people. It was not possible to be long in his company without realising that he looked at what was around him through eyes quite different from one's own. He saw men and women as machines walking, their appendages of ears, nose, hands oddly stuck on, their activities from speech and eating to excretion and copulation stutteringly awkward and comic. Allen rightly called his way of thinking profoundly unEnglish, and said the shorthand expression for it might be Cartesian. Lewis certainly resembled Descartes in being a man of supreme intelligence who rejected purely rational thought in favour of what seemed to him evident truths based on his individual and extraordinary perceptions. Descartes, however, proceeded from the basis that the power of thought is the proof of selfhood ('cogito ergo sum') to deduce the existence of God. Lewis's perceptions were used to assert the power of art, and he applied them to a view of society that, except in his last years, was remote from religious feeling. He saw the society he lived in as undergoing drastic and revolutionary changes in the decades between the Wars. 'My mind is *ahistoric*, I would welcome the clean sweep,' he wrote to me in 1937. 'I could build something better, I am sure of that, than has been left by our fathers.' The 'something better' he identified as a finer art, which would be achieved in a society revering works of art as the greatest products of civilisation. And he took it for granted that he was capable of producing such works.

An approach of this kind is inimical to British ways of thought and feeling which, especially in the Victorian and Edwardian periods, permitted and even welcomed eccentricity in its artists, but did not expect a personal announcement of genius. Lewis aroused suspicious dislike also by the variety of his talents. He first became known as a near-abstract visual artist, the most important figure connected with Vorticism, the movement he founded although Ezra Pound gave it a name. Then he became known as a writer of novels and short stories, some of them satiric. He was always ready to defend and explain his work in essays and articles, and to dissect the work of others with a frankness often resented. From the early 1920s until his death in 1957 he supported his own art works with a philosophical, political and economic analysis of society that suggested possible directions in which social power would develop, and looked at which of these directions might be most beneficial to art.

All this work—the novels and stories, along with the criticism, exposition, discussion and denunciation—was done with an exclamatory jocular freedom very similar to the form of his conversation, although the conversational tone was heightened on the page. Eliot was not alone in calling him the greatest English prose stylist of the century. Others found him unreadable because of the very qualities Lewis's admirers regard as virtues, although few went so far as Anthony Quinton who called Lewis the worst prose writer of the century. Certainly the style was unique, rapid and exclamatory, learned yet vividly colloquial. He discussed complex philosophical questions with the jovial slanginess of a man arguing with others in a pub. This style is not, as it looks, artless, but the product of careful design, devised as the best means of conveying messages about the need for and nature of the changes in society that Lewis, writing in the Twenties, expected to see emerge.

In his fiction the style is thicker and more complex, but still infused with the same frantic energy. His rendering of dialogue is, again, entirely original, revealing the hesitations, repetitions, clichés and inanities of common conversation with the faithfulness of a tape recorder put into

3

a room where the speakers are unaware of its presence. The dialogue that looks natural in most novels is in fact highly artificial, changing and improving the way in which most people speak. The dialogue which Lewis gradually perfected in *The Apes of God* and the novels of the following decade sometimes looks strange on the page, but corresponds to the actual nature of conversation.

This style, whether the finest or the worst of the twentieth century, was utterly unacademic, alien equally to the discreet grey-suited manner in which literary and social criticism was written in the two decades from 1914 onwards when Lewis became celebrated, the moral concern and analytic zest of British Leavisites and American New Critics that left them unconcerned with any style at all, and to more recent structuralists and deconstructionists who would shudder away from a manner so insistently individual, and an approach offering the lie direct to their view that an author is of little or no importance beside his infinitely variable text.

To have so many talents, to write always with the arrogant assumption of genius, to outrage the canons of literary establishments in every period: perhaps all this was enough for Wyndham Lewis's writings to have roused feelings of dislike and anger. But there were other reasons too, connected with his personality, his philosophical stance, and the political views that stemmed from it.

ii The Ungentle Art of Making Enemies

Lewis was both truculent and shy, could be elaborately polite and blisteringly rude. Minor examples of both aspects of his personality have stayed in my memory. When his first autobiographical volume *Blasting and Bombardiering* came out, I asked if he would sign my copy. He glared at me and said he never did that kind of thing, an untruth manifest to me from the signed and dedicated copies in the library of my brother AJ, with whom he was friendly. A couple of years later, however, in 1939, Lewis said he would like to paint my portrait. I said, truthfully, that I could not pay for it. 'Have you got £10?' he asked. 'You have? Very well, then.' I was too crass to appreciate the generosity of the suggestion, yet the very crassness that let me think a portrait painted practically for nothing called for no special thanks probably appealed to Lewis. He deprecated, indeed disliked, any expression of personal feeling. The request for his signature may have seemed to him a bit of fawning sentimentality, my casual acceptance of the idea that a tenner was adequate payment for an oil painting admirably offhand.

There were times, however, when Lewis's behaviour would have offended anybody. A desire to dominate, distrust of rivals, resentment of those who provided the financial patronage he needed, contempt for most women and many men, and suspicion of others' motives and actions, were features of his character. Like many other paranoiacs Lewis often did have something to complain about: his belief that he suffered as a visual artist from the relentless enmity of Roger Fry after a bitter quarrel in 1913 in which right was on Lewis's side, and later of Kenneth Clark who succeeded Fry as arbiter of Britain's artistic establishment, was well founded. He opposed himself to such figures, derided them, and suffered for it. But his attitude towards friends and admirers, especially those who gave him financial support, was also often deeply antagonistic. The painter Edward Wadsworth and his wife Fanny, Sydney and Violet Schiff, Richard Wyndham, are only a few of those who found that the attempt to ease the material conditions of Lewis's life was rewarded with savage caricatures of them in his fiction. By the end of the Twenties Lewis was isolated in the British literary scene, and in 1927 the book-length, almost one-man magazine he founded bore the title *The Enemy*. There was, he said in the editorial to the first of the three issues that appeared, no ' "movement" gathered here (thank heaven!), merely a person; a solitary outlaw and not a gang', and he went on to say that this one-man magazine was a guarantee of total independence. 'There will be nobody with whom I am dining to-morrow night . . . whose susceptibilities, or whose wife's, I have to consider.' And it is true enough that he did not consider them.

So far the personal. The other reasons for the alienation of Lewis from British artistic society after 1927 were connected with his ideas. His extreme individualism had by now been formulated into a philosophy radically critical of many shibboleths respected by the intellectual society of the period. His ideas are elaborated in the body of this book, but as they developed during the Twenties they can be put simply in the form of a few propositions:

1   *Freedom* is a word always on the lips of those who regard themselves as progressive thinkers. More freedom for everybody

is regarded as an obvious and absolute good.

2   This is an illusion. Very few people, including those who talk most about it, wish to be free. Freedom implies individuality in life and thought, a concept that would terrify most people if they ever really contemplated it. On the contrary, what the mass of men and women want is to be like other people, live in similar houses, wear similar clothes, enjoy similar pleasures.

3   The press, wireless, cinema, all encourage this illusion of freedom, while in practice urging conformity.

4   The intelligentsia are no less conformist than the mass. They wear a different uniform and admire different works of art, it is true, but their accepted ideas and admired art-works are always in tune with what is intellectually fashionable at any given moment.

5   The intelligentsia's approach to politics as to literature (even when they claim to be totally 'unpolitical') accepts the word 'revolution' as an absolute good like 'freedom', while always evading or rejecting the genuine article. They play with 'revolution' like children with a ball—and indeed they wish to be children, often proclaiming the virtues of the naive painting, the child's innocent eye. He coins a phrase for them: they are *revolutionary simpletons*, in life as in art.

6   But genuine revolution is very much a fact of modern life. The world society dominated for so long by Europe, by liberal ideals and the rule of the ballot box, is doomed to extinction. The form taken by revolution in Russia is one possibility, the Fascist state developing in Italy under Mussolini another.

7   The political tendency of the modern world is towards the growth of international organisations that will eventually eliminate national boundaries and national feeling. The natural result of mass production is not merely uniformity of clothes, appearance and thought, but also a much greater degree of association between groups with common interests like chess, health, homosexuality. The social tendency of this uniformity is also towards the breaking down of those barriers against change embodied by the institution of the family. The advance of feminism, closely linked with the development of homosexuality, is eroding and will finally destroy the family as a factor of social importance.

8   The decline of nationalism and its replacement by an international

world order, a melting-pot of all nationalities and races upon the American model, is both desirable and inevitable. A world state, 'with a recognised central world-control', would eliminate the need for war. The desire most people feel for conformity will be satisfied by the press, which will find each year fresh amusements for the 'little man' and his wife that will convince them of the novelty and originality of their lives, supplemented by the arbiters of fashion who will decree changes in clothing, house decoration and the arts. In this society the intellectual will be a separate figure, honoured not as a 'great man', but given isolation and the opportunity of working without interference 'as the chosen vessel of our human intelligence'.

This is a greatly simplified version of the ideas advanced in the stream of books Lewis poured out in the Twenties: most notably *The Art of Being Ruled*, *The Lion and the Fox*, *Time and Western Man* and *Paleface*. On a mundane level it is startling, sixty years later, to see how prophetically right he was in relation to the demise of the family, the standardisation of clothing and its unisexual nature, the rise of feminism and homosexuality, the immense growth of what he called 'associational life' through the development of specialised interests, and the control exerted over all our lives by gigantic international cartels and the press. He was also dramatically wrong about the fading of national feeling, the elimination of national boundaries, and the acceptance of an international world order.

But the force and importance of his ideas rests much less on whether they 'came true' or remained unfulfilled, than in the way they ran counter to the stance of almost all Western social and political thinkers of the twentieth century. To place a low value on human life as such, and to make the assumption that some lives are important, most of no interest or value, outraged the conventional beliefs of Lewis's own time, and even more the pieties of ours. To ameliorate the wretched lives of the poor, reduce infant mortality, ensure that the old die in comfort and dignity—these have seemed to almost all twentieth-century social thinkers ends that cannot possibly be questioned, and all politicians pay lip-service to them. Lewis, however, scorned the attitudes from which these practical good works sprang, saying that 'To attach, as the humanitarian does, a mystical value to *life* itself, for its own sake, is as much a treachery to spiritual truth as it is a gesture of "humanity" '. Thoughts of this kind emphatically expressed made Lewis enemies among liberal thinkers, and an open contempt for all art that he regarded as merely fashionable, like the Russian Ballet created by Diaghilev ('He has used and degraded all the splendid material on which he could lay his hands to the level of *Gentlemen Prefer Blondes* [if you make the "blonde" a gentleman] . . . The Russian Ballet is the Nineties of Oscar Wilde and Beardsley staged for the High-Bohemia') made him detested by many more who might have been thought his natural allies. Just as Dostoevsky was the Great Antagonist for fellow Russian writers and artists in the latter part of the nineteenth century, the expositor of extreme pan-Slavic and Christian views that could not be ignored because of the brilliance with which he expounded them, so Lewis is the Great Antagonist for twentieth-century social reformers.

The present generation of British intellectuals who insist that more university education must involve a lowering of standards owe a debt to Lewis, although their objections are usually made from a Plain Man standpoint with which he would have had little sympathy. Much nearer to his attitude in the Twenties and Thirties was that of W.H. Auden when in an early poem he wrote that

> The few shall be taught who want to understand,
> Most of the rest shall live upon the land;
> Living in one place with a satisfied face
> All of the women and most of the men
> Shall work with their hands and not think again.

Essential to the well-being of a civilisation is the existence of a class whose intellectual superiority is acknowledged: that is the core of the argument put forward by Lewis with immense vivacity and a wealth of instances. It is an argument that, as our culture becomes wider and thinner, its characteristic works at once more popular and less serious, has even more application in our own time, but its only exponents now are those who want to turn back the clock: none of them would, like Lewis, 'welcome the clean sweep'. Their criticism does not look forward to a new world: they simply want to return to an old one.

The conclusions reached through the social and philosophical analysis of these books can be, and were, criticised from another point of view. At the end of the editorial introducing *The Enemy* Lewis said: 'If I am asked, "What

8

are your Politics?", I can truly answer I have none', and he even thought of calling the magazine *No Politics*. In 1931, however, his *Hitler*, based on a series of magazine articles published in the preceding year, offered a view not unfavourable to the Nazi movement and its Führer, an attitude that did not change when the Nazis came to power in 1933.

Lewis was a revolutionary who wished to see the overturn of European liberalism, and saw in Communist Russia, Fascist Italy and Nazi Germany harbingers of a new and potentially finer society. He did not particularly favour one kind of rule or another, and so was able to reply in 1934 to a questionnaire asking whether he supported any political party or creed: 'Politically I take my stand exactly midway between the Bolshevik and the Fascist—the gentleman on my left I shake with my left hand, the gentleman on my right with my right hand. If there were only one (as I wish there were) I'd shake him with *both* hands.' As the Thirties wore on, however, and political feelings among intellectuals became increasingly Left-wing, Lewis's left hand disengaged itself from the Bolshevik gentleman, by way of some pamphleteering books that attacked Left-wing politicians and their fellow-travellers. They gave no explicit support to Right-wing movements, but these books (*Hitler*, *Left Wings Over Europe* and *Count Your Dead: They Are Alive*) made him a figure not merely neglected but positively ostracised. It is not an exaggeration to say that he became the most hated writer in Britain. This was particularly so among the group I have elsewhere called the Pragmatists among the intelligentsia of the time, the working-class intellectuals and professional men and women who regarded the theatre, the novel and the artist's canvas as vehicles for social propaganda. Lewis was not a propagandist for Nazism as Pound was for Italian Fascism, nor a latently anti-Semitic supporter of the Fascist ideas of Charles Maurras like T.S. Eliot, nor did he proclaim the wisdom of the blood like D.H. Lawrence, or believe like him that homage to a leader is the highest form of collective being. Nevertheless, he gave more offence than any of them, an offence neither forgotten nor forgiven when, after Munich, he wrote *The Hitler Cult: And How It Will End*, and in the unhappily-titled *The Jews: Are They Human?*—a title derived from the best-selling *The English: Are They Human?*—said without qualification that the 'diatribes of the antisemite' were 'ugly nonsense'. None of this changed the almost total disapproval with which he was regarded by British and American intellectuals. Nor did the fact that after World War II he stated again his belief in the melting-pot of the United States as an ideal basis for the rootless society this man of the world approved. 'The most conspicuous advantage of being American . . . is surely to have turned one's back on race, caste, and all that pertains to the rooted state.' *The Enemy* was a title Lewis took to himself partly as a joke, but he found the term taken seriously in relation both to his personality and his ideas.

It is right to admit what some of Lewis's admirers have sought to evade or deny: that what he envisaged as the good society was authoritarian, not democratic. A good society, he thought, was one that made the mass of people content and offered freedom to original thinkers and artistic creators, and he believed the liberal societies of Europe encouraged only the second-rate. Stated thus harshly the position offends. If it is put a little differently, however, we can all agree that writers and original thinkers are often 'at odds with their time' and sometimes hostile to it, and are denied appreciation by Philistines and bureaucrats. This self-congratulatory murmur of agreement is based on the assumption that *we* are much more enlightened than those Philistines and bureaucrats. Have we not laughed with rather than at Bernard Shaw's outrageousness, said that we don't understand quite what *The Waste Land* was all about but some of the lines are beautiful, come away from *Waiting For Godot* calling it marvellous theatre? The self-satisfied ease of such reactions seemed to Lewis worse than simple ignorance. To see a Shaw play without bothering about its possible meanings, to read Eliot and watch Beckett without understanding that they were expressing despair at the decay of a civilisation—such superficial reactions would have disgusted him. His basic requirement of those who looked at his pictures and read his books was that they should respect the artist as, by nature of his calling and achievement, a superior being: and that, in the twentieth as in most other centuries, was a condition not likely to be fulfilled.

iii Reasons for Reading Lewis

Wyndham Lewis is a unique figure in twentieth-century art and literature. Nobody else has combined his several qualities: the production of thousands of drawings and perhaps two hundred oil paintings, many of which hang in art galleries around the world; more than a dozen works of fantastic and realistic fiction; a whole series of books analysing social and political movements of the period, and the philosophies behind them; pungent book-length pamphlets supporting his own socio-political position; volumes of literary criticism, art criticism and poetry; autobiographical reminiscences.

He is acknowledged now as a major figure in twentieth-century British art, but his literary genius has been much less appreciated. In his lifetime he became less famous than notorious, a man whom most British publishers steered clear of because they thought him likely to offer them scandalous or libellous work, and whom the major American publishers ignored after the early Thirties. The posthumous acknowledgement he expected has been granted only in part. Some of his books have been published in paperback, and the Black Sparrow Press in California has reissued most of the fiction and some non-fiction in handsome editions, but the very fact that the reissues come from a small firm in California rather than one of the New York publishers suggests the disregard Lewis still suffers. A handful of critical studies have been published, but they are a trickle beside the flood of works about the contemporaries with whom his name was linked, Eliot, Joyce and Pound.

Certainly Lewis brought some of this neglect on himself, as already suggested, by his disregard of the usual civilities of literary life, his paranoiac suspiciousness, and the carelessness about possibly libellous references that led to the withdrawal or suppression of three books in the Thirties. But that is only part of the story. One basic problem is that few works by Lewis lend themselves to simple classification as fiction, literary criticism or philosophy. *Snooty Baronet*, for instance, is undoubtedly a novel, but one that veers away into criticism of behaviourist doctrine, an attack on D.H. Lawrence, and a philosophical approach to the nature of violence prefiguring that of Camus in *L'Etranger*. The first part of *The Childermass* is formally fiction, but much more a discussion of contemporary philosophies and political attitudes, while the second and third parts, completed more than a quarter of a century later, outline philosophical and religious attitudes very different from those in Part One. The literary criticism, even when dealing with apparently straightforward subjects like the work of Hemingway and Faulkner, is always likely to look at such work from an unusual point of view. Consideration of Hemingway's deliberately simple prose leads to an examination of the relationship between American and

11

British use of language, and the use of the 'neutralised vowel'—a vowel which has made immense progress since Lewis observed it in 1934. And in relation to Faulkner, Lewis catches a phrase from a short story about a flash and a glare, and enlarges on it: '*A flash, a glare*—that is what Faulkner's books are intended to be—a very long flash and a chronic glare, illuminating a "doomed", a symbolical landscape—centred in that township of the Old Dominion symbolically named *Jefferson.*' Such insights lead to the conclusions in which the Hemingway hero is labelled 'The Dumb Ox', and Faulkner is called a moralist with a corn cob. Leavisites, structuralists and deconstructionists would all agree that this is not the way in which criticism should be written, and it is true that Lewis as literary critic has no 'method'. His approach is wholly individual, offering an interpretation of a writer's work linked to his own interests and attitudes. Its justification is that the insights offered are often extraordinary. His view of the Hemingway hero and of Faulkner's attitude may be disputed, but it will not be forgotten.

The problem of disentangling one thing from another—fiction from politics and personalities, literary criticism from its linguistic and social implications—enriches his best writing, giving it a subtlety and flexibility denied to work produced from the standpoint of an orthodoxy. This book is meant primarily for those who know little of the work, and have found that little not easy to understand. It is designed to show that Lewis was at his best a great literary artist, and that his insights into the nature of twentieth-century society were unique. His ideas may be at times no more congenial than those of Nietzsche, but that should not prevent us from appreciating the accuracy of much he foresaw, or the force of arguments that are rarely considered let alone answered, or the nobility behind his belief in an aristocracy of intellect.

The book is divided into sections, each chronological, with passages of exposition and explanation, an arrangement that has the advantage of showing the nature of Lewis's thought, and the changes over the years in his view of what was possible and desirable by way of developments in our civilisation and our art. Those changes were considerable. In World War I Lewis saw service as a bombardier before becoming an official war artist, and although he spent World War II in the USA and Canada, both wars greatly affected his thinking. The revolutionary of 1914 who expressed a desire to 'Kill John Bull With Art' and was moving towards complete graphic abstraction, held views very different from those of the man who published in 1954 *The Demon of Progress in the Arts*. The arrangement also makes it possible to show, through a course roughly biographical, the relation of these changes to the buffets Lewis suffered in the latter part of his life. The necessary simplifications mean that something less than justice is done to the complexities and subtleties of Lewis's thought. There are places where if he had been allowed to speak for himself at greater length, the effect would have been both more powerful and more entertaining than my attempts to convey his meaning briefly. But such abbreviations were inevitable in a book meant as an introduction to one of the greatest stylists and most original thinkers of the twentieth century.

The last phrases are not used casually. Lewis was more greatly and variously gifted than any of his artistic contemporaries, his understanding deeper, his mind more audacious. He was also personally injudicious, arrogant, a man who throughout his life rode the tiger of intellectual pride, yet sometimes produced wretchedly slapdash work in search of the popularity he despised. Ezra Pound was right when he wrote of the young Lewis: 'You cannot be as intelligent as he was, in that sort of way, without being prey to the furies.'

A Note on the Texts

Lewis's punctuation, and his handling of capitals and lower case lettering, were both distinctly idiosyncratic, and have been preserved as nearly as possible. The various extracts appear as they were first printed in book form with the exception of *Tarr*, where the revised edition has been used for reasons given in the text. This involves minor occasional inconsistencies, because some publishers insisted on imposing their house style on Lewis's work, but it seemed to me truer to the spirit of the writing than an attempt at conformity. Where I have moved from one passage to another within a given text this is indicated by dots.

I have retained the sub-titles used in the non-fiction works. Sometimes their application to the passage chosen from a particular section is not obvious, but replacement of the existing sub-titles by others of my own would have been both confusing, and an intrusive interpretation of Lewis's ideas.

In *The Enemy 2* Lewis explained his use of lower case when writing of nationalities, saying that his eye was offended 'by the spectacle of a host of capital letters sticking up on a page, and drawing the eye to words that do not seem to call for this emphasis or singularity more than those around them'. He therefore made the 'concession to human feelings that results in the spelling of "a Briton" or "a Singalese" with a capital letter', but 'when used adjectivally I have suppressed the "caps", for I felt that it would be so exaggerated a susceptibility that would pursue me with its indignation outside the substantival class that I could safely disregard it.'

The distinction between Lewis's texts and editorial exposition of them has been made by a reduction in type size between the main body of the text and editorial contributions.

PART ONE

PHILOSOPHY, POLITICS SOCIETY

In the first of his two autobiographical volumes, *Blasting and Bombardiering*, Wyndham Lewis ignored his early years, beginning around 1914. That, he said, was better than starting with the bib and bottle. Since this is not an investigation of his psychology but an examination of his work and ideas, a paragraph about his background seems sufficient here.

Percy Wyndham Lewis was born in November 1882, the only child of Charles Edward Lewis and an English girl named Anne Prickett. The 'old Rip', as Lewis later called his lively and dashing but idle American father, was fond of hunting and sailing, and the boy was born in Nova Scotia aboard his father's yacht. When Lewis was eleven the old Rip ran off with a red-haired housemaid, and Anne gave the rest of her life to the care of her son. With help from her husband's family she sent him to Rugby where he was bottom of his class, then to the Slade School of Art, and later supported him in the seven years he spent wandering around Europe, with long stays in France, Germany and Spain. In this time he sired the first of five illegitimate children, and contracted also the first of several venereal infections. He returned to England in 1909, began to write and publish the stories later collected in *The Wild Body*, and in 1912 exhibited some of the paintings and drawings done under the influence of Cubism, which a year or two later had developed into the near-abstractions labelled Vorticist.

Whatever may have been the exact course of Lewis's reading through these years, the ideas of Nietzsche and the emphasis on violent and extreme solutions to life's problems in Dostoevsky held an evident attraction for him. In Paris he attended Bergson's lectures, but rejected the essential optimism about the *élan vital* that lay behind them. His Vorticist paintings and drawings emphasise hardness, rigidity, intensity, force. Human figures are turned to mechanical shapes, the philosophy behind their creation the opposite of Bergsonism, or of Bergson's philosophical pupil Bernard Shaw. This, though, was a philosophy at that time only vaguely formulated. The editorial from *Blast* 2 (1915), 'A Super Krupp—or War's End', written before Lewis was in the Army, shows the drift of his thinking at this time and the letters written from the trenches in France to Ezra Pound, in spite of their characteristic detachment, show the effect the experience of war had on him. The = sign in these letters is a form of punctuation Lewis used at this time. 'The Code of a Herdsman' (1917) is his first full expression of Nietzschean, or Ibsenite, ideas about the superiority of the lonely man. It is also an excellent example of Lewis's humour (rule 4), his passion for a kind of play-acting secrecy (rule 7), his indifference to class distinctions and insistence on an aristocracy of the intellect (rule 6), and his intellectual contempt for women (rule 12). The 'Code' is a vital document in relation to Lewis's ideas, exemplifying what later made some people detest him, while the manner in which those ideas were expressed could be found either deplorable or wonderfully comic.

from BLAST 2

A Super-Krupp—or War's End.

People are busy reading into this huge political event prognostics for the satisfaction of their dearest dreams.

The PEACE-MAN says: 'Here at last is such a tremendous War that it will exterminate even War itself.'

Another sort of man says: 'One good thing about this War is that it will de-democratize France considerably. France has been unbearable lately.'

Another says: 'Here is the chance of their life for the ruling classes.'

Or from another direction: 'Social revolution is nearer because of this senseless conflict.'

Among artists, the Futurist will naively reflect: 'The energies awoken by all this, the harder conditions, etc., will make a public after the War a little more after my own heart.'

Another sort of artist, again, thinking of his rapidly depreciating 'shop', says triumphantly: 'This War with all its mediaeval emotions' (for it gives him mediaeval emotions) 'will result in a huge revival of Romanticism.'

I happen, as an artist, to be placed about where Probability and Desire harmoniously meet and mingle. And it seems to me that, as far as art is concerned, things will be exactly the same after the War as before it. In the political field this War may hasten the pace in one direction or another. All art that matters is already so far ahead that it is beyond the sphere of these disturbances.

It is quite useless speculating on the Future, unless you want some particular Future. Then you obviously should speculate, and it is by speculations (of all sorts, unfortunately) that the Future is made. The Future, like the Truth, is composed of genial words.

Artists are often accused of invertebrate flexibility, in their 'acceptance' of a time. But it is much more that they change less than other people. A good artist is more really 'of his time' and therefore makes less fuss about his accidental surroundings. He has exactly the same attachment to his time (and reproaches those who don't show such an attachment) that he has to his family and his country. It is the same thing.

Well, then, I should be perfectly content that the Present Time should always remain, and things never change, since they are new to me, and I cannot see how the Port of Rotterdam can be bettered; and an A.B.C. shop is a joy for ever.

There are one or two points, despite this, that it may be useful to consider.

IS THIS THE WAR THAT WILL END WAR?

People will no doubt have to try again in 20 or 80 years if they REALLY like or need War or not. And so on until present conditions have passed into Limbo.

19

Perpetual War may well be our next civilization. I personally should much prefer that, as 18 months' disorganization every 40 years and 38½ years' complete peace, is too anarchic except for Art squabbles. In the middle ages a War was always going on somewhere, like the playing of perpetual football teams, conducted by trained arquebussiers, etc. This permanent War of the Future would have a much more cynical and professional character.

Trade usually attracts the Corsicans of the Modern World. With the future for War so precarious as it has been lately, the tendencies of the Age against it, idleness or common virtues rather than ambitious brains, have gone into the career of Arms. Will it be worth any bright boy's while, after this War, to devote his attention exclusively to Strategies?

War has definitely and for good gone under the ground, up in the air, and is quickly submerging itself down to the bed of the ocean. In peace time, now, the frontiers will be a line of trenches and tunnels with miles of wire and steel mazes, and entanglements crackling with electricity, which no man will be able to pass. Everything will be done down below in future, or up above. Tubes will be run from the principal concentration camps inland.

French soldiers may emerge from a hole in the pavement in Unter den Linden on the declaration of War half-a-century hence, or England be invaded under the North Sea.

A sort of immense in-fighting has been established everywhere, with hosts of spies and endless national confusions.

A Super-Krupp is the best hope for the glorious future of War. Could Krupp only combine business ability with a Napoleonic competence in the field, the problem would be solved! We might eventually arrive at such a point of excellence that two-thirds of the population of the world could be exterminated with mathematical precision in a fortnight. War might be treated on the same basis as agriculture.

Have you ever considered what a state of delirious contentment hundreds of old military gentlemen, strategists and War-writers, must be in: A battle bigger than Gravelotte somewhere in Europe every week—sometimes two or three in a week! Oh! the unexampled richness of material to work on; the delightful problems of Napoleonic versus Moltkean strategy each day provides! I wonder that some of these red-faced old gentlemen do not burst with satisfaction—blow up like a well-placed bomb.

As to Desirability, nobody but Marinetti, the Kaiser, and professional soldiers WANT War. And from that little list the Kaiser might have to be extracted.

On the other hand, you cannot help feeling that the Men of Thought have interfered too much with other people's business latterly. This immense sentimental interference is not even the province of Thought. Most men who are naturally articulate and therefore have something to say on this as every other subject, are not pre-eminently interested in military operations; and, on the other hand, they are sufficiently good-hearted and conscious of the endless private misery a modern War causes. All men cannot, and never will be, 'philosophic men.' So what are they going to be: Soldiers and politicians, a good many, I expect; and much happier and more amusing that way than in any kit the Men of Thought would invent for them.

Do not let us, like Christian missionaries, spoil the savages all around us.

————

There is a tragedy of decay and death at the end of all human lives. It is all a matter of adjustment of tragedy: a matter almost of Taste—where to place the Tragedy, like where to place a blackness in a picture. But this is perhaps rather consolation than anything else. And it would be no consolation for the people this War will have crushed with grief.

to EZRA POUND

8/6/17 [8 June 1917]

My dear Pound. I have had a day or two full of incident and movement. = The night before last I was gassed in my sleep (lethal shells): the sentry did not apparently know that I was sleeping in dugout, and omitted to wake me. However, by about eleven I had recovered from that, and proceeded to an O[bservation].P[ost]. on the top of a hill. From there I saw an immense and smoky struggle for a village: saw tanks advancing, cavalry etc.: tanks hit, air fights—panorama of war, in fact. Then in afternoon I returned to my Battery, and in late afternoon walked up with my Battery commander to the line gained a few hours before: through the desolation of the Bosche concrete dugouts in a wilderness of charred spikes that was formerly a wood, everything not trenches [was] pits and gashes: dead Germans lying about like bloody waxworks: and up to present line which was too confused to be present. We passed through a field Battery that was being shelled, though quiescent itself, and there I came nearest to a black shell-burst: about twenty yards, twice. They were coming over every few seconds. I picked up a copy of Voss's Gazette in the German lines, & have been applying my German dictionary to it. = So I covered a good deal of ground yesterday along roads to the O.P., across country to the front line, and saw a lot of War. I have been particularly lucky in dropping into the midst of a very big attack. The attack has been especially successful, and today is like a quiet day in the country; no row, fine sun, the map-room; waiting for an aeroplane to come along & signal she is ready: a half hour's shooting, more calm etc. etc. – I hope: For I want to sleep tonight. = I still have not got your letter sent me at the Base. But I expect in a day or two it will arrive. Tell Miss S[aunders]., if you see her, to send me a copy (type-written or otherwise) of the first 8 pages (the doubtful pages) of the Soldier of Humour. I should probably have time to put that right. — My compliments to Mrs. Pound. Yrs

W.L.

P.S. Do not print Soldier of Humour until I have made that alteration. = As to photographs: that funny one with my legs apart mustnt be reproduced, since the paper will come to England. The second batch I had printed is not bad (or some of those will probably do). Get Miss S. to procure two or three (I will send her money). Her address is the same.

W.L.

14/6/17

My dear Pound. I have just got your second letter (of May 30th.) At the same time I received a letter from another quarter describing your latest choreographic exploits in Maida Vale. The One Step, as I understand it, is just the same as the Fox Trot, only it is twice as quick. It also, requiring more acrobatic skill, is less adapted for luxurious degustation of your mate. – A double-twinkle is a thing that should immediately be learnt. – I know no official wriggle: you can make them up as you go along. = That 'alert' photo is napoo. There are others, that I trust you have by now, more fit for international, rather than purely national, consumption. = I have got the first pages of the 'Soldier of Humour', which I will overhaul & return. (You see the date at the head of the letter).

This morning is peaceful: the enemy is now much farther away, and we are temporarily derelict among 12″ railway mountings, horse lines: minor Headquarters are even moving up among us. I expect we shall have to go pretty soon. Yesterday once more I took my way to the forward intelligence O.P. We were shelled out of it yesterday morning, the side of the dugout being disorganized by an 8″ shell. = Imagine a stretch of land one mile in depth sloping up from the old German first-line to the top of a ridge, & stretching to right & left as far as you can see. It looks very large, never-ending and empty. There are only occasional little groups of men round a bomb-dump, or building a light railway: two men pushing a small truck on which a man is being brought back, lying on his stomach, his head hanging over the side. The edge of the ridge is where you are bound for, at the corner of a demolished wood. The place is either loathesomely hot, or chilly according to the time of day at which you cross it. It is a reddish colour, and all pits, ditches & chasms, & black stakes, several hundred, here & there, marking the map-position of a wood. Shells never seem to do more than shave the trees down to these ultimate black stakes, except in the few cases when they tear them up, or a mine swallows them.

The moment you get in this stretch of land you feel the change from the positions you have come from. A watchfulness, fatigue and silence penetrates everything in it. You meet a small party of infantry slowly going up or coming back. Their faces are all dull, their eyes turned inwards in sallow thought or savage resignation; you would say revulsed, if it were not too definite a word. There is no regular system of communication trenches yet; this is the bad tract, the narrow and terrible wilderness. As a matter of fact it only becomes clearly unsafe as you approach the ridge. You get nearer to the shell bursts on the crest, until the nearest black cloud is only a hundred yards away, on the road at the skyline. Perhaps to your right, half way up, there has been heavy shelling, but not near enough to require craft, & the noise is inconsiderable. There are shrapnel bursts overhead almost continually, but for some reason absurdly high and ineffective. = As to the ridge: I have been three times. Yesterday as we got within a hundred yards of the road there was suddenly a swooping whistle: my commanding officer shouted <u>down:</u> we crouched in a shell-hole, and a 5.9 burst about 15 or 20 yards away, between us & the wood—about 3 shell holes away, you could say, they were so regular thereabouts. Another came over about 15 yards nearer the wood, & at the third, actually in the wood, we concluded it was the wood corner they were after, & proceeded. The road at the top runs along the front of the wood for about 100 yds; the O.P. on the edge of the wood, being about 40 yds from where we struck the road. This road for its own sake is being shelled constantly, & because the Bosche imagines that there are machine gun emplacements at farther end. He also imagines that the wood is bristling with batteries; & is fatuous enough, in addition, to believe that his beautiful concrete dugouts are being used by our men. (You notice how guarded my language is.) As we reached this road, four black bursts came in succession halfway down the short stretch we could see. Straight for those bursts we made: but I shall not repeat that often. Nothing else came over as it happened. But as soon as we had reached the handsomely concreted German dugout, three 5.9's dropped just outside the door. This goes on the whole while up there. = Shall I or shall I not ask to go up there again tomorrow? There is nothing there you cannot imagine: but it has the unexpected quality of reality. Also the imagined thing and the felt are in two different categories. This category has its points. I will write you further on the subject of War. Do not expect my compositions to be well-worded, as letters (my letters) are only meant to be chat and slop. —Remember me to Mrs Pound. Yrs

<u>W.L.</u>

18/6/17

. . . My latest experience is being nearly blown out of bed by a large shell. It occurred at 2.30 this morning. It rained earth & stones on my roof, but fortunately was some yards away. The conscientious enemy is almost [?] certain to repeat his work this morning. We have been taking the magnetic bearing of the line of the shell-craters, and meditating on his possible intentions. But his overnight proceedings admitted of several interpretations. Anyhow he has pitted our position with holes big enough to bury a horse in. He has had aeroplanes over photographing them this morning. = Two of his planes were brought down together yesterday near us. = I am under the impression that he uses his guns more flexibly than we do: more as a man does a rifle, & less as a large fixed machine. He also is much more difficult to follow in his timing:—for we cannot be difficult at all! On the other hand we send over about ten to his one . . .

The Code of a Herdsman

(A set of rules sent by Benjamin Richard Wing to his young friend Philip Seddon inclosed with a letter. Under the above title now edited.)

1   Never maltreat your own intelligence with parables. It is a method of herd-hypnotism. Do not send yourself to sleep with the rhythm of the passes that you make. = As an example of herd-hypnotism, German literature is so virulently allegorized that the German really never knows whether he is a Kangaroo, a Scythian, or his own sweet self. = You, however, are a Herdsman. That is surely Parable enough!

2   Do not admit *cleverness*, in any form, into your life. Observe the accomplishment of some people's signatures! It is the herd-touch.

3   Exploit Stupidity. = Introduce a flatness, where it is required into your commerce. Dull your eye as you fix it on a dull face. = Why do you think George Borrow used such idiotic clichés as 'The beams of the descending luminary—?' He was a great writer and knew what he was doing. = Mock the herd perpetually with the

grimace of its own garrulity or deadness. If it gets out of hand and stampedes towards you, leap on to the sea of mangy backs until the sea is still. That is: cast your mask aside, and spring above them. They cannot see or touch anything *above* them: they have never realized that their backs—or rather their *tops*—exist! They will think that you have vanished into Heaven.

4   As to language: eschew all clichés implying a herd personality. Never allow such terms as Top-Hole, Priceless, or Doggo to pass your lips. Go to the Dictionary if you want an epithet. If you feel eloquent, use that moment to produce a cliché of your own. Cherish your personal vocabulary, however small it is. Use your own epithet as though it were used by a whole nation, if people would have no good reason for otherwise accepting it.

> *Examples of personal epithets.*
> That man is *abysmal.*
> That is an *abysmal* book.
> *It was prestigious!* ⎫
> Here comes that *sinister bird!* ⎭ Borrowed from the French.
> He is a *sinister card.* (Combination of French and 1890 Slang.)
> He has a great deal of *sperm.*
> I like a fellow with as much *sperm* as that.

Borrow from all sides mannerisms of callings or classes to enrich your personal bastion of language. Borrow from the pulpit, from the clattering harangue of the auctioneer, the lawyer's technicality, the pomposity of politicians. = Borrow grunts from the fisherman, solecisms from the inhabitants of Merioneth. = 'He is a preux, ah, yes-a-preux!' You can say—'ah-yes-a-preux' as though it were one word, accent on the 'yes.'

5   In accusing yourself, stick to the Code of the Mountain. But crime is alien to a Herdsman's nature.

6   Yourself must be your Caste.

7   Cherish and develop, side by side, your six most constant indications of different personalities. You will then acquire the potentiality of six men. Leave your front door one day as B.: the next march down the street as E. A variety of clothes, hats especially, are of help in this wider dramatisation of yourself.

Never fall into the vulgarity of being or assuming yourself to be one ego. Each trench must have another one behind it. Each single self—that you manage to be at any given time—must have five at least indifferent to it. You must have a power of indifference of *five* to *one*. All the greatest actions in the world have been five parts out of six impersonal in the impulse of their origin. To follow this principle you need only cultivate your memory. You will avoid being the blind man of *any* moment. B will see what is hidden to D. = (Who were Turgenev's 'Six Unknown'? Himself.)

8　Never lie. You cannot be too fastidious about the truth. If you must lie, at least see that you lie so badly that it would not deceive a pea-hen.—The world is, however, full of pea-hens.

9　Spend some of your spare time every day in hunting your weaknesses, caught from commerce with the herd, as methodically, solemnly and vindictively as a monkey his fleas. You will find yourself swarming with them while you are surrounded by humanity. But you must not bring them up on the mountain. = If you can get another man to assist you—one, that is, honest enough not to pass his own on to you—that is a good arrangement.

10　Do not play with political notions, aristocratisms or the reverse, for that is a compromise with the herd. Do not allow yourself to imagine 'a fine herd though still a herd.' There is no *fine herd*. The cattle that call themselves 'gentlemen' you will observe to be a little cleaner. It is merely cunning and produced with a product called *soap*. But you will find no serious difference between them and those vast dismal herds they avoid. Some of them are very dangerous and treacherous. = Be on your guard with the small herd of gentlemen!

11　You will meet with this pitfall: at moments, surrounded by the multitude of unsatisfactory replicas, you will grow confused by a similarity bringing them so near to us. = You will reason, where, from some points of view, the difference is so slight, whether that delicate margin is of the immense importance that we hold it to be: *the only thing of importance* in fact. = That group of men talking by the fire in your club (you will still remain a member of your club), that party at the theatre, look good enough, you will say.

27

Their skins are fresh, they are well-made, their manners are good. You must then consider what they really are. On closer inspection you *know*, from unpleasant experience, that they are *nothing* but limitations and vulgarities of the most irritating description. The devil Nature has painted these sepulchres pink, and covered them with a blasphemous Bond Street distinction. Matter that has not sufficient mind to permeate it grows, as you know, gangrenous and rotten. Animal high spirits, a little, but easily exhausted, goodness, is all that they can claim.

What seduced you from your severity for a moment was the same thing as a dull woman's good-looks. = This is *probably* what you will have in front of you. = On the other hand, everywhere you will find a few people, who, although not a mountain people, are not herd. = They may be herdsmen gone mad through contact with the herd, and strayed: or through inadequate energy for our task they may be found there: or they may be a hybrid, or they may even be herdsmen temporarily bored with the mountain. (I have a pipe below myself sometimes.)

There are numerous 'other denominations.' Treat them as brothers. Employ them, as opportunity offers, as auxiliaries in your duties. Their society and help will render your task less arduous.

12 As to women: wherever you can, substitute the society of men. = Treat them kindly, for they suffer from the herd, although of it, and have many of the same contempts as yourself. They are a sort of bastard mountain people. = There must be somewhere a female mountain, a sort of mirage-mountain. I should like to visit it. = But women, and the processes for which they exist, are the arch conjuring trick: and they have the cheap mystery, and a good deal of the slipperiness, of the conjuror. = Sodomy should be avoided, as far as possible. It tends to add to the abominable confusion already existing.

13 Wherever you meet a shyness that comes out of solitude, (although *all* solitude is not *anti*-herd) naïveness, and a patent absence of contamination, the sweetness of mountain water, any of the signs of goodness, you must treat that as sacred, as portions of the mountain.

However much you suffer for it, you must defend and exalt it.

On the other hand, *every* child is not simple, and *every* woman is not weak. = In many cases to champion a female would be like springing to the rescue of a rhinoceros when you notice that it had been attacked by a flea. Chivalrous manners, again, with many women are like tiptoeing into a shed where an ox is sleeping. = Some children, too, rival in nastiness their parents. But you have your orders in this matter. Indifference where there should be nothing but the *whole* eagerness or compunction of your being, is the worst crime in the mountain's eyes.

14 Conquests have usually been divided from their antitheses, and defeats from conquests, by some casual event. Had Moscow not possessed a governor ready to burn the Kremlin and the hundreds of palaces accumulated there, peace would have been signed by the Czar at Bonaparte's entrance. = Had the Llascans persevered for ten days against Cortés, the Aztecs would never have been troubled. Yet Montezuma was right to remain inactive, paralysed by prophecy. Napoleon was right when he felt that his star was at last a useless one. He had drained it of all its astonishing effulgence. = The hair's breadth is only the virtuosity of Fate, guiding you along imaginary precipices. = And all the detail is make-believe, anyway. Watch your star soberly and without comment. Do not trouble about the paste-board cliffs!

15 *There are very stringent regulations* about the herd keeping off the sides of the mountain. In fact your chief function is to prevent their encroaching. Some, in moments of boredom or vindictiveness, are apt to make rushes for the higher regions. Their instinct always fortunately keeps them in crowds or bands, and their trespassing is soon noticed. Those traps and numerous devices you have seen on the edge of the plain are for use, of course, in the last resort. Do not apply them prematurely. = Not very many herdsmen lose their lives in dealing with the herds.

16 Contradict yourself. In order to live, you must remain broken up.

17 The teacher does not have to *be*, although he has to *know*: he is the mind imagining, not the executant. The executant, the young, svelte, miraculous athlete, the strapping virtuoso, really has to give the illusion of a perfection. = Do not expect *me* to keep in

29

sufficiently good training to perform the feats I recommend. = I usually remain up on the mountain.

18 Above all this sad commerce with the herd, let something veritably remain 'un peu sur la montagne.' Always come down with masks and thick clothing to the valley where we work.

Stagnant gasses from these Yahooesque and rotten herds are more dangerous often than the wandering cylinders that emit them. See you are not caught in them without your mask. = But once returned to our adorable height, forget your sallow task: with great freedom indulge your love. = The terrible processions beneath are not of our making, and are without our pity. Our sacred hill is a volcanic heaven. But the result of its violence is peace. = The unfortunate surge below, even, has moments of peace.

———————

'1918–1926 is a period marked "strictly private",' Lewis said in *Blasting and Bombardiering*, and he talked about going underground in those years. In fact he emerged quite often at dinner parties and in the company of friends, although it is true that this was a period of intensive reading and research in which he published very little.

It was early in this period that he went on a cycling tour in France with T.S. Eliot, and that they met James Joyce, an occasion memorably described in the autobiography. One might suspect invention or exaggeration in the account, except that its basic details are confirmed in Richard Ellmann's biography and Joyce's letters. The 'nondescript garments for the trunk' were in fact a suit.

from BLASTING AND BOMBARDIERING

First Meeting with James Joyce

James Joyce had come to Paris from Zürich. In the summer of 1920 I went there with Thomas Stearns Eliot. We went there on our way to the Bay of Quiberon for a summer holiday, which his wife said would do him good. We descended at a small hotel, upon the left bank of the River Seine. It was there I met, in his company, James Joyce for the first time. And it was the first time that Eliot had seen him, too. Joyce was the last of my prominent friends to be encountered; last but not least.

It had been agreed before we left London that we should contrive to see Joyce in Paris. And Eliot had been entrusted with a parcel by Ezra Pound (as a more responsible person than myself), which he was to hand to Joyce when he got there. We did not know at all what it contained. It was rather a heavy parcel and Eliot had carried it under his arm, upon his lap, as it was too big to go in a suitcase.

At that time I knew very little indeed about Joyce. He 'conveyed nothing' to me, I was in the same position as the white-coated doctor I mentioned in my introductory remarks—except that I did not, in my person, resemble James Joyce in any way, whereas certainly the doctor did, and yet had not even heard of his double.

Beyond what Ezra Pound had told me, which was mostly apologetic (the good Ezra assuming that I should laugh at him for his over-literary respects and genuflexions) I knew nothing. That was the situation. It was in consequence of this that in our subsequent intercourse Joyce and myself were often talking at cross-purposes.

I had not read *The Portrait of the Artist* nor *Dubliners*. *Exiles* and *Chamber Music* I had never heard of, *Ulysses* had not, of course, yet made its appearance. But Joyce, on the other hand, had, I am persuaded, read everything I had ever written. He pretended however not to have done so.

In very marked contrast with Joyce I was indifferent as to whether he had followed the fortunes of Tarr and Kreisler or not. There was no arrogance at all in my indifference. But, as it is easy to suppose, since their author assumed I had read all his books (*Ulysses* included although it had not been published) but was pretending like himself to have forgotten, things were at first very involved. Bad jams occurred in the dialogue, in both directions.

It does not follow that a couple of authors, when they come face to face need meet as 'authors'. But aside from everything else, James Joyce

31

was in a superlative degree the writer of books, the champion Penman, and breathed, thought and felt as such. We had been starred together on many occasions. He saw me as a Penman, too, and as a champion—one I expect he thought he could easily 'put-to-sleep'. It was quite impossible, under these circumstances, to encounter Joyce otherwise than as one of a pair of figures in the biography of a big Penman—I, of course being the interloper. For the biography would be one devoted to *him*, not to me. And finally why I on my side was indifferent was of course because I had no feeling for history. I was in fact a chronological idiot. A burlesque situation!

But this light comedy was sufficiently curious for it to be worth while to go into yet more detail. *Some* pages of the 'Portrait' I had read, when it first appeared as a serial in the *Egoist*, a paper edited by Miss Harriet Weaver. But I took very little interest. At that time, it was of far too tenuous an elegance for my taste. Its flavour was altogether too literary. And as to its emotional content, that I condemned at once as sentimental-Irish. Even now, for that matter, I feel much the same about *The Portrait of the Artist*, with the important difference that I have obliged myself to read a great many more books, in the meanwhile, many of which suffer from the same shortcomings, as I see it. So I do recognize the *Portrait of the Artist as a Young Man* to be one only of a large class, and of its kind a very excellent example.

On my side my first meeting with James Joyce was (at first) devoid of any particular interest. I found an oddity, in patent-leather shoes, large powerful spectacles, and a small gingerbread beard; speaking half in voluble Italian to a scowling schoolboy: playing the Irishman a little overmuch perhaps, but in amusingly mannered technique. Soon I was prepared to be interested in Joyce for his own sake. I took a great fancy to him for his wit, for the agreeable humanity of which he possessed such stores, for his unaffected love of alcohol, and all good things to eat and drink.

What should have been a momentous encounter, then, turned out to be as matter-of-fact a social clash as the coming together of two navvies, or the brusque *how do you do* of a couple of dogs out for a walk. The reason: just my inveterate obtuseness where all that is historic and chronological is concerned. It is because I cannot see things as *biography*. I have not got the Barretts of Wimpole Street mind. My insensitiveness in this respect is

32

to blame if all this part of my narrative is literally *flat*, like a Chinese or a Japanese picture.

I have gone ahead like this, outrunning the physical, to take all surprise out of these happenings, as a preliminary disinfection. Also I have hoped to drive home the fact that I have nothing up my sleeve, in these harmless exercises.

Returning, however, to my narrative of the physical encounter. T.S. Eliot—need I say the premier poet of Anglo-Saxony?—T.S. Eliot and myself descended at a small hotel. The Eliot fan will appreciate this way of putting it. He will see I know my Eliot. The hotel was nearer to the quays of the Seine than to the central artery of the Saint Germain quarter. It was the rue des Saints Pères, or it may be the rue Bonaparte: no matter, they are all the same. Our rooms were the sort of lofty, dirtily parquetted, frowsily-curtained, faded apartments that the swarms of small hotels in Paris provide, upon their floors of honour. These small hotels still abound.

T.S. Eliot ringing for the chasseur, dispatched a *petit bleu* to James Joyce. He suggested that Joyce should come to the hotel, because he had a parcel, entrusted to him by Ezra Pound, and which that gentleman had particularly enjoined upon him to deliver personally to the addressee; but that it would likewise be a great pleasure to meet him. This was accompanied by an invitation to dinner.

An invitation to dinner! I laugh as I write this. But at the time I did not know the empty nature of this hospitable message, seeing to whom it was directed!

The parcel was then placed in the middle of a large Second Empire marble table, standing upon gilt eagles' claws in the centre of the apartment. About six in the evening James Joyce arrived, and the Punch and Judy show began.

Joyce was accompanied by a tallish youth, whom he introduced to Eliot as his son. Eliot then introduced me to Joyce. We stood collected about the shoddily-ornamented french table, in the décor of the cheap dignity of the red-curtained apartment, as if we had been people out of a scene in an 1870 gazette, resuscitated by Max Ernst, to amuse the tired intelligentsia—bowing in a cosmopolitan manner to each other across Ezra's prize-packet, which was the proximate cause of this solemn occasion.

When Joyce heard my name he started in a very flattering fashion. Politely he was galvanized by his historic scene, and then collapsed. It was as if he had been gently pricked with the ghost of a hat-pin of a corsetted demirep out of the Police Gazette, and had given a highly well-bred exhibition of *stimulus-response*. Suppose this exhibition to have been undertaken for a lecture (with demonstrations) on 'Behaviour', and you have the whole picture. He raised his eyebrows to denote surprise and satisfaction at the auspicious occasion; he said *Ah! Wyndham Lewis* civilly under his breath, and I bowed again in acknowledgement, at the repetition of my name. He then with a courteous haste looked around for his son, who was heavily scowling in the background, and effected an introduction. His son stiffened, and, still scowling, bowed towards me with ceremony. Bringing my heels together, unintentionally with a noticeable report, I returned the salute. We all then sat down. But only for a moment.

Joyce lay back in the stiff chair he had taken from behind him, crossed his leg, the lifted leg laid out horizontally upon the one in support like an artificial limb, an arm flung back over the summit of the sumptuous chair. He dangled negligently his straw hat, a regulation 'boater'. We were on either side of the table, the visitors and ourselves, upon which stood the enigmatical parcel.

Eliot now rose to his feet. He approached the table, and with one eyebrow drawn up, and a finger pointing, announced to James Joyce that *this* was that parcel, to which he had referred in his wire, and which had been given into his care, and he formally delivered it, thus acquitting himself of his commission.

'Ah! Is this the parcel you mentioned in your note?' enquired Joyce, overcoming the elegant reluctance of a certain undisguised fatigue in his person. And Eliot admitted that it was, and resumed his seat.

I stood up: and, turning my back upon the others, arranged my tie in the cracked Paris mirror—whose irrelevant imperfections, happening to bisect my image, bestowed upon me the mask of a syphilitic Creole. I was a little startled: but I stared out of countenance this unmannerly distortion, and then turned about, remaining standing.

James Joyce was by now attempting to untie the crafty housewifely knots of the cunning old Ezra. After a little he asked his son crossly in Italian for a penknife. Still more crossly his son informed him that he had no penknife. But Eliot got up, saying 'You want a knife? I have not got a knife, I think!' We were able, ultimately, to provide a pair of nail scissors.

At last the strings were cut. A little gingerly Joyce unrolled the slovenly swaddlings of damp British brown paper in which the good-hearted American had packed up what he had put inside. Thereupon, along with some nondescript garments for the trunk—there were no trousers I believe—a fairly presentable pair of *old brown shoes* stood revealed, in the centre of the bourgeois French table.

As the meaning of this scene flashed upon my listless understanding, I saw in my mind's eye the phantom of the little enigmatic Ezra standing there (provided by our actions, and the position of his footgear at this moment, with a dominating stature which otherwise he scarcely could have attained) silently surveying his handiwork.

James Joyce, exclaiming very faintly 'Oh!' looked up, and we all gazed at the old shoes for a moment. 'Oh!' I echoed and laughed, and Joyce left the shoes where they were, disclosed as the matrix of the disturbed leaves of the parcel. He turned away and sat down again, placing his left ankle upon his right knee, and squeezing, and then releasing, the horizontal limb.

With a smile even slower in materializing than his still-trailing Bostonian voice (a handsome young United States President, to give you an idea—adding a Gioconda smile to the other charms of this office) Eliot asked our visitor if he would have dinner with us. Joyce turned to his son, and speaking very rapidly in Italian, the language always employed by him, so it seemed, in his family circle, he told him to go home: he would inform his mother that his father would not be home to dinner after all. Yes, his father had accepted an invitation to dinner, and would not be back after all, for the evening meal! Did he understand? To tell his mother that his father—But the son very hotly answered his father back, at this, after but a moment's hestitation on account of the company: evidently he did not by any means relish being entrusted with messages. It was, however, with great hotness, in yet more resonant Italian, that the son expressed his rebellious sensations when the imperturbable Jimmie handed him the parcel of disreputable footwear. That was the last straw—this revolting, this unbecoming packet. Having exchanged a good number of stormy words, in a series of passionate asides—in a good imitation of an altercation between a couple of neapolitan touts, of the better order—Joyce, père et fils, separated, the latter rushing away with the shoes beneath his arm, his face crimson and his eyes blazing with a truly southern ferocity—first having mastered himself for a moment sufficiently to bow to me from the hips, and to shake hands with heroic punctilio. This scene took place as we were about to leave the small hotel.

An 'Age Group' meets Itself

James Joyce, having disposed of his foreign-bred offspring, Ezra's embarrassing present, and his family arrangements for the evening, turned to us with the air of a man who has divested himself of a few minor handicaps, and asked us where we would like to dine and did we know Paris well, or would we commit ourselves to him and allow him to conduct us to a restaurant where he dined, from time to time, not far from where we were just then, and at which it was possible to get a good meal enough, though he had not been there lately.

We replied that we would gladly go with him to the restaurant he mentioned; and so he led the way in a very business-like fashion: he bustled on ahead of us—if the word bustled can be used of a very spare and light-footed cosmopolitan gentleman: he selected a table, took up the Menu before we had sat down, asked us what we liked, inspecting the violet scrawl to ascertain what was available in the matter of *plats du jour*. And before we could say Jack Robinson he had ordered a large and cleverly arranged dinner as far as possible for all palates, and with a great display of inside knowledge of the insides of civilized men and the resources of the cuisine of France, discovering what wines we were by way of liking if any. And he had asked for a bottle to start with to introduce the soup. And so on, through a first-class French repast, until we had finished, he pushed on, our indefatigable host: then, at a moment when we were not paying particular attention, he called for the bill: and before either of us could forestall him, he had whisked out of his breast pocket a handful of hundred-franc notes, and paid for this banquet; the wine, the liqueurs, the coffee, and added to it, it was evident, a lordly pourboire. Nor was it ever possible for T.S. Eliot or myself to pay for the smallest thing from that time onwards.

If we were in a taxicab with James Joyce, out he would spring in front of us. And before even we reached the pavement the fare was settled and the cabman was pocketing a disproportionately massive tip: whereas in a café no beer or coffee, whoever had ordered it, was ever paid for by anyone but the eminent recipient of the parcel of old shoes. Nor was there any means, whether that of physical violence or urgent persuasion, to redress this in the long run most burdensome balance in favour of us.

We had to pay his 'Irish pride' for the affair of the old shoes. That was it! He would not let us off. He was entirely unrelenting and we found it impossible to outmanoeuvre him.

Eliot and myself agreed that short of paying for meals before they were ordered, or knocking Joyce down every time he rushed forward to settle the taxicab fare, and holding him down while the other paid, there was no means of escaping. Ours was the female rôle of economic exemption, with its attendant humiliation, if regarded from the ancient standpoint of masculine convention. When alone with me Joyce would occasionally relax to the extent of allowing me to pay for an occasional drink of my own, never his, however. And even this was much later on.

Towards T.S. Eliot Joyce maintained a punctilious reserve. In alluding to him, with me, he would say 'Your friend Mr Eliot,' as if Eliot had been an obscure family friend, with whom I happened to be travelling, and who, out of polite humanity, must be suffered to accompany us. As to mentioning his writings, or as to ever a passing reference to him as *a poet*—that was the last thing that it ever occurred to Joyce to do, it seemed. Eliot perhaps had been accepted as the messenger sent by Ezra Pound with a pair of old shoes; to whom, if you like, out of courtesy to the good if misguided Ezra, Joyce offered hospitality. I was a different matter. But then, in any case, it was not I who had been the bearer of old shoes!

What part the old shoes really played in the comedy I do not know. Contemptuous, tolerant, discreetly correct, the author of *The Portrait of the Artist* did not seem best pleased with what was not a pleasantry, but something else, of course—though exactly *what* it might be I am unable to decide. I do not suppose, for instance, that, in a spirit of heavy mischief, Ezra in fact calculated, in handing Eliot the securely wrapped-up parcel, upon these *particular* social effects. Or had he perhaps? Why no: it would have taken a different mind from that of Pound to foresee the stilted occasion, the ceremony of the handing over of the brown-paper parcel; that atmosphere of highly continental or cosmopolitan formality, of Irish social pomp, of solemnly-smiling transatlantic reticence, on the part of this biliously handsome paladin, and myself there genuinely uninterested at the unpacking, an unmoved observer! On the contrary I believe this little matter arose from the romantic charity of a man who, on a certain side, is unsusceptible to the influences of the external world of human stimulus and response. It was the work of a charitable egotist.

When I remarked that James Joyce betrayed no knowledge of the identity of 'Your friend Mr Eliot', that statement demands some qualification. There was, indirectly, one occasion, during our first meeting, upon which he showed that he was conscious of Eliot's existence, apart from the fact of his happening to be travelling in France in my company.

This was when, as we sat together in the restaurant to which he had taken us (having breathlessly and with overpowering host-at-all-costly resolution ordered a full-course meal) he said to us—toasting us obliquely and ever so airily as he tasted his Château La Tour Rose with lung and tongue at once—'It appears that I have the melancholy advantage of being the eldest of the band,' or words to that effect. Band was not the word, nor group, but I cannot recall it nearer than this. He referred, of course, to the literary band, or group, comprised within the critical fold of Ezra Pound—the young, the 'New', group of writers assembled in Miss Weaver's *Egoist* just before and during the War. And of course Pound, Joyce, Eliot and myself were all within about five years of each other in the matter of age. At that time I imagine Eliot was about thirty, Joyce about thirty-six and I a year or two younger than him. So far as the classification of people by ages goes, we did certainly make, or we do make if you like a perfect 'age-class'.

Surely the vanity of classification, however, was never better exemplified, than in the persons of these four *Zeitgenossen*! We are all familiar with the solemn groupification that occurs every year or so of, usually, a half-dozen 'poets' or artists, introduced to the world by their impresario as the team chosen (by him if not by destiny) to represent the absolutely newest generation. To-day these teams age and disintegrate with alarming rapidity. But new ones take their place. And always the rationale of their assemblage is that their members were all born of women about the same time.

Well, sure enough, the birth years of Mr Pound's little circle, including Mr Pound himself, were 'all sprinkled up and down', as Eliot once remarked to me, 'the Eighties of the last century'. And if being born in a stable makes you a horse, why then being born in the same years is liable, perhaps, to make you an identical human product. A mechanical theory at the best, for the purposes of the literary pigeonholing of a complex society this method is useless. According to this simple-hearted rule, Herr Adolf Hitler is as like as two peas with any Cantonese or Peruvian born at the exact minute of the Eighties of the last Century at which Herr Hitler saw the light—irrespective of place, traditions, individual ancestry, glandular, nervous, and other bodily make-up—race, religion and what not! Here we have the time-philosopher's classification with a vengeance!

But in the first place, even the *time* factor does not accord with this classification. In the Atlas Mountains to-day, or in the Tibetan hinterland, the inhabitants are anything but *Zeitgenossen* of the citizens of Chicago or of Fascist Rome. They are existing in what is the equivalent of our European feudal age. They are the contemporaries of Bayard and La Palice—or of Roland and Oliver—much more than of Litvinov and Count Ciano.

So, as to the little age-group implicitly recognized in James Joyce's remark—with a solemn sidelong wrinkling of the nose and eye, meant for that busy Manager, and propagandist, Ezra—four people more dissimilar in every respect than himself, myself, Pound and Eliot respectively, it would be difficult to find. There is only one sense in which any such a grouping of us acquires some significance—we all got started on our careers before the War. This was, I believe, an advantage. In other respects, Joyce brought up by the Jesuits—in Ireland—in the 'Celtic Twilight'—trained as a medico—thereafter exiled in Trieste and Switzerland, and becoming an Italianate Irishman: what a different set of circumstances are those to the origins for instance and early environment of Eliot? Born under the shadow of the famous New England puritanism, but transplanted to a city south of the Mason and Dixon Line, returning to Harvard and sent into another hemisphere to get a polish at Oxford, and subsequently drafted to Germany to finish this complicated process of training. Hardly can you compel such disparities at all into a class. Substitute place for time, and suppose two people born upon the same square foot of ground, one in the age of William the Conqueror and one in 1937—one a Negro and one a Norman. It would be in vain to classify them according to identity of *place*, and hope for any fruitful results.

Our Lady of the Sleeping-Cars

Eliot and myself remained in Paris for some days, I forget how many. All of our time was passed in the hospitable company of James Joyce. Paris might have been his demesne, though he had only been there a month—he only knew a few streets at that period and would lose himself between Invalides and the Chamber of Deputies and was uncertain of his whereabouts even in the Latin Quarter, once he was off his beat.

Our stay was one long fête. Except for our hotel bill—which he made no attempt, as far as I know, to settle—we lived free of charge. A party would be suggested by us: and although of course Joyce paid for it, it was still *our* party. And then we could not refuse to accept a return banquet, to cap our banquet; when, in the nature of things, and hoping that *this* time we might outwit this implacable *payer*, we proposed yet another meeting—on our own ground, at some restaurant of our own choosing; but always with the same result.

To the last Eliot was treated distantly, as I have said. And this did not make these transactions any the more palatable for 'poor Tom'.

'He does not take much notice of me!' he drawled one day, with sardonic resignation, when we were discussing the problem of how to stand our eminent colleague a glass of beer—agreeing, of course, that in fact it was a feat beyond our powers, for, with the best grace we could, we had admitted defeat by this time. 'But *you* might I should have thought do something about it,' he said, with heavy melancholy mischief.

'I have expostulated with him in private and in public,' I answered. 'He does not appear to understand. He thinks he is obliged to pay. He has some idea that he *must*.'

I encountered, a little later on, a similar phenomenon to this in Venice. There I met Mr Francis Meynell for the first time. I was introduced to him by Osbert Sitwell, at a large café in the Square of St Mark's one evening. There were about ten people at our table I should think, and I was astonished to find after a time that Mr Meynell always paid for the successive rounds of drinks.

On expressing some reluctance to continue under this régime of enigmatical patronage, and making some expressive movement, indicative of my intention to break the spell, I was stopped by Osbert Sitwell, who whispered, in a purring, nasal, *chuchotement* which gives a special flavour to that gentleman's asides, that it was 'no use'.

This puzzled me still more. And as Osbert Sitwell remarked that I was still not satisfied that all was as it should be, he explained, still under his breath, that Francis Meynell felt obliged, on account of his political opinions, to be responsible for the bill. Mr Meynell was 'very sensitive', that was all I really understood. He was an outstanding Radical, so it was a case of *noblesse oblige*.

The logic of what he told me appeared entirely satisfactory to Osbert Sitwell, and I raised no further objections, though completely mystified.

Here at all events is what looks like a clear case of the same sort of fixed idea; namely that refreshments *must* be paid for by one member of a party and by no other member: indeed that drinks must be stood to all within sight: that there is *a duty* to do so, imposed upon a particular person.

As to what I am persuaded was the true motive of the embarrassing liberality on the part of James Joyce, to return to that, it never I think, occurred to Eliot to allow for the emotional weight of the Pair of Old Shoes. He put it down to an attack of objectionable openhandedness, to which, as an Irishman, he supposed, Mr Joyce was probably subject; and which our presence stimulated to an unprecedented degree. Joyce was showing off, he was probably always showing off: and his native aggressiveness caused him to affect to be icily unaware that he was in this way entertaining, nay over-entertaining, an angel, an angelic, an

41

archangelic poet of great promise, with a brood of brooding Prufrocks behind him.

'I find our friend,' said I, 'very affable and easy, don't you, if a shade stilted?' But Eliot found him definitely burdensome, and *arrogant*. Very arrogant.

'I do not think he is *arrogant*,' I said, astonished at this description of Pound's proud protégé, who seemed to me to be a civil, unassuming man enough, of agreeable and accommodating manners, except for his obsession regarding economic independence, which was harmless after all. If he really got a kick out of dashing on the tips of the little patent leather shoes (so unlike those dilapidated stogies dispatched by Ezra) towards the desk of a restaurant and putting us under obligations, according to suburban money-canons, well, there was no great harm at all.

'He may not seem so!' Eliot answered, in his grim Bostonian growl. 'He may not seem arrogant, no.'

'You think he is as proud as Lucifer?'

'I would not say Lucifer!' Eliot was on his guard at once, at this loose use of the surname of the Evil Principle.

'You would not say Lucifer? Well I daresay he may be under the impression that he is being "as proud as Lucifer", or some bogtrotting humbug of that order. What provincials they are, bless their beastly brogues!'

'Provincials—yes!' Eliot agreed with contemptuous unction. 'Provincials.'

'However he is most polite.'

'He is polite.'

'I have never succeeded in getting out of the door *behind* him, have you? He is very *You First*. He is very *After you!*'

'Oh yes. He is polite, he is polite enough. But he is exceedingly arrogant. Underneath. That is why he is so polite. I should be better pleased if he were less polite.' Eliot was very grim.

'I personally don't care if he *is* arrogant—all I ask, in the words of the New England literary chanty, is "a little god-darned seevility and not much of that!" But I should be surprised if he is really arrogant.'

'No-o?' Eliot was impressed by my persistence. 'You may of course be right. It doesn't matter.'

'Not much really.'

I puzzled over this charge of 'arrogance'—it was quite a new reading for me of this perhaps after all enigmatical discovery of Ezra's, who only a few hours before had sung us a love song, all about a young lady who was ill, who indeed was dying, whose death would be the heartbreak, the despair, of the male voice, all of the most disarming passionate bel canto.—I could not see, frankly, where the arrogance came in. This Dublin gondolier might be poor and proud, but he could not be arrogant. That did not go with gondolier.

In these years Lewis had several love affairs and as many quarrels, found it increasingly difficult to sell his paintings because of opposition from Roger Fry and Fry's Bloomsbury associates, and was in financial straits only slightly eased by money from friends, which he accepted while resenting the need for it. The reason for his reclusion was the production of an immense analysis of post-war Britain, and by extension of Europe, and by further extension the United States, to be called *The Man of the World*. The varied aspects of this work, and the way in which Lewis slipped from one of them to another, disturbed his friends, and in the end he accepted Eliot's advice that he should concentrate on one book at a time rather than planning eight or ten. Or at least he accepted the advice to the extent that he decided to divide *The Man of the World* into several volumes. The extent of his energies became manifest when *The Art of Being Ruled* appeared in 1926, *The Lion and the Fox* and *Time and Western Man* in the following year, *The Childermass* in 1928 and *Paleface* in 1929. In this same period his satiric fiction *The Apes of God* was being written, and stories written earlier were collected and published as *The Wild Body*. In correspondence Lewis mentions other works of fiction which remain unpublished, although parts of them exist in manuscript.

The Art of Being Ruled is a key book, almost *the* key book to read as a guide to understanding Lewis's ideas, the way his mind worked, his ability to absorb an enormous amount of information about everyday aspects of life and then demonstrate the social implications of the links between them—and also the disconcerting jumps he sometimes made when doing the linking. Some of the views that seemed outrageous in 1926 are now conventional wisdom. The idea that the thoughts and actions of people can be controlled through the adroit use of publicity, not just by commercial organisations but also by the agents of government, is commonplace today when opinion polls are called for on every subject from the use of washing powders to the standing of political parties, the moral rights or wrongs of atomic energy power stations, and legalised abortion. What Lewis called 'the doctrine of *What The Public Wants* . . . the notion of *the will of the greatest number*' has today been enormously enlarged so that it is used by all governments in many forms. Floods of figures are produced to suggest that 'in real terms' conditions which appear to be worsening are improving, opinion polls to show that the puppets who make up the Public are truly the arbiters of their various societies and nations, their rulers merely agents who carry out 'the will of the greatest number'. And the manipulations are made with such dexterity that people do not understand what is happening, and will say that they don't believe all they read in the papers or see on TV when the whole cast of their thought has been formed by the very media they are decrying.

Lewis's general vision of contemporary society has already been suggested, and the extracts show particular aspects of his thought. Here he is writing about the illusion of freedom.

from THE ART OF BEING RULED

'Bolshevism and the West'

The european community which participated at the great change-over from the predominantly agricultural to the industrial age presented us with the French Revolution, which was made possible by the super-agriculturist dreams of Rousseau. While these people bustled into factories, or were driven into them, building themselves more rigidly and irretrievably into a mechanical urban life, they exploded in dreams of bucolic 'freedom'. Pictures of the 'freedom' of the noble savage and the child of nature excited them to a great outburst at the very moment when (as they must from their own point of view have regarded it had they not been so full of a false and exotic emotion) they were enslaving themselves more thoroughly to men. So it has been in the name of nature always that men have combined to overthrow the natural in themselves.

For their instinct to be so fallible, where, it would seem, so much is at stake for them—for them to proclaim so ardently that they wish to be 'free' and nature's children, and yet, in effect, to carry through great movements that result in an absolute mechanization of their life,—can only mean one thing. It must mean that they do not really know what they want, that they do not, in their heart, desire 'freedom' or anything of the sort. 'Freedom' postulates a relatively solitary life: and the majority of people are extremely gregarious. A disciplined, well-policed, herd-life is what they most desire. The 'naturalistic' form that eighteenth-century revolution took was because all violent revolution is saturnalian. A rare saturnalia is necessary for most people, but it exhausts their passions, and the rest of the year they are anything but their saturnalian selves. The few years of youth is such a saturnalia: but youth, in that case, is not synonymous with life.

That men should *think* they wish to be free, the origin of this grave and universal mistake, is the (usually quite weak) primitive animal in them coming into his own for a moment. It is a restless, solitary ghost in them that in idle moments they turn to. The mistake can be best appreciated, perhaps, by examining a great holiday crowd. How can these masses of slowly, painfully moving people find any enjoyment in such immense stuffy discomfort, petty friction, and unprofitable fatigue, you may ask yourself as you watch them. They ask themselves that, too, no doubt, most of them. That is the saturnalian, libertarian, rebellious self that asserts itself for a moment. But if they *have to choose* between what ultimately the suggestions of the 'free' self, and the far steadier, stronger impulse of the gregarious, town-loving, mechanical self, would lead to, they invariably choose the latter. So to be 'free' for one person is not what to be 'free' for another would be. Most people's favourite spot in 'nature' is to be found in the body of another person, or in the mind of another person, not in meadows, plains, woods, and trees. They depend for their stimulus on people, not things. So inevitably they are not 'free' nor have any wish to be, in the lonely, 'independent', wild, romantic, rousseauesque way. In short, the last thing they wish for is to be free. They wish to pretend to be 'free' once a week, or once a

45

month. To be free all the time would be an appalling prospect for them. And they prefer 'freedom' to take a violent, super-real, and sensational form. They are not to the manner born where 'freedom' is concerned; and so invariably overplay it, when they affect it.

━━━━━━━

The following passage from later in the same chapter 'Bolshevism and the West' is written in contradiction of Bertrand Russell's view (shared by many) that all change in the world of the Twenties was likely to be tentative and gradual, that 'it is no use to try things until people are more or less ready for them', the 'things' being radical social changes. Lewis advances a whole cluster of contrary views emphasising the increase of standardisation and uniformity—again, processes now much more obvious than they were in his day.

from THE ART OF BEING RULED

If the rulers of the world wished it to develop on marxian lines, which ultimately is not at all likely, it would develop like that. Were these rulers world-rulers, either an open or unavowed centralized government, or a confederacy of closely knit international interests, they would have the power to impose any orthodoxy they chose from China to Peru. They would be able to make the matron in Yokohama and Dublin simultaneously appear in a dress of lotus leaves, a vest of mail, a ballet-dancer's skirt, or a crinoline: to shave her head, or dangle her hair in plaits; to see that she had seven lovers, or to see that she confined herself to her husband: to decree that she only had sexual intercourse on prescribed days; that in the grip of *fashion*, so much more effective than that of *law*, she was a confirmed vegetarian one week and a hearty beef-eater the next. Every thought and action of both herself, her husband, and her family could be rigidly controlled without her knowing it, actually, if it amused them to leave her in ignorance of her puppet-like servitude. And she would be quite happy. All these things in any case can be observed around us in an imperfect, primitive form to-day.

Already the standardization coming in the wake of the compounding of local national interests has made our civilization very uniform; sport, the cuisine, the centralized fashion-control, and so forth, imposing this unity more thoroughly every day. Without insisting on this tendency, the evidences of which are so accessible and universally recognized, it is legitimate to say that those differences between individual and individual in our community, or between the various western nations, the differences to which Mr Russell refers, are potentially a matter of the past. That past was truly nationalist and regional. To-day neither the motive nor even the possibility of these differences between nation and nation exist. And the change has not been 'gradual', like biologic growth; but swift, like the effect of the appliances of the human will precipitating the leisurely habits of nature.

With individuals it is the same thing. As the opportunities for individual business enterprise diminish, the great trusts relieving the individual of any particular initiative or energy more thoroughly every day, and as the mechanical pressure of public opinion, aiming at a highly organized uniformity, makes any personal irregularity increasingly prohibitive and not worth while, the differences between individuals, either in mentality, or personal appearance, or individual habits, disappear. They were the exuberant marks of a disordered age, before the doctrine of an economic uniformity had become also a social law. The 'individual' tends rapidly to disappear, as do national characteristics. In this, too, Mr Russell is using an argument for 'gradualness' depending on conditions that no longer have any reality. For the pace, even, at which this standardization and drawing together is proceeding is in itself one of the most excellent arguments against his theory of a leisurely, conservative growth.

This *uniformity* is the object of much abuse and protest on the part of the stereotyped regionalist reactionary. But does he not contradict the reality responsible for his protest? China for the Chinese, for instance, is the regionalist cry. But when China was actually for the Chinese, a Chinaman never saw, from year's end to year's end, anything but a Chinaman. Did he complain of this 'uniformity', then? Regionalism, Merrie England, etc., is in reality a movement to substitute one uniformity for another: a small one for a big one. The really fanatical regionalist, confining himself entirely to Puddletown and its parish pump, would be surrounded by an absolute 'uniformity' of puddletownians.

A visit to *St Joan*, and a consideration of that play in the context of what he had already been saying about the inadequacy of Russell's gradualism, blends happily with Lewis's general argument that in future governments will become more conscious of their power and its potentials, and use it more ruthlessly. His prevision did not go so far as to contemplate the present position, when most of the world's governments quite calmly accept the use of torture as a necessary aspect of policy—while, of course, denying its existence, or saying that it occurs only in isolated cases of which senior officials were in ignorance. The files of Amnesty International tell a different story.

The criticism of *St Joan*, or of the attitudes behind it, is the more effective because Lewis acknowledges the 'very noble understanding' at the play's origins. At the same time it conveys something of what those who regarded themselves as progressive thinkers found uncongenial about Lewis—many of them thought 'the swan-song of English liberalism' exemplified in the play the most congenial, and indeed the only song to sing. The more general criticism of Shaw's status as philosopher-king that follows emphasises again Lewis's belief that human life *in itself* is not of value. It is only what humans make of it, what sort of society they create, that *may* be valuable. It follows, of course, that some lives are important, others are not, a view outraging all modern egalitarian beliefs.

from THE ART OF BEING RULED

Violence and 'Kindliness': Mr Bernard Shaw and Mr Bertrand Russell

In a general way Mr Russell has a habit of discussing things that are in full swing to-day as though they belonged to a very distant future. Thus he says that *some day* it may be possible, in place of violence, for the ruler to attain his ends by means of other forms of coercion.

It is not necessary, when we are considering political consequences, to pin our faith to the particular theories of the ductless glands, which may blow over, like other theories. All that is essential in our hypothesis is the belief that physiology will in time find ways of controlling emotion, which it is scarcely possible to doubt. When that day comes, we shall have the emotions desired by our rulers, and the chief business of elementary education will be to produce the desired disposition, no longer by punishment or moral precept, but by the far surer method of injection or diet. The men who will administer this system will have a power beyond the dreams of the Jesuits, but there is no reason to suppose that they will have more sense than the men who control education to-day.

By 'sense' here Mr Russell means—what? That these rulers, with governmental power infinitely magnified, will still wish to *rule*; get all they can out of their fellows, in short, rather than live, and use the power they have seized, 'for the good of' mankind. 'Sense' does not mean anything more than that, however: it would show very little 'sense' if they applied themselves to these good works, instead of enjoying their power. The words he uses, such as 'kindliness' and 'sense', are characteristically weak and modest. Such graceful modesty will not to-day meet the case. And the 'kindliness' of Mr Russell or Mr Shaw has an unpleasant sound of moral charlatanism, of the virtue *à bon marché* of the immensely prosperous old liberal England; that again will not answer the case. No one but a great saint can tread that road to-day and be respected. Vegetarianism and geniality are a mockery for our present danger and need.

In seeing Mr Shaw's play, *St Joan*, it was difficult to resist the suggestion that the cast had been furnished by the anglican clergy. The 'kindliness' of the Earl of Warwick, the 'kindliness' of the Bastard, the 'kindliness', in different ways, of everybody on the stage (with the exception of the admirable actor who took the part of the bishop of Beauvais) was overwhelming. It could have been produced by no machinery except that of anglo-saxon protestantism, livened up a little bit for the occasion by irish charm. The poorness of the language (when such things as 'green fields' had to be mentioned by Joan of Arc, who booed cheerlessly the thin journalese with which she was provided, this was forced on the attention)—the incessant rattle of stale, clever argumentation—the heartiness and 'kindliness' pervading everything—the chill of a soulless, arty, indefatigable 'rational' presentation of the theme—must have an increasingly depressing effect on the audience it seems destined to attract, if it is not softened or otherwise modified in new interpretations. It is the swan-song of english liberalism staged for the post-war suburbs of London. The 'kindly' twinkle in Mr Lyall Sweete's eye, his massive gladstonian jaw and bulky person, is the symbol of that strange thing, part humbug, part fierce possessiveness, part real gentleness and goodness, that has served the white race so ill.

Why it is necessary to expose and condemn this humanitarianism, with the especial local colour conveyed for us in the word 'kindly' ('kindliness' having such a different sense to 'kind'), is because it is a sort of spiritual nineteenth-century vulgarization of the great fanatical compassion of which it is a degenerate, genial, tepid form; a half-measure, embalmed in rationalistic discourse.

It is always 'on the right tack': it never reaches any effective position. *St Joan*, for example, has for its theme a very noble understanding of the unhappy situation of the saint. But Mr Shaw, in spite of himself, desecrates it with his weak-minded, chilly worldliness, which is *plus fort que lui*. He seems to 'give away', to betray, at least artistically (which in a play is naturally everything), his heroine. He is resolved to show the world this situation, but he has not the power. He laughs, twinkles, and cackles to hide his incompetence where this task is concerned.

In the preface of *Back to Methuselah* there is similarly a fine humane motive at work. But what happens at the end? Well, of course, the play. But Adam and Eve are in the same predicament as Joan of Arc where their presentment by Mr Shaw is concerned. They speak the jargon of the city tea-shop; as you read you fancy them in bathing drawers, a London bank clerk and his girl, great Wells readers, extemporizing in a studio the legend of the creation, prompted, mephistopheles-fashion, by Mr Shaw: and the preface remains the play.

'Nobody noticed the new religion in the centre of the intellectual whirlpool,' he says, referring to the master-work of his maturity. He now reveals this latent 'new religion', which turns out to be Bergson's *élan vital*. He writes: 'Darwinism proclaimed that our true relation is that of competitors and combatants in a struggle for mere survival, and that every act of pity or loyalty to the old fellowship is a vain and mischievous attempt to lessen the severity of the struggle and preserve inferior varieties from the efforts of Nature to weed them out.' But in the surplus life in which he suggests, as human creatures, we should live, he has nothing very positive to offer, except his 'new religion', that is, Bergson's *creative evolution.*

He misrepresents his hero Nietzsche, whom he interprets as follows: 'Nietzsche, for example . . . concluding that the final objective in this Will was power over self, and that the seekers after power over others and material possessions were on a false scent.' This sense is certainly not obtained from a reading of Nietzsche's works. 'Power over others' came very vividly into the programme of that philosopher. Again, as a persuasive engine the exhortation to 'self-control' does not seem the best; it smacks of the Y.M.C.A. straight talks to young men. All his persuasiveness is haunted by this sort of vulgarity of mind: almost less than any famous english writer has he what Arnold would call a 'celtic' tact. He inccssantly (when his criticism is finished and his persuasion begins) suggests the sunday school, or the 'straight and hearty, man to man' talk.

How, finally, these things can be summarized, is that both Mr Shaw and Mr Russell fail as artists, they have no dramatic sense above the rhetoric of the anglican pulpit. Although they can convince us of their sincerity, they would not be able to convince a stranger from some other system of things, because there is no vibration in their words or universal significance in their gestures. They are just words, opinions, that they have been unable to fuse, and which they have not the force to dramatically present. And their humanitarianism is a poor, prosaic food, meant for a cruder animal existence, and a much easier and more fortunate one, than ours.

Vegetarianism and Capital Punishment

The eating of meat and the execution of criminals are the two acts that bring out more intensely than any others all our perplexities as 'human animals.' It is difficult to come to any decision about them without appearing either a brute or a humbug.

At the root of both of these questions it is advisable to place the not

51

necessarily inhuman proposition that life is in itself not important. Our values make it so: but they are mostly, the important ones, non-human values, although the intenser they are the more they imply a supreme, vital connotation.

To attach, as the humanitarian does, a mystical value to *life* itself, for its own sake, is as much a treachery to spiritual truth as it is a gesture of 'humanity.' We execute a criminal for a variety of frivolous reasons, and often kill the wrong one. The manner of the administration of our law is thoughtless and brutal usually. But the theory of capital punishment (if the 'punishment' of the *too-just god of the law* could be abstracted from it) is as humane as possible. A higher value than all he can allege in his favour—namely, the fact that he is *alive*—we consider is threatened by the most violent and extreme criminal. It is his 'violence' that we are seeking to eliminate by destroying him. It is the principle of non-violence that he menaces by his existence: which is a superhuman one. We know that to improve our conditions as animals we must banish violence from life. We put a 'value on life,' a *violence value*, as it were. The assassin or poisoner cannot plead that he should live *because he is alive*, when it is *life*, and in addition the only thing that gives life a supernatural value, that he is attacking.

'It is sometimes necessary to kill men, as it is always necessary to kill tigers,' Mr Shaw admits in the preface from which I have already quoted. And many people hold that it is very often necessary to kill men as it is necessary to kill sheep in prodigious numbers. (Shaw is saved by his vegetarianism from extending his permission to massacre.) But are the tiger-men untamable? Or could they not all be trapped and put in a Zoo, where the humane crowds could examine them at leisure?

One of Mr Shaw's principal intellectual weaknesses is his optimism where the success of taming is concerned. That is the liberal's old and terrible mistake. The permission to slay the tiger-man is belated. And the 'kindliness' shown to the man-eating tiger-man has accounted for the slaughter of more sheep-men than any simple brutality could ever have done: the theory is so humane, but in practice it is so inhuman. So the point is reached at last when all the liberal men can say is what we have heard Mr Bertrand Russell saying: 'Failing that' (the world being saved by 'kindliness'), 'it seems that the solution which the Houyhnhnms adopted towards the Yahoos, namely extermination, is the only one; apparently the Yahoos are bent on applying it to each other.' This is a rather bloodthirsty point of bitterness for the liberal (surveying the sanguinary chaos for which he is responsible) to have reached!

The intricate problem of capital punishment cannot be dealt with, of course, here, in a few passing observations. For my purpose, however, it is enough to say that the rhetoric of death and of the law, devised as a 'punishment' and a deterrent, is one thing, and the question of regarding the loss of life itself (apart from the needless tortures of trial and execution) as inhuman or not, is another.

In general, it can be asserted that the characteristic humanitarian attitude reposes on an exaggeration of the importance of crude and concrete *life* itself. Life, *tout court*, plays too great a part in that attitude.

The cruelty of the law, on the other hand, errs in assuming a sensitiveness that is certainly absent in the majority of violent criminals. That accounts for the 'deterrent' notion. In general, men seem disposed to think that other men are greater cowards than in fact they are. Animal courage is the most underestimated of common facts. It seems that people are not as a whole so attached to life as they are supposed to be, or they are attached differently. About the animal world of Darwin's 'struggle for existence,' with which Mr Shaw's preface to *Back to Methuselah* principally deals, men must be even more mistaken. Many of the situations observed by Fabre and other entomologists can only be accounted for in the way that Weismann, to Mr Shaw's horror, accounts for them. Here is the passage in which he discusses this point:—

> And the darwinians went far beyond denying consciousness to trees. Weismann insisted that the chick breaks out of its egg-shell automatically; that the butterfly, springing into the air to avoid the pounce of the lizard, 'does not wish to avoid death, knows nothing about death,' what has happened being simply that a flight instinct evolved by Circumstantial Selection reacts promptly to a visual impression produced by the lizard's movement. His proof is that the butterfly immediately settles again on the flower, and repeats the performance every time the lizard springs, thus showing that it learns nothing from experience, and—Weismann concludes—is not conscious of what it does.

Battle itself, or murder even, is probably not horrible for living creatures, only *thinking about* those things. Action, mechanical functional

53

activity without reflection, probably leaves no room for the conception of death. Although it is disputed, it is still a widely held belief that primitive men did not understand or reason about death, as they were ignorant of the circumstances of their coming into the world.

We have the well-known statement that the horse in the burning stable is very difficult to get away. He moves into the flames if left alone: he does not wish to leave the fire, which he does not understand and which fascinates him. He is like the child who has never burnt his fingers, but likes and is attracted by the pleasant flame. Without accumulating instances or going farther into this, it seems likely that the bird being fascinated by the snake is having what we should call a 'fascinating' experience, perhaps unique in its life. Until it is killed, which naturally terminates its pleasure, it is having 'the time of its life.' The snake, it is true, is an artist, and that Mr Shaw would hardly understand. But many insects develop mesmeric head-dresses and symbolize their destructive purposes with emblems of terror and power that probably make the insect-world, for their victims, a place of delight.

To take two of the homeliest examples: it is probable that the mouse enjoys its half-hour with the cat when it is caught very much. Then who can doubt that the spinster or susceptible widow with a small bank account enjoys every minute of the time during which she is being destroyed by some homicidal impostor for her money? And the soldier, except when he is inactive and has to think and imagine instead of act, is no doubt usually having a most enjoyable time. He likes acting better than thinking, habit is strong; and he will find ways of acting even when thrown on his own resources, and in a situation more favourable for thought.

To conclude, the vast mistake, exemplified so well by Mr Shaw, is that he does not realize that men are tigers, wasps, and wolves, or parrots, geese, sheep, and asses, or the humdrum monkey, rather than men. He is, in short, too anthropomorphic. For all his lifetime of raillery and scolding he has not realized quite what sort of animal he has been talking to. 'The creatures that we see around us are not men: there is some perversion, the cause of which we cannot penetrate,' Rousseau would have told him. I think that his is a creditable and amiable mistake; but it puts him (and those of his persuasion) in a weak position where the science of life is concerned.

Sometimes, of course, he will pretend to understand, as when he is describing the embarrassments of the ruler:—

Good-natured, unambitious men are cowards when they have no religion. They are dominated and exploited not only by greedy and often half-witted and half-alive weaklings who will do anything for cigars, champagne, motor-cars, and the more childish and selfish uses of money, but by able and sound administrators who can do nothing else with them than dominate and exploit them. Government and exploitation become synonymous under such circumstances; and the world is finally ruled by the childish, the brigands, and the blackguards.

That statement is full of confusions, because he has only half come out of his shell into the light of reality. For example, he admits that even 'able and sound administrators' can find nothing better to do with 'unambitious men than *dominate* them.' ('Exploit' is only an emotional redundancy: for who ever heard of a ruler not getting something out of his rule?) But then he winds up with his 'children and blackguards,' immediately forgetting his admission of the 'able and sound administrators' into the picture. Yet (if such people exist, and he says they do) these 'able and sound' personages would surely have something to say to their 'childish and blackguardly' rivals, and not necessarily leave them to have the last word and the world to be 'finally ruled' by them?

What Mr Shaw does not add, but should, is that 'unambitious men' would far rather be ruled by a 'brigand' or a 'child' (whom they can understand) than by Mr Shaw. For that would require a measure of 'ambition' that is unfortunately by no means common. That is the fallacy of the philosopher-king that we are brushing against.

Mr Shaw has been a sort of mocking and 'mischievous' conscience to middle-class England for a good many years. People have put up with him because (in his capacity of 'a conscience') he was such a respectable thing to have. He has been the one thing that has saved their face—while all the time he has been persuaded that he was putting them dreadfully out of countenance! But he has often been angrily accused of treating the public with contempt. The mistake emphasized above shows him, of course, in an opposite light—the mistake in virtue of which, bursting with optimism and friendliness, he approached the public brimming innocently with highly intellectual conversation, as though cheerily exclaiming, 'Ah, you old villain, I'll make a philosopher of you before I'm done with you!' The public has smiled and smiled—and remained a villain. Horatio wrote in his tablets in vain where Mr Shaw was concerned.

In the nursery in which the 'blackguardly' children (who 'will do anything for cigars, champagne, and motor-cars') rule the unambitious children (whose appetites do not aspire to these exciting luxuries), and in which Mr Shaw has sat like a very genial uncle, a 'kindly' twinkle in his eye, humorously recommending the unambitious to revolt, there is a great deal of bloodshed. The game of government goes on, and it is a game that no philosopher has ever been able to interrupt seriously for a moment. The children die in shoals, the philosopher is aghast. But they hardly know they are dying—in the way, at least, that the philosopher understands it. The villains of the play (namely, the children fond of champagne and cigars) are as intent on the game, and as childlike, necessarily, as the others. The presence of a grown-up (a philosopher like Mr Shaw) is useful; it enables them to be more ferocious than ever. The 'freedom of speech' in which he is able to indulge is their sanction, it gives an air of *fairness* to anything that happens. (Mr Shaw especially, would give an air of *fairness* to almost anything. His mere presence at the most disgraceful spectacle would confer a certain respectability on it.) The philosopher stands wringing his hands, and the bloodshed redoubles in violence. A paroxysm of slaughter supervenes. When it abates, the voice of the philosopher is heard imploring the children not to cut off the tail of a mouse that they have caught: 'Ever since (Darwin) set up Circumstantial Selection as the creator and ruler of the universe, the scientific world has been the very citadel of stupidity and cruelty. Fearful as the tribal god of the Hebrews was, nobody ever shuddered as they passed even his meanest and narrowest Little Bethel or his proudest war-consecrating cathedral as we shudder now when we pass a physiological laboratory.' In the listlessness and exhaustion ensuing on what was perhaps the biggest beano that has ever occurred, the voice is heard exclaiming: 'Neither the rulers nor the ruled understand high politics. They do not even know that there is such a branch of knowledge as political science; but between them they can coerce and enslave with the deadliest efficiency, even to the wiping out of civilization, because their education as slayers has been honestly and thoroughly carried out. Essentially the rulers are all defectives; and there is nothing worse than government by defectives who wield irresistible powers of physical coercion.'

The scandal of these childish sports is, however, probably about to receive the attention of a more efficient principle of order than that of the irresponsible philosopher. Instead of the ineffective sporting 'fairness' of moral authority, there will be the justice of force. Let us suppose that that turns out worse than things have always been. At least the attempt is on novel lines, the old factors of failure are as far as possible eliminated. And at least the power engaged has shown from the start a sympathetic understanding of the adage, 'Boys will be boys!' which commutatively could be expressed, 'Animals will be animals!', which is more than can be said for the author whose views I have been discussing, who wishes that all the children would grow up, which is impossible. Animal life would never support the strain of his too ambitious programme.

Death and blood and all the problems arising in connection with them are, then, the central difficulty with us as 'progressive' animals. No one could object to wars for an instant if they were like the Valhalla wars, in which the dead rose up and rode home to a good dinner once the battle was over. It is the fact that they are supposed, rightly or wrongly, to be *real* that makes them objectionable. And I have just indicated what lines the solution of that secular problem would take here. A few further remarks of a general nature may define a little more the answer intended.

The philosopher at all times is opposed to violence: at least, it is very seldom that he is not, Sorel and Nietzsche being exceptions. The philosophic man inveighs against violence ostensibly on other people's behalf. Really he is speaking for himself: not only has he no mandate, but he would be found on careful investigation not to have the sanction of life, for his humane contentions. As in the play or novel, drama or violence is a highly prized ingredient, so it is in life, which the majority of people do not take so seriously as the philosopher. The philosopher is apt to regard life (*tout court*) as precious and full of mysterious power and sanctity, because his own is so full of interest and vitality. That is probably not the general view: most people cannot develop any such flattering conception of their personal existence.

The faith and conviction of the philosopher imposes itself on them when they come in contact with it. But when they get out of touch with this influence—which tends to attach so much *importance* to everything—they naturally pitch their tone much lower, and a fatalism or frivolity where life and death are concerned is the result.

'(Shakespeare) developed that curious and questionable art of building us a refuge from despair by disguising the cruelties of Nature as jokes,' says Mr Shaw. If this is a true account of shakespearean humour, then it was not Shakespeare who invented it. The popular mind is at one with Shakespeare in that respect. And it is actually a characteristic of philosophy that enables it to reach this 'questionable' condition, if Schopenhauer's definition holds, namely, that the true philosopher is to be recognized by a constant sense of the *unreality* of the things by which he is surrounded.

How then is bloodshed or violence to be regarded? Essentially as an excess, nothing more: for if you see life not in compartments, but unified as one appetite, violence is a sadism merely, a degeneration the powerful ruler would ban. The roman mortuary games, and their eventual overwhelming extension into an official bloodbath, were the sign of the decline of authority and power.

No 'moral' or ethical value can stand for a moment against the intoxication of death, and such values are of no service except in secure and peaceful times. Nothing but the most dreadful force can deal with a licence of that sort that has got its head. Therefore there are times when any resolute ambitious force must be supported.

Where violence is concerned the aesthetic principle is evidently of more weight than the 'moral', the latter being only the machinery to regulate the former. One is an expedient, whose pretensions can easily be exploded: the other is the thing itself. As measure is the principle of all true art, and as art is an enemy of all excess, so it is along aesthetic lines that the solution of this problem should be sought rather than along moral (or police) lines, or humanitarian ones. The soberness, measure, and order that reigns in all the greatest productions of art is the thing on which it is most useful to fix the mind in considering this problem. The blood of the roman circus; the cheap pastry of stuffy and sadic romance, with its sweet and viscous sentimentalism, which was manufactured with such success by Proust; the highly spiced incestuous pastry of Freud; the *exaggeration*, emphasis, and unreality of all forms of common melodrama, are all in the same class, and are vulgar first, and evil because of that: the ethical canon must ultimately take its authority from taste. It is a higher form of the appetite that leads to excess, that leads to the measure of aesthetic delight. Sadistic excess attempts to reach roughly and by harshness what art reaches by fineness.

We have been looking so far at the first sections of the book, called 'Revolution and Progress' (revolutionary social change Lewis saw as inevitable because of the development of new industrial techniques) and 'Agricultural Thought and Industrial Thought'. The book now moves on to sections concerned with the 'small man', the mass or the herd. Borrowing, with acknowledgement, a phrase from Goethe, Lewis divides people into 'natures' (original thinkers or artists) and 'puppets' (the mechanical, obedient remainder). The puppets, of course, do not understand their own mechanical quality, but wish to be real people, with original thoughts, genuine personalities. The following passage comes from the chapter 'The Contemporary Man "Expresses His Personality" '.

from THE ART OF BEING RULED

The Contemporary Man 'Expresses His Personality'

Generally speaking, it can be said that people wish to escape from themselves (this by no means excluding the crudest selfishness). When people are encouraged, as happens in a democratic society, to believe that they wish 'to express their personality,' the question at once arises as to what their personality *is*. For the most part, if investigated, it would be rapidly found that they have none. So what would it be that they would eventually 'express'? And why have they been asked to 'express' it?

If they were subsequently watched in the act of 'expressing' their 'personality', it would be found that it was somebody else's personality they were expressing. If a hundred of them were observed 'expressing their personality,' all together and at the same time, it would be found that they all 'expressed' this inalienable, mysterious 'personality' in the same way. In short, it would be patent at once that they only had *one* personality between them to 'express'—some 'expressing' it with a little more virtuosity, some a little less. It would be a *group personality* that they were 'expressing'—a pattern imposed on them by means of education and the hypnotism of cinema, wireless, and press. Each one would, however, be firmly persuaded that it was 'his own' personality that he was 'expressing': just as when he voted he would be persuaded that it was the vote of a free man that was being cast, replete with the independence and free-will which was the birthright of a member of a truly democratic community.

Here, in this case, you get an individual convinced that he is 'expressing his personality': that he has a thing called a 'personality,' and that it is desirable to 'express' it. He has been supplied with this formula, 'expressing the personality,' as a libertarian sugar-plum. He has been taught that he is 'free,' and that it is the privilege of the free man to 'express his personality.' Now, if you said to this man that he *had* no personality, that he had never been given the chance to have one, in any case, in the standardized life into which he fitted with such religious conformity: and secondly, that he did not *want* to have a personality at all, really, and was quite happy as he was,—he would reply that you might be very clever, and might think that you were funny, but that *he* was the best judge of whether he possessed a personality or not: that as he 'expressed' it every Saturday afternoon and evening and on Sundays, he probably knew more about it than you did; and that in consequence your gratuitous assumption that he did not want one was absurd, as well as offensive. If he were a savage Robot, he might confirm this statement by directing a blow at your head.

The truth is that such an individual is induced to 'express his personality' because it is desired absolutely to standardize him and get him to rub off (in the process of the 'expression') any rough edges that may remain from his untaught, spontaneous days. Where the avenues of 'expression' suggested to him are more 'original' and sensational (as in

Germany, where the *Rhythm-army of naked male life*, the *Joy Group*, or *Naked Men's Club of Sun-Pals* would perhaps attract him), the case is no different, but he is of course then far more convinced, even, that his personality is being 'expressed.' But, drawn into one orbit or another, he must in the contemporary world submit himself to one of several mechanical socially organized rhythms. There is really less choice every day: the number of group-personalities available, of course, diminishes just as the number of newspapers decreases. And it seems impossible to dispute that, as regards this side of life, and leaving aside the threat of unemployment and fresh wars, people have never been so happy. The Not-Self (and *not* the self at all) is the goal of human ambition. And not 'freedom,' or the eccentric play of the 'personality,' but submission to a group-rhythm, is what men desire.

It should be emphasised that no quotations, even these fairly lengthy ones, can fully convey the book's argument and the verve and humour with which it is developed, even though the general drift is, I hope, apparent. Other aspects of the book that show Lewis's prophetic quality are those dealing with the disintegration of the family (a commonplace to us, but a novel concept in the Twenties), the rise of feminism, and its links with sexual inversion. Lewis says he takes no side in arguments about male–female relationships, and that 'if anything women represent, I believe, a higher spiritual average', and may even justify the mystical and creative qualities attributed to them by primitive races. With a side glance at the ironic fact of Proudhon, the very model of a nineteenth-century revolutionary thinker, supporting the idea of the family, Lewis states his own position. He is opposed to the family, because it is in the modern world an institution of authority that no longer has the reason for existence it had in primitive societies. Nowadays, he says, it is massaged into the shapes they prefer by 'mercantile despots, more or less benevolently patriarchal', or in today's language multi-national organisations. To these the family is a bulwark against rebellion and anarchy, and so it continues to exist, a product of 'this unreal, materialist world, where all "sentiment" is coarsely manufactured and advertised in colossal sickly captions, disguised for the sweet tooth of a monstrous baby called "the Public." ' Anybody who has watched a family soap opera, non-existent when Lewis wrote, will recognise the picture.

Feminism Lewis saw as part of the class, sex and age wars with which he also dealt, all of them movements furthered by both capitalists and socialists for their own political and economic reasons. The social purpose—distinct, of course, from the desire of individual feminists for 'freedom'—he regarded as the provision of cheap labour, carried out in factories and shops to commercial profit, instead of in the home. 'Ten honest wives daily performed in the way of washing, cooking, and so forth, what two could perform under a communal system of the Fourier type, or that being introduced in Communist Russia. The remaining eight would then be available for other forms of work.' The effect of this would be to 'break up and root out all those little congeries of often ill-assorted beings; and terminate the terrible age-long tête-à-tête of the husband and wife, chained to each other for the practical purpose of perpetuating the species, which could now be effected more successfully *without* this often unhappy union.' Much of this anticipates the present situation in Western countries—equal pay and equal prospects for the sexes, and frequent changes of sexual partners—but Lewis viewed feminism not as an egalitarian movement, but as a struggle for domination between the sexes. He linked this with what was then called sexual inversion, which he saw spreading in the West. How right he was in this, and in the view that homosexuality would spread so that it became fashionable and even commonplace, any comparison of the Twenties and the Eighties shows. Some remarks, like that about the taboo on generic terms like 'feminine', surprise one by having been written then rather than now. The sex-war itself Lewis saw as a struggle essentially socio-political, not merely a desire for a different form of sexual activity. The following passages exemplify these ideas, and emphasise that the writer has no objection to the physical practices that, then and now, disgust some who think them 'against nature'. It is the social implications of homosexuality, as of feminism, that concern him.

from THE ART OF BEING RULED

The Matriarchate and Feminine Ascendency

All orthodox opinion—that is, to-day, 'revolutionary' opinion either of the pure or the impure variety—is *anti-man*. Its terms are those of a war or insurrection still, although theoretically the war is over and the position gained. But subtly and in the nature of things, it is no longer a question of adjusting an inequality, but of advancing (as of a *superior* nature) the qualities of the 'down-trodden,' of the 'weaker' sex. On the scientific, or the pseudo-scientific, front of the world-movement of sex reversal, it issues in the form of a great deal of insistence on the phenomenon of the Matriarchate. The Matriarchate tends to be represented as a more absolute thing than it ever was, and as in a sense the *natural*, the *primitive* social organization. Such a war as the 'sex war,' as was to be expected, does not end in a stabilization in which the man and the woman exist on *equal* terms. It necessarily ends in a situation in which feminine values are predominant.

That the 'sex war' is not at the finish (whatever it may have been at the start) an egalitarian movement is certain. It is not an insurrection with an egalitarian watchword any longer, but a 'war' for domination, not 'equal rights.' The nietzschean notions that converted in the vague general mind the darwinian formula of *a struggle for existence* into that of *a struggle for power* operates here as elsewhere. In innumerable books and articles on the subject this tendency can be traced. A highly characteristic one is *The Dominant Sex*, by Matilda and Mathias Vaerting. (Whether the order in which their names are printed is a survival of the days of chivalry, or is a token of the surrender of Mathias, we are not told.)

Abusing and over-using the slender evidence of the Matriarchate, these writers' theory is that sometimes men have ruled the world and sometimes women: that the pendulum swings backwards and forwards: but that *equal rights*, or a rule shared equally by both, is only a transitional state, and is not the characteristic one. That one or other should be the *top dog* is the natural condition.

There is, indeed, a tendency towards fixity in the relationship of power between the sexes, whatever that relationship may be. But there is a still stronger countervailing tendency towards change, towards progressive modification. The relationship of power is subject to the laws of motion. The present authors' researches seem to justify the contention that the movement of the relationship of power between the sexes is undulatory, or that it resembles the swing of a pendulum. Automatically, masculine dominance is replaced by feminine, and feminine by masculine. In the swing from the prevalence of one form of sexual dominance to the other, the pendulum necessarily traverses the stage in which there is a balance of power between the sexes: this is the phase of equal rights.

This movement, however, does not seem to be a simple oscillation. We do not find that the power of one of the sexes continuously diminishes, while that of the other continuously increases. The subordinate sex experiences from time to time reverses in its march to power, these reverses being followed by fresh advances . . . The dominant sex, on the other hand, the one whose power is declining, will win occasional victories even during that decline . . . The highest point of the movement of the pendulum is that at which the reversal of the movement begins. After the dominance of one of the sexes has been pushed to the pitch of absolutism, and when the power has reached a climax, the descent into the valley of equal rights begins.

These writers excuse themselves presumably for the unsatisfactory nature of the evidence on which they have to rely for this mechanical and well-ordered picture by inventing something like Freud's *Censor*. They imagine a despotic and marvellously thorough sex soul, carefully erasing all traces of the rule of the sex recently dispossessed.

It will be seen that the Vaertings deal in a type of historic psychology like the fatalism of the *decline and fall* of all empires; although for the foundations of their statements they have to get into the vague, 'vast,' convenient region of proto-history and unlimited pre-history. But as to any movement on the part of these two minds to question the desirability of 'empire' and *domination* at all, you would look in vain for it.

If this mechanical oscillatory movement were, for the history of which we have any reliable record, correct, then would it not be strange to find these 'rebel minds,' because a certain mechanical movement has always taken place, accepting it for all time? Should not the 'progressive' ticket oblige its holder to something different to that? Is not, in fact, the historic attitude the very negation of 'progress'—if 'progress' is to break the spell (for is it not that?) of mechanical necessity? So the historic conservatism of such mechanistic writers throws them into the sort of strange opposition with their 'revolutionary' label that we have noticed occurring elsewhere. Their evidence is collected on the same principle as that directing the inquisitorial procedure in which the functions of judge, attorney, jury, etc., were vested in one person: their evidence of the order and value of that extracted by torture and hypnotic suggestion.

To wish back the patriarchal family (with the *patria potestas* of the roman domestic despot at the end of the reactionary road, or the slave-wife) because feminism seems to be rapidly becoming affected to a vast scheme of political exploitation; or because men, not yet free of women, have not the necessary initiative to institute a secondary war, to hasten the dissolution that has begun, and which, as things stand at present, falls most heavily on them,—is the natural reactionary gesture. Men do not do anything, but they are dissatisfied. They feel too guilty in their capacity of hereditary 'tyrant' or 'sultan' to say much openly. And 'chivalry' is a great obstacle to declaring war.

The recommendation of Christ to the Rich Man has already been mentioned in connection with the Man as an emblem of sex-authority. The surrender of the Plain Man to the feminizing woman was a piece of chivalrous nonsense, if it was not coercion. So christianity is responsible for it, since chivalry dictated it; unless force covers the whole transaction. But if the Rich Man, when he had given up his possessions, should howl like Timon because he was not then of so much importance, he would be a poor christian. It is against christianity that man should turn, the source of all his sexual woes. These two actions—that of surrendering any wealth you may have accumulated or inherited, and that of surrendering the privileges acquired and inherited by the caste or sex to which you belong—are highly to be commended, in my opinion. But what is not usually recognized is that they are of exactly the same order: just as a magnanimous christian self-sacrifice in sex is the same as it would be in race. According to any worldly standard they are both excessively stupid.

The 'right' of the child to freedom from family control is of a piece with the 'right' of the woman to an 'independent' existence. They and the rest of the sex innovations and theories of the family are in the nature of factory regulations, nothing more. The multitudinous mollusc in the body of which these changes occur has to be found a soft or a sentimental reason for everything that happens in such a tender and respectable place. But the real reason, although matter-of-fact enough, is not from the public point of view threatening or alarming. The truth *always* has to be hidden, whether it is good or bad. In itself it causes alarm: *any* truth is impossible to utter.

Sorel writes: 'Marx, as is known, proposed this law, that "every class which, successively, has seized power has sought to safeguard its newly acquired position of mastery by imposing on society conditions calculated to ensure it (the conquering class) its own revenue." Several times the same principle is employed by him in attempting to predict what would happen to the world as a result of a proletarian revolution. It is in this way that he comes to announce the disappearance of the *bourgeois* family, because the proletarians will not find themselves in conditions likely to permit them to practise this type of sexual union.'

Since the great masses of the people are not likely to be in a position to prolong the family arrangement based on an individual 'home' (marriage, and the family circle to which the European is accustomed), it will be abolished. That is the economic fact at the bottom of 'feminism.' Given industrial conditions, the Plain Man and the Plain Woman will be better off if the unit of the family is abandoned. But that consideration would perhaps not have been sufficient to bring this revolution about. It is an economic adjustment primarily: after that a great deal of relief from responsibility, and from a too constant conjugal *tête-à-tête*, is to be laid to its credit.

The Piecemealing of the Personality

Race is the queen of the 'classes': but in Europe to-day its power is very slight—for one reason, because it lacks all organization or even reality. But there are less fundamental ones, but usually far more present to our consciousness in everyday life, needing the greatest attention, and involving a variety of ritual. The other 'classes,' it is true, have never been recognized as of the same standing as *race*. As a *casus belli* they have been inferior to it. None of these other differences, or the membership of any of the other classes, was recognized as a pretext for taking life. Race or nationality, on the other hand, has, in the modern world, been recognized as a sanction for murder by every State. But this sanction usually had only 'nationality' to repose on, which was a very different thing to race. Marx, with his 'class war,' indirectly demonstrated the absurdity of these privileges of race—especially when it was not *race* at all. The success of his system has shown how easy it is to substitute, in a disorganized, non-racially founded society, any 'class' for the classical 'racial' unit of the State.

Once 'war' between classes started spreading, from the teaching of Marx, it did not stop at social 'class,' naturally. Schopenhauer, for instance, early in the last century, called women the 'short-legged race.' So women were thenceforth one *race* and men another *race*. The idea of race substituted itself for that of sex. But where there are *races* there are *wars*. The 'sex war' was soon in full swing. Schopenhauer himself, it is interesting to recall, was one of the first in the field. He early in life flung himself on a strange woman whom he found conversing on the staircase of the house where he lived, and threw her downstairs. For this pioneer engagement, however, he was forced for the rest of his life to pay a crushing pension to this crippled member of the enemy 'race.'

Women are notoriously unamenable to strictly *racial* mysteries. The classical example of this is that of the Sabine women deciding, as it is supposed, to remain the property of the Sabine ravishers rather than return to the defeated men of their own race.

The child is the 'class' that is most nearly associated with the sex-classification: or rather, the age-difference it represents. 'The child is father to the man': and the child is, as primitive societies saw, actually a different being, in spite of physiological continuity, to the grown man into which he develops. It is the case of the worm and the butterfly—only in inverse order, the butterfly coming first. So Master Smith and Mister Smith are as different almost (when they are the same person at different ages of Smith's career) as though they were offspring and parent.

But the difference diminishes when you are dealing with *Isaac Newton*, or even with Clara Vere de Vere, in place of poor 'Smith.' The more highly developed an individual is, or the more civilized a race, this

67

discontinuity tends to disappear. The 'personality' is born. Continuity, in the individual as in the race, is the diagnostic of a civilized condition. If you can break this personal continuity in an individual, you can break *him*. For *he* is that continuity. It is against these *joints* and sutures of the personality that an able attack will always be directed. You can divide a person against himself, unless he is very well organized: as the two halves of a severed earwig become estranged and fight with each other when they meet.

A good demonstration of the rationale of this piecemealing of the personality for attack was given the other day by a caricaturist. He divided his celebrated victims into their Young and Old Selves: in this way he had them in half, like hydras, and made the angry tail discourse with the fiery head. But you can effect far more than this. You can with luck cut men up so thoroughly that they become almost 'six-months men,' as they might be called, rather than men of one continuous personal life—than 'life men.' It is only necessary to mention the central subject of the very effective and fashionable plays of Pirandello, to show how, systematically presented in a dramatic form, this segregation of the 'selves' of which the personality is composed can affect the public mind.

But there is no way in which people differ, however minutely, that does not supply material for a 'war.' And the general contention throughout this essay is that they cannot have too much of 'class': that people's passion for 'class' and for reposing their personality in a network of conventional 'classification,' is not often realized. Where war is concerned you must, of course, disregard entirely the humanitarian standpoint. *Passively* men may even enjoy war, as the bird enjoys being drawn irresistibly to the fang of the snake. The blowing off of heads and arms is a very secondary matter with the majority of people. But that does not justify you as a responsible ruler in abusing this insensitiveness.

When really well mixed into a good, strong group, men are so many automata: they hardly notice any disturbance, like a war. But that the conscious self (in so far as it remains) of the average human being is terribly bloodthirsty and combative, much as I should like to, I find it difficult to credit. *By themselves* people are, every one admits, averse to fighting: it demands too much energy. Perhaps a really *perfect* group, or class, to prevent itself from dying of inanition, would favour war, as a stimulant. But I think the more the question is examined, the more certain it is that people *for themselves* (not for others—they enjoy seeing other people fighting, and dying, naturally), and *in the mass*, prefer eating, sleeping, fornicating, and playing games of skill to killing each other. And even if *the happiness of the greatest number* is not so individual a matter as Bentham supposed—even if the happiness of dying, let alone living, with a huge crowd of people must have a serious claim on our attention—nevertheless the individual, betrayed momentarily by some collapse or etiolation of the communistic medium, does object very strongly to dying. As *an individual* he is all for not dying or being crippled—that *is* the law of nature. And the ruler who bases his action on the stability of this Artificial Man of communism constantly risks sinning against God.

The Physiological Norm and the 'Vicious'

Of all the tokens of the flight of the contemporary european personality from the old arduous and responsible position in whose rigours it delighted, now made too hot for it, there is none so significant as the sex-transformation that is such a feature of post-war life. A few years ago this topic would have been exceedingly difficult to deal with in a book destined for public sale. Even to-day it is not an easy one, but for rather different reasons.

On what tone are we to address ourselves to the consideration of this inverted fashion, abstracting ourselves, of necessity, from any prejudices we may feel for the purpose? Dr Matignon (*Archives d'anthropologie criminelle*), the great authority on China, said that he had never heard a Chinese express any disapproval of sexual inversion except that it was universally agreed to be bad for the eyes. Until quite recently european society took a very severe view of it; which dislike was apparently a sort of tradition in any case among the germanic peoples. Genuine, fully developed physical inversion in men is probably quite rare: in a time unfavourable to its practice it makes a sort of martyr of the individual born with it—a martyr to his glands, like 'the painter called Sandys' in the limerick, or in the sense that we say 'a martyr to the gout.' People regard it askance as a kind of possession; and in many rough communities every misfortune would befall these delinquents of natural processes, whose quite simple and harmless topsy-turvydom was associated with witchcraft and treated on that basis. Even so late as the famous 'nineties the english courts made a martyr of that description of Oscar Wilde. He became almost a political martyr, other countries using his well-advertised agony to point to the philistinism of England. A very amiable and charming person, he awakened the chivalrous instincts everywhere, like a very attractive maiden in distress. And as he possessed to the full the proselytizing zeal that usually goes with sex inversion (as with any other intensification of sex), he prepared the ground with his martyrdom, ecstatic recantations, eloquent and tearful confessions, and the great prestige of his wit, for the complete reversal of the erotic machinery that has ensued or is ensuing.

An admission of complete *moral* blindness and indifference, although it might be damaging under certain circumstances, will not be misplaced in handling this subject. But there is another aspect of the matter that also claims attention. There are many people, perhaps, who would be lacking, as I am, in *moral* sensitiveness, and who would yet be in some way physically offended by practices 'against nature.' This would be extremely unreasonable, as I have already suggested; for to an impartial taste, divinely exempt from participation in either normal or 'abnormal' joys, as we call them, their 'normality' would be just as offensive. They might very well offend the most fastidious god more than the object of *their* disgust; for their 'norm' would be merely the dislike or revolt of the senses against something *different*, not part of their personal norm or system. It would, in short, be the animal self-complacency and self-love that thinks itself 'natural' and engaging, and everything else 'unnatural' and disengaging.

The physical is the only aspect that interests the majority of people, however: which makes the non-physical impracticable as a basis of discussion, or at least very difficult. That there is any other side to a fundamental thing of common experience—about *themselves*, in short—they require much persuading. Nevertheless, the attempt has to be made, since the subject is important.

There is still, of course, one thing, but that a physical and exterior one, that plays an important part with many people in any such question as this. A drunkard soon develops a red nose and a generally inflamed, bloated, and dissipated appearance. Red noses are for some reason universally disliked by both men and women. So in the case of the drunkard, although no one would be likely to raise any objection to or experience any disgust at the physical act of pouring into the mouth a probably attractively coloured liquid, the result of this action in the long run is the red nose by which people are generally repelled for some reason. The 'Nancyism' of the joy-boy or joy-man—the over-mannered personality, the queer insistence on 'delicate nurture,' that air of assuring those met that he is a 'real lady,' like the traditional music-hall 'tart' who is always a 'clergyman's daughter,' the grating or falsetto lisp, or the rather cross hauteur of the democratic teashop waitress—are to some human norm almost as central as that which resents the red nose, or the big paunch, offensive.

But the drunkard is at peace with his red nose, probably, and left to himself can live on terms of mutual respect with his paunch, no doubt. Some human norm—the same one, perhaps, that is outraged by the red nose—hates the rat and the beetle. But its idea of the rat is not at all that which the rat has of itself; it loves its swift, clammy sausage of a body as much as the human being does his hairless, erect machine. That erect, conceited human norm may yet have to bend to the will of the rat or the serpent, and go about on its belly near the ground. And then it will be just as pleased with itself as at present: and indeed be happier relieved of the white man's burden *cum* the human burden *cum* its amazing moral rectitude.

I suggest that it is only the over-instinctive person, the slave of the human-all-too-human norm, who would be such a stickler for the 'natural' as the reactions sketched above imply. It is this unfortunate conservative human-all-too-human norm that we are incessantly combating. It is even that Old Adam in the 'Nancy' that makes him so satisfied with his humble eccentricity, and insignificant loudly-advertised change of gear—like the exultant cackling of a hen who had laid an egg of an, for it, unwonted calibre.

It is not, alas! by victories of such modest proportions over our too rigid physiologic norm that we can hope to break it down, if that is our intention. We merely flatter and preserve it by such indirect attentions.

But in order to advance a little farther into the physical problems involved in such a scrutiny, let us take the objections of the conventional bridegroom on his marriage night to evidences of unchastity in his bride. Marrying, the man of the approved masculine type is distressed and disillusioned if he finds that some one has forestalled him in the tasting of this fruit. The gilt is off the gingerbread. This painful situation we usually take at its *face* value. We think we know what we mean by the gingerbread, and where it is situated. It is on the *physical* plane, in short, that we believe this deception to have occurred. In this, I think, we are wrong.

Suppose, for instance, that the disappointed bridegroom learns that, instead of being deflowered in the course of a love intrigue, his bride has been deflowered against her will on a lonely road by a tramp. Then the situation changes for him at once. There is a flood of bitter tears on the part of the bride; he folds her in his arms and all is well. *For it is not the physical fact that has disturbed his repose of mind.* It is the person, *she*, gazing at him out of her lovely, *personal* eyes, that it has caused him such a disagreeable shock to find he was not the first with. The act of deflowering, it is true, occurred, technically, on the physical plane. But that—were there no *person* attached to it—would be of no more importance than something happening to an automaton: no more than the daily dirtying of the hands, which are washed and then they are clean again: no more than the figure in the Bois, in Mallarmé's prose poem, observed embracing mother earth. For it is a person, a mind, that he has married; incarnated and expressed, it is true, by a certain body. But that body is, in a sense (in the things that happen to it, if that is possible, independently of the mind), as unimportant by itself as the materials by which it is surrounded—its clothes, the tables and chairs, dust on the road, or bricks of the house. Disconnect it from the *person*, if that may be, and it is *dead*. In short, the body outraged by the tramp would be a *corpse* only. The body enjoyed by an earlier lover would be *alive*. In the latter case it would be *she*—Daphne, Joan, or Elizabeth. It is the personality he is in touch with when he looks into her eyes (and not a bit of flesh—that is, as flesh, of the same impersonal order as a bit of cloth, a lump of clay, a sponge, a vegetable) that all the trouble is about.

This illustration will, I hope, suffice to suggest to us that in all such things the physical event is of very little importance by itself. In the case of sex, more than anything else, the fuss is supposed to be about that, and localized to physical experience. In reality we are always dealing with something else. It is in this misunderstanding that morals thrive. The shallow disgust or indignation of the moralist is installed in an elementary materialism that appeals directly to the animal machinery of combat or rut. Its pompous censure is able to surround, as though with an aureole of intelligence and martyrdom, something that is—what? If we paused to think what it is we should no doubt laugh at the conjuring trick: the piece of sardonic illusionism to which we all surrender. But when that comic screen had been removed, at the heart of the tissue would be found the same entelechical reality which gives significance to all the material life we know.

But that physical delusion, with all its mocking symbolism, that has roused us to protest or repulsion—clasping to our hearts, with no repulsion, an almost identical object ourselves!—is of the very essence also of the practice responsible for it. The moral indignation, or loudly expressed disgust, of the Plain Man or the Plain Woman is the twin and complement of that self-satisfaction and sense of outrageous discovery that is the incentive on the other ('unnatural') side of this sexual pale.

The sex revolution of the invert is a *bourgeois* revolution, in other words. The *petit bourgeois* type predominates: a red tie, or its equivalent in the approved badges of sexual revolt, tells its theatrical tale. The puritan conscience, in anglo-saxon countries, provides the basis of the condiment, and gives sex inversion there its particular material physiognomy of *protest* and over-importance. How moral, essentially, the anti-moral stimulus must be is not difficult to grasp, when you are privileged to witness its operation in the English or American. And so the 'vicious' circle is described.

The Intolerant Tradition of the Anglo-Saxon

These disparaging remarks (for in employing the epithet *petit bourgeois* I have gone as far as human vituperation will go) do not, of course, apply to those people whom a displacement of the sex psychology marks out for physical paradox. The most agreeable inverts to be met—and every one, in post-war society, meets a great number of every sort—are the true-blue inverts: those who, whatever the orthodoxy of the moment, would certainly be unaffected by it, and would be there busy with all the rather complicated arrangements incident to their favourite pursuit. This male-pole type of invert is often entirely free from that feminine bias, resulting in caricature so often, of the female of the genus; or that of the convert to inversion, the most fanatical of all. What this male invert thinks of his female it is impossible to say without being one yourself. But certainly he gives the impression of being much more *male* in the traditional and doctrinaire sense than any other male. His pride is often enormous in his maleness. If perhaps a little over-fine and even mad, he can meet on equal terms the male of any other species—either the lion, the male of the farmyard-fowl, the Samurai, the powdered male gallant of the Stuart stage. The frantic and monstrous cock, that notorious nobleman, *Monsieur le comte de Six Fois*, of the Casanova dispensation, he would easily put to flight.

Just as there are a few born revolutionaries, but in great numbers people who are 'revolutionary' because other people are: so in the ranks of each respective legion of revolt to-day there is the small nucleus of 'pukka' material, the 'regulars,' and the sheeplike indoctrinated majority. So it is that the neglected, despised, and rejected adept of Sodom, so well described in his formerly outlawed state by Proust, suddenly finds himself, owing to one of those freaks peculiar to political life, the leader of a highly disciplined host. It must be an Arabian Nights entertainment for some of the more hardened old perverts. All their life they have been chivied from pillar to post, till very recently living in the shadow of the Oscar Wilde case, the British equivalent of the *affaire Dreyfus*. Then all at once, as though by magic, they find themselves Princes of Sodom: every university in Christendom is pouring out, as thick as herrings, shoals of their natural prey, duly indoctrinated and suitably polished. They must rub their old heavily painted eyes and pinch their corseted ribs to ascertain if they are dreaming or not.

If the physiology of abnormal love as of normal love does not seem to you a matter of great importance; if you have not the puritan itch or the spur of an over-sharp vanity to make such things important and, indirectly, mentally exciting; if 'righteousness' as Arnold would say, or sanctimoniousness as Butler corrected him, is not your strong point, —there, you would think, must be an end of the matter as far as you are concerned. But you would find very soon that you had reckoned without your host. First of all you would discover that other people were not so accommodating as yourself. Indeed, a violent and jealous intolerance, you would begin to notice, accompanied most people's devotion to a sex fashion, as indeed to any other fashion. You would find, if you began to examine the machinery of fashion, that all fashions to-day tend to be organized on religious lines; and that, where sex especially is concerned, the same puritan spirit, in the anglo-saxon countries, that made people in the anglo-saxon past such intolerant maniacs where 'immorality' and all sexual 'enormities' were concerned, makes them also, when they are recruited to an *opposite* fashion, just as snobbishly intolerant on behalf of the 'immorality' to which they have gleefully, and without a sense of diabolical naughtiness, surrendered. You will perhaps recall the traditional *laissez vivre* of the French, and the wide measure of liberty left to personal taste—so that in the streets of Paris (the home of fashion) it has always seemed impossible to astonish or attract the attention of the passer-by, by even the most revolutionary costume: whereas any departure from fashionable convention has been met, always, with fierce resentment or fierce ridicule in England. Oscar Wilde invariably referred, I have been told, to 'Get your hair cut!' as the english national anthem.

Far more important, you would find that this prairie-fire of sex revolution (of feminism and then of inversion) altered fundamentally the status of ideas socially. As the psychic element existing in even the simplest sexual operation escapes people, so the percurrent nature of a great sex fashion is either not understood or not admitted. Certain people, highly educated and belonging to millionaire circles, indulge in an ancient, universally prevalent, 'vice' or pleasure, of a privileged and exceptional kind, which, because it seems to contradict nature's arrangements, we call 'unnatural.' And there, for most people, is the end of it. It is on the pleasure or distraction basis alone that discussion of it is relevant.

That attitude resembles another obtuseness that sees in the newspaper, cinema, or wireless only one of the innocent, non-political distractions of mankind: or that attributes 'serious' political significance solely to the Parliament and Crown. 'Mr Gossip' in the newspaper is a harmless, idle, 'gossipy' fellow. The novel, again, is as little of a 'political force' as little Jackie's new rag doll or scooter. Those weighty columns that occupy the centre of the *Times*, dealing with matters of patent consequence; or (to contrast with the mere novel) a political history of England, for instance—they are the only things worthy to rank as 'politics.' It is the mistake illustrated elsewhere by a cutting from the *Sporting Times*.

The social value of ideas, you would find altered, then, by this revolution in a novel sense. Not only was it a case of one set of ideas being exchanged for another set, as usually happens. But in place of anything in the shape of an *idea*, a *sensation* had been installed, you would discover. The very organ responsible for the making of an idea would be looked at askance. The sex revolution started as sex, but had ended as something else, rather in the way that religious ecstasy may begin as religion and end as sex. The various forms it had taken since the war did not, as they became more 'social' and less 'political,' become less militant. So this revolution had often little to do with sex ultimately. And then, of course—at last—it might enter your head that *in the first place*, too—not only in its result, but in its first motive—it was not sexual either. 'The socialists wish to abolish the family, *because it costs too much!*' we have heard Proudhon saying. (It is strange that the 'socialists' so early in the day should have been preoccupied to that extent with ways and means and displayed such an anxious foresight!) May it not be, too, that all the phases of the sex revolt—from the suffragette to the joy-boy—are equally *political* at the start—as they certainly become at the finish? Is it not the same old hag that in a 'morality' would be labelled Power, and for whom pleasure, in the simplest sense, means very little, who has pupped this batch of related fashions?

The Taboo on Generic Terms, and the Abstract Creature of Democracy

As the result of the feminist revolution, 'feminine' becomes an abusive epithet. When you say that the *salon* world, society, is essentially a *feminine world*, you encounter that difficulty for which provision has already been made. The number of generic terms that you may not use increases daily. This is natural in a period of radical upheaval. Classifications which people wish to transcend are indicated by them: so when you say 'feminine' it is as though you said 'women before the revolution.' Any term of differentiation is taboo. The recognition of the human standard of industrial standardization, the abstract 'man' without narrowing specifications, is *de rigueur* in forms of address. That is the ultimate stage of the *democratic* system. It is not, I need not point out, what we regard as the goal of revolutionary thought. For us, as for Sorel, it is the last decadence of that false-revolutionary movement that began with the great monarchies in Europe in the sixteenth century. It is of the essence of democracy, not of radical social revolution and non-democratic revaluation.

The central question, then, is still (and in this part of our discussion as much as elsewhere) that of differentiation or non-differentiation. Some things, which from every human standpoint we should regard as bad, feeble, corrupt, or even imbecile, we should nevertheless regard as good and profitable in their destructive capacity. But their essential degeneracy remains. They are, like the mercenaries, to be got rid of as soon as possible.

So, with these things in mind, we can go on with our questions. Whether it would be better, as it appears to you, if the world were peopled by and society composed of persons differing from each other in certain well-marked ways (not necessarily the ways in which they have so far differed, perhaps very different ones or modifications of them)? or would it amuse you more if they were all on one pattern?

Sex is one of the capital respects in which people differ from each other. And as far as sex is concerned, one of four things can happen. People can either be divided (1) into men and women as we know them—into people, roughly, like President Roosevelt, Nurmi, Dempsey, or Bernard Shaw, to take at random some notorious *men*, on the one hand; and Signora Dusé, Lady Diana Manners, Jane Austen, and Mary Queen of Scots on the other, to take some celebrated *women*: or (2) they can resolve their secondary sex characteristics and become either *all feminine* or (3) *all masculine* (approximating to one or other of the poles illustrated above); or (4) evolve some one undifferentiated human type, at least as far as sex went, unlike either of the two that we know.

At present a fusion is taking place: carried to its logical conclusion, it would result in a standardization on the feminine side of the secondary sex-barrier. This appears to me a less promising adjustment than that which No. 4 of my table would produce. No animosity to women, but rather a feeling of the psychic lopsidedness that would result, accounts for this preference.

Perhaps the exact half and half would be a solution—not so good, I believe, however, as No. 4. The latter would involve a new creative element. It would not always be reminding people what a close shave it was that they had not divaricated to one side or the other.

As I am not occupied with prophecy, but with things as they present themselves to-day, it is with the second eventuality that we are confronted—that is, with an increasingly feminine world. This, under correction, would be more puritanic and fastidious, more excessive and emotional, than a masculine one. No make-weight of typical masculine phlegmatism would *deaden* it. More uniquely alive to the things of the moment; more docile and mercurial; more burdened with and swayed by the tidal movements of the unconscious—finally, more *unconscious*, less 'intellectual': that is what, for convenience, I call 'feminine.'

Once more, perhaps, it will be better to insist that it is not meant that (1) 'all women' are more 'emotional' than any man; (2) that some cannot be as indifferent to hamperingly polite rules as the standard man; (3) that women cannot be as 'phlegmatic' or as highly 'intellectual' as that same not very inspiring standard.

A miner or drayman gets from his occupation a certain body and habits, and the majority of women get certain well-defined characteristics from theirs; both inherit others. So we can forbear from argument as to whether the drayman could not be made into a picture-postcard beauty, or the woman made to support the heaviest drudgery. We know that the women of Dahomi are reported (or were by Burton) to be hardier and more masculine than the men, and to do the heavier field-work; and that if the drayman makes his fortune, his grandson, who goes to Eton, is not so big and rough and may become very small and smooth. We are obviously talking of realities as we find them, and not as some interested propagandist would arrange them.

'Call Yourself a Man!'

And it is in the experiences of war time that we must seek not only the impulsion, but in some sense the justification, of male sex-inversion, apart from its rôle in relation to the disintegration of the family unit. As a war-time birth it can be regarded as a reply to the implications of *responsibility* of those times: nature's *never again* in the overstrained male organism.

After the war it was reported that french mothers (who had lost masses of expensive children at the moment when their long task of nurture was about to be rewarded) were vociferating, as they probably did, that they would bring no more children into the world to be brought up and then killed. But more than the mothers, during the war no doubt men too were saying to themselves subconsciously that at last, beyond any doubt, the game was not worth the candle: that the Heroic Age was nothing to this: that the 'kiss' they would receive 'when they came back again,' if they ever did, did not make them look any less foolish as 'heroes,' but more so; and that the institution of manhood had in some way overreached itself or got into the caricatural stage.

Men were only made into 'men' with great difficulty even in primitive society: the male is not naturally 'a man' any more than the woman. He has to be propped up into that position with some ingenuity, and is always likely to collapse.

We have defined with some care what was intended by the term 'woman,' and we can now do the same for the term 'man.' The term MAN implies a variety of indispensable but not necessarily pleasant things, quite independently of the specific sex characters, although it can only be attached to an individual falling within the sub-division of the adult male. The identification by means of sex-character on the part of adult males has always been a source of mortification to women and children: and at the present juncture some more neutral term should be substituted for it if we are to divert female energy into a less competitive and imitative channel. There is no visible alternative to this except that of abandoning entirely to women the attributes associated with this term. Either the *word*, or the attributes for which it stands, would have to be given up. Otherwise women must still insist on being 'men'; and war to the knife over that ridiculous name, and the ghastly privileges that accompany it, must result.

A man, then, is made, not born: and he is made, of course, with very great difficulty. From the time he yells and kicks in his cradle, to the time he receives his last kick at school, he is recalcitrant. And it is not until he is about thirty years old that the present European becomes resigned to an erect position.

There are very many male Europeans to-day who never become reconciled to the idea of being 'men' (leaving out of count those who are congenitally unadapted for the rigours of manhood). At thirty-five, forty-five, fifty-five, *und so weiter*, you find them still luxuriously and rebelliously prostrate; still pouting, lisping, and sobbing, spread-eagled on their backs, helpless and inviting caresses, like a bald-stomached dog.

With infinite difficulty 'a man' is, in the first place as a baby, put upon his feet, and invited to toddle. A period elapses which is the equivalent of the life of many a large-sized animal before he can walk on his hind legs at all respectably: and few men ever become entirely at ease in the erect position. So that eventually he should be able to get about without danger to himself and other people—cross the road, mount a bus, and so forth—infinite pains are expended on him. He is taught during ten years a host of symbols to prepare him for the subsequent feats of independence expected of him: and at every moment of his tutelage he is resentful and rebellious. *He does not want, if he can possibly help it, to be a man*, not at least if it is so *difficult*.

And to the end of his life he is not persuaded of the point of it all; and when he reflects about it, regards all this preparation and fuss (for *nothing*, or so little—for what is the famous adult life for which all preparation is made?—that it is hardly worth mentioning) as a meaningless evolution.

So 'a man' is an entirely artificial thing, like everything else that is the object of our grudging 'admiration.' Or if there is an exception to this rule, it is the abnormal or exceptional man, whom we worship as a 'hero,' and whose unnatural *erectness* arouses almost more hatred than surprise. Prostration is our natural position. A wormlike movement from a spot of sunlight to a spot of shade, and back, is the type of movement that is natural to men. As active, erect, and humane creatures they are in a constantly false position, and behaving in an abnormal way. They have to be pushed up into it, and held there, till it has become a habit only to lie down at night; and at the first real opportunity they collapse and are full length once more.

The snarling objurgations of the poor man's life, such as '*Be* a MAN!' (banteringly and coaxingly) or 'CALL YOURSELF A MAN!'(with threatening contempt), arouse 'the man' in the male still: but we can confidently look forward to the time, now, when this feminine taunt will be without effect.

A sense of DUTY is what we call the system of psychological injunctions (painfully learnt and easily discarded) by which all the useful actions of social life are effected. But that sense, in its turn, depends on the vanity: and the vanity requires its regulation food, which gets scarcer every day. Although all people depend for this staff of life, like a populous island for its nourishment, on other people: since few are such monsters as to grow it themselves.

But the vanity even is not such a primary thing as is usually supposed. CALL YOURSELF A *MAN*! at once puts it in motion. But it depends on the concept MAN for its effectiveness. And that is a belief, like a belief in God. Reduce a man's vanity below a certain point, or destroy his capacity for belief, and he subsides into his natural and primitive conditions.

The *instinct of self-preservation* would be dragged in as a hypothetic support of the man attacked with the remark, CALL YOURSELF A *MAN*! But the instinct of self-preservation is artificial too. It is the result of training and experience. Before a child has burnt its finger or is sufficiently documented about what will ensue if it puts its fingers in the fire, it is not afraid of fire. What it is painfully acquiring during the years of its gradual propping up and training in erectness, is a *personality*. Without a *personality* there is no instinct of preservation: or rather, the less personality there is, the less horror is there at the idea of losing it. Many animals whose lot it is to be eaten are probably *willingly* eaten, as has already been suggested. When the male of the epira is devoured by its mate in the midst of its tumescence, that is part of the fun.

The average civilized man is so precariously erect that it is almost laughable to watch him at times: on those occasions, for instance, when from vanity or a sense of duty he is addressing himself to a distasteful and difficult task—like looking at pictures in a gallery, reading *Das Kapital*, or watching a good play. The grinding boredom you realize that he must be experiencing makes a mechanical hero of him—as a very heavy machine that lifts itself into the air, and flies like an eagle, could be termed *a hero* in the way of a machine. The gravitational pull from the prostrate depths of the abyss which he had to sustain should earn him, on these occasions, any title he might covet.

It is not more natural for one sex than for the other to be heroic or to be responsible, then.

The position of the male to-day, and the symbolism of the word MAN, are purely artificial: no more for one sex than for the other are the heroic ardours, 'intellectuality,' *responsibility*, and so forth, that we associate with the male, *natural*. Men had grown to regard them as natural, because in the first place they had seemed profitable. But now the rewards associated with the exercise of these manly duties are a little flat and stale. The depreciation in the value of the psychological side has brought down with it in some obscure way the physical or sensual side. (The psychological element in the *reward* for 'the man' was, of course, the vanity element in the notion of power.)

The industry, courage, and responsibility of the male are artificial, and have only been sustained and kept in place by a system of rewards, like everything else in this world: reward that has sometimes been of the nature of loot, and sometimes of a juridical nexus. (We will examine in a moment the nature of these rewards.) The male has been persuaded to assume a certain onerous and disagreeable rôle with the promise of rewards—material and psychological. Women may in the first place even have put it into his head. BE A *MAN*! may have been, metaphorically, what Eve uttered at the critical moment in the garden of Eden.

The large, bloated, and sinewy appearance of the male, again, is partly the result of manual work or physical exercise, but is the result as well of thousands of years of ACTING THE MAN. The more muscular frame of the male, and his greater hardihood, are illusions, like everything else about him, provisionally and precariously realized, but no more stable than the muscular development produced by some intensive course of physical exercise, resulting in the inflation of this system of muscles or that. He is blown out by vanity into a *bigger* and *bonier* creature than his consort, like Shakespeare's Ajax. *He is in reality just the same size, and of just the same sort.*

82

The male is by nature (uninflated by vanity and physical exercise) as muscleless, slight, and as we say 'feminine,' both physically and mentally, as the female. There is no mysterious *difference* between the nature of the sexes, except the secondary differences we have been considering. If you persist in referring to 'the woman' not only as 'the woman' but as 'the sphinx' (as a certain contemporary intellectual *énergumène* does), what word would you have left for yourself?

Remove the arbitrary psychological machinery that in this way constitutes the mere male 'a man,' or tamper with it too much, or overtax it, and he collapses and becomes to all intents and purposes a woman. The functional difference, then, alone separates them. It is only functional differences that separate any one thing from another. If the duration of this collapse were at all considerable, even a functional readjustment would probably occur. The extreme rapidity with which these collapses occur (both in the specifically adipose bulk of the female, and the secondary muscular 'manliness' of the male) has been witnessed since the war.

In more primitive times than ours the exaggerated dimensions of the northern male—who vaingloriously blew himself out, and tiptoed himself up, till he was over six feet high, and weighed fifteen stone—has probably been the cause of our northern stock sticking culturally as it has done. The little mediterranean man would not have understood these 'manly' monstrosities: nor could he have done what he did if he had allowed himself any such functional specialization. For this *size* actually suggested to our ancestors perhaps the idea of an independent *function* (like the female's procreative one)—the function, namely, of the 'fighting machine.' Northern neighbours, or neighbouring northern tribes, would flash their eyes at each other, and blow themselves out till they hardly had room for any more spectacular sinew, and then fling themselves on each other in mortal combat. Their 'manliness' became a mania.

The last part of the book asks what kind of government will make the majority happy while giving freedom to the herdsmen, bearing in mind that industrial societies are being forced into social change by the nature of technological advance, and that the centripetal gathering of power is both inevitable and desirable. It is taken for granted that some sort of socialism will come, although for Lewis the word meant social control of the means of production and distribution, and had nothing to do with equality.

This does not mean that he lacked human sympathy. 'The european poor become poorer every day: whatever the reason may be for this, you cannot, unless you are a heartless fool, do nothing. And there is an immense instrument to your hand (in socialism), especially organised for the correcting of this terrible situation.' It seemed to him that what were called 'democratic' governments did nothing, hence were heartless fools. Lewis, in 1925, was ready to applaud those who deliberately changed the nature of society—the rulers of the Soviet Union and of Italy, later those of Nazi Germany and, under Roosevelt's Presidency, the United States. That the rulers of those states, although not fools, might be far more heartless than those they replaced did not—in 1925—seem to him likely, any more than such a consideration ever occurred to those who for many years supported the Soviet Union as an ideally democratic and efficient state. Lewis expected the absolutist state to be no less humane than the more or less liberal governments of Europe. As for Everyman, 'can this poor man be the loser—has he *anything* to lose?—by his rulers shedding the pickwickian masks, the socialist noses, the kindly liberal twinkles of the european egalitarian masquerade?' We know now that Lewis was mistaken, and that many of them had a great deal to lose, yet his position was neither inhuman nor ignoble, and was far nearer reality than that of the myriad liberal intellectuals who regarded the Soviet Union, Moscow trials and all, as a dream come true.

At the end Lewis restated his case for the new society. Man is by nature peaceful, yet engages in ever more destructive wars: and this sickness, if not cured, will eventually be mortal, making an end to all we mean by civilisation. The remedy must be the world-state, which will cause the withering or suppression of national feeling under centralised control. It is accepted that more wars and revolutions are likely to come before the world-state is achieved. The final chapter, which asks for the intellectual to be valued as a benefactor of society, is finely moving whether or not the argument is accepted.

from THE ART OF BEING RULED

The Great Development of Associational Life

Everything assumes an increasingly associational form. A vast system of interlocking syndics—pleasure syndics, work syndics, sex and age syndics, vice and race syndics, health syndics, and valetudinarian syndics—is imposed. In *Sodome et Gomorrhe* Proust shows the working of this very well in his analysis of the powerful instinctive freemasonry of the pederast. But the Philatelist, the Anti-Semite, the Rollsite, or the Daimlerite, the Player of Chess or of Mah-Jong, can form equally well-cemented brotherhoods.

The associational habit in its present development is the result of mass production. It is fostered in the interests of economy in our overcrowded world, and people are encouraged to get as quickly as possible into the category that offers the nearest approach to what they require or what they can hope for, and there remain. The mass mind is required to gravitate to a standard size to receive the standard idea. The alternative is to go naked: the days of made-to-order and made-to-measure are past. The standardization of women's dress, which is effected by the absolutist machinery of fashion, is the type of all the other compulsions tending to a greater and greater uniformity and standardization. There a colour—'nigger-brown,' for instance—is imposed. The great syndic of the manufacturers, dressmakers, etc., agree on 'nigger-brown,' and so the world flowers universally in 'nigger-brown' for a season, with perhaps a streak of mushroom-pink exuviae from the last season. In the interest of great-scale industry and mass production the smaller the margin of diversity the better. The nearer the fashion is to a uniform the bigger the returns, the fewer dresses unsold—for where there is little difference in cut, colour, and fancy there is the less temptation to be individualistically fussy. When there is so little essential difference between one costume and another, the difference is so slight it is not worth holding out about.

This closer and closer enregimentation of women, with the rhythmic seasonal changes of sex-uniform, is effected without difficulty by simple fiats of fashion. The overpowering instinct for conformity, and the horror of antiquation or of the eccentric, sees to the rest. In all this vast smooth-running process you see the image of a political state in which no legislation, police, or any physical compulsion would be required: in which everything would be effected by public opinion, snobbery, and the magic of *fashion*. We have, historically, in the hebrew state, a type of non-executive state such as might be arrived at on those lines. The legislature, of the greek city-state sort, did not exist; of all coercive administrative machinery, only the judiciary was required. God did the rest, or rather the teachings of *righteousness*, the anxious fanatical conscience of the citizen, and a great system of ritual. That is an example of moral rule, or rule by opinion, as opposed to rule by physical force: of much more effective *interior*, mental, domination, in place of a less intelligent *exterior* form of government. Theocratic and theurgic forms of government are the highest form of democracy—a kind of super-democracy, in fact.

The ideas of a time are like the clothes of a season: they are as arbitrary, as much imposed by some superior will which is seldom explicit. They are utilitarian and political, the instruments of smooth-running government. And to criticize them seriously, especially to-day, *for themselves*, would be as absurd as to criticize the fashion in loofahs, bath-mats, bath-salts, or geysers, in children's frocks or soft felt hats.

Those who actually like uniformity are naturally open to an unflattering suspicion. If, for instance, you protest too much that 'all men are much the same'—does it not mean perhaps that you *wish* all men to be much the same? You have no hope of benefiting by a general recognition of their being otherwise? You see your interest best in a *degradation* of men, rather than in a belief in their potentialities and in the excelling of some? If you reply that I or another are similarly arguing for privilege or discrimination because we have a personal interest in such an arrangement, that would have to be accepted by us. There would be no dishonour in such a conclusion to the argument. At all events, that is the danger run by the person too emphatic for the uniform. Again, the physical size of a living organism at any given moment of time is of the same value as the size of a stone. A man six foot high and a stone six foot high are both six foot. But since the man is living, goes on, and multiplies himself in space, there is no meaning in comparing them in that way. By saying that the stone is alive, only living slower, you do not alter the matter on our plane, which is alone the plane on which we are conscious, and about which we are talking. Outward uniformity is highly deceptive in any case.

The associational herd-instinct has one peculiarity that is very much to the point. The higher up in the scale of intelligence and vitality people are found, the less do they care, or are they able, to associate with each other and lend each other help. The inherent weakness of this natural isolation is the cause of all human misfortune, since the inventive individual is constantly exposed to destruction in a way that the uninventive, mechanical, associational man is not. Had the best intelligences at any time in the world been able to combine, the result would have been a prodigy of power, and the result for men at large of the happiest.

What makes the present time, then, so hopeful a one is that in the ever closer and more mechanical association of the great masses of people into an ever more and more rigid system of clans, societies, clubs, syndics, and classes, the original man is more and more forced out of these groupings, since there is no play for the inventive or independent mind within them. All these *odd men out* stand at present glaring at each other as usual, remarking perhaps to themselves that adversity brings them strange bedfellows. But the time must arrive when *they*, too, in spite of themselves, form a sort of syndic. That will be the moment of the renascence of our race, or will be the signal for a new biological transformation. While the philosopher of the sort of Mr Russell, of the author of *The Anatomy of Melancholy*, or of Professor Richet, would be swept down into the underworld of subconscious automatism, wringing their hands, in attitudes of apocalyptic despair.

Earlier in this essay it was remarked that: 'Left at the mercy of this vast average—its inertia, "creative hatred," and conspiratorial habits where the "new" is concerned—we shall always checkmate ourselves; and the more we "advance," the more we shall lose ground.' But if this inertia (1) is *satisfied* by a businesslike organization of its desire (its *What the Public wants* requirement), and if (2) this inflexible organization severs it entirely from all the free intelligences in the world, which it more and more isolates, then a new duality of human life (introducing perhaps a new species, and issuing in biological transformation) would result.

That is why, far from molesting or subjecting to damaging criticism (of a vulgarizing description) the processes of *stultification* which are occurring, everything should be done (publicly, and at large, of course) to hasten it. So it can be truly said with fullest good sense that whenever you see a particularly foolish play, read an especially idiotic article, full of that strident humbug to which we are so accustomed, you should rejoice. Mental food changes people in the same way as what they eat and the climate of their habitat. Those who like or can stomach what they are given in Western democracies to-day will change and separate themselves naturally from those who reject or vomit at that fare. A natural separation will then occur, and everybody will get what he wants. 'Nature's ethereal, human angel, Man,' will become segmented, and the divorce will be to the good of both these sections which are being forced apart.

How Much Truth Does a Man Require?

Sorel draws our attention to what he affirms is the importance of the *anticipatory* spirit by a quotation from von Hartmann:—

> The melancholy which is spread like a *presentiment* over all the masterpieces of greek art, in spite of the life with which they seem to overflow, is witness that individuals of genius, even in that period, were in a condition to penetrate the illusions of life, to which the genius of their age abandoned itself without experiencing the need to control them.

And Sorel comments on this to the effect that 'there are few doctrines more important for the understanding of history' than that of *anticipation*, reminding us of Newman's use of it in his researches in the history of dogmas.

This melancholy presentiment of the truth, that the tragic drama possessed in Greece, enabling it to tear aside the veil of illusion, as Shakespeare did so terribly in our own time, was a possession (in both senses of that word) not shared by greek philosophy as a whole. Heraclitus, the 'dark,' the 'weeping,' philosopher, owned it. But the platonists were busy, as in their capacity of teachers and healers they were bound to be, with happier pictures. The artist's truth is in this way the deeper and more terrible. His classical tragic task of providing a *catharsis*—his diabolical rôle of getting as near to destruction and terror as that is possible without impairing the organism—requires of him a very different disposition to that of the philosopher.

When the tragic artist takes life in hand for representation, secondary characteristics disappear as he manipulates it. It is at life itself, rather than at our particular social life of the moment, that his terrible processes are directed. His 'truth,' if it were not deadened by a rhythmical enchantment, would annihilate us. But the philosopher, he who is responsible for the Utopias, although he may have his 'presentiments' as well, is typically engaged in bestowing life, not in pretending to take it away—however salutary that threat may be in the event. He heals the wounds inflicted by natural science, or tries to; dovetails his midwifery with the purges of the more terrible form of artist; investigates life's gentler and nobler possibilities with the serener sort of artist. So he defines his discursive functions: showing himself as indispensable as the dock leaf is for the nettle, and claiming to stand between man and the artist, as well as between man and the man of science. He is the *lover*, his wisdom or system his carefully collected nest.

That our contemporaries have an aversion, as Sorel says, to 'every pessimistic idea' is indisputable. But what people have not had? He means, however, that they refuse to take on even so much of the harsh truth as is necessary for life's bare preservation. But they get their truth all right, in spite of themselves. Mechanically it reaches them, without their knowing how, by way of the vulgarization of scientific thought. They actually get much too much, far more than what would be a suitable ration. It is plainly the popularization of science that is responsible for the fever and instability apparent on all sides. To withhold knowledge from people, or to place unassimilable knowledge in their hands, are both equally effective, if you wish to render them helpless. As Einstein is reported as saying in conversation, the characteristic danger to human society is that the outstripping intellect will destroy the backward mass of men by imposing a civilization on it for which it is not ready.

The question, of course, remains if it will ever be ready. That is the capital question where its destiny is concerned. It is on the answer to that that all political thought must repose. What has been suggested in the foregoing pages is that ample evidence has been accumulated by now that *men, as a whole, will never be ready*. Instead of sitting down and abusing them as the man of the type of Robert Burton does—or as Professor Richet has just done, and as have numbers of other philosophers, ecclesiastics, etc., in the past,—and instead of fixing an eye of hatred on them, and deciding that they must die, as Swift did, or coolly blasting them (with the gesture, oddly enough, of benediction), as Mr Shaw does with Ozymandias, a quite different course, luckily, to-day presents itself.

In 1849 Lange wrote: 'Should it not be clear to every reasonable man that civilized Europe must enter into one great political community?' Earlier Goethe was a constant advocate of a world-state, and of the suppression of nationality. In other words, he was an 'internationalist.' To-day, in spite of very great efforts to artificially preserve 'national' frontiers, these frontiers being a more disreputable farce than at any former period, *automatically*—the automatic defeating conscious strategy most plainly in this instance—internationalism is becoming a fact. The standardizing of giant industry and its international character will have it so, in spite of the international industrialists. When all Russians wore beards and all Americans were clean-shaven, it was much more easy to make them believe, respectively, that they were of different clay. But 'nationality' is the one thing that cannot be manufactured. Once you have destroyed, or allowed to be destroyed, the ancient customs and arts of a country, you cannot reimpose them. The Maypole or Jack o' the Green in the Council-School festivity is too evident a lie: it is like a sphinx in St Paul's, or a carthaginian galley on the Spree.

There is to-day a new reality; it is its first appearance in terrestrial life—the fact of political world-control. To-day this may be said to be in existence, and to-morrow it will be still more of a fact. Neither can it be hidden—short of destroying everybody's sense of reality altogether. People no doubt could be persuaded that they did not see the sun and moon: but the effort to assimilate this gigantic lie would destroy their brains altogether, and universal imbecility would ensue.

Thereby the whole problem of government is altered. New methods are suggested that formerly circumstances did not allow people even to imagine. With a world-state and a recognized central world-control, argument about the ethics of war would become absurd. More profitable occupations could then be found for everybody. In a society organized on a world-basis, 'revolution' would not be encouraged, either, any more than to-day it is encouraged in fascist Italy or soviet Russia.

The idea for which Professor Perry stands, that of the comparatively recent growth of war, and of the fundamentally pacific nature of man, when not trained or organized as a 'fighting machine' (for it is only as a machine, even, that he can fight—by himself he is not very pugnacious or brave), is supported by a great deal of very good evidence. And there seems no reason at present why this period of chaotic wastefulness should not be regarded as drawing to a close. In order to wind it up, further wars and revolutions may occur. But they are not any longer necessary. There is no even political excuse for them. There may soon therefore no longer be any reason for the despairing philosopher to inquire, 'Who made so soft and peaceable a creature, born to love mercy, meekness, so to rave, rage like wild beasts, and run on to their own destruction? How may Nature expostulate with mankind, "I made thee a harmless, quiet, a divine creature!" etc.'

For we know quite well what makes such a soft and peaceable creature into a warrior—it is his rulers in the course of their competitive careers who effect this paradoxical transformation in their extremely soft subjects. If all competition were eliminated—both as between the small man and the big, and respectively between the several great ones of this earth—then this soft and peaceable, or 'mad, careless, and stupid,' creature would be spared the gymnastics required to turn him into a man-eating tiger. It is also absurd, and even wicked, to attempt to turn him into a philosopher. He should be left alone and allowed to lead a peaceful, industrious, and pleasant life, for we all as men belong to each other.

The optimism of socratic thought might even be rehabilitated, and not seem so aggravating as Sorel found it. His serene picture, without coming true, might no longer enrage: the 'presentiments' of the prophets and artists could be taken or left—left by most people, who would hum and buzz as monotonously and peaceably through their life as even the most fortunate bee. Those who had a taste for other forms of life, or who were bred, by means of eugenics, to a different existence, would not rage against their soft and peaceable fellow-man as formerly. For every one would be perfectly satisfied.

Different Magics

In the Mind and Body war, the war of Sensation against Intellect, the war of the high and the low-brow, the war of women and men, you are expected to be obediently, conventionally, militant. If you agree, and if in the first, for instance, your occupation thrusts you into the ranks of the Mind, then you have imposed on you an attitude of artificial hostility to the Body. This may be against your nature, which disposes you to be friendly to both. The same through the whole list. The intolerance, the militancy-to-order, the savage partisanship imposed on you on every possible subject, is a conscription that, intellectually, you must learn to evade.

'Qui terre a, guerre a' is a French proverb. But without 'terre' it is apparently the same thing. Everything is done to make people wish to be animals rather than men. A writer in the *New Leader* recently quoted what purported to be a letter from a perplexed correspondent. It expresses very well the widespread discouragement of the moderately ambitious man:—

> 'What is the use of being told about books (he wrote) when I can't read them! I haven't the money to buy them, and nine times out of ten my local library hasn't got them; or if it has, there is a list as long as your arm of people waiting for them.'
>
> Beginning on this personal note, his argument proceeded to wider considerations, raising the whole question of the value of civilization for the poor. A progress in culture, he said, meant a reduction in happiness; the more complicated a man's needs became, the more refined his tastes, the greater their liability to be outraged. The man who is used to good books is revolted by the sunday papers that satisfy his fellows; the man who likes good music is a martyr to noise and shudders every time a barrel-organ comes down his street; the man who recognizes a lovely building when he sees it, turns in loathing from the squalid ugliness of our towns.
>
> If he be rich he can to some extent obtain compensation for the pain his cultivated tastes cause him, by spending time and money on their satisfaction. He can only shudder away from a world of savages and hooligans and shrink into himself in pride and disgust.

'Thus (my correspondent ended) if I had to choose to-day between being a pig happy or being Socrates unhappy—and wisdom seems to point to the necessity of being one or the other—I should plump for the pig-stye every time.'

To be 'happy' is the object of the person illustrated in the letter. If you want to be 'happy' you must not be a man, but a pig. And that that is especially true to-day is indisputable. Well, the Circe of Capitalism is able to achieve this for our shipwrecked world. We can either decide among ourselves, or draw lots, as to who shall be happy and who unhappy.

There is a story that in the early days of socialism a certain labour leader had organized a demonstration in Trafalgar Square. Thousands of strikers assembled, and large forces of police were reported as approaching from all directions. The organizer of the demonstration passed round the word that all the manifestants, at the first sign of the police, should *sit down*. In due course the police appeared: they rushed furiously into Trafalgar Square from Whitehall, Cockspur Street, and the Strand. But a non-resisting human carpet was spread out at their feet: the entire crowd, as ordered, was *sitting down on the ground.*

Some of the revolutionary movements in full swing to-day are an unconscious adoption of this method of meeting the difficulties of the time. It was a particularly good way, and one that people cannot be blamed for adopting. The only magic that the ruled have at their command in face of the demands of the ruler is such as balked the police in the above story. Complete industrial obedience would, no doubt, absolve you from constant doses of war and revolution. The corrective of civil disobedience since the world began has been military discipline, war, and blood-letting.

Fourier refers to the *magical* effect of the capitalist transformation of his day in words already quoted:—

One is ready to believe in magic on seeing kings and empires thus circumvented by a few commercial sophisms, and the race of monopolists, stockjobbers, *agioteurs* exalted to the skies . . . who employ their influence in concentrating masses of capital, in producing fluctuations in the price of products—ruining alternately all branches of industry.

93

We have got used to the money magicians. We are all under their spell. The Good European (perhaps Nietzsche's 'Good European' was after all a mockery), the *Brave* European (*brave* as in german), is not very good at magic. He is very good at war, however. Of this he is very proud indeed: any time you ask him to fight and show how good he is at war, there is no holding him. What a pity he is not a better magician, and, on the other hand, a less remarkable fighter! Oh, that 'fighting face' of the novelette!

Celui qui sera mon curé, je serai son paroissien (Whoever will look after me can call me his client) is a *good* proverb for a good man, or 'Good European.' 'Whoever will be my Circe, I will be his swine' would be the proverb for the writer of the letter quoted above. That argument turns on the question of the desirability of 'happiness,' which each man instinctively resolves for himself.

Happiness is the chief material also in the construction of Utopias. Christ's is the most famous and the nearest to socialism. And the Utopia of Christ can conveniently be compared with the Utopia of the Ford industrial colonies or the ideal working-class community of Port Sunlight.

Christ's millennium was the old jewish dream of a land of promise. The hard cash of suffering and enslavement that the Jew was willing to pay down, in vicarious atonement, through his long genealogical sequences, passed on to the sombreness of the puritan: the 'dogged old jewish optimism' vanished: and the European must have a very imperfect notion of the dream of Jesus.

'However much, therefore, Christianity may have insisted on renouncing the world, the flesh, and the devil, it always kept in the background the perfectly jewish and pre-rational craving for a delectable promised land. The journey might be long and through a desert, but milk and honey were to flow in the oasis beyond.' Beyond the puritan's savage gloom there was no Valhalla, however, much less the delectable oasis indicated above by Santayana—the honey-pot of the hebrew faith.

However, whatever Christ's Kingdom of Heaven may have meant to his followers, there are certain elements in it that are accessible and generally understood. The difference between it and Port Sunlight, say, is this. Lord Leverhulme promised what he could perform, whereas

Christ was in a very different position. The former was more honest, and, if allowed to, would, I think, in the fullness of time, have been a greater *benefactor* (measured by material cleanliness and comfort) than Christ. Port Sunlight is (in more senses than one, as I have suggested) a certainty. There is no *last shall be first* about it; it is a dead level of sanitary life—sunlit, but not pretending to be Heaven. (It would be impossible for a man to say that he had Port Sunlight inside him, as he can say that he has Heaven within him.)

On the other hand, is Christ, promising what most likely can never come about, for that reason less of a benefactor than Lord Leverhulme or Henry Ford, promising what certainly can and will (most likely) come about? Christ's perfection was full of impossibilities, on the mundane plane, and to stage them he had to take his audience *out of life* altogether. His doctrine was a drug: beneath its influence men saw their wrongs being righted, saw the 'oppressor's wrong, the proud man's contumely,' punished, and humble faith rewarded, the last first and the first last. Is it the action of an honourable man to give people these flattering visions? Is not the modern benefactor of big business (possibly sometimes of the type against which Christ inveighed) really the eternal *rich man* justifying himself, stealing a march on the magician and so-called Saviour? Even if this whitewashing of the whited sepulchre only resulted in a sanitary tiling such as we associate with lavatories and hospitals, is not perhaps this stone that the Builder rejected (namely, the *rich man*) becoming the headstone of the corner?

But does he not also get much more out of it than Christ? it might be objected. Even there it is not certain that Ford or Lord Leverhulme could not make good their claim for a bigger halo than Christ's. I have no means of knowing what exactly the author of Port Sunlight got out of life, or what Henry Ford is still enjoying; but I should think that probably, on the model of most millionaires, they both must have led a harassed, frugal, lonely existence, full of distrust and indigestion. The experience of Christ—like a lyrical poet dying young, under romantic conditions, worshipped by throngs of people attracted by his personal magnetism, living to some extent the rosy dream that he recited daily—this experience sounds on the face of it more enviable than that of a modern millionaire.

'Malheur à celui qui en rit, il ne comprend pas l'esprit humain, sa fière originalité, petits esprits qui n'apprécient pas ce qui dépasse la vulgarité d'un salon, les étroites limites d'un bon sens vulgaire.' So Renan writes of those who are apt to laugh at the holy passion of Sainte Thérèse, or other saints and madmen. 'Malheur' indeed, and we must not be too hasty in taking Port Sunlight into our hearts in the place of the full christian or other dream.

But is not Christ's too exceptional a phantasy for the average of human desires? The more discriminating arrangements of the hindu heaven—or system of heavens—respond probably more accurately to the reality of human wishes.

The Politics of the Intellect

That when I am speaking of the intellectual I evidently experience no shame (reflecting on the compromising nature of my own occupation), that I do not pretend to be 'a plain, blunt man,' is true.

Far from that, it is my effrontery to claim that men owe everything they can ever hope to have to an 'intellectual' of one sort or another. And that is true both of the business magnate and his meanest employee. I claim further that the intellectual is the only person in the world who is not a potential 'capitalist,' because his 'capital' is something that cannot be bartered. What he deals in, even when it gives him power, gives him no money.

For this splendid and oppressed class nothing is done in the social revolution. But that it is a refuge for the scum of every other defeated class—or any class temporarily lying low—is true. And it is no doubt the great mass of pseudo-artists, writers, and so forth who discredit it. Therefore, when the agitator hurls his abuse at the intellectual, if he would be more specific and pick out the sort of figures that abuse the shelter of the too hospitable intellect, he would be doing a service.

The intelligence suffers to-day automatically in consequence of the attack on all authority, advantage, or privilege. These things are not done away with, it is needless to say, but numerous scapegoats are made of the less politically powerful, to satisfy the egalitarian rage awakened. The intellect, so exposed, so helpless in such a case, suffers most of any category, which is a danger to all of us. It is our own brain we are attacking—while the stomach looks on and laughs 'to see such sport.'

The possession and exercise of intellectual power in no way affects a person to a class enjoying political ascendency. There is nothing 'aristocratic' about the intellect: its noticeable simplicity makes it unpromising to look for analogies to it in a complex society at all. An early society would offer better parallels, and indeed in many primitive communities the chief or leader is chosen as the man known to have the best head. But the word 'aristocratic,' with its implication of a crowd within the bigger crowd, organized for the exploitation of the latter, is peculiarly inapt for the essentially individual character of the intellect.

The intellect is more removed from the crowd than is anything: but it is not a snobbish withdrawal, but a going aside for the purposes of work, of work not without its utility for the crowd. The artificial barriers that an aristocratic caste are forced to observe are upheld to enhance a *difference* that is not a reality. It is because they are of the same stuff as their servants that they require the disciplines of exclusiveness. In the case where an aristocratic régime represents a race ruling as the result of conquest, as has generally been the case, often the aristocrat is inferior in every respect to the subject population—that is, except in organization for war.

The primitive, 'democratic,' picture of the intellectual leader living his life simply among the people, with admirable simplicity and without fuss, has too many ready illustrations in history to require specification. But this leader claims the authority of the function that he regards as superior to any mechanical dominion of physical force or wealth. Also it is not for his own sake that he claims it; in this he resembles the king. More than the prophet or religious teacher he represents at his best the great unworldly element in the world, and that is the guarantee of his usefulness. It is he and not the political ruler who supplies the contrast of this something remote and *different* that is the very stuff of which all living (not mechanical) power is composed, and without whose incessant functioning men would rapidly sink back to their mechanical origins. The objectionable *difference* that is such an offence, or can be made to look so, is the very sign by which he should be known and accepted.

The life of the intelligence is the very incarnation of freedom:

97

where it is dogmatic and harsh it is impure; where it is too political it is impure: its disciplines are less arbitrary and less *political* than those of religion: and it is the most inveterate enemy of unjust despotic power. In its operation it is less violent and more beneficent than religion, with its customary intolerance of emotional extremes. It does not exercise power by terror or by romantic pictures of the vast machinery of Judgment and Destruction. It is more humane than are the programmes of the theological justiciary. And its servants are not a sect nor an organized caste, like the priest or the hereditary aristocrat, but individuals possessing no concerted and lawless power, coming indifferently from all classes, and living simply among other people. And their pride, if they have it, is because of something inside themselves which has been won at no one else's expense, and that no one can give them or remove from them.

But if you want to take him at his lowest, there is an intellectual who is the most valuable specialist in the service of capital. The capitalist would have neither machine-guns nor aeroplanes nor bombs without this intellectual: for he could not invent these things or anything else himself. The intellectual is thus a 'worker.' What the capitalist does occasionally is to stir up the other workers against this highly salaried, specialist worker.

For the intellectual workman in general it is necessary to claim isolation and freedom from interference: that is, if the best intelligences of the race are to work for us and produce their best results. This greatest and most valuable of all 'producers' should be accommodated with conditions suitable to his maximum productivity. He should not, if that were to be realized, be regarded (and hated) as the 'great man,' but regarded, more scientifically, as the chosen vessel of our human intelligence. He should be no more the object of envy and dislike than Dempsey is because an unmatched gladiator. And he should be relieved of the futile competition in all sorts of minor fields, so that his purest faculties could be free for the major tasks of intelligent creation.

It is easy to see how the passing of democracy and its accompanying vulgarities, owing to which any valuable discovery has to fight its way in the market-place—and the better it is, the bitterer the opposition—must facilitate this putting of the intelligence on a new basis. The annihilation of industrial competition and the sweeping the board of the Small Man, commercially and socially, should have as its brilliant and beneficent corollary the freeing for its great and difficult tasks of intelligence of the first order.

Our minds are all still haunted by that Abstract Man, that enlightened abstraction of a common humanity, which had its greatest advertisement in the eighteenth century. That No Man in a No Man's Land, that phantom of democratic 'enlightenment,' is what has to be disposed for good in order to make way for higher human classifications, which, owing to scientific method, men could now attempt.

The Art of Being Ruled is the tree from which all Lewis's social and philosophical ideas, and some of his artistic ones, sprout, a fact he acknowledged by frequent quotation from the book in later writings. *Time and Western Man* and *The Lion and the Fox* are two offshoots, the first concerned with the philosophy of what Lewis calls the 'time-mind' as exemplified here particularly by Spengler and Bergson, and by the effects of that philosophy on Joyce, Gertrude Stein and other modernist writers living in Paris. The links between the writers and the 'time-mind' are distinctly tenuous, the definition of it vague. We have understood already that Lewis is in favour of the intellect and opposed to sensation, and he identifies any philosophy concerned with history and chronology as anti-intellectual. Hence the attack on Spengler, about whom it is said that no systematic philosopher can make anything 'out of the mystery-clouded far-echoing symbols "Past" and "Future".' Lewis shows very effectively the deliberate romantic vagueness of Spengler's language, and his difficulty in dealing with any civilisation, like those of Greece and Egypt, that did not regard time as a pre-eminent factor in human life, and he has fun with Spengler's view of an imagined struggle in Leonardo da Vinci 'between the hand and the soul'. He is equally entertaining about Bergson and A.N. Whitehead, but the argument as a whole is too diverse, and its linking to recognisable artistic works too uncertain, to convince. It is really the shortcomings of a certain kind of *art* that Lewis is approaching through this elaborate analysis of Time philosophies, and his argument against them is basically the Johnsonian commonsensical one against Bishop Berkeley's idealistic solipsism when he kicked a stone and said, 'Thus I refute him.' Lewis's own artistic preferences were for the hard, clear and satiric as opposed to the romantic and idealistic, but he fails to make convincing connections between idealistic art and idealistic Time philosophy. The mathematician J.W.N. Sullivan, one of Lewis's most intelligent admirers, put it well when he said: 'You seem to regard it [Time philosophy] as a sort of pestilence that has now, you hope, reached its maximum.'

Whatever may be its deficiencies as an ordered argument, *Time and Western Man* bears further witness to the range and elasticity of Lewis's mind. It should be added that some of his most acute critics value the book very highly, W.H. Pritchard saying that 'the philosophical criticism seems worthy of more serious consideration than it had by any historian of ideas engaged in describing the philosophic situation in the first twenty years of this century', and Hugh Kenner calling it 'one of the dozen or so most important books of the twentieth century'.

If it seems odd that an extract from *Time and Western Man* is included under 'art and literature', it may look stranger still to find the study of Shakespeare, *The Lion and the Fox*, discussed here: but this masterly analysis sees the dramatist primarily through the socio-political Lewisian spy-glass. The result is a wholly original view of Shakespeare, and indeed of all the Tudor plays, as work produced under the shadow of Machiavelli. Of course Lewis does not mean by this that the playwrights were all students of *The Prince*, although he quotes Chapman writing of 'schools / Now broke ope in all parts of the world, / First founded in ingenious Italy, / Where some conclusions of estate are held / That for a day preserve a prince'. It is the *shadow* of Machiavelli that informs the work of these writers, a particular way of thinking about life, and so about society.

from THE LION AND THE FOX

Machiavelli in Elizabethan Drama

The master figure of elizabethan drama is Machiavelli. He was only known through the french of Gentillet, if that: but he was the great character of supreme intrigue that, however taken, was at the back of every tudor mind. Elizabethan drama—'the first terror-stricken meeting of the England of Elizabeth with the Italy of the late renaissance'—was more terrified of Machiavelli than of anybody. The Borgias, Sforzas, Baglionis, Malatestas, Riartes were of far more importance to the elizabethan dramatists than any of their own eminent countrymen. Familiarity bred contempt in the long run. But during its flourishing period the english stage went constantly to the schoolmaster of manslaughter, Machiavelli—and his political paradigms chosen in conformity with his Borgia worship—for its thrills.

Had there been thirty years ago in Europe a theatre as impressionable and active as the elizabethan, it is certain that we should have had a body of plays reflecting the human-all-too-human doctrines of Nietzsche, with 'aristocratic' supermen in the principal rôles.

Mr Bernard Shaw, it is true, produced a 'Superman,' of sorts; but his Superman was dressed in Jaeger underclothing and ate nuts, instead of being a blond beast, its jaws dripping with human blood. The nietzschean frenzy was queerly translated into the genial posing and prosing of a victorian literary puppet, rendered excessively voluble through the 'celtic' bias. Certainly no galvanizing horror could possibly be extracted from that or any other figure of Mr Shaw's: the inveterate cackle of the dialogue would alone preclude any thrill. The strangely unreal geniality and playfulness in *St Joan*, again (that seems written to be played by a cast of elderly anglican curates), is a deadly atmosphere for such a heroic subject, of course, and produces a most painful effect. Indeed, as it was presented first in London, it was difficult to escape from the feeling that most of the actors—with all their very 'kindly' but, of course, mischievously twinkling eyes, and breezy, capable manner—were not in reality of a more elevated calling than that of an actor; and that for some reason they had decided—attracted perhaps by the 'religious' nature of the subject—to take part in that performance.

In any case when Nietzsche came there was no great european theatre—the Scandinavians having produced the last effective thing of that sort: and so the superhumanity influences found other outlets— even such inappropriate ones as Mr Shaw was able to provide—on the principle, probably, of 'any port in a storm.' Machiavelli, on the other hand, three centuries earlier, was much better served, and precisely in England of all places.

Apart from the theatre, however, Nietzsche had nothing to complain about. Europe was deeply affected by his doctrines, and found a better way, perhaps—certainly a more sensational one—of giving them effect—namely, in real life. In France they were given hospitality by a crowd of writers—Remy de Gourmont is an instance: in Italy Marinetti and Papini collected them; and many vitalist strongholds ran up the flag of the *Ubermensch*. And—without necessarily dramatizing the central conception, or making operas of Zarathustra—everywhere people were saturated with these bird-of-prey, ruthless, 'a-moral' ethics.

Before all that—and in a sense the father of it—was the great shadow of Bonaparte, who provided England with her biggest 'scare' since the Armada, and impressed on Europe the image of the type of gigantic material success he symbolized. From his commissariat officer, Stendhal, to the Wall-Street millionaire, this picture of relentless personal aggrandisement served as model.

Mr Edward Meyer has catalogued three hundred and ninety-five references to Machiavelli in elizabethan literature. As to his influence in England, Dr Grosart wrote: 'I have suggested to the biographer of the renowned Machiavelli (Professor Villari of Florence) that an odd chapter might be written on the *scare* his name was for long in England: so much so that he came to be regarded as an incarnation of the Evil One himself.'

If three hundred and ninety-five direct references can be found to Machiavelli in elizabethan literature, it is everywhere steeped in his philosophy and what his philosophy represented. Webster, Massinger, Ford, Marston, Tourneur, Middleton are all indebted to him so heavily that either in the form of revulsion or delight they could be called the children of Machiavelli. *The Unnatural Combat, Women beware Women, Antonio and Mellida, The Insatiate Countess, The Changeling, The Revenger's Tragedy*, etc., would not have existed in the form in which they did without the showmanship and propagandist zeal of Machiavelli.

Marston was the first eminent machiavellian. He was entirely subjugated. The following lines can be cited as examples of his machiavellism:

Why, by the genius of that Florentine,
Deepe, deepe observing, sound brain'd Machevell,
He is not wise that strives not to seem fool.

This will recall Iago's profession:

> For when my outward action doth demonstrate
> The native act and figure of my heart
> In compliment extern, 'tis not long after
> But I will wear my heart upon my sleeve
> For daws to peck at: I am not what I am.

Iago is a typical elizabethan *Machiavel*. With him we can associate, as among the best known, Barabbas, Aaron, Eleazar, Angelo and Mendoza (in *The Malcontent*). A remark of the latter is among the most full-blooded of the elizabethan machiavellisms, and also relates Machiavelli, in its bombast, to Nietzsche:

> We that are great, our sole self-good still moves us.

Meyer insists on the influence exercised over Marlowe by Machiavelli. And his successors, Greene, Shakespeare, Jonson, Marston and Webster, inherited this.

... The great *fox and lion* figure which went with this political machiavellian obsession, invariably used to express it, is well illustrated by Nash:

> Want cannot be withstood, men can do no more than they can do: what remained then, but the fox's case must help, when the lion's skin is out at the elbows.

But in the long run the English got over their fright, and 'saw through Machiavelli'—'Machiavel, thou art an ass!' (*The Distracted State*) dates from 1641. The English were getting cleverer. It may be that, having suitably diluted his creed for British use, and absorbed him, this 'seeing through' would ensue. In *Volpone* (iv.1) Jonson ridicules the popular scare. Chapman in *All Fooles* ridicules the popular conception of Machiavelli. But while it lasted the rage and counter-rage was immense: and it became a component of all subsequent english psychology, just as the *italian* infatuation has never disappeared.

———————

The conflict between lionish and foxlike impulses in those who rule other human beings is at the centre of Machiavelli's commonsensible and candid doctrine, and his conclusion is that a combination of the two is necessary for the wise ruler.

Lewis contends that Shakespeare, like other playwrights in his time, was much influenced by these doctrines concerning the nature and use of power, and was not the natural conservative seen by many critics, but 'a sort of feminine genius', rather a contemplator than a sublimated actor in relation to the action of the plays. 'He was the *ideal spectator*, we could say', with the qualification that this spectator was much moved by the actions he describes, so that the curses of Caliban and Thersites were also momentarily their creator's, and that 'far from being a feudal poet . . . [he was] much more a bolshevik (using this little word popularly) than a figure of conservative romance'.

How does this fit the figure of the lion and the fox? The instances given are very varied, and Lewis has valuable things to say about the contrast between the chivalric feeling represented by Cervantes and the 'scientific spirit' of the Renaissance or Shakespearean mind, but that is a side issue. The lion/fox duality is summarised as 'the contest or the tragedy arising from the meeting of the Simpleton and the Machiavel, the Fool and the Knave'. More conventional names would be Hero and Villain, but it is the complementary nature of these opposites that Lewis insists on. The Simpletons or colossi are Othello, Lear, Antony, Macbeth, Coriolanus, their complementary opposites the men and women of the world who bring them down.

from THE LION AND THE FOX

Othello as the Typical Colossus

Of all the colossi, Othello is the most characteristic, because he is the simplest, and he is seen in an unequal duel throughout with a perfect specimen of the appointed enemy of the giant—the representative of the race of men at war with the race of titans. The hero comes straight from a world where Machiavelli's black necessities—the obligation, for animal survival, for the lion to couple with the fox—are not known. He is absolutely defenceless: it is as though he were meeting one of his appointed enemies, disguised of course, as a friend, for the first time. He seems possessed of no instinct by which he might scent his antagonist, and so be put on his guard.

So, at the outset, I will present my version of Othello; and anything that I have subsequently to say must be read in the light of this interpretation. For in Othello there is nothing equivocal, I think; and the black figure of this child-man is one of the poles of Shakespeare's sensation.

Who that has read Othello's closing speech can question Shakespeare's intentions here at least? The overwhelming truth and beauty is the clearest expression of the favour of Shakespeare's heart and mind. Nothing that could ever be said would make us misunderstand what its author meant by it. Of all his ideal giants this unhappiest, blackest, most 'perplexed' child was the one of Shakespeare's predilection.

The great spectacular 'pugnacious' male ideal is represented perfectly by Othello; who was led out to the slaughter on the elizabethan stage just as the bull is thrust into the spanish bull-ring. Iago, the *taurobolus* of this sacrificial bull, the little David of this Goliath, or the little feat-gilded *espada*, is for Shakespeare nothing but Everyman, the Judas of the world, the representative of the crowds around the crucifix, or of the ferocious crowds at the *corrida*, or of the still more abject roman crowds at the mortuary games. Othello is of the race of Christs, or of the race of 'bulls'; he is the hero with all the magnificent helplessness of the animal, or all the beauty and ultimate resignation of the god. From the moment he arrives on the scene of his execution, or when his execution is being prepared, he speaks with an unmatched grandeur and beauty. To the troop that is come to look for him, armed and snarling, he says: 'Put up your bright swords or the dew will rust them!' And when at last he has been brought to bay he dies by that significant contrivance of remembering how he had defended the state when it was traduced, and in reviving this distant blow for his own demise. The great words roll on in your ears as the curtain falls:

> And say besides, that in Aleppo once . . .

Iago is made to say:

> The Moor, howbeit that I endure him not,
> Is of a constant, loving, noble nature.

But we do not need this testimony to feel, in all our dealings with this simplest and grandest of his creations, that we are meant to be in the presence of an absolute purity of human guilelessness, a generosity as grand and unaffected, although quick and, 'being wrought, Perplexed in the extreme,' as deep as that of his divine inventor.

There is no utterance in the whole of Shakespeare's plays that reveals the nobleness of his genius and of its intentions in the same way as the speech with which Othello closes:

> Soft you; a word or two before you go.
> I have done the state some service, and they know it.
> No more of that. I pray you, in your letters,
> When you shall these unlucky deeds relate,
> Speak of me as I am; nothing extenuate,
> Nor set down aught in malice: then, must you speak
> Of one that loved, not wisely, but too well;
> Of one not easily jealous, but, being wrought,
> Perplex'd in the extreme; of one, whose hand,
> Like the base Indian, threw a pearl away,
> Richer than all his tribe; of one, whose subdued eyes,
> . . . .
> Drop tears as far as the Arabian trees
> Their medicinal gum. Set you down this;
> And say, besides, that in Aleppo once,
> Where a malignant and a turban'd Turk
> Beat a Venetian, and traduced the state,
> I took by the throat the circumcisèd dog,
> And smote him—thus.

And it is the speech of a military hero, as simple-hearted as Hotspur. The tremendous and childlike pathos of this simple creature, broken by intrigue so easily and completely, is one of the most significant things for the comprehension of Shakespeare's true thought. For why should so much havoc ensue from the crude 'management' of a very ordinary intriguer? It is no great devil that is pitted against him: and so much faultless affection is destroyed with such a mechanical facility. He is a toy in the hands of a person so much less real than himself; in every sense, human and divine, so immeasurably inferior.

And say besides, that in Aleppo once.

This unhappy child, caught in the fatal machinery of 'shakespearian tragedy,' just as he might have been by an accident in the well-known world, remembers, with a measureless pathos, an event in the past to his credit, recalled as an afterthought, and thrown in at the last moment, a poor counter of 'honour,' to set against the violence to which he has been driven by the whisperings of things that have never existed.

And it is *me* who are intended to respond to these events, as the Venetian, Lodovico, does, when he apostrophizes Iago, describing him as:

More fell than anguish, hunger or the sea!

The eloquence of that apostrophe is the measure of the greatness of the heart that we have seen attacked and overcome. We cannot take that as an eloquent outburst only: it was an expression of the author's conviction of the irreparable nature of the offence, because of the purity of the nature that had suffered. The green light of repugnance and judgment is thrown on to the small mechanical villain at the last.

Professor Bradley in his elaborate analysis of Iago says that many people have seen in Iago one of the traditional Machiavellis of the time; but he repudiates that parentage for him. Yet it hardly seems a thing about which there can be any dispute. There is no question of Shakespeare's finding this *particular* duplicity in the figure of Machiavelli. But it is certain that Iago is a variety of the recognized stage Machiavelli type. Will anyone believe that if a philosophy of duplicity and ruthless mechanical intrigue, directed to the reaching of a definite material end, had never been written by Machiavelli: if Cesare Borgia had not supplied him with a living illustration and hero (as Napoleon was Stendhal's vast living confirmation and original): and if the italian nature had not stood for *intrigue*, of a bold and relentless description, that Iago, the italian 'villain' of this italian story, would ever have been created?

In Act I, scene 1, he reveals himself at once, without the least delay or coyness, both to Roderigo and to the audience.

There is nothing that Iago says, in the displays of his mental workings with which we are accommodated, that would be inappropriate in the mouth of any solicitor, stockbroker, politician or man-about-town in England to-day, or in Shakespeare's day. He possesses the same pride in his *cunning*—tells you with a wink that *his* thoughts are not worn on his sleeve but in a deep and secret place, where they cannot easily be found.

There is something at once commonplace and maniacal, 'normal' and mad, about the way he speaks of his hiding-place, his mind:

> In following him, I follow but myself;
> Heaven is my judge, not I for love and duty,
> But seeming so, for my peculiar end:
> For when my outward action doth demonstrate
> The native act and figure of my heart
> In compliment extern, 'tis not long after
> But I will wear my heart upon my sleeve
> For daws to peck at: I am not what I am.

The last words are the supreme bombast of such people. *I am not what I am.* The small and shoddy, when it meets its kind, knows it at once by this sign—namely, *that it is not what it is.* Both are the votaries of the goddess whose oracle these words convey. Shakespeare's own words—*I am that I am*—where in his *Sonnets*, through all the veils of his beautiful rhetoric, he is, as Wordsworth said, 'unlocking his heart'—are similarly the supreme defiance of the rarest nature, for ever over against the dark equivocal crowds saturated with falsity.

When Robert Browning denied that Shakespeare was capable of such an action as 'unlocking his heart' (as Wordsworth said that he did) he classed himself with more nicety than he knew. The romantically machiavellian and 'detached' *'Robert Browning you writer of plays'* as he calls himself, with his social obsession ('the need of a world of men for me'), his vitalist habit of mind and proliferous spawning-powers, judged Shakespeare with that essential, romantic conventionality that he brought to all his judgments. So the 'impersonality' dogma, popularizing the method of exact science, is, when applied to individual character or to the arts of life, an expression of the at once commonplace and demented cunning, pride in which is stigmatic of the man of the crowd of our day. But later in this book I give more attention to the subject of impersonality. I show how it is the characteristic myth of science, how in that sense it is a form of personality; and how the instinctive and conscious mind is sacrificed to it.

The secret of Iago, then—if there could be any secret about Iago's nature for an intelligent spectator of the play in which he occurs, for he is as candid as it is possible to be to the audience and to everybody except his victim—is that this particular Everyman is the bluff, commonplace, quite unvillainlike, little 'man of the world,' mobilized to destroy a great shakespearian hero. Bosola is a complicated renaissance figure, but Iago is so great a creation because he is not that at all, but just the man-in-the-street of any time or place since the emergence of *homo sapiens* on our scene. This plain man is, of course, deeply marked by professional, racial and other stereotyping effects of circumstance; and Iago, for instance, is the *blunt soldier*, and has other characteristics of his calling. But at heart it is one figure, the animal human average.

Most Shakespeare critics, however, when they come to write about Iago, use more or less the language of his wife Emilia on the discovery of his treachery, or of Lodovico, or Gratiano: his 'motiveless malignity' is supposed to be motiveless because it is assumed to be so unusual and so deep. Professor Bradley scouts the idea that his own repeated explanation of his behaviour is to be accepted; and although he will not admit that it is motiveless, with Coleridge, he considers his villainy without parallel in its depth and degradation, and goes off hunting for motives of the most unusual sort (to match the *unusualness* of the crime).

He implores the reader to remember that Iago *under no circumstances* ever tells the truth! Should the reader forget that for a moment, one is almost made to feel he might find himself entrapped by this spartan dog as poor Othello was.

All this appears to me very far from the truth. The most obvious thing about Iago is that he never lies, and is as open (in his villainy) as the day, as we have already said.

He always tells the truth when speaking to the audience or to himself. It is a stroke of genius of Shakespeare to make him always called *honest*—when his actions are so deliberately dishonest, and yet when his nature, rough and direct, does, in another sense, perfectly answer that description.

The villainy of Iago did not seem to Shakespeare, from all appearances, very exceptional, although very black. Also he accounted

109

for it, fully, even, on several occasions, out of Iago's own mouth. In Act 1, scene 3, Iago's soliloquy seems a very straightforward and reasonable explanation of why he intends 'to pay out' his master:

> I hate the Moor;
> And it is thought abroad, that 'twixt my sheets
> He has done my office: I know not if't be true;
> But I, for mere suspicion in that kind,
> Will do as if for surety. He holds me well.
> The better shall my purpose work on him.
> Cassio's a proper man: let me see now;
> To get his place, and to plume up my will,
> In double knavery,—How, how?—Let's see:—
> After some time to abuse Othello's ear
> That he is too familiar with his wife.
> He hath a person, and a smooth dispose,
> To be suspected; framed to make women false.
> The Moor is of a free and open nature,
> That thinks men honest that but seem to be so;
> And will as tenderly be led by the nose,
> As asses are.

That is a very close statement: or again (Act II, scene 1):

> He'll prove to Desdemona
> A most dear husband. Now, I do love her too;
> Not out of absolute lust (though, peradventure,
> I stand accountant for as great a sin),
> But partly led to diet my revenge,
> For that I do suspect the lusty Moor
> Hath leap'd into my seat: the thought whereof
> Doth, like a poisonous mineral, gnaw my inwards;
> And nothing can or shall content my soul,
> Till I am even'd with him, wife for wife;
> Or, failing so, yet that I put the Moor
> At least into a jealousy so strong
> That judgment cannot cure.

Iago is a professional soldier, a 'man of action,' like Othello; and in a sense he is *simple*, like Othello. When he says the Moor is of a constant, loving, noble nature he admires those qualities. He does not sneer as he says it, their psychology has enough in common, just as their way of life has, so that, in spite of his immense respect for the tortuous, he can also admire the open and truthful.

Being in this sense *simple*, like Othello; and believing that Othello has cuckolded him, he reacts to this event in as violent and primitive a way as Othello does. He is, like Othello, very touchy where the faithfulness of his wife is concerned, and likes the idea of being pointed at as a cuckold just as little as Othello does. In other ways, also, Othello has treated him without very much consideration: but the ostensible plot of the play is really the revenge of the sex-vanity of a subordinate on his chief, the revenge taking the form of inspiring his chief with the same feelings of jealousy and wounded vanity that he has experienced himself.

But it is much more than a sex-revenge—*sex* in its way being as deceptive as *money* is in itself a human incentive. It is also, as it were, a *race*-revenge, the vengeance of the small nature upon the great nature.

To conclude the consideration of this question by returning to the conflict we supposed between the worldly soul of man and a champion of the superhuman idealism—the factor that has produced all those astonishing achievements that men have felt separated them from the other animals—where should we look for our champions? We have agreed that it would probably be from among Shakespeare's colossi that the champion on one side would be taken; though perhaps, because of the historic reference, and the magnificence of the traditional setting, the Antony of *Antony and Cleopatra* would be better than Othello. But if you were matching Othello or Antony in this way, who would you choose for the vulpine rôle?

Ulysses is a great myth traditionally representing 'the world,' but his cunning is almost heroic; and there would be the same objections to him, on those grounds, as to the jesuit. Yet (in a sense since they are real champions) it would probably be Ulysses, the jesuit, or the transformed shaman that you would choose. (The matching of a woman and a man is too unnatural.) You would not get the David and Goliath contrast in stature, but you would get a more exciting spectacle. The pathos of the 'little pin' and the 'good-bye king,' the meanness of the instrument used to destroy all greatness, is perhaps too intense, in principle, for artistic expression. That is why tragedy is not the purest art. The contests of pure art would be like the battles of the norse heroes in heaven. They would ride back after the battle to Valhalla or some more congenial Elysium, the wounds and deaths abolished by magic at the termination of each day. Only heroes would participate; and no reality would mar their vigorous joys.

———————

In an appendix Lewis sees Shakespeare, like all the greatest artists, as international. A truism, one might say, but for a writer concerned with the links between race, class and sex, this was a supreme distinction, and the view that emerged was unusual.

from THE LION AND THE FOX

Race and the Person

Sometimes the fashionable error of the moment is to neglect the factor of race, as though there were no such thing as race, but only classes or nations or empires; and sometimes it has been the fashion to exaggerate that factor, as though there were not such a thing as persons, but only races. *Class* in these adjustments is, of course, the great rival of *race*: it is also a very much easier thing to fix. Race is for the most part too obscure a force for us to be able to organize it into anything coherent, so it is perhaps rightly ignored. In an art-form like elizabethan drama, if the race factor could be got at, it might tell us a great deal more than anything else—as it goes deeper and farther back—about the impulses at work in it, giving it its peculiar physiognomy. But it is the one thing that it is impossible to chart. We can only argue, rather uncertainly, from the results, and inductively work back to a supposed origin; where some particular idiosyncrasy, oddly flowering and challenging our curiosity, suggests a new road to the virgin regions behind us.

These remarks apply of course to Shakespeare as well as to his contemporaries. But our contention here is that they apply differently and less. At this point it may be well to ask if, to start with, we are prepared to deny the significance of race altogether? That—from what has been said above—is evidently not the case. A man's *race* is the most interesting thing about him, usually—*class* is a parvenu category compared to it. But Shakespeare's race (not his nation), if we knew it, would *not* be the most interesting thing about him.

The belief on which I am basing my statement here can be summarized as follows. Not only genius, as we call the greatest development of conscious personality, but all personality, is raceless for all practical purposes: for the characteristic work of personality is to overcome the mechanical ascendancy of what is imposed on it by birth and environment. So, since it illustrates itself essentially by triumph over race, class and fashion, these things are rather what it is *not*, than what it *is*. It is, however, true that in this struggle it uses aptitudes and forces that it derives from the things it is destined to combat.

In Shakespeare's case there is less temptation than in that of almost anybody to occupy ourselves with where he came from: for where he got to is a matter of such great and universal interest that it would be sure to dwarf his origins, as it dwarfed his immediate environment. However far back you went down the stream of his blood, you would not be likely to meet anything so worth your attention (however picturesque) as himself.

We can suggest more clearly what we mean, perhaps, by other examples. Supposing you were talking to an enthusiast for 'french civilization,' the fact that Flaubert was 'a Frenchman' would be very much in Flaubert's favour. But most Frenchmen, as everyone who has travelled in France must have rapidly discovered, are very much like Bouvard and Pecuchet. Therefore, in dragging in 'the Frenchman' in Flaubert's case, you would be arriving at this surprising result: you would be advertising Flaubert on account of his racial or national association with Bouvard and Pecuchet! It would surely be far truer to say that it would be reasonable to be a little endeared to the average Frenchman on account of his fellow-countryman, Flaubert; or because he spoke the language of Racine. This is the extreme personalist-position, the opposite to the first one to which you would be committed in the above illustration—namely, that in which you ended by congratulating Flaubert on belonging to the same stock as Bouvard and Pecuchet . . .

The foregoing remarks in no way dispose of the interest in race for us: all they are designed to do is to put us on our guard where unbridled racial romanticism is concerned, and to hint at the ridiculous situations we inevitably arrive at if we pursue that enthusiasm too far. If it were suddenly announced, with a wealth of proof that it was impossible to controvert, that Shakespeare was a Chinaman, I should of course know at once—in the present state of science and politics and with what I know of the press—that it was intended in England to establish some sort of alliance with China. I should expect to see the announcement followed by a clever forgery described as a 'recently discovered play of Shakespeare's,' with as many points of resemblance to the philosophy of Confucius as Hamlet has to Montaigne. But supposing I heard, and *believed*, that Shakespeare was a Chinaman, I should then feel no surprise; it would require no readjustment at all in what I thought about him. For I should know that he must be as unlike most Chinamen as he was unlike most Englishmen. But because you say that the position of an individual such as Shakespeare to his race-class-time context is exactly that of the child to his parents, it does not mean that you deny the beauty and propriety of filial love; nor that you would deny that the outward appearance of every creature roughly follows the lineaments of father and mother. It would only involve a suspicion that very strong race-characteristics in an individual, in their face, gait or mental disposition, probably means, at all events to-day, that they are not the highest examples of their kind; that had they been more creative and mentally active they would not have been content *to repeat*—even physiologically: nor would they have followed mechanically the rules laid down by nature and humdrum tradition.

But race is a very great reality: and were we not dealing with such a figure as Shakespeare we should certainly not have been compelled to go into all these uncomfortable details. How amusing it is, for instance, to speculate whether the pictorial attainments of the modern Jew has its rationale in the turanian intermixture, showing itself so often in the features of jewish immigrants. Or, again, renaissance Italy is one great ethnologic question-mark. The largely oriental slave-population of Rome far outnumbered the native Romans, and these along with the hordes of slaves employed on the latifundia must subsequently have left

114

huge deposits of human stocks, opposite to those provided by northern invasion.

Any analysis of a great creative period—and we are concerned with that too—must have this chaotic spot in its centre: the incalculable factor of racial intermixture. For it needs only a few men, or even one man, to give a novel turn and a strange power to a supposedly 'national' movement. In a mind like Shakespeare's a whole necropolis comes to life. And he made a good use of his ghosts. In such a risorgimento who is to say what ultimately is the value even of Stratford-on-Avon and the Bankside theatre business? The special conditions we have applied to the individual must also be applied to any exceptional creative group; the same alibis must be, perhaps, employed. The strangest ghosts must have trod those elizabethan stages, as they always assemble wherever life becomes suddenly incandescent.

———————

Colour is part of race, 'not only controversial [but] for the human being of symbolical importance . . . The most humble Babbitt possesses something enviable, to which, besides, intellectually and socially, he has no right—namely his "pale" face.' How absurd, then, of whites to envy those of another colour, black in particular, and to discover 'primitive' virtues in their simplicity, their art, their unconscious wisdom. *Paleface* is a high-spirited, entertaining attack, not on blacks but on their white culture-worshippers, particularly D.H. Lawrence and Sherwood Anderson. It is the absurd romanticism of this idealisation of black culture, its exaltation of feeling and rejection of thought, that are Lewis's chief targets. He has good boisterous fun with the absurdities of Anderson's *Dark Laughter*, and attacks effectively Lawrence's view that primitive 'consciousness' is superior to the white 'consciousness' by which it has been defeated. But the chief interest of this book-length pamphlet is its stress on the limitations of white civilisation, and the forceful reiteration of an internationalist view with particular emphasis on the possible role of the United States. The whites who 'overran the world, and with the help of their rapidly developing Science, enslaved the greater part of it, wiping out entire races and cultures, were possessed of a meagre cultural outfit, and only a borrowed religion'. They were, it is said, less 'civilised' than

115

the Aztecs, Mayans and Indians they subdued, they wiped out the American Indian, enslaved Negroes, and 'subjugated the highly civilised Hindu'.

Is this, then, a criticism of Paleface civilisation, a suggestion that it might be succeeded by something better of another colour? Not exactly: indeed, not at all. While criticising the Paleface, Lewis is not at all in favour of those who suggest like Spengler that white decline should now be accepted. He invokes an imaginary Plain Man asking Spengler: 'Why do the Western governments want to smash up their own property?' Spengler's reply that the decline is inevitable is found unacceptable, no better than the Fabian idea of the inevitability of gradualness. Lewis's own position is outlined in the last chapter, extracted below.

from PALEFACE

A Final Proposal: A Model 'Melting-Pot'

There are, in the specifically *moral* nature of the situation in which we find ourselves, factors that I do not propose to investigate. There is the contradictory spectacle, which we can all observe, of our institutions, as they dehumanize themselves, clothing themselves more and more, and with a hideous pomposity, with the stuff of morals—that stuff of which the pagan world was healthily ignorant, in its physical expansiveness and instinct for a concrete truth, and which, for the greatest peoples of the East, has never existed except as a purely political systematization of something irretrievably inferior, a sentimental annexe of a metaphysical truth. It is natural that 'the Congo' should 'flood the Acropolis' (though I am not sure that I did not misunderstand the Princess) when we see the attitudes of Renaissance culture, as illustrated by the great french stylists, being subtly combined with the militant emotional gloom of the Salvation Army: when the Salvation Army marches weeping, in jazz-step, into the study of Montesquieu, then the crocodiles *are* on their way to Hellas.

What I shall especially neglect is to analyse the artificial character of this puritanic gloom, settling in a dense political smoke-screen about us, gushed from both official and unofficial reservoirs. I shall confine myself to remarking that the person who meets all these sham glooms with an anguished *De Profundis*, instead of a laugh (however unpleasant), is scarcely wise, though he may be good. To see a vineyard in the sun surrounded by armed federal officers of the law, who prevent anybody from taking the grapes and making them into wine, is absurd, more than anything else. Foodstuffs rotting upon the quays while people are starving, is a fact that should be met, if at all, not by stylistic theologic melancholy, that seems obvious. Or again, the abstruse principles of the manufacture of paper-money, like the arbitrary non-manufacture of a healthy and pleasant wine, and all that results from one as from the other—of gloom and a sense of the *difficulty* of everything—this is not the material for profound heart-searching groans, although that is the correct unofficial response, it is true. But a reader of this book will be left with those sums or equations on his hands, to work out or not, as he may feel inclined. I have made it clear, I think, how the *ethical*, introduced into the physical problem of the Melting-pot, produces a gloomy and passionate infusion: that is all I set out to do. With a definite proposal, one that has been made often before by many people, I will bring this essay to a close.

In America the expression Melting-pot has been coined to describe the assimilation of european nationalities in the United States, and now of the negro population, ten million strong, which has begun in earnest. In Europe we have no such expression, for the excellent reason that there is no assimilation in progress. If the United States possessed fixed areas in which Danes, Spaniards, Germans, Negroes, Irish and so forth were segregated, as we are, each settled in certain states, with fortified frontiers, taught only their mother-tongue and unable to converse with the inhabitants of the next state, then there would be no Melting-pot there either. America without its Melting-pot would simply be another Europe, plus a Black Belt and a few Chinatowns.

There is a radical contradiction between the european and american way of regarding this problem. Perhaps because it is so much taken for granted, this difference passes for the most part unnoticed by us. Whereas the rulers of America are committed to fusion (however dissimilar the racial stocks) in one form or another, in Europe the question does not even arise. Since the French live upon one side of the Rhine and the

117

Germans upon the other, or the English and the French upon opposite sides of the English Channel, there is no 'problem' as to their mixing: indeed the great majority of Germans or Frenchmen or Englishmen never see a member of the neighbour-nation except during such times as their respective governments decide appropriate for a mass-meeting, as it were, and they are despatched to kill one another with bomb and bayonet. Even then it is only the infantry who see members of the 'enemy' nation at all distinctly: and it is possible for an infantryman to pass many months in the Line without catching sight of more than a few of his european neighbours, and these mostly dead specimens, or even nothing more than their facetious skeletons.

Of these two attitudes—the melting and the non-melting—the American appears to me by far the better: I am heart and soul upon the side of the Melting-pot, *not* upon that of the Barbed Wire. That is why I have called this book 'The Ethics of the *Melting-pot*,' and not 'The Ethics of the Barbed Wire.' But what a terribly sad thing it is to reflect that literally millions of Basques, Finns, Scotsmen, Danes, Normans, Prussians, Swiss, should be kept rigidly apart while in Europe, by the intensive perpetuation of purely historical frontiers (which the Versailles Treaty has made even more numerous and complicated than before), whereas if they emigrate to America they are liable suddenly to be hectored for an opposite reason—namely because they show some slight compunction in coupling with a jet-black Kaffir. Personally I consider that they are quite wrong in looking down upon the transplanted Kaffir: but it is far more stupid of them (if, say, a Swede) to look down upon a lovely Basque, or (if a Bavarian) to look down upon an industrious Gasconesse. Yet have they not always been taught to do that, at least since the rise of the national idea in Europe or since the time of the great religious schisms?

My own view is that the Melting-pot should be set up in Europe, upon the spot. Instead of posters on our walls which say 'Join the Royal Air Force and See the World,' there should be posters (and offices in every district to deal with applicants) saying, 'Marry a Swiss and See the World,' or, more jocularly, 'Get spliced to a Finn, and Get About.'

What can there be against it, except that it would be impossible to have wars any more in Europe? If it is objected that there is no unifying principle in Europe to compare with *americanization*, it is necessary to recall that only five centuries ago the whole of Europe possessed one soul in a more fundamental way than America can be said to at this moment, and the actual appearance of its towns must have been at least as uniform as today (and that is very uniform), though in a more agreeable fashion. As to the individuals of the various races, there is no obstacle there. In the valleys of the Pyrenees, for instance, you meet with a great many people physically as like as two eggs to the inhabitant of Devonshire, Derby, Limerick, or Caithness: a swiss peasant woman is in character and physical appearance often so identical with a swedish, english, german, or french girl, that they might be twin sisters. This everyone must have remarked who has ever travelled to those countries. It has always been fratricidal that these people should be taught to disembowel, blind and poison each other on the score of their quite imaginary 'differences' of blood or mind, but today there is less excuse for it than ever before. So why not a *Melting-pot?*—instead of more and more intensive discouragement of such a fusion. Europe is not so very large: why should it not have one speech like China and acquire one government?

But feeling about Europe in that manner, and all too familiar with that situation, the spectacle of the rather feverish opposite to that attitude, wherever these same Europeans leave their countries and live in the proximity of people so different from themselves as the Negroes or the Chinese, cannot but occur to one as a very sudden and from some points of view unsatisfactory reversal. On the one hand you have too absolute a segregation, on the other too absolute a freedom to mix. America is the child of Europe entirely, except for the Negroes and in Mexico and south of Panama the Indians, and the two problems should not be dissociated. What happens to Europe is of great importance to America, and vice versa—what happens to America, that other-Europe, must be of great moment to us.

This essay is much more to propose that we set up a Melting-pot in Europe—which would be as it were a Model Melting-pot, not at the boiling-point but cooking at a steady rate day in day out—than to venture any criticism of the principle underlying the american or african Melting-pot or, alternatively, Colour Line. Indeed a quite irrational attitude is often adopted by the American to miscegenation. Another factor of 'inferiority' feeling has its roots in a profound misunderstanding of the true situation. The American is apt to accept the false european attitude towards 'race,' as it is called. It is a common experience in talking to Americans to hear some magnificent human specimen (who is obviously the issue of say a first-class Swede and a magnificent Swissess, with a little Irish and a touch of Basque) refer to himself as a 'mongrel.' It is inconceivable, yet indeed that is how such a 'mixed' product is apt to look upon this superb marriage of Scandinavian, Goth and Celt—all stocks as closely related in blood—if it is 'blood' that is the trouble—as the brahmanic caste of India. Merely physically this epithet is given the lie: for all you have to do is to look at this sterling type of 'mixed' American to admire the purity of line and fine adjustment achieved by the conjunction of these sister stocks. Far from being a 'mongrel,' of course, he is a sort of super-European: the best of several closely allied stocks have met in him, in exactly the same way as was constantly happening in the noble european families—where the issue of a marriage between nobles, whether from England and Italy or Spain and Russia, did not constitute a 'half-breed,' but rather a more exalted feudal product, so subtly 'mixed.'

Some racial mixtures are not so fortunate as others, however, it is necessary to allow: the indian and spanish mixtures, in say Peru or Mexico, have not proved really very good. The Barber of Seville that peeps through the Inca removes him from Mozart, and yet does not make a good Indian of him, though there are exceptions. But practically all european intermarriage presents no problem at all, and is indeed politically much to be desired, as certain to abolish the fiction of our frontiers and the fiction of the 'necessity' of war. The asiatic elements in Southern Spain, Italy and Russia aside, the European is as much of one blood as are the inhabitants of the British Isles, and in many instances more so—for instance the Bavarian and the lowland Scotch are man for man as nearly one race (to look at them, as well as in their character) as you could find anywhere at all. If they spoke a common Ido the Austrian with his *Spielhahnfeder* and *Eichenlaub* stuck in his *Steierhut* would melt into the Crofter without noticing he had left his native village.

But (until they reach America, and all have to speak english, or, in Latin-America, spanish) the great difficulty is language. In discussing such a question as this we always get back to the problem of Babel. It is in the interest of the Melting-pot that every European should wish to learn Volapuc as I do, or to have some language picked for him that it shall be agreed all shall speak and that he can easily learn and speak—woo his possibly distant bride in, and talk over all those subjects of common interest with his brother at the other extremity of Europe, which since the decay of latin as a universal tongue no one has been able to do. I cannot imagine any person in Europe who, when the matter was presented to him in that light, would not plump for some Volapuc: but if there is anywhere a person who would not, how slender his reasons must be compared to those a Dutchman say in Africa could allege for refusing to mate his daughter with a Cape-Black or a settler from the Dekkan! And yet even the Dutchman would not be right, would he?—how much more wrong then would not the man in Europe be who stood out, for in fifty per cent. of the cases he would be vetoing a closer match than could be made even in the home-village at any given time—for I would guarantee to match a young man in a Devon village better in the Canton of Berne than would be possible probably, at any given moment, in his own english district.

On the other hand if the Dutchman in Africa had ten daughters and seized the other end of the stick (after a reading of Plomer) so fanatically as to pester them all to choose upon the spot a Black bridegroom, that would be a sentimental extreme that it would be perhaps allowable to deplore: if he should embellish his persuasiveness with highly-coloured abuses of all owners of a pale skin, then he would definitely become irritating and perhaps even absurd, and if his ten girls took him and flogged him no one could find it in his heart to blame them, though if called to a Grand Jury it would be necessary to send the whole of the ten girls to jail of course, for they should not, strictly speaking, flog their father, either, however misguided, as potentially his whiteness would be the symbol of their consanguinity and the ultimate reason for their objecting to the break-up of their pigment. This last illustration touches upon a complexity which (in rare instances, so far) qualifies the absolute simplicity of this question—the problem of the *gaga* Paleface Pap who reads Plomer or Du Bois. But—as I have prophesied—he will be dealt with by his children or grandchildren, when he disinherits them and leaves all his money to the female Kaffir cook.

What in these concluding pages it has been my intention to stress is that the fiery ethics of the Melting-pot are conjunctly european and protestant in origin more than anything else (though the gallic invention of the 'great nation' plays its part as well). The fanatical ill-temper and the black intolerance that accompany the discussion and propaganda for 'race-fusion' can be traced to these sources, when they cannot be directly traced to the equally intemperate ethical zeal of the 'radicalist' righteousness.

At this time the Anglo-Saxon is no longer paramount in North America: but his language is still the general speech, and american civilization is in its main principles anglo-saxon. The alternation of emotional indulgence in liberalist programmes (and anglo-saxon 'radicalism' is newer and more heated liberalism, merely) and unintelligent race-prejudice, with which distressing see-saw we are so familiar, is anglo-saxon, is it not? Neither the Spanish, Portuguese nor French as colonists have handled their respective Melting-pot in that manner. The latin tradition, more tolerant, catholic and mature, has not sentimentalized about the deeply-pigmented skin, nor fixed upon it, on the other hand, a stigma. You would not be so likely to get adepts of jazz in a Black Belt in a latin land, nor the ferocity of lynching neighboured by anti-White tracts, written by Whites, nor a universal thunder of psalms from Black and White throats mixed, and evangelist extremes of intolerance and hysterical expansion—it would be more likely you would find a firmer attitude, more satisfactory to both sides, far less superstitious, in the Latin.

Yet, although it is necessary to fix, for any such survey, the anglo-saxon responsibilities, they are not all anglo-saxon, and the nationalism of Europe as a whole is to blame, I think, both for the excesses of the 'Nordic Blondes' or what Mencken calls the 'Ofays,' where they occur, and for the excesses of their satirists and detractors. Must we not agree that it is the artificial principle of european *separatism* (of all the Irelands, Ulsters, Catalonias, Polands, Czecho-Slovakias and the rest) transplanted to America or Africa, that, there, is apt to issue in a quite new form in a hotbed of separatist, or of fusionist, passion—which in the near future may wreck those societies as it is wrecking ours?

If (to show my enthusiasm for fusion) I may allow myself a strikingly *mixed* metaphor, it is at the fountain-head that we should establish our Melting-pot—an example to all other Melting-pots. And it is here in Europe that we should start a movement at once for the miscegenation of Europeans—with *each other*, that is—Asia and Africa could be considered later, no doubt, for incorporation in our Model Melting-pot.

———————

Those who believe Lewis to have been a rabid racist and nationalist may blink at this unequivocal advocacy of miscegenation, accompanied elsewhere in the book by a contemptuous reference to 'the most intense and inveterate [racial superstition] the world has ever known', that of Jewish inferiority. The jocularity of tone, as in those remarks about the Afrikaner who insisted on his ten daughters all marrying blacks, will infuriate those who think serious suggestions must always be solemnly made, and it should be noted that Lewis's internationalism does not imply a belief in equality. The proposed melting-pot is a blend of nations and races, supported not because of any idea about equality, but in the belief that in it irrelevant and outmoded nationalist sentiments will rapidly disappear.

It may seem extraordinary that a man who regarded the United States as a model melting-pot should have written a study of Hitler before he came to power that was not unfavourable, and certainly it represents an about-turn, or at least a shift of some degrees, in Lewis's attitude. The book is also the first unhappy demonstration of something that was inevitable: in the production almost yearly of book-length pamphlets dealing with current political and social questions, the background of research was sketchy, sometimes almost non-existent. Lewis relied on cuttings from newspapers, gossip, and his own necessarily limited observation. What he says about political theory is always perceptive and intelligent. When he deals with the current policies and attitudes of governments in Britain, France and Germany, however, he is often retailing, commenting on, and drawing deductions from, newspaper stories.

The result in *Hitler* is a number of assertions that, even in 1931, were obviously wide of the mark. In Hitler, it is said, 'we have a "Man of Peace" ', somebody who is 'not a sabre-rattler at all'. What about his attitude to the Jews? A friendly Englishman or American should 'say to the Hitlerite that he takes the Jew too seriously', and no doubt Hitler himself, once in power, would 'show increasing moderation and tolerance' to the Jew, as he would certainly not make war. 'He would, I am positive, remain peacefully at home, fully occupied with the internal problems of the *Dritte Reich.*' All this was not merely wrong, but a contradiction of what was plainly set down in *Mein Kampf.* The journalist who said, when the original articles appeared, that Lewis lacked knowledge of the German situation in general and the Nazi movement in particular, was not far from the truth.

If one digs deeper, Lewis's favourable view of Hitler sprang from his belief that an authoritarian society, ruled by those who combined the qualities of Machiavelli's lion and fox, offered the best hope for an enduring peace. Through much of the Thirties the Nazi movement seemed to him to hold the possibility of such a society, and so he gave it implicit approval, although never more than that. To do so meant jettisoning the model melting-pot, and trying to square the desire for an international government and individual freedom with praise of Hitler as 'the most unassuming and simple of men' who had 'sacrificed himself, literally to a principle; that of national freedom' (*Left Wings Over Europe*, 1936). Of this book, and of *Count Your Dead—They Are Alive* (1937), there is little good to be said, except that they are written with Lewis's never-failing verve, and that they deploy some effective arguments against believing any of the propaganda coming from the Soviet Union and its fellow-travellers. By contrast with this scepticism, Hitler's speeches and intentions are viewed with almost total credulity.

These books are the worst of Lewis, and they had a disastrous effect on his reputation. In the one-man magazine he had founded in 1927 he adopted the role of *The Enemy*, one of the 'six most constant indications of different personalities' advocated in 'The Code of a Herdsman', but that was a stage Enemy whose activities were in part an intellectual game. Lewis was now, however, regarded as a real enemy, no voluntary outlaw but a man expelled as unacceptable to the tribe. Pound's outspoken support of Mussolini was regarded as mere eccentricity, but Lewis was hated, perhaps less for his view of Hitler than for his increasing hostility to the Soviet Union and his contempt for the many intellectual travellers of the Communist Party. As the Thirties neared their end he felt some need for a mending of fences. In a short book, *The Jews: Are They Human?* (1938) he praised Jewish courage, intellect and honesty, and ended with the following chapter, expressing unexceptionable views.

from THE JEWS: ARE THEY HUMAN?

A New Deal for the Jew

In this last chapter of my short book I will draw what seems to me the necessary conclusions. Any intelligent discussion of the 'Jewish Problem' must, I think, lead to much the same results.

1   The 'Jewish Problem' is not inherent in the nature of the Jewish People, but in (*a*) the character of the Christian nations, and (*b*) their attitude towards the Jews.

2   It is the Christian nations who have taught the Jews bad habits, not the other way round.

3   We Anglo-Saxons and other Europeans, should reform ourselves: by so doing we should be liquidating the 'Jewish Problem.' Our own undesirables, and the more irresponsible elements among the Jews, would be discouraged simultaneously, and would disappear.

4   Our attitude to the Jews was in the first instance the outcome of our religion.

5   The Jew did not like the Christian 'heresy', as they considered it. They insisted, with consummate lack of tact, upon their own religion. They were an opposition shop. Our priests reacted violently. Also the part the ancestors of the Jews were described as playing at the climax of the drama of our profoundly sensational cult, gave our forefathers a horror of them.

6   As objects of dislike, and even of *horror*, they became at once cowed and sullen. This reacted unfavourably upon their disposition, as it would have done upon ours.

7   With Eighteenth and Nineteenth Century 'enlightenment' all this tended to diminish in intensity. At last the Anglo-Saxons discovered, to their surprise, that the Jews were human after all.

8   Then a nation of fiery pastors, gone pagan—and military to the marrow—but still full of gothic superstition, turned upon

125

their Jews and drove them forth, denouncing them as devils in human form, who were after their girls. Other nations followed suit.

9   That brings us up-to-date. All is naturally confusion. All these 'refugees' are headed for the Anglo-Saxon world.

10   What are we to do? Are we to go back and begin all over again (but without the excuse of Christianity) thinking of these people as accursed, as unclean, and as branded with the mark of Cain?

11   There can be only one answer to that: a unanimous NO. Of course we cannot.

12   But we must do something more active than just not go back. We must make up for the doings of the so-called 'Christians' of yesterday—who degraded the Jew, and then mocked at him for being degraded. We must give all people of Jewish race a new deal among us. Let us for Heaven's sake make an end of this silly nightmare once and for all, and turn our backs upon this dark chapter of our history.

═══════════

Few people read this little book, and of those who did some will have disliked the light-hearted way in which Lewis said that the generally rather stupid Englishman found the 'brainy' Jew 'a useful sort of bird' to have around, the 'sharp-witted underling' of 'a lazy and stupid master'. That was not how the English or perhaps any other Jew wished to be regarded.

In his second volume of autobiography *Rude Assignment* Lewis came near to admitting his errors. 'A nationalist I have never been. But I believed, say twelve years ago, that the doctrine of national sovereignty was an indispensable guarantee of freedom . . . I regard that as archaic thinking. Such group freedom is no longer possible nor is it desirable.' *The Hitler Cult*, published in December 1939 but begun more than a year earlier, after the Munich pact, not only offered a totally different view of Hitler, now seen as 'more an entranced medium than anything else', but marked also a return to the internationalism of the decade before 1930, and explained the logic of this changed view.

from THE HITLER CULT

Sovereign-Nationhood

Wherever I go to-day I hear people talking about a Federal scheme, the object of which is to induce the great democratic states of the West, especially Great Britain and America, to abandon their national sovereignty, pool their resources, have a common Parliament and armies under one direction. The establishment of something that would resemble the British Commonwealth of Nations, but more centripetal, is, I suppose, the idea.

Let me say at once that I am in favour of such a scheme: and if France, Spain, Portugal, and the Scandinavian countries would join it so much the better. Let me also say that I have not always been in favour of arrangements of this order, I have tended to advocate individualist political structures: small units as against big ones. And I will explain why—for there are things against as well as for, and it is important that everybody should be in possession of the arguments against, before they are invited to vote on it. This is not the usual practice in a parliamentary democracy. But both sides *should* be heard.

Here then is the case against the surrender of sovereign rights, and against a great merger of this kind. The main argument runs on the same lines as that used against any monopoly or trust: namely, it would be too big, and the interests of the individual would suffer accordingly.

As recently as two or three years ago I favoured that small unit—the nation. 'For years to come the whole world will be busy answering the question: "Are you for the super-state of internationalism, or for the sovereign state of non-international politics?" ' So I wrote in 1936. And my answer then was that I preferred the sovereign state—preferred decentralized government to centralized government. Or, as I put it, I was for *the part*, rather than for *the whole*. I was for 'those who wish to retain the maximum freedom for *the parts*: and to withhold unreasonable and too oppressive power from *the whole*. For *the whole* would be only a verbal figment,' I added. 'It would mean government by a handful of individuals.'

'The part' seems to me at present just as much a 'verbal figment' as

127

'the whole.' It also means government by a handful of individuals, and by no means the most representative. Whether the unit thus *mis*-represented comprises forty million or four hundred million souls makes little difference.

When I stated that, should we follow the Geneva road of the League of Nations Union, then 'the destiny of England, perhaps for centuries to come, is to be decided in a Swiss city by a motley collection of gentlemen whose names most of us are unable to pronounce,' I was overlooking the fact that the Parliament that sits in London is so peculiarly unrepresentative of the real interest of England that 'a motley collection of gentlemen' in Geneva could not be any worse, and, in spite of their unpronounceable names, might be considerably better.

It is a very powerful argument in favour of retaining sovereignty and independence, that 'out of sight is out of mind,' and that power ought to be vested in the hands of people who are in daily contact with those they are to rule. Even such a short way away from the Scottish Border as is London, it is far enough for a Parliament sitting in London to forget or overlook the peculiar needs and problems of Scotland. That is a very powerful argument. But how much more valid it would be if the Parliament sitting at Westminster did not forget and overlook just as much the peculiar needs and problems of *Londoners*, who are right there under its nose!

I have had my eyes fixed upon the political scene now for six years without intermission. My conclusions to-day differ, not unnaturally, from those arrived at earlier. More every day I am convinced that to isolate any part of that Whole is impracticable. We should let the whole thing rip. Our instincts as men born to a great tradition of human freedom is to hold back what we can from the political merger. The monster business concern is 'soulless,' we say; the monster state must be the same. But monstrous and 'soulless' wars to stop the merger—to stop *Earth Ltd* coming into being—are no solution. Such wars, in any case, can only be undertaken by mergers. (Grossdeutschland is a merger.) One monopoly is much the same as another: though if I have to be part of a vast concern I prefer it should be a trust that has swallowed up the English. I want to be with them, wherever I am, on a *my country submerged or afloat* principle!

Some years ago I hoped to be *only* with the English—for us to be distinct. Now, after a great deal of close observation, I see that is impossible. I have to have my England diluted, or mixed. Dear old Great Britain has to take in partners. I believe if we could all of us have made up our minds to that earlier we could have avoided a general war. No one would have taken on *all* the Anglo-Saxons and their satellites.

But the most compelling argument of all in favour of the great international merger is that it has already occurred. That surely should be an argument to put a stop to all argument. Even the anarchists, for all their rigid isolationism, are a part of the system they oppose. And as for us, have not we taken to barter?

What I mean is that whether nations merge politically or not, they cannot keep out the *Zeitgeist* or isolate themselves from the spirit of their neighbours. Ideas pay no attention to frontiers; they slip in and out like elves. But since it is only the soul of a nation that is worth preserving, once we recognize that that long ago has *merged*, however exclusive it may have desired to be, the political and economic side of it is unimportant. It is not worth having great nationalist wars if there are no true nations left to fight about.

Before the Great War Sir Norman Angell wrote a book entitled *The Great Illusion*. And the Great War in due course proved itself a Great Illusion, and Sir Norman Angell very properly got the Nobel Peace Prize. For if people had listened to him there would have been no war.

This famous book exposed the futility of nationalist war, seeing how interlocked—that is to say, internationalized—were all national economies. Nations *could* not act as if they were detached, or even semi-detached, any longer. If they persisted in doing so they would suffer for it. Such was Sir Norman's argument.

There is, however, another equally 'great illusion,' as I have just indicated, and I wish that someone would write a book to demonstrate it at the present time. I should like to see a long and duly statistical book written to show how the economic interlocking is not the only one, and how that spiritual identity to which I have referred must prove even more embarrassing for the isolationist.

The opposition *blocs*, Totalitarians on the one side and Democrat-Marxists on the other, are poles apart politically, it is generally believed. And indeed it is true that in almost every respect we are superior to them.

Yet if the Totalitarians affect to despise and to oppose democracy and communism, why there is nothing easier than to show how deeply the Germans are 'tainted' with Marxism, or how democratic a demagogue like Hitler is, all allowance made for the strange form democracy must take when popped into field-grey and jackboots.

Nor do *we* entirely escape this horrid system of spiritual barter. Every day we import some Totalitarian trick—just as eggs with *Heil Hitler* on them get through our defences.

The individual national systems as typified by their governments, are in every case too corrupt, too stagnate, and in some cases even too ludicrous, to make any intelligent European observer feel over-conservative. If France, Italy, Spain, and England joined up, the resultant state, when it brought forth its composite executive—sitting in Paris, of course—could scarcely prove to be less good than are the individual governments as they exist to-day. The insularity of the English would be modified, the French receive an access of 'steadiness,' the Spaniards lose some of their *grandeeism*, and the Italians lose Mussolini (with about as much regret as a man loses a stiff neck).

How greatly some federal scheme for the Western democracies would appeal to me is obvious from what I have said. But we must be realist, and we have to ask ourselves if it is likely to happen.

Were you to propose to-morrow to the French and English nations that they should amalgamate, even the majority, their respective 'publics,' quite apart from the wealthy and influential minorities, would be stunned at the idea. They would receive your proposal at first with incredulity, ridicule, and distrust.

Should you propose to either, on the other hand, that they should *attack* and destroy the other, they would understand that at once. Owing to the *Entente Cordiale* they would be a little astonished at first; but in a very short time they would come to see that their neighbours were a lot of treacherous blackguards, and the sooner they were pushed off the earth the better.

The prospective federalist will find it none too easy to reverse what for so long these unfortunate people have been encouraged to think. The Government and the Press of all countries have exploited national sentiment too thoroughly for it to be possible, without long preparation, to bring them to take seriously such a merger. And the people of the United States have been taught to regard Europe as a backward, impoverished, quarrelsome, and unscrupulous part of the world ever since 1920. That cannot be undone in a day.

However that may be, the effort should be made. The more 'sovereign states' that cease to be sovereign the better for all of us. And it is not perhaps too much to hope that the fact of a common tongue, English, will start the rot; disintegrate these stupid barriers.

———

Lewis spent the war years, the most miserable of his life, first in the USA, then in Canada. In 1942 he wrote to the poet Theodore Spencer, who taught at Harvard: 'We are heading for an economic freeze-up of so total a kind that life upon this continent—or this planet, rather—will become impossible for any person not ensconced in some occupational, salaried niche. Already I am shivering a little: six months hence I shall be frozen to death.' No such niche was offered to him; he found it increasingly difficult to get any literary commissions, and was reduced in Canada to painting portraits of local celebrities who were sometimes dissatisfied with the result, and demanded (as he told me later) a little off the nose, or a more emphatic chin. This personal experience, and the events of the War, made him more than ever an internationalist, and in *America and Cosmic Man* (1948) he returned to the idea of the United States as an ideal melting-pot, a potential model for the future society in which rootless ahistoric Cosmic Man would live peacefully and flourish.

from AMERICA AND COSMIC MAN

The Case Against Roots

There is something I have never seen seriously challenged: namely, this notion that to *have roots* (as if one were a vegetable or a plant) is a good thing for a man: that to be *rootless* is a bad thing for a man.

The exact contrary, of course, is the case. References to that subject are to be found in my first part: but this is the place to take it up and re-assert what to me seems very plain: to be rooted like a tree to one spot, or at best to be tethered like a goat to one small area, is not a destiny in itself at all desirable. It is a matter of surprise that the bluff of the *rooted* boys has never been called—I mean radically so, by a plain statement of the excellence of what is the opposite of rootedness.

As we have with us, in my own person, as good an illustration as can be found, I will take myself. I am just as much at home, if not more so, in Casablanca as in Kensington; feel in no way strange in Barcelona—like equally Paris, London, or New York. I feel most at home in the United States, not because it is intrinsically a more interesting country, but because no one really belongs there any more than I do. We are all there together in its wholly excellent vacuum.

The sight of the *root* depresses me; and I know in that country that everyone has left his roots over in Poland or Ireland, in Italy, or in Russia, so we are all floating around in a rootless elysium.

Never having been in the West, I cannot say what it feels like to be there. But in the Mid-West and East, where I have lived, it feels just grand to be drifting around in a sea of Poles, Lithuanians, Irish, Italians, Negroes, Portuguese, French and Indians. It is the kind of disembodied feeling that I like.

But to be perfectly earnest. No American worth his salt should go looking around for a root. I advance this in all modesty, as a not unreasonable opinion. For is not that tantamount to giving up the most conspicuous advantage of being American, which is surely to have turned one's back on race, caste, and all that pertains to the rooted state?

American citizenship is in a different category to any other citizenship. The ceremony of initiation that accompanies the acquisition of citizenship is of a peculiarly solemn character suggestive of something more (as indeed it is) than a mere transference of allegiance from one government to another. The rite is of a religious order: in becoming an American, it is not a nationality that is being assumed, but a new way of life, universal and all-inclusive in its very postulates: in a New World in which a new type of man is destined to appear.

Tolstoi had much to say about patriotism; it bore the imprint of his massive common sense, and abhorrence of the tricks by which men are enslaved. In order to demonstrate what becoming American is *not* (I mean ideally, of course, and historically) I will quote a passage from *Christianity and Patriotism*, an essay wherein Tolstoi is vigorously engaged in the task of attempting to unseal people's eyes. The myth of the starry-eyed Russian peasant and his veneration for the 'little father' and so on is his target.

'They talk of the love of the Russian masses,' he writes, 'for their faith, the Tsar, and their government, and yet there will not be found one commune of peasants in the whole of Russia, which would hesitate for a moment, which of the two places to choose for colonisation— (1) Russia, with the Tsar, the little father as they write in books, and with the Holy Orthodox Faith, in its adored country, but with *less* and *worse* land, or (2) without the little father, the whole Tsar, and without the Orthodox Faith, somewhere outside of Russia, in Prussia, China, Turkey, Austria, but *with some greater and better advantages* . . . For every Russian peasant the question as to what government he will be under (since he knows that, no matter under what government he may be, he will be fleeced just the same) has incomparably less meaning than the question as to whether, I will not say the water is good, but as to whether the clay is soft and as to whether there will be a good cabbage crop.'

No one I hope would be so determined an idealist as to deny that there are *any* immigrants to the U.S.A. who have shifted themselves over there for precisely the reason described by Tolstoi in the above passage: in the pleasurable expectation of better conditions of life, better wages, less interference, less war. But should one of these immigrants suddenly take it into his head, in later years, to *leave* the New World, then there would I believe be something more difficult to dispense with than the Tsar, the little father, or the Orthodox Faith to deter him.

How shall we define this? It is very different from pious attachment to the soil, which scarcely exists in America, or to historic tradition. No: it is attachment to the *absence* of these things. It is attachment, I should say, to a slightly happy-go-lucky vacuum, in which the ego feels itself free. It is, it seems to me, something like the refreshing anonymity of a great city, compared with the oppressive opposite of that, invariably to be found in the village. Everything that is obnoxious in the Family is

133

encountered in the latter: all that man gains by escape from the Family is offered by the former. The United States is full of people who have escaped from their families, figuratively.

'Freedom and irresponsibility are commutative terms': such is a definition of freedom proposed by me in a book published in 1926. The more he is beset by duty, the less free a man is. I am not saying the more happy he is, nor would I resist the rejoinder that you can have too much of a good thing. Here I am doing my best to define, wherever it leads, something I have constantly felt in that country, as I have lived in its cities. London is a village compared to New York. One has a most pleasant disembodied sensation, as I have remarked, among all those herds of Italians, Germans, Jews, Irish, Negroes. You at last are *in the world*, instead of just in a nation.

There are few friendships in America such as exist in Europe. Every man is *a little bit* your friend, and will call you Bill or Fred or Jim after he has known you half an hour. But you will never become *his* Bill: there are too many other Bills for that. Friendship is a responsibility!

I am quite serious when I say that this is what Heaven must be like—agreeably inhuman, naturally; a rootless, irresponsible city (for everyone is agreed that Heaven is a city, so what the confirmed agriculturist will do is difficult to see), where the spirit is released from all the too-close contacts with other people (others who get 'in your hair,' or are all the time 'underfoot') but where everything is superficially fraternal.

Now having analysed something I have invariably felt all about me, while in America, I will return to the citizen, making up his mind to emigrate *out* of it. Where he would be going there would be no Americanism—there would be something far more solid; there would be friendships that chain down—a marriage that was, of all things, a friendship as well—there would be tradition telling you it 'wasn't done,' or that it *was*—saddling you with a thousand duties and obligations. Would he like all that after his prolonged immersion in this sort of ether? He would not.

My definition of freedom ('freedom and irresponsibility are commutative terms') would have, no doubt, to the dutiful ear equivocal implications, perhaps sound like invitations to licence. My 'rootless Elysium' likewise would have a lawless sound: would appear to be located in an equivocal region, not subject to the moral law.

But let us, to the best of our ability, challenge the ascetic prejudice, which, if you analyse it, would ultimately be seen to deny all real freedom to anybody. Let us, if anything, go too far in the other direction, rather than surrender to that prejudice.

Then the standards that enthrone Duty at the expense of the happiness of the individual belong essentially to fiercely competitive systems. They are standards proper to a state of chronic emergency; which is descriptive of our modern societies, for ever eyeing a neighbour known to be subject to accesses of homicidal mania and who does not disguise the fact—far from it—that he has a revolver in his pocket. The emphasis upon Duty, to the exclusion of all the epicurean values, is the natural result of such conditions.

America, however, is outside that area where nations are crowded up against each other, groups of rival diplomats engaged in that apparently absorbing game in which our lives and fortunes are the stakes. Until quite recently, rather, this has been the case: the air-age has closed up the ocean gaps. Then Americans are in the main people who have escaped, or whose ancestors escaped, from the rigours experienced in such societies as ours. They could at last relax somewhat, were able to put down their guards and be at peace, enjoy a freedom from interference they had never known up till then. They could discard the major part of duties and obligations, since what had dictated their imposition had been left behind. The Puritans, the Huguenots, the *émigrés* of '48—whether politics or religion had driven them out of their native land—all moved *outside*, out of the area of great pressure, into an area where the pressure was lifted from them and they could breathe freely. They would suddenly have the sensation of walking on air, of having been delivered of an incubus. For millions of people America has been as near heaven as they will ever get. If it did not go on being heaven, it always remained different to any other place.

Was this flight to America (a sort of suicide, as the nationalist would see it) immoral: a flight from Duty? The refugee blackens his motherland by the mere act of leaving it in this very pointed way.

Criticism is always involved in flight, from a country as from a wife: but it was usually from what they regarded as the wrong kind of duties and allegiances that men effected their escape. William Blake, for instance, typifies the spirit in which men have usually passed over into this great international sanctuary. His friend Tom Paine had gone there, and Blake, at a certain moment, was preparing to pass out through the 'Western Gates,' as he called them. Here is the poem, 'Thames and Ohio,' in which he gave expression to his discontents, and his expectations of a better life:

> Why should I care for the men of the Thames
> And the cheating waters of chartered streams,
> Or shrink at the little blasts of fear
> That the hireling blows into mine ear?

> Though born on the cheating banks of Thames,
> Though his waters bathed my infant limbs,
> The Ohio shall wash his stains from me;
> I was born a slave, but I go to be free.

That is what they all have said—'I go to be free.' And America is the place in which all these dreams have forgathered. Is it surprising that occasionally in the air one thinks that one detects something so far not met with; the electric intoxication of the air breathed by prisoners set free? The American air is conditioned by these immigrant multitudes, hollow with the great *ouf*! with which they have turned their back upon the European world.

(I ought, perhaps, to say that *our* America, at the opening of what has been called the 'atomic age,' is not any longer across the seas. Instead, it is a time, not a place: namely, the cosmic era which lies beyond the ruin and disintegration of atomic war.)

To turn back for a moment to the propaganda of *rootedness*: most of it emanates from governments, by the agency of their newspaper Press and other channels, emotional Jingo purpose behind it. They desire a sedentary population, for the same reason that feudal lords wanted to be able to put their hand on their personal militia.

But the moment you get rid of the 'sovereign state,' you will hear no more about 'roots.' Cosmopolitan values will displace immediately the 'root.' An authentic World Government would have the desired effect, though that is only a first step, and a full world society is necessary. Then there would be no further inducement to keep people fixed to one spot, nor to promote romantic values regarding their hereditary fixity.

So glorification of rootedness is bound up with conditions which have at last, as might have been foreseen, reduced us to a bankrupt slum—which is what the Socialist Government of England inherits from generations of men who have put class before country, but were too stupid even to keep healthy and intact the milch-cow of their privileged order.

The ruler is traditionally anything but a rooted person. Kings had roots in every country, just like a modern American, and so had many nobles too. It was only poor Hodge who was quite certain to have a good firm root. The higher you went in the social scale—when Europe was 'Christendom' prior to the nationalist era—the less the root business would have any meaning.

Today the parliamentary rulers, who have succeeded the kings and archdukes, take every opportunity of travelling outside their national frontiers. Their roots must get frayed a good bit, from so much moving about, and this is in general an excellent sign. We should always welcome movement of any kind.

Now I arrive at the goal of these particular observations. The 'rootless Elysium,' as I have called it, enjoyed by the great polyglot herds in the American cities, is what will come to exist everywhere after universalism is established: after the final change-over from a plurality of competitive nationalist societies to one great cosmic society. And for the new principle of brotherhood, and the essential de-snobbing of the various racial stocks, we can depend, I suggest, upon the atom bomb. It sounds ridiculous put in that way. But all our behaviour is ridiculous, and there is no rational road to a more sensible world.

When that change has been effected, it is obvious that there cannot but be an immense *relaxation* of the kind experienced by the earlier immigrant to the United States. Consider how the elimination of one great department of our political life labelled 'Foreign Affairs,' with its corollary, 'War,' would revolutionise our lives. The change would be far greater than it is easy to imagine. Were we informed that our span of life was henceforth extended to an average of two hundred years—the man of forty becoming the man of a hundred—that would have a very great

137

effect upon our lives, would it not? But hardly greater than will this change I am discussing.

Few people are conscious how much space all that stupid activity occupies, what is called 'defence' or 'security.' Nor is it quantitative only. It does not merely with its brutal bulk monopolise the space allowed for us to live in. It impregnates and colours everything about it: the shape of our minds is determined by it. Literature, and some of the greatest of it, is filled with an obsessional tension. Men are shown there as little fighting animals, whose lot it is to fight other little animals like themselves—and nothing else. We might be bull-terriers, for all certain of our other attributes, not concerned with fighting, play a part. Philosophers whom we have been taught to regard as among the wisest of mankind are no exceptions.

All the nightmare of austerity—Duty ruling each man's life from the cradle to the grave—which was Plato's idea of a model 'Republic,' is an excellent illustration of this. Human life in society was reduced by him to a military problem. The only state he was able to imagine was a 'Sovereign State,' as we call it today, all of the life of which was conditioned by *other* sovereign states, next to which its citizens dwelt in a tense watchfulness, armed to the teeth.

So grim, and cruelly dull, a pattern of a state could never have occurred to him had Plato lived in a world in which state-sovereignty had been abolished, or had never existed. He then presumably would have thought of something slightly less disagreeable. If you reply that Plato was a member of a military aristocracy in decay, attempting to introduce a super-Spartan discipline, we only come back to the same point. An Athenian Junker, who was one of the most extraordinary intelligences that ever existed, composes an account of the perfect state, and as such it is laughable. It turns out to be a convict settlement. Its purpose—collective training for the slaughter of other men (probably Spartans).

Let us imagine, however, this republic of Plato's in full swing—should the conception of the state embodied in it have been adopted, and such a state been set up in Attica or elsewhere. Then let us suppose that as a result of some tremendous catastrophe (such a disaster for the human race as a war in which atomic bombs were freely used in large numbers, half of the population of the world wiped out), the 'sovereign state' was at last abolished. What would happen to the republic on the platonic model, just established? An immense relaxation would, of necessity, at once ensue: an abrupt deflation of the entire social structure. Its constitution would be from that moment quite meaningless—its purpose, in the new dispensation, unattainable. For men would have abandoned the age-old habit of mutual slaughter. To train all day long so that you might be in good trim to smite your neighbour hip and thigh would be pointless. To subordinate everything in life to *that* would now, fortunately, have become criminal, just as it would be to wipe out the family in the neighbouring flat, or to bludgeon to death the rival tailor, or apothecary, across the road. To subordinate free speculation, art (Plato would have abolished free speech and free creation), the delights of the family (Plato would have made women public, and so destroyed the family) and all the adjuncts of a happy life to a programme of power, would now be regarded as maniacal, and be dealt with accordingly. Your neighbour had unexpectedly become your brother. You might train to defeat him at bridge or chess, or excel him in the rugged splendour of your rock-garden, but you might no longer plot and prepare to take his life.

Were you a citizen of this platonic republic, it is easy to see what, under these circumstances, your sensations would be like (assuming you were not a Guardian). You would feel all your rigid little world agreeably dissolving about you. The relaxation would be almost painful—like the blood bursting into an arm long constricted: or like a Trappist's tongue beginning eagerly to move, the vow of silence suddenly cancelled. All the springs that had held you tensed up, like a fierce tomcat upon a dark night, would snap.

I have been conjuring up these images of admirable relaxation to give an idea of what America has been, and to some extent still is. A fine irresponsibility and innocent egoism survives, to be a preview, in this peaceful checkerboard of races, of the world to come. There men will be able to jettison a good deal of responsibility—to gain for the advantages of their ego what the winding-up of Mars and Co. makes generally available. And, finally, one does not have to be ashamed of happiness!

On the philosophic side, the Utilitarian, as against the intuitive, is the path to take at this time. For everything that is not Utilitarian has failed us. The principle of the Greatest Pain of the Greatest Number has for far too long held sway.

It is with great diffidence that anyone today mentions such a thing as *happiness*. And the Puritan is still with us, to chide us, if we speak of pleasure. A famous American political lady, in face of the universal destruction that threatens us at the hands of Heavy Water, delivered herself of the aphorism—'Either men must love each other or die.' As an improvement on that I suggest the following: 'Either men must pursue Happiness, or perish.' There is no middle course.

So-called 'austerity,' the stoic injunction, is the path towards universal destruction. It is the old, the fatal, competitive path. 'Pull in your belt' is a slogan closely related to 'gird up your loins,' or the guns-butter metaphor. It is fight-talk language. Let us call to mind—for it may save us—the saying of William Blake: 'Curse braces—Bless relaxes.' Which is the moral of all my foregoing arguments.

Let us hope that in England minds will gradually turn towards the cosmic, or universalist, age ahead, and not be lured back to 'big-shot' politics. Luckily we have a Socialist Government, which is here to stay, and which will make this vastly more simple. My stressing of Happiness places me upon the epicurean side of this old argument. As to epicurean teaching, as that affected the destinies of Rome, 'the anti-patriotic tendency of its teaching contributed to that destruction of national feeling which was necessary to the rise of cosmopolitanism.' This is stupidly stated; but it will show you how any doctrine of that sort—one smoothing the way for 'cosmopolitanism' as it is called by the above writer—is liable to be criticised as unpatriotic. When you hear that, all you need do is to recall the bloody path along which the great 'patriots' of all great nations have led us. Let us pray for the rise of 'cosmopolitanism,' rather than more of the same patriotic poison. When I substituted the pursuit of happiness just now for brotherly love, I did not mean to dismiss that. Of course men have to acquire the habit of brotherly love as well.

Cosmic Society and Cosmic Man

The logic of the geographical position and history of the United States leads only, I believe, to one conclusion: namely, the ultimate formation of a society that will not be as other societies, but an epitome of all societies. If a nation, then it must be a super-nation: so inclusive of all the various breeds of men, all the creeds, and fads, and philosophies, that its unity must be of quite a different character. It can only be something more universal than the Roman Empire, because its metropolitan area is coterminous with its imperial area. It has been built or is being built from outside, many different peoples and cultures converging on it—either, as that regards the people, as refugees, or as slaves or what not: people have moved in to make it, it has not moved out, like a spider constructing its web, to embrace all outside itself. Nor is it an endemic culture, moving out to modify other cultures, and subdue them to one standard, namely, its own. It has no original culture of its own (except for the Negro contribution, which is African): it is eclectic.

Of course, all the peoples of the earth will not move into North America, but in the end there will be larger or smaller segments or pockets of all of them there. Now, if, like many Americans, you aver that all the different stocks present already are not in fact going to mix, thoroughly to merge into a homogeneous mass, but instead will remain, as in large measure they still are found, isolated from each other (in great cities, inhabiting separate wards or districts, or sprinkled over the country in discrete racial and religious settlements) then that is going to be a very odd kind of nation—if it is a nation that is intended, of the usual sort.

At present all these various stocks—and even religions—enjoy an anything but uniform social status. As I pointed out at an earlier stage, race has tended to be class in America. Economic disparity, even, is not more productive of class feeling than blood. In fact, to have a son-in-law of a racial stock not highly esteemed—say a Greek, or Peruvian—would be more embarrassing to parents than to have one of 'poor boy' origin.

In Canada, for instance, there is the most impassable race-barrier separating the English-Canadians and the French-Canadians: on the English side this is interpreted as indicative of a racial superiority,

141

enjoyed by themselves *vis-à-vis* the 'Peasoups.' The fact that a majority of French-Canadians have Indian blood does not improve their chances of social equality with the Nordic Blonds; and catholicism is a peculiarly unpopular religion with the latter-day Puritans of this isolated and backward country.

The 'Wop' in the States, as elsewhere I have indicated, is a much lower grade citizen than the Nordic (especially one with an English name). The Negro is naturally out of the picture altogether, from the standpoint of marriageability, as is also the 'Chink.' If either of these elements moves into a street, everybody else moves out. You have to be a remarkably poor White to take a coloured mate, or to tolerate a coloured neighbour. ·

The equilibrium is, however, highly precarious. Present conditions will not survive any major shock to the political and social system—such as a record slump, or a war which rocks America to its foundations, in the way the war that has just ended has shaken the British Empire. As to Negro and White, that situation at present approaches a bitter climax. If anyone believes that this huge population of Africans is going to remain as it is, an insoluble black lump, they will fairly soon be undeceived. The Negroes of the United States cannot be shipped out, as once they were shipped in, nor do even the most hostile suggest that. But they cannot remain there and continue to be treated as animals, whom you could no more marry than you could mate with a baboon.

That dark lump *will* melt, spread out and colour the entire human contents of the States, until 'American' will mean somebody with that dusky intermixture. As the traditional supremacy of the 'Nordic' dies out (and the instability of American family-wealth, and the violence of economic change, accelerates the disappearance of this social advantage) all the other race-barriers will rapidly dissolve.

Whether America has a Big Business Fascism, or some sort of change to a Socialist economy, will not alter the outcome, except that the latter would precipitate the process of miscegenation. If it were a Business-Fascist economy, with America's penetration of Asia greatly stepped up, that must result in the impoverishment of the white population. Cheap Asiatic labour—which would doubtless be used in America proper, as well as on the spot in Asia, in affecting disadvantageously the home labour market, and in reducing the living standards of the masses, would overcome snootiness of a racial order.

The policy of both the Socialist and his enemy the Capitalist would work out identically as regards the white and coloured population. The former is committed to the non-recognition of race discrimination, the latter is the natural protector of all coloured people, because they work for less money.

Why one takes any interest in this so-called Pot, and the problems of its melting, is very simple. We lock ourselves up aggressively, or are locked up, in that antiquated group-pen the 'nation,' and pretend to be a 'race,' and a mighty fine one too, as did par excellence the National Socialists. But in America you have a powerful country of great size which at least cannot call itself a 'race.' Like everybody else, it takes on the competitive attitudes, the Jingo emotionalism. But those devoutly hoping for an international order naturally see in America the thin end of the wedge. The requisite raw material is there, namely the great variety of races present—all that is needed for the manufacture of Cosmic Man.

But 'cosmic man,' as I have called him: would not the arrival of this hybrid be a bad thing? Should such creatures be encouraged? The answer is that in the event of a World Government (which man has been trying to bring about for so long, and there is good reason to suppose may now, with the help of nuclear energy—after a final conflagration—obtain) with a single government controlling all the affairs of the earth, a cosmic society would be a necessary corollary, as distinct from the mere Administration. It probably would not be very satisfactory for everybody stolidly to go on behaving as if nothing had happened: it would be better for man to unanchor, and circulate. In order permanently to banish the parochial or tribal spirit, that would be the best course.

The idea of a federative World Government—which is the most popular at present, because men so hate the prospect of rendering up their identity—might involve only a mechanical administrative change, a spiritual *status quo*: consequently it should be rejected. War out of the way (and let us hope its twin, the profit-system with it) very little local government would be necessary. The latter serves to keep alive the ancient territorial rivalries.

It is not enough to have a central administration alone then. Some fresh approach to the problems of living in society should go with such a change. This is where the United States is so useful. It is not interesting only because it is a 'melting-pot.' That might perfectly well be as dull as it sounds. What makes it so worthy of everybody's attention is the fact that in America there is, as nowhere else, the basis of a cosmic ethos. Even their gregariousness belongs to an, as it were, deep emotional fund, a sort of communal pooling of all the cordial reactions of man. But to this I will return presently.

For a World Government when first formed to have a genuinely cosmic society there already, practising—and preaching—all the collective virtues appropriate in a world state, would be of great value. The example of a kind of universalised Everyman would prove infectious. And the new war-free, tolerant, nationless world society—arrived at last at the point reached by the forty-eight States of the Union—could do worse than take for its model American citizenship (purged of its nationalism, of course).

It is comprehensible that many people should be disinclined to accept the idea of a cosmic society, and so of a cosmic man. Human conservatism is fathomless, and when it comes to *roots*, habit is another name for those roots. But it is most difficult to see how any fairly intelligent man or woman could question the desirability of a World Government.

To take its minimum claim: a World Government could scarcely be as bad, however imperfect it might be, as a number of governments, or so-called 'sovereign states.' For the main incentive to be bad would be lacking. A large proportion of the crimes of governments arise from the existence of *other* governments. Just as a man all by himself, alone on the earth, would be debarred from committing most of the recognised crimes, which require the presence of two or more people (apart from ill-treating the animals, there is not much he could do), so if there were only one government in the world, it would have had removed from it the possibility of committing many major crimes. It could still, if so disposed, commit a great number of crimes against the people it governed. But at least it would have inter-governmental war removed from its repertoire of crime.

War is a major crime of government—there is none so great, where it is *total* war, *levée en masse*, with all that that entails: paralysis of all the creative functions of the community for years on end; squandering of the nations' wealth, which otherwise employed would abolish poverty entirely; brutalisation of millions of men; fearful catastrophes of every kind in the private lives of 'unimportant' people, men, women and children; mental regimentation of communities; by appeals to the vanity, the causing everyone to have a stake in his own misfortune; the death in youth of multitudes, maiming, impairing of health, of opportunities in life—but I need not continue the catalogue.

A World Government appears to me the only imaginable solution for the chaos reigning at present throughout the world. Many would agree that it is desirable, but very unlikely, in their view, to materialise. Such is, and always has been, the logical goal of civilised mankind—though usually men have said, 'We must give our law to the barbarian.' It has been imperialist.

The Greeks had the notion of Cosmopolis, they were too power-hungry and contentious to do anything about it. The Romans made the attempt: it was the Roman World and imperial, but became highly cosmopolitan. That fell to pieces, and in succession to it a theocratic universalism was attempted. But Christendom was the reverse of a reign of peace. Luckily, they had only battleaxes and bows and arrows, instead of the weapons of wholesale slaughter which we possess, or there would have been very little left, so remorselessly did the Sermon on the Mount impel those Christians to homicide. Christianity, as a unifier, became a bad joke long ago.

With a start of surprise (followed by apathy) we find ourselves in the presence of the so-called Atom Bomb. Perhaps that will do what the Sermon on the Mount failed to accomplish. That this will come to pass *before long*—that the inhabitants of this planet have not only the chance, but the certainty, of again enjoying one government instead of a plurality—may, I believe, with complete confidence be predicted . . .

If it occurred to you to wonder how the Americans—without some beautiful old village at the foot of a down to love and cherish, that had been there perhaps since it was a Gesith, in the days of the eorls and ceorls—can without all that be so attached to their strange, rootless, restless, polyglot world, the answer is they like it that way. They only have a country to live in that is not much more *theirs* than the valleys and green meadows of the ocean. But the disdain of 'rootlessness,' they would

145

declare, is a bluff or a superstition. *Roots* are the last thing they want. Released from all the stocks of Europe, Africa and Asia, they enjoy what is, in fact, a *cosmic* sensation. Their citizenship, about which they make so much fuss—and a justifiable fuss—is a kind of world-citizenship model A. For here is the beginning of the new world, which must one day be everywhere, when the term 'American' would be as irrelevant as Polish, Irish, or Arab.

This is, I repeat, the only possible meaning of the U.S.A.—to be the place where a Cosmopolis, as the Greeks would call it, is being tried out. Either the United States is (1) a rather disorderly collection of people dumped there by other nations which did not want them—a sort of wastepaper basket or trash-can; or (2) a splendid idea of Fate's to provide a human laboratory for the manufacture of Cosmic Man. It is, I feel, quite certainly the second of these alternatives.

Cosmic man is, however, not merely being manufactured in the flesh but also in the spirit. A cosmic society must have a cosmic culture: and that is being provided for it, at colossal expense and the deployment of a fantastic pedagogic apparatus. The cultural centralisation in America, for so vast a place, is abnormal. New York, with its massed publishing houses, its swarm of art dealers (as headquarters of the book-racket and picture-racket) and control of theatrical reputations (both for playwright and player) is as much the cultural centre of the United States as Washington is the political centre. And it is a long way from New York to Texas or to Idaho.

New York's intellectual authority is feebly disputed at times by the Middle West. You will have heard the saying: 'New York is not America.' For a Texas Ranger, or a man growing potatoes in Idaho, it of course is not. In all cultural matters, however, it is that absolutely. It is the Mecca of all women, who play a so much more important role in America than elsewhere, it is the headquarters of Fashion, as Paris is in Europe, and its hotels are always full of visiting provincials.

That there is a cultural melting-pot in America as well as a racial—that it melts a great deal more effectively than the latter: that it is part of a vaster melting operation, going on all over the world, not stopping at frontiers, so that the young man in Birmingham, Warwickshire, and in St Louis, Missouri, is apt to be reading just the same books or literary reviews, and looking at photographs of the same pictures or buying the same musical records, let me repeat, before moving on to the next chapter, in which I explain how the cultural life of America functions. Science, naturally, is already internationalised, the pharmacologist or biochemist in Chicago or New York is in touch by letter with workers in the same field in India, South America, Europe. That is 'culture,' too, and it is enjoyed in common.

Naturally, there is nothing farther from the thoughts of most of those engaged in these cultural activities in America (most of them no doubt violently nationalistic) than a cosmic society of the future, or that they are in fact engaged in preparing the way for a 'cosmic man'—a perfectly eclectic, non-national, internationally-minded creature, whose blood is drawn—more or less—from all corners of the earth, with no more geographical or cultural roots than a chameleon. Yet it is to that end that their activities will imperceptibly lead. They cannot be a cultural centre: they can only be a place that things blow through from the outside. But in the end, so conditioned, they will insensibly produce the sum of all assimilations, a cosmic fruit, indeed.

This book, published in 1948, was Lewis's last statement of importance about politics and society, except those implicit in his fiction. Apart from the years in the Thirties when he supported what he called the doctrine of national sovereignty, he was a convinced internationalist. He wished to see a world government, an intermixture of races and peoples, and came increasingly to regard the United States as a model—not, of course, a perfect one—of such a society. He made the large assumption that a future world government would be benevolent.

The battering Lewis received from life, and the quirks of his personality, made him forget some of the injunctions in 'Code of a Herdsman'. He should have stayed on the mountain, and not have become involved in that sad commerce with the herd. As he reiterated hopes and warnings, Lewis did so in terms sometimes strident and in writing often slapdash. Yet his vision of society was neither commonplace nor ignoble, and the mistaken involvement in day-to-day politics does not invalidate his insights into the nature of Western society in his time and our own. Much of the shape of the world we now live in was forecast more than half a century ago in *The Art of Being Ruled*.

PART TWO

ART AND LITERATURE

The pattern of thought established, the lines of social and philosophical beliefs laid down, there is little need for further explication. Lewis's criticism, and his imaginative work as an artist on canvas and in print, are uncommonly coherent, the art works an exemplification of the ideas, the criticism firmly based in his view of society.

The Caliph's Design ('Architects: Where Is Your Vortex?') of 1920 is the work of the ahistoric revolutionary. The Caliph demands of his two talented architects that a street in a new city shall be built in accordance with the design of 'a little vorticist effort that I threw off while I was dressing'. If they fail they will be executed. 'Within a month a strange street transformed the heart of that cultivated city.' The parable is used to offer a vision of the new, inspired by an exultant belief rather like the innovative fury of Russian visual artists after the Revolution that anything was possible, including the dismantling of all 'stylistic architectural rubbish', and the development of something entirely new from the box model of the skyscraper.

from THE CALIPH'S DESIGN

The Bull Sounds

We are all agreed as to the deplorable nature of the form-content and colour-content around us. But there agreement ceases.

The divergence of opinion gathers round the following points:

151

Is it not preferable to have every manifestation of the vulgar and stupid constantly, in an appetising, delicious form (something like the 'highness' of game), at the disposal of our superiority and wit?

What would Flaubert have done had France not bred Bouvards and Péchuchets with rabbit-like fecundity? Can nature ever be thanked enough for Sir Sampson Legend, Mantalini, Boswell's Johnson, Falstaff or any such types of Comedy, composed of the nastiest excrement and washiest imbecilities? No one would diminish by one ounce the meat of art that resides in folly or deformity; or see snobbery, gluttony or cruelty reduced by one single exemplaire, once his mind was fixed on the benefits that the aesthetic sense has received from their abundance in Nature!

A less self-indulgent satirist like Aristophanes, it is true, will attach a stink or some disgusting attribute to his absurd character, relying on the squeamishness of his audience, sending his characters about like skunks. But most authors are not so moral as to poison our pleasure with these gases. A stupid form is for the painter the same food as a stupid man for a writer like Gogol or Flaubert.

So it is very debatable whether without the stimulation of stupidity, or every bestial, ill-made, tasteless object that abounds in life to-day, the artist would be as well off and well nourished. Would he not be in the position of a satirist, like Flaubert, without a Bouvard, or of an artist like Boswell without his rich and very unusual dish? The irritation with the particular French folly that surrounded him, and that Flaubert ate every day as regularly as his breakfast; the consequent pessimism that became the favourite manure for his thoughts; we cannot see Flaubert without that, any more than we can conceive of Rousseau the Douanier without his squab little bourgeois, and blank, paunchy little villas.

The point rather lies in the *attitude* that was Flaubert's and that was the Douanier's. Flaubert hated Bouvard, and considered the vulgarity and idiocy that he witnessed a very sad and improper affair. The Douanier, on the other hand, probably admired his Bouvards very much. It was with a naively respectful eye, it may be assumed, that he surveyed the bourgeois on Sunday, and noted his peculiarities like a child, directly, without judging.

Shakespeare, it is true, must have relished the absurd or deformed more consciously; and Dickens made a cult of it. But with Shakespeare it was against a vast background of other matter, and as comic relief, or used in farces, and so labelled. It has never amounted to what has practically become, in our day, a *rejection* of anything as dull or useless unless it lends itself to our appetite for the comic or the 'queer.'

But Wilde's antithetic glitter, when used in journalism, may become the most wearisome thing on earth. We long, confronted by such a monotony of inversion as we get in Mr G.K. Chesterton, for instance, for a plain 'dull' statement. In the same way, if the villainous stupidity that has always been around every man since the world began (only he has belaboured it with one hand while caressing it with the other) became something like the religion of the educated—such education, that is, as enabled you to enjoy it—and its pursuit and enjoyment the one topic and habit of life, should we not sigh for the old variety; the hero, the villain, the lovely lady and the Comic Relief? Should we not also, if embedded in some bric-à-brac of stuffed birds and wax flowers, and the languors of the 'aesthetic period' of the article I cite later in this pamphlet, look towards Karnak, a plain French provincial town, or almost anywhere—with eyes of longing?

Surely all this sensibility of the 'queer,' the 'amusing,' the divinely ugly, the exquisitely vulgar, will date, and date very quickly.

There would to-day, in the 'modern' section of the art-world, be as great an outcry if some philistine proposed that the lovely embellishments of our streets, coloured signs, posters, beautiful police-stations and bewitching tiled Tube stations should be pulled down, as there would have been formerly, and is still by the 'beauty-loving public,' when some 'picturesque old bit' or decaying cottage is removed.

But, with men trying their hardest to eliminate ugliness, injustice, imbecility and so forth from the world, has there ever been any absence of these commodities for the sweet, or bitter, tooth of the artist? Is there ever likely to be? It is true that the artist can gorge himself to-day probably as never before. But is that the best thing for his talent?

If twenty Christs charged abreast anywhere in the world, you would still get in a remarkably short time, and within a half-hour's walk of their super-calvary, some such monument as the First Pyramid, the result of such a block of egotism as had never been seen before, to show you the weakness of the humane corrective. But I do not believe you would ever get a pyramid builder without Christian hysteria.

Even in order to appreciate the 'banal' you must not have too much of it. And you must *pretend* you do not like it even if you are incapable of liking anything else. The reactionary Prussian theorists of war—good, beneficent war—tyranny, and so forth were less useful than the Pacifist, and less intelligent.

The arrangement seems to be that you spend half your time destroying the cheap, the foolish, the repellent; and the other half enjoying what is left over after your efforts! This evidently being how we are intended to live, there is no excuse for slackness in the carrying out of your unpleasant duty: that is to desire equity, mansuetude, in human relations, fight against violence, and work for formal beauty, significance and so forth, in the arrangement and aspect of life.

But to conclude. The great line, the creative line; the fine, exultant mass; the gaiety that snaps and clacks like a fine gut string; the sweep of great tragedy; the immense, the simple satisfaction of the surest, the completest art, you could not get if you succeeded in eliminating passion; nor if you crowned imbecility, or made an idol of the weak.

Whereas you can always get enough silliness, meaningless form, vulgar flavour to satisfy the most gargantuan or the most exquisite appetite.

The Politician's Apathy

What is this ugliness, banality, and squalor to which we have been referring? It is simply what meets your eye as it travels up practically any street in London to-day, or wanders around any Hotel lounge or Restaurant, or delects itself along the wall of the official galleries at Burlington House. Next, what influences go to the making of this horrible form-content and colour-content that we can either offer up a prayer of thankfulness for, take no notice of, or occupy ourselves with modifying, in our spare time? Exactly what set of circumstances, what lassitude or energy of mind working through millions of channels and multitudes of people, make the designs on match boxes (or the jokes on the back of some), the ornamental metalwork on the lamp-posts, gates, knife-handles, sepulchral enclosures, serviette-rings, most posters, ornamented Menu cards, the scenery in our Musical spectacles, chapter-headings and tail-pieces, brooches, bangles, embossments on watches, clocks, carving-knives, cruets, pendants in Asprey's, in Dobson's, in Hancock's windows in Bond Street; in fact, every stitch and scrap of art-work that indefatigably spreads its blight all over a modern city, invading every nook, befouling the loveliest necks, waists, ears, and bosoms; defiling even the doormat—climbing up, even, and making absurd and vapid the chimney pot, which you would have thought was inaccessible and out of sight enough for Art not to reach; for the cheap modern thousand-headed devil of design not to find it worth while to spoil?

We are all perfectly agreed, are we not, that practically any house, railing, monument, wall, structure, thoroughfare, or lamp-post in this city should be instantly pulled down, were it not for the 'amusement' and stimulus that the painter gets out of it?

A complete reform (were it not for the needs of the painter who *must* have his bit of banality, bless his little heart!) of every notion or lack of notion on the significance of the appearance of the world should be instituted. A gusto, a consciousness should imbue the placing and the shaping of every brick. A central spectacle, as a street like Regent Street is, should be worked out in the smallest detail. It should not grow like a weed, without forethought, meaning, or any agency but the drifting and accident of commerce. A great thoroughfare like Regent Street develops and sluggishly gets on its ill-articulated legs, and blankly looks at us with its silly face. There are Bouvards and Pécuchets in brick and stone, or just dull cheerless photographs. There is no beautiful or significant relief, even, in this third-rate comic spectacle.

Do politicians understand so little the influence of the Scene of Life, or the effect of Nature, that they can be so indifferent to the capital of a wealthy and powerful community? Would not a more imaginative Cecil Rhodes have seen that the only way an Empire such as he imagined could impress itself on the consciousness of a people would be in some such way as all ambitious nations have taken to make the individual citizen aware of his privileges and his burden? Whether in the weight of a Rhetoric of buildings, or in the subtler ways of beauty signifying the delights and rewards of success won by toil and adventure; in a thousand ways the imagination of the multitude could be captured and fixed. But beyond the obvious policy of *not* having a mean and indolent surrounding for the capital of what sets out to be an 'Empire,' simply for human life at all, or what sets out to be human life—*to increase gusto and belief in that life*—it is of the first importance that the senses should be directed into such channels, appealed to in such ways, that this state of mind of relish, fullness and exultation should obtain.

It is life at which you must aim. Life, full life, is lived through the fancy, the senses, consciousness. These things must be stimulated and not depressed. The streets of a modern city are depressing. They are so aimless and so weak in their lines and their masses, that the mind and senses jog on their way like passengers in a train with blinds down in an overcrowded carriage.

This is worse, again, for the crowd than the luckier individual. The life of the crowd, of the common or garden man, is exterior. He can only live through others, outside himself. He, in a sense, *is* the houses, the railings, the bunting or absence of bunting. His beauty and justification is in a superficial exterior life. His health is there. He dwindles and grows restless, sick and troublesome when not given these opportunities to live and enjoy in the simple, communal crowd manner. He has just sense enough to know that he is living or not living. Give him a fine, well-fed type of life, a bit dashing and swanky, suitably clothed, with a glamour of adventure about it, to look at, and he is gladdened, if his own stomach is not too empty. Give him fine processions, and holidays, military display. Yes, but there is something you are going to omit. By the deepest paradox he knows that the plaster objects stuck up in Oxford Street outside Selfridges for Peace Day are not a symbol of anything but commerce; in which he equally, though not so successfully, is engaged himself. There is nothing there that he could not do himself, and they do not reach his imagination. Similarly, it is not such a tremendous critical flight as you would imagine for him to connect in some subtle way in his mind these banal plaster statues with the more careful but even more effusively mean Albert Memorial, or any other monument that meets his eye. Yet these he knows are the monuments that typify the society of which he is a unit. This putrid dullness, hopeless deadly stare of almost imbecile stupidity, that he is confronted with in the art offerings from those above, as in their persons, can hardly be expected to stimulate him, either to buoyancy, obedience, or anything but boredom.

So if there are a hundred reasons why Painters should oppose any modification of the appearance of our works, which is *Perfect* in the quaintness of its stupidity, there is no reason why the politician should feel obliged to protect it.

How the Fact of Style Obstructs

The parable of the Caliph's design describes the state of mind which must be that of every healthy and active artist living in the midst of the blasphemous stupidity, too much so even for health, that surrounds us to-day. But alas! although like the Caliph, a vorticist, I have not the power of life and death over the Mahmuds and Hasans of this city. Otherwise I should have no compunction in having every London architect's head severed from his body at ten o'clock to-morrow morning, unless he made some effort to apply a finer standard of art in his own art-practice. I would flood those indolent commercial offices, where architects pursue their trade, with abstract designs. I am sure the result would be to cram the world with form and intention, where to-day, as far as it is beholden to the architect, it has no discernible significance or aesthetic purpose of any sort.

There is no reason at all why there should not be a certain number of interesting architects. I can also see no reason why this pamphlet should not bring them forth. I should be very proud of that, and watch their labours with great interest. This, I think, is such a modest optimism that I am sure you will allow it. I should like to see the entire city rebuilt on a more conscious pattern. But this would automatically happen should an architect of genius turn up who would invent an architecture for our time and climate that was also a creative and fertilising art-form. The first great modern building that arose in this city would soon carry everything before it; and hand in hand with the engineer, and his new problems, by force of circumstances so exactly modern ones, would make a new form-content for our everyday vision. So all we want is one single architect with brains, and we will regard him with optimism.

Now the question of form-content is obviously one of importance to every painter. Almost any painter, sculptor, or designer of an actual type to-day will agree with you that Cheapside, Piccadilly, Russell Square, Marylebone Road, are thoroughly dull and insignificant masses of brickwork, laid out according to no coherent plan, bestially vulgar in their details of ornament, and in every way fit for instant demolishment. Similarly, he will agree that any large and expensive West-End restaurant is an eyesore, and a meaningless sham.

Similarly, when you say to him that it is about time something were done to get rid of this graceless and stupid spectacle, he will agree, but will quickly change the subject. Every law of common-sense precludes any possibility of an appreciable modification of this detestable sight. He will either imagine that you are out for some Utopia, or he will think that your notions hardly agree with the fashionable fad-idea that all is for the best in the best of all possible worlds—that whatever reality, accident, or your neighbour, that is, flings at your head, your head should resound to, if it is empty, as it ought to be.

Of course there are good arguments against you. I have made use of those arguments myself. We have just been envisaging them in the section of this pamphlet headed 'The Bull Sounds.' But we will proceed to sift out more thoroughly the Painter's argument; this time not only the painter or the amateur, but any painter.

Style, he will say, can transform anything into gold. Take a convenient example. Should Rembrandt in one of his pen-drawings have had a more interesting type of architecture before him for subject matter, in place of the country mills by the side of the Dutch canals, would this better form-content have made his drawings better drawings? You must answer to that: 'No, it would not.' But a windmill is a rough and simple contrivance, and there is a sad difference between the rough beauty and fitness of such objects stuck up centuries ago in Holland, and similar rough and simple objects built to-day. One would do better to imagine a Rembrandt, working in the same way that he worked, doing similar drawings in an industrial country like England or Germany at the present time. Still you have to admit that as fine an artist as Rembrandt would, by the magic of his use of the medium he chose, by his line, by his tact of simplification and elimination, make a *New* thing of anything, however poor the original. And so, in considering if it is worth while to change a single brick, even, or the most trifling ornament, however offensive, you would be compelled to admit that, as regards the production of the finest type of art you would be no better off. The best half-dozen artists of any country, as regards the actual beauty and significance of their work, do not depend on the objective world for their success or stimulus.

As to all the thousands of artists, not amongst the most able or imaginative, or possibly able to do something, it is another story. *They* depend on Nature, on the objective world, for their stimulus or their taste. Set a rather poor artist down in a roadway, ask him to draw a street of houses in front of him. If the houses were of a good and significant build, he would be more likely to do a good and significant painting than if they were such clumsy, and stupid, lineless, massless, things as we invariably find ourselves in the midst of to-day. If he has no particular invention or vision of his own, he depends on Nature a good deal. Nature must do half the work.

But the fallacy in the contention about a good artist is this. That although he does not depend on Nature, he certainly depends on life, and is subject to its conditions. And this surely re-acts on his painting. If he starves, is disturbed in his work, or has to do some horrible type of present-day commercial painting or designing to make a living, then his independence of objective form and colour-content is of little use to him.

Where the Painter would Benefit

Apart from my conviction on this subject, a useful way of illuminating it will be to consider how I, or an artist like me, stands towards it on the practical ground. It reduces itself to this: I have nothing materially to gain by your adopting these theories. You are perplexed: painters are everywhere perplexed. I make you and them a present of this analysis of these perplexities. I see the shapes that you would see did the world for the moment contain more stimulation and effort in the related arts.

I do not need to have a house built with significant forms, lines, masses, and details of ornament, and planted squarely before my eyes, to know that such significance exists, or to have my belief in its reality stimulated. But *you* require that. I am, or any painter you can see is, obviously here to do that. I am at your disposal in this respect. But that is primarily a work for you and not for me. I can get on quite well, the artist always can, without this material realisation. Theoretically, even, a creative painter or designer should be able to exist quite satisfactorily without paper, stone or paints, or without lifting a finger to translate into forms and colours his specialised creative impulse. It should be the same with the painter, the architect, or the sculptor as it is with the composer of music. The Interpreter is really only in the same category as the bricklayer, or at best a foreman of works.

Still, I suffer somewhat all the same, from this lack of readiness, or really of aptitude, on your part, to employ me usefully. And every true artist I know, painter or sculptor, is in the same box. The trouble is this: It does not matter what objective Nature supplies. The inventive artist is his own purveyor. But the society of which he forms a part, can, by its backwardness, indolence, or obtuseness, cause him a series of inconveniences; and above all, can, at certain times and under certain conditions, affect his pocket adversely and cause him to waste an absurd amount of time. When no longer able to produce his best work, it would not be a waste of time for a painter or for a writer to lecture, for example, on the subject of his craft. The propaganda, explanatory pamphlets, and the rest, in which we, in this country, have to indulge, is so much time out of active life which would normally be spent as every artist wishes to spend his time, in work, in a state of complete oblivion as regards any possible public that his work may ever have. Yet were one's ideas on painting not formulated, and given out in the shape of a lecture, a pamphlet, or a critical essay, an impossible condition would result for an artist desirous of experimenting.

So when I say that I should like to see a completely transfigured world, it is not because I want to *look* at it. It is *you* who would look at it. It would be your spirit that would benefit by this exhilarating spectacle. *I* should merely benefit, I and other painters like me, by no longer finding ourselves in the position of freaks, the queer wild men of cubes, the terrible futurists, or any other rubbish that the Yellow

160

Press invents to amuse the nerves of its readers. (Do you suppose that the art-man who reports on the French Show in Tottenham Court Road and describes the 'horror' of these pictures, really *thinks* that they are in any way blood-curdling? No. He knows for every extra curdle he makes an extra quid.) It naturally does not please me, or any other painter who paints pictures that appear extravagant according to the pretty and facetious standard of this time, to be described as a wild man, or a bolshevik in paint. No pleasurable thrill accompanies these words when used about one's own very normal proceedings, since they appear to the painter the *only* normal proceedings in the midst of the detestable capers of the usual mild lunatic asylum we have to inhabit.

The Public Chosen

The Public I should like for this pamphlet is a rather different one than that to which painters usually consider it worth while to address themselves. In the first place, any individual belonging to the rank and file of the Royal Academy is fond of regarding himself as 'a Craftsman'; as a specialist of the most prodigious, horny, paint-and-dust-grimed, mediaeval sort. The more furibundly ignoble his paintings, the further he retires into the technical mysteries of his craft. And so lay opinion he scorns.

Then another pale exists, an even funnier one, beyond which stand those multitudes who have not been taught a delightful faintness, a cheap catch of the voice, and the few dozen snobbish tricks of thought and hand coined in each decade for the lucky young rich. A board school master, an excise clerk, a douanier, for that matter, are usually approached if at all with every nuance of amused condescension that a disgusting stereotyped education can breed.

How sick such men must be with the wearisome and endless trifling that they have come to associate with the word Artist!

I write in these notes for a socially wider and not necessarily specialist public.

Architecture

Architecture is the weakest of the arts, in so far as it is the most dependent on the collective sensibility of its period. It is so involved, on the other hand, in utility, and so much a portion of public life, that it is far more helpless than painting and literature in the face of public indifference. Sculpture shares with it some of this helplessness. There are many good sculptors wasted to-day as thoroughly as anyone can be, through the absence of such conditions as are needed to give them their chance of natural expression. Had Gaudier Brzeska lived, he would be doing an odd door-knocker or two, and an occasional paper-weight, or portrait busts, for a living, with all the limiting circumstance that personal vanity sets to that form of art work. There only remains for the sculptor, as for the painter, the art exhibition, and the freak-selling or commercial-selling of the dealer's shop. A man like Archipenko, for instance, quite capable of finer things, is reduced to stunt-sculpting of a dilettante sort, on a small scale, it may be assumed of a precarious nature on the material side.

Have you ever met an Architect? I do not mean a well-paid *pasticheur*, who restores a house or runs one up, in Tudor, Italian, or any other style. But a creative architect, or a man with some new power in his craft, and concerned with the aesthetic as well as the practical needs of the mass sensibility of his time? I have not. And what is more, should you wish to approach this neglected subject and learn more about it, you will find nothing but a dismal series of very stupid books for your information and reference. The best treatise I have so far come across is W.K. Lethaby's handbook, 'An Introduction to the History and Theory of the Art of Building.' It appears to me to be as sound a book as possible: and if everybody were of Mr Lethaby's opinions we should soon find that the aspect of this lifeless scene had changed for the better. And this voice for the right and active vision comes from the unlikeliest quarter. For Mr Lethaby, I understand, is Chief Lecturer on Architecture in the South Kensington School.

Listen to this admitted academic authority on the subject:

Modern armoured concrete is only a higher power of the Roman system of construction. If we could sweep away our fear that it is an inartistic material, and boldly build a railway station, a museum, or a cathedral, wide and simple, amply lighted, and call in our painters to finish the walls, we might be interested in building again almost at once. This building interest must be aroused.

We cannot forget our historical knowledge, nor would we if we might. The important question is, Can it be organised and directed, or must we continue to be betrayed by it? The only agreement that seems possible is agreement on a scientific basis, on an endeavour after perfect structural efficiency. If we could agree on this we need not trouble about beauty, for that would take care of itself.

Experience must be brought back once more as the centre of architecture, and architects must be trained as engineers are trained.

The modern way of building must be flexible and vigorous, even smart and hard. We must give up designing the broken-down picturesque which is part of the ideal of make-believe. The enemy is not science, but vulgarity, a pretence to beauty at second hand.

What do you make of that? Does not Mr Lethaby, Professor of Architecture in the South Kensington Schools, speak to you in a tone seldom heard in the art-schools? What English professor of painting would you find recommending his pupil to paint in a manner 'smart and hard'?

Such books as C.H. Caffin's contain nothing very useful. He refers to the Woolworth Buildings in New York in the following way:

> Up to the present, the noblest example of this new movement is the Woolworth Buildings, which is not only the tallest of the tall buildings, but a monument of arresting and persuasive dignity. Such a building supplies an uplift to the spirit. Etc.

The Woolworth Buildings, one of the tallest in New York, consisting of 51 storeys, is a piece of rudimentary ecclesiastical nonsense, 25 of its storeys being a spire. It is in every way less interesting than the less ambitious skyscrapers, which are at least enormously tall boxes, and by their scale 'uplift the spirit' that wishes to soar so high, far more than this monstrous, dull, Anglican church: that is not a church, however, and has not even that excuse for its stupid spire.

In this connection, we hear a great deal of rubbish talked about the sky-scraper. The sky-scraper, for the most part, is a tall box. So far it has been nothing but that; except where, as in the Schiller Theatre Building in Chicago, or the famous Woolworth Buildings, some dreadful intervention of art has converted it into an acre-high advertisement of the modern architect's fatuity.

It has been a fashion lately to admire the sky-scraper in its purely engineering form, and other forms of quite plain engineering construction. But a box is always a box, however high. And when you think of the things that could have been done by a liaison of the artist's fancy, once more, with all these works of engineering genius, you wonder that there is not one single example which one can quote of such a structure.

In the case of a dynamic shape like an aeroplane there is neither any reason nor any need for the association of engineering inventiveness with that of the artist. All such machines, except for the colouring of them and a possible deliberate camouflaging to modify their shape, not to deceive the eye of the enemy but to add significance or beauty to their aspect, develop in accordance with a law of efficient evolution as absolute as a tiger, a wasp, or a swallow. They are definitely, for the artist, in the category of animals.

When we come to the static cell-structures in which we pass our lives there is far more latitude and opportunity for the inventiveness of the artist.

To begin with, let us by all means reduce everything to the box. Let us banish absolutely the stylistic architectural rubbish. But even as to the shaping of the box or series of boxes let the artist be used.

For if you say that the design and ornament over the body of the building is the same as the clothes on a man's back, there is still something to be said about the naked shape of the man or even for his skeleton. The nature of the body or of the skeleton will decide what the character of the clothes must be. So the artist should come in long before he usually does, or give a new consciousness to the shaping of the skeleton of the Engineer. This should be invariable, not occasional: that is when the first painters or sculptors have been used for this purpose, instead of the horrible stock architect.

Remy de Gourmont has the following notion on the subject of the decay of architecture in our time:

> Voilà le point capital de l'explication pourquoi on avait au moyen-age le sens de l'architecture: on ignorait la nature. Incapables de jouir de la terre telle qu'elle est, des fleuves, des montagnes, de la mer, des arbres, ils étaient obligés, pour exciter leur sensibilité, de se créer un monde factice, d'ériger des forêts de pierre.
>
> La nature s'ouvrit à l'homme parce que la France et le centre de l'Europe furent sillonnés de routes, parce que les campagnes devinrent sûres et d'un commode accès.

And he goes on to fancy that perhaps when Nature has become too cheap, through its general accessibility, and men tire of it, that Art and Architecture will once more have its turn.

Since a narrow belt of land like the Nile valley is more crowded with buildings, or their remains, than any other territory, and since the character of those buildings, the source of all subsequent constructions, was evidently determined by the nature of the landscape of Egypt, the hills, palms, and so forth, with which, further, the builders were at least as familiar as any men could be with Nature, de Gourmont's theory would appear to be nonsense. It displays the listless and dull eye that a usually keen journalist can turn to this Cinderella of a subject.

Child Art and the Naif

The Child and the Naif are two of the principal mainstays of dilettante criticism in this country. And this 'phenomenon' with all the sentimentality of which its exploitation clearly is susceptible, is one of the trump cards in the Amateur's game, and a fruitful source of confusion. It is one of the most obvious avenues, flooded with an effusive critical craft, by which the thoroughly undeserving can slip through into a position of artificial respect.

'The Young Visiters' is swelling into fabulous editions. Pamela Bianca, a child of nine, is fawned on by the hoary great. The Omega

Workshops have had an exhibition of children's drawings. The Naif, too, is a doll-like dummy that the trader on sentiment pushes in front of him in stalking the public. The Naif is an elastic phenomenon and of earlier date, as regards his boom, than the Child.

The Slade School produces regularly a certain number of naifs. They are frequently the most sophisticated individuals imaginable. Beyond the fact that they wrestle with a slight incompetence, in addition to possessing a pretty feeling for the sentimentalities of rustic prints, although they never by any means capture the native charm of those, they are no more naive than Mr Horatio Bottomley. None that I know are half as good manufactured naiveté as George Formby. They are very cunningly simple, and their graces and queernesses pall as swiftly as the tiresome mannerisms of a too clever child, exploiting its childishness.

There are two types of Naif: the Child-Naif, and the Primitive Naif. It is difficult to decide which is the more boring of the two.

The Child-Naif usually starts from a happy combination of an ingrained technical incompetence and of a 'nice feeling' for the things of art. He is distressed that this 'nice feeling' should be wasted owing to his lack of power, and hits on the happy idea, or gradually drifts into the habit (a sort of progressive *collage*) of bringing his lack of painter's prowess and his nice feeling for art together, and producing the very marketable commodity, Naiveté!

Or he may be a bit more definitely naive than this. The woodenness of his figures or trees, his rickety line, may really have a pathetic charm for him. He genuinely pities his little wooden figures for being so wooden and silly looking (a manner of pitying himself). He is sorry for himself through them! And this sensation becomes a necessity with him; he goes on doing them. If he has been touched enough; or, more likely, if his is a nasty theatrical self-love, other people are touched, and he in turn touches a little regular income in consequence!

Or the more general pathos may be absent. The weak pathetic line, and silly meaningless forms, the unreal colour, are the object of a certain emotion: something that I can only describe as a technical pity; a professional pathos. The best is made of an unfortunate limitation. This Naif may even become perfectly bumptious and self-satisfied in course of time, everything turning out, in the practical sphere, for the best: by the same process that produces the infantile swank of the deformed.

The Primitive Naif may evolve rather in the same way as the Child-Naif, or he may not. It may be a refuge of incompetence. Or it may be a romantic mode, teutonic in character. Then the Child-Naif and the Primitive Naif sometimes come together in the same artist.

There is no such thing as the *born Primitive*. There is the *Primitive* in point of view of historical date, the product of a period. And there is the *Primitive voulu*, who is simply a pasticheur and stylist, and invariably a sentimentalist, when not a rogue. When he is not specially an *Italian* or *Flemish Primitive*, but just a *Primitive* (whatever period he flits into *always* a Primitive), he is on the same errand and has the same physiognomy as the Period-taster, or any other form of dilettante or of pasticheur. The Primitive voulu acrobatically adapts himself to a mentality of a different stage of social development: the pasticheur merely, en touriste, visits different times and places, without necessarily so much a readjustment of his mind as of his hand.

As to the Child proper. Of course the success of 'The Young Visiters' is partly due to its domestic appeal, partly due to its character of a sentimental curiosity. The distillation of Middle-class snobbery, also, presented in this pure and objectionable form, is sure to 'attract a wide public.'

Pamela Bianca, whose drawings are to be found in a publication called the *Owl*, in *Vogue*, and so forth, is like Daisy Ashford at least in one point: that *she is not a child*. She may be nine years old, and 'The Young Visiters' may have been written by a child of two. But they both have every sad relaxed quality of the average adult mind. They are as extinct as that. Pamela Bianca's 'libido' has naively devoured the Douanier's Fête National. But that is the nearest she has come to naiveté. Otherwise she imitates Beardsley or Botticelli, or some fellow-child, with as sophisticated a competence as any South Kensington student. She is very exactly the aesthetic peer of the professional painters who run the *Owl*.

The growth of the mind and of the body is so often not parallel, some people's 'mature' lives so long, others almost non-existent, that it is difficult to know where you are dealing with the art product of the child, or the child-like art of the adult.

Presumably a powerful nature develops at once, disregarding the schedules of human growth and the laws of probation. William Blake was a case of a being who took little notice of the dawdling ritual of growth. On the other hand, many individuals, highly developed in adult life, have shown no precocity at all.

Genius no doubt has its system of working in a man, all the facts of the case—the best time to strike—the mental resources—the character of the gift to be hatched—in its possession.

As regards the Naif, Rousseau the Douanier is the only great naif as far as I know. In his case Nature made on the one hand his Douanier's calling a water-tight case against sophistication; and then put something divinely graceful and simple—that we associate with 'childhood' and that that abstraction sometimes has—at his disposal for the term of his life.

Nothing seemingly could corrupt or diminish it; and it brought with it, like a very practical fairy, or a sardine tin with its little key, an instrument with which to extract all the genius from within this Douanier of forty or fifty years old.

To return to the Child proper. The only case in which the drawing of a child is of value, is when it possesses the same outstripping or unusual quality that the work of a very few adult artists possesses. The adult in question may have accomplished nothing himself as a child. But the drawing of the child would seem perhaps to be his work at a more immature stage. It is not the question of Child or Adult. It is a question simply of the *better being*. Both belong to an exceptional type of being.

There is also a fresh and delicate charm of very young life that some children, not many, have the power of infusing into their drawings. And there remains the melancholy fact that no infant's pictures could be duller than the average adult's. And therefore there is every bit as much justification for exhibiting any twenty children's scribbles as there is for exhibiting those of any twenty professional painting adults.

Machinery and Lions

The Futurists had in their idée fixe a great pull over the sentimental and sluggish eclecticism, deadness and preciosity of the artists working in Paris.

But they accept objective nature wholesale, or the objective world of mechanical industry. Their paean to machinery is really a worship of a Panhard racing-car, or a workshop where guns or Teddy bears are made, and not a deliberate and reasoned enthusiasm for the possibilities that lie in this new spectacle of machinery; of the *use* it can be put to in art. Machinery should be regarded as a new resource, as though it were a new mineral or oil, to be used and put to different uses than those for which it was originally intended. A machinery for making the parts of a 6in. Mk. 19 gun should be regarded apart from its function. Absorbed into the aesthetic consciousness it would no longer *make* so much as a pop-gun: its function thenceforward would change, and through its agency emotions would be manufactured, related, it is true, to its primitive efficiency, shininess, swiftness or slowness, elegance or power, but its meaning transformed. It is of exactly the same importance, and in exactly the same category, as a wave on a screen by Korin, an Odalisque of Ingres, a beetle of a sculptor of the XVIII. dynasty. Ingres lived in the midst of a great appetite for the pseudo-classic: the Egyptian sculptor lived in the presence of a great veneration for the beetle. Korin's contemporaries possessed a high susceptibility and sentiment for the objects of the natural world. Korin's formal wave-lines is the same impulse as Balla's Linee Andamentali: the Beetle and the Odalisque are both sleek and solid objects! Ingres probably did not believe in the Odalisque as an Odalisque, although realising the admirable uses to which she could be put. The Egyptian probably found the beetle objectionable until transformed into stone. And there should be no obligation to supply veneration, or to behave like a religious fanatic about a sausage machine or a locomotive: other people can supply that, indeed should do so about something or other. If the world *would only build temples to Machinery* in the abstract then everything would be perfect. The painter and sculptor would have plenty to do, and could, in complete peace and suitably honoured, pursue their trade without further trouble. Else what is the use of taking all the useful Gods and Goddesses away, and leaving the artist with no rôle in the social machine, except that of an entertainer, or a business man?

Imagine Koyetzu, Signorelli, or the sculptor who carved the head of Akhenaton or of the wife of the Sheik-el-Beled, alive painting and carving, to-day. They would have been in the profoundest sense the same artists. But just as a painter may use one medium one day and another the next; so far more than simply traces of the fact that they had seen the machines that play such a part in our existence would be found in their inventions. Just as the sculptors of Nineveh put the lions that were such immediate objects in their life, to good use in their reliefs; or the painters of the Sung period the birds and landscapes found by them in their wilfully secluded lives; so it was inevitable to-day that artists should get into their inventions (figures, landscapes, or abstractions) something of the lineaments and character of machinery. An artist could excel, no doubt, who never suggested in his pictures acquaintance with anything more ferrous than a mushroom. But you would not be liable, I suppose, to pick a quarrel with the artists of Asshur because they used the lions at their door?

This ground has to be gone over, and thus much reasserted, for the purposes of the new adjustments I propose.

The Artist's Luck

The best artists of the Sung period lived a secluded life, very luckily for them. It was considered the thing to inhabit the fairly distant country and live in intercourse with the objects of Nature. When this fashion passed, and a painter had to live within hailing distance of the court, the pictures produced showed an immediate decline in quality. That is *one* lesson.

The scenes in the Assyrian bas-reliefs from Nineveh were produced by an artist who led an unlucky kind of life. He was hurried about by the king in his razzias and hunts: no sooner had the party (a marauding or a hunting one) returned to the city than the harassed sculptors had to rush to their workrooms and produce by the next morning a complete series of bas-reliefs describing in what was apparently considered a flattering way the exploits of their diabolical idiot of a master. For no sooner had he slept off the fatigue caused by the last of an incessant series of displacements than he insisted on seeing what he had looked like to his band of performing sculptors during the last week or two. Their heads probably fell like apples in an autumn wind; though there

170

is seemingly no record of his ever having had sculptors enough to build up their skulls into a pyramid. How they succeeded in doing such good lions it is difficult to say. Perhaps the ones who did the good lions were left in peace sometimes. But on the whole, a sculptor fated to work for Asshur's deputy would no doubt have regarded the Sung hermit as the luckiest old yellow crab that ever painted.

It has occurred to me that we might be worse off than we are. But I can see no reason why we should not be better off: hence, partly, this pamphlet.

But this view of the options open to the modern artist soon changed. The various technically revolutionary movements in art had, Lewis thought, now performed the necessary service of clearing away the nineteenth-century stylistic rubbish, or as he put it more politely: 'After a period of productivity which has burnt itself out and come to an end, [the painter] has to readjust and renew vision and virtuosity and develop the necessary material for a new term of creative work corresponding with the changed aspects and ideas of his time.' Had Lewis lived in the Soviet Union he would probably have remained one of those formalist artists eventually proscribed by Stalin, but the nature of British society in the Twenties gave little encouragement to such work. He had never been a completely abstract artist, and from the early Twenties onwards his work contained only abstract elements, used in the service of rendering human figures in formalised or fantastic guises. He also began to exploit his mastery of line in the drawings and portraits that have fixed several of his contemporaries permanently in the eye of posterity. The article 'After Abstract Art', which appeared in the *New Republic* in 1940, is perhaps the furthest point he reached in calling for the replacement of abstraction by the attempt to 'imitate what is under our eyes', but to do so through a super-naturalism quite different from the literary approach of the Surrealists.

171

After Abstract Art

In an article printed recently in The New Republic I announced the death of 'abstract art'. I implied that the final liquidation of all of these anti-natural movements, in the visual arts, is imminent. At this prospect I was frankly elated. Our 'abstract' adventure (I recapitulate) revealed one great objection to high-hatting nature. On the one hand a certain polar emptiness; on the other an, in the long run, equally disconcerting tropical redundance, a romantic excess, is what happens in a visual art when the objective datum of the visual field is abandoned.

So much for the technical obstacles. Quite as noteworthy are the psychological complications—'Difficult painting', like caviar, is a thing of which there cannot be very much: and its consumption, again like that great delicacy, is confined to the plutocratic crust of our society. For an artist, to be 'difficult' is either to die or to go to live with Croesus and his satellites in a glittering dreamland. And the contemporary Croesus is, alas, a consummate savage.

Now snobbery *re* the 'difficult painter' is indicative of a barbarous *lack* of interest in art: just the same as too exotic dishes suggest enfeeblement of the taste as much as of the appetite. Snobbery does not originate in the studio, but in the salon, of course. The painter can hardly be a snob. All painting—Corot, Chardin or Giotto; Rouault, Rembrandt or Blake—delights him. So it is not in him that the appetite is wanting: although in some societies the painter may be the only man who regards a painting otherwise than as an exhibit, a possession or a counter in a game. Art that is too gamey reveals the presence of an undesirable order of patron, as much as human flesh appearing on a menu would justly be regarded as an outrage by the 'Club des Cent' (not to mention anything so suspect and Anglo-Saxon as the Food and Wine Society). And some of the most fashionable painting today has been hung too long.

Seeing how exclusively pictorial art has become an expensive condiment, valued by its barbarous user in proportion to its kick, no wonder 'difficult' painting has been compromised, and the whole of painting been shot to pieces economically. From the moment Croesus—ably abetted by the millionaire picture-dealers and fashionable experts—cast his gorgon-eye upon a blank blue canvas, with two pink spots at its centre and a scarlet triangle up in one corner—gazed at it bleakly and found it *good*, the doom of all that was not *blank* was sealed.

Then came the Child, with its fascinating scribbles, and the adult that sat at the feet of the Child, and then the inmate of the asylum, with *his* fascinating distortions; and we were all set for a number of decades, if not forever. But politics, seemingly, are coming to our rescue. Such an unlikely instrument as the New Deal, even, has played its part.

Freedom for the painter is what this new dispensation spells—nothing less than freedom; for better or for worse, of course. Freed of the snobbish obligation to excel in oddity, as if they were running a freak-show, all but a decimal percentage of professional painters will breathe freely once more. The dangers inherent in this freedom are obvious. Those in a decimal minority, in a free community, are not always the least endowed. You do not need to tell me that. But before you shudder at the thought of those dangers, you have to inspect very conscientiously the condition of art, as we find it today, and ask yourself what is likely to happen—or *not* to happen—if that state of affairs endures.

All that our abstract experiment of twenty years ago did for painting, it seems, was to substitute sensationalism for the cultivation of the senses, and to clap down upon the practice of painting a snobbery of the most withering description. The hatred for art in all its forms which is such a characteristic of that well-groomed barbarian, the 'socialite', and his strange new prompter, the 'art-expert', has found in these snob-values the satisfaction of its animus. So we have arrived at the stagnation which we see today.

In this freedom-for-the-painter slogan there is a paradox. For it was in the name of freedom that as abstractionists, or cubists, or what not, we set out to explore beyond nature. Yet the constraint and unfreedom that have provoked what is now happening are very much of a reality. Nature—the nature of Holbein, of Ingres, in distinction to that of the photographer—is not respectable. And such conventions are found cramping by most artists.

That this freedom that is now being won for painters will be used to paint simpering photographs of an obnoxious sweetness, and scenes of an enervating domestic bliss—the kitten playing with the ball of wool, and the child nestling in its mother's lap—is certain. That is what complicates the process, and freezes the hoorah upon our lips.

Here we arrive at the question—since it evidently has become a question everywhere—of what to do next in art, so as to restore painting to its old position of creative mastery: so that it should cease to be a plaything—a joke—of the rich. For several decades it has had the status of a dwarf at the court of a king of Castille. It is surely time it ceased to waddle and grimace at the heels of some scented playboy, or playgirl, and remembered some of the things it had done, better worth doing than that, since it first came on the scene, in Greece and China.

The Federal Artists' Project is now an old, and I am afraid stale, story. It must, I suppose, be allowed, too, that you cannot *stick art onto life*: life itself, and the shells in which life is lived, have to be altered first. Nevertheless, Mr Roosevelt has done more for the art of painting than any other public man alive, in any country in the world.

His gesture is so entirely unique that it cannot be enough, or long enough, applauded. Why should we complain that the statesman gives too little heed to art, if, when at last the rule is broken, as in the case of Mr Roosevelt, and a great deal of youthful talent is unearthed, you put yourself on your guard, mobilize all your critical faculties, as if an unworthy attempt had been made to make you an intellectual sucker?

'Post-office art' is, a great deal of it, far better than gallery art. I would much rather go to the Twenty-third Street Post Office in New York City than to most picture exhibitions. Although it is an unnecessarily hideous hall, and the colour scheme not of a kind to induce people to linger (and one can see that, in a post office, that had to be guarded against), I never go there to buy a stamp but what I admire some new dexterity or piece of invention on the part of the artist.

As to the type of art, these Federal Artists' Project murals naturally reflect the tendencies of the last few decades. But in a 'new deal' for the artist the technical problem is of far less importance than the psychological, or if you like the political. When the state steps in, and throws the doors of its post offices open to the artist, what it is doing more than anything else—and this is generally overlooked, or insufficiently stressed—is taking the destinies of the art of painting out of the hands of the 'socialite', the dealer and the expert. That is the thing of capital importance.

The kind of art, as I have remarked, is unimportant. To imitate what is under our eyes; to develop those imitations into generalized (*super-natural*—but not *super-real*) realities; and beyond that, and in a more general way, to care for, and to influence people to observe, the visual amenities, and to banish as far as possible from the visual field all that is degrading or stupid, all that is of trivial or slovenly design and texture: these are great human functions, surely, that people neglect to their cost.

———

As so often, he was swimming against the tide. Within a decade a kind of automatic abstraction was beginning to find favour in the United States, and a minimalist version of it in France. Lewis did not live to see the triumph of minimalism or the worship of Jackson Pollock, but there can be no doubt that he would have excoriated the first as the kind of art 'in which nothing is preferred to something', and the second as exemplifying the infantile sensationalism he had opposed all his life.

In *The Demon of Progress in the Arts* (1954) he pointed out what was happening in British art, while praising the current generation of artists whose work he had reviewed for several years in *The Listener* as 'the finest group of painters and sculptors England has ever known'. The title of one chapter in the following extract, 'There is a Limit, beyond which there is Nothing', expresses his objections to the kind of 'pure' abstract art which in its randomness and casualness denies any role at all to the intellect.

from THE DEMON OF PROGRESS IN THE ARTS

The Cause of the Heterogeneity in the Fine Arts in Our Time

If you go through the picture-galleries of Italy or of Germany where old masters are hung, ranged according to period, there is a great homogeneity in the paintings of each period, so that you know at once when you are among the canvases of such-and-such a school. This homogeneity of the works of any time, or school, continues up to French Impressionism. You then find yourself among painters so different as Manet and Monet, as Degas and Whistler (nocturnes). Within a few decades you reach Van Gogh, John Sargent, and Gauguin. A few decades more and you would be surrounded by Cubists, Futurists, religious pictures by Rouault and Augustus John. As you advanced from decade to decade the confusion, the lack of homogeneity would grow. In England today (1954) you would be among pure Impressionists like Coldstream, those who prefer carpentry to paint, like Pasmore, traditionalists like Augustus John, Post-Impressionists like Trevelyan. We have reached a point at which there is not much money to be extracted from the painting of pictures, and artists pursue their fancies: so you find side by side painters of all sorts of schools. There is still a certain amount of mild excitement when a few people are under the impression that they are *des avant-gardes*, and still exhibit a little superiority about those who are not so far ahead as themselves. The I.C.A. provides them with a rallying ground.

Now, the proliferation of schools began with the bitter hostilities between the classicists and the romantics at the beginning of the nineteenth century. This was a war between the new and the old. The battle between the new and the old has continued up to the present moment. The only difference is that for a long time almost any group is denounced as 'old' at the end of about ten years of life. Since this group of noisy denouncers is in its turn denounced in a decade, or half a decade, or even twelve months—this has meant that very soon there were dozens of schools and groups claiming to be *le dernier cri*, the quintessence of revolution, so much the latest thing that they are almost out of sight, as are some of the dimmest of the Abstractists in post-war Paris.

This heterogeneity is not an explosion of rugged individualism, but, on the contrary, quite the opposite. The personality is surrendered to some small well-disciplined group: it is always as groups that they advance to the attack upon the obsolete. If the contemporary scene could be confined to any one of these groups, it would seem a very homogeneous period.

What is the explanation of this universal disunion? In the eighteenth and in the seventeenth centuries there was the homogeneity of discipline, the like-thinking of a classical norm. The turning-point was political; the age of political revolution was followed by the era of perpetual revolution in the arts. Halfway through the last century the revolutionary zest, the turmoil of schools, the roaring of slogans and watch-words began to assume a crazy intensity. But at present, halfway through the twentieth century, revolution, of a visual kind, appears to have become stabilized at a point which is as far as it is possible to go technically, without disappearing altogether—without the visual arts committing suicide. There are several abstract schools on the continent which the slightest push would tip over into the blankness of the great zero. It is my belief that we are approaching the point where there will be no visual arts at all, of a serious kind. On the one hand, the 'advanced' gestures, the project-foolery, will become stabilized; on the other hand, something like the Royal Academy will survive (unless there happened to be an authentic social revolution), trying to be a little vapidly go-ahead here and there, but still remaining a market-place for portraits of people who regard an oil-painting as a symbol of the sitter having arrived. Real whole-time painting, of the kind practised by the old masters, will not even pretend to exist any longer. This is not quite yet more than speculation.

All these pretentious little crusades, or gestures of revolution, certainly date from the period of the French Revolution at the end of the eighteenth century; although receiving their first impetus from a social revolution, the subsequent upheavals related purely to technical modifications. In the first decades of the last century painting, to start with, merely mirrored the mighty battle of the new and the old; so there was a grand cleavage into two schools of painting, the classicism of Ingres standing confronted by the romanticism of Delacroix or Géricault. A new factor becomes apparent after that: namely the invasion of the visual arts by the spirit of scientific discovery—the French painters were seized by the desire to make their imitation of nature more scientifically exact. They studied the theory of colour and this eventually led to the following system: (1) the colours were, as usual, squeezed out upon the palette; (2) the colours were not mixed with one another, neither on the palette nor on the canvas; small dabs of each colour were transferred intact from palette to canvas; (3) the theory was that the colours would mix in the eye of the spectator—they must never be allowed to mix anywhere else, but to preserve their original purity. The Pointillistes adhered most rigidly to this rule, and were the culmination of these experiments. A borrowing of a quite different kind from science, in the present century, was jeeringly named Cubism. So, from the middle of the last century, a pseudo-scientific impulse has been apt to start some school; reflected from science, there has been the impulse incessantly to perfect, constantly discarding what has been bettered, like yesterday's model in the motor-car industry; and last, but not least, the fiery millennial zeal of the social revolutionary emotionally galvanizing everything, and instilling the painter with a quite irrational belief in the *rightness* of his *latest* mannerism.

For the last hundred years the art-student has found himself at the centre of a brawl between old and new, assailed by the claims of schools or of leading artists to be ahead in the race, or to possess some secret of technical up-to-dateness. When I was an art-student in Paris in the first years of the century, it was reported that leading artists, like Picasso, had passed into a new 'period'. Picasso had begun his career with a 'blue period', for instance. No student would be in the swim who did not develop, himself, a green period, say, or a saffron one. To eliminate from the palette all but one colour appeared to these people the most easily recognized way of having a 'period'. I can give you another illustration of what *period* means in the life of the painter. Once a week, I think it was, a group of painters formed the habit of meeting in the large first-floor of 'The Newcomes' in Fitzroy Street, not long before World War One. I remember, on one occasion, Walter Sickert dramatically announcing, in a rhyme which still rings in my ears:

Mr Ginner's
Painting thinner.
Mr Sicker's
Painting thicker.

This meant of course, that the painter, Charles Ginner, was entering upon a 'thin period'; whereas Walter Sickert was going thick—was having a 'thick period'.

The pictures of the more authentic masters of the past did not suddenly develop curious rashes—you do not find Rembrandts or Titians of certain years all of a crude green or a crude blue colour. But the mercurial masters of the budding century had to give the student-mass a new sensation every few years, or even, sometimes, if they felt they were losing ground, every few months, by *going red*, or by *going blue*. Then the students would follow suit and in the *Salon des Indépendants* the fashionable colour would appear everywhere.

Let me return, now, to the question of the heterogeneity of the arts in the modern age. We have not one manner, as in the past, but dozens of ways of expressing ourselves. It will be obvious from this that the individuality of the artist is the last thing you are likely to find. Each artist conforms to one or other of the violent orthodoxies of the moment. Women are obedient to the annual fiats of fashion from Paris, and an artist has no more individuality than has a woman, whose only desire is to conform to the fashion. So when I speak of the freedom of the artist in my next section, it cannot mean that the artist is personally, or individually, free. That is not a thing that could possibly happen anywhere today.

Amateur Artists

Ours is an age, inevitably, of amateurism of the fine arts: there are a countless number of people who are identified as artists, and most of them, even where they have had a little training, remain amateurs. Thirty years ago, for instance, while the middle-class still had money, 'art' was very often chosen as a career by a young man who had nothing in particular he wanted to do. It was an attractive way of doing nothing. It did not mean that any talent whatever was possessed by this young man; if he had told himself to start with that he had talent, he very soon found that he had been mistaken. These conditions were productive of a great number of what passed as professional artists. As the British Empire became a less and less attractive place to do nothing in (to be a soldier for instance), such a 'profession' as this became an obvious refuge. But this no longer could be regarded as a solution, I suppose, when the welfare state took over, and the middle-class family no longer had the money to pay for so expensive an education.

This accounts for quite a few of the amateurs technically professionals. Then, at the end of World War Two, upon demobilization (when the State stepped in, with a lavish financing) a number of young soldiers adopted the career of an artist. Quite apart from either of these two classes of artist, there is the enormous quantity of young men of all classes who find their way every year into provincial art-schools or into the Royal College of Art and other large metropolitan academies. There are, of course, nearly as many women as men studying to be some kind of artist. Talent is not often met with; but a great number of more or less youthful people are trained as artists: and it is from among this horde that the stunt crusades are recruited—the more violently untalented would no doubt soon drop out, if it were not for the opportunities offered the dud in extremism.

The army of technicians required by commercial art (which has turned the art-schools into a group of specialized classes, dressmaking, poster-art, or what not), this today is the most solid cause of the swarming of young men and women to which I have referred. But if there were, instead of these conditions, a small number of professional artists, for the most part lucratively employed, then there would probably be no extremism. Extremism is symptomatic of a vacuum—a time in which there is no rationale for visual expression. It would be quite impossible to persuade any professional artist (at a time when such a profession was intact) to indulge in unpopular adventures.

For quite a time it has been so unwelcome to point out the realities of the present period that a sort of conspiracy of silence has developed. Everyone pretends, including the horde of impoverished artists, the professional pundits, the picture-dealers and so on, everyone pretends that we enjoy normal conditions, and even that art is flourishing. This is the necessary background for what I am shortly to examine—the institutional unreality, as also the costly 'cultural' bluffs inaugurated by the state, to conceal the growing absence of culture behind these imposing façades.

Those who are Accessible to an Extremist Glamour

The visual artist, alone in his studio, if of a technically inventive disposition, is easily tempted to go back and imagine himself a primitive, or to go forward into the future and imagine himself in a society far more intellectual, and sensitively receptive, than the one in which he finds himself. Then naturally, works will be produced which may seem very queer indeed to the public.

If technically a brilliant performer—as was, for instance, Pablo Picasso—the artist will be unwilling to abandon traditional achievement entirely. The great skills he has acquired it will give him delight to employ, and he will continue existing, to some extent, upon the plane of Leonardo or of El Greco, he will have a dual personality. In the case of Picasso, we find him producing, side by side, works as abstract as a coloured rug, and others quite naturalistic, if strongly marked with his personal idiosyncrasies. Otherwise, if there is no inducement of that kind to cling to naturalistic form and colour, if the artist's power is very moderate, an artist may use his paint and brush, or his chisel, to create forms and combinations reminiscent of the rough sketches of the engineer and the carpenter rather than the artist; indulge himself in 'advances' which are so far removed from normal sensuous experience as to alienate him entirely from any possible public, except, in such a time as ours, the snobbish patron or pundit, not necessarily an intelligent or sensitive man, who cares to spend his life among very strange images indeed. But the readiness on the part of an artist to step over into a type of fanciful engineering is usually due to the fact that the visual arts have no very great attraction for him, he has no roots in the sensuous reality, or he would not be willing to desert them. Whatever he did in the way of experiment (and let us remember that the word *experiment* is the word used to account for these departures from the practice of visual art that we inherit from all past ages, whether Greek, Far-Eastern, or Italian Renaissance), *that experiment would be within the regions of visual sensibility—never outside them.*

It is all a question of whether the individual artist is one of those rare ones who are greatly gifted, and if he has acquired, in the course of a long training, a great deal of traditional power; in a case of that kind there would be no chance that he would allow himself to be dragged off into the problematical wilderness of the future. He would be too satisfied to find himself where he was, to listen to the aesthetic excursionist. It is unimaginable that the man who painted the portrait of Thomas Carlyle and that of Miss Alexander, were he today of vigorous middle age, would break up his perfection, and launch out into the abstract. With a young man, not yet fully trained, it is another matter. If the glorious reality of his gifts is not yet visible, present to his eyes, he might do anything. Nevertheless, it is usually those of very little talent who furnish the little crowds of people painting empty abstractions, or sticking together lengths of heavy iron, or platinum, or tin, which goes under the name of sculpture.

There is a Limit, beyond which there is Nothing

I am writing this not long after the death of Stalin, and there is a general feeling that, perhaps, the new rulers of Russia are going to modify the aggressive policy of the old leader. For the time being to speak of a third world war would be unpopular, but it still, unfortunately, is something which might happen at any moment. In the case of a third disaster of this kind, and one of unspeakable 'totality', the position of the fine arts, and the other great civilized forms of expression, would be profoundly changed, if the arts did not disappear altogether. So anything one says about the future is provisional: and anything one says about the present must have a certain unreality because of the 'cold war', which dislocates our national economies, and always has implicit in it the hottest war yet.

Having made this necessary statement, let me proceed. In the last section I spoke of Picasso's great traditional power, in painting and drawing, which he acquired when he was young. That was a period over fifty years ago; it was a time when Europe was at peace, and when it was possible laboriously to prepare for the career of a painter in a society unable even to imagine impoverishment, disposed to patronize all the arts and to spend considerable sums of money at the picture dealers and at the annual exhibitions. How vastly different that was from the present time goes without saying: all one need say is that an art student had leisure to build up the technical abilities which he required. Does he enjoy those conditions today? He certainly does not, and that solid mastery is not to be looked for in a time like the present. Artists are able to conceal the fact that this power is not possessed by them: to become an extremist of the most irrational stamp is one of the most obvious ways. Eighty years ago French impressionism offered a concealment of the same kind for the incompetent; but it was not a tenth as good a means of evasion as that provided by the arid bluff of *Réalités Nouvelles*, and all similar extremism.

Now, if you will consider the case of a young Englishman of eighteen or nineteen today, who feels he has an aptitude for painting; if, with me, you will examine the influences shaping his young mind, I believe you will find out a great deal about the position of the fine arts at the present moment. First of all, he will have visited the dealers' galleries, the R.A., have read the contemporary art journalism, possibly have gone to Paris. If he is a bright young man, he will imagine himself in the future an extremist: youth is always attracted by extremism. But it is not only that. What else is there for a bright young man to imagine himself? *There is no painting today worthy of consideration between extremist painting and the Royal Academy.* This is the essential fact that you must try to understand if you want to put yourself *au courant*. So a long traditional training would be the last thing he would think about. The fact that Reg Butler received four thousand five hundred pounds would be an enormous advertisement for extremism, suggesting to the bright young man that *even economically* extremism was a good bet. So there would not be much likelihood that he would do more than learn how to be a very extreme painter, or a frightfully advanced sculptor.

What is being done in England on a small scale, is being done in France in a big way. If you go to Paris and try to find a painter not an extremist, and not the French equivalent of the Royal Academy—one who is highly thought of—you will be disappointed. There is no such painter. There is a rash of total abstraction, and of near-abstraction. Under these circumstances, it is safe to assume that in France the bright young man will think the same thoughts as the bright young man in England.

What does this mean? It means, I think, that there will be no more artists (painters or sculptors) possessing the great traditional accomplishment which is possessed by Pablo Picasso, or, in this country, Augustus John or Jacob Epstein may be cited as possessing, or, to take an advanced artist, Henry Moore.

I will end this section by saying that, as far as I personally am concerned, I do not object to the extremism of Henry Moore or of Graham Sutherland. In my own work I pushed at all times to that limit, although doing fairly traditional work as well. Having made this statement, let me add that extremism is not *necessary*. It is all right; some people tend to be extremist, and some are not extremist. There is no merit in extremism; although at the present moment it is a universal fashion. What I am arguing about in this book is that an easily defined limit exists in painting and sculpture, in music, in the theatre, in literature, in architecture, and in every other human art. There are daring drivers who enjoy driving along the edge of a cliff, whenever the opportunity offers. All I am saying is that there is such a thing as driving *too near* the edge of a cliff. There is no sense in shooting over it. It is quite simple; beyond a certain well-defined line—in the arts as in everything else—beyond that limit there is *nothing*. Nothing, zero, is what logically you reach past a line, of some kind, laid down by nature, everywhere.

As you must understand, we have reached the point at which a quite final position has to be taken up. It is where you have to say *yes* or *no*.

Because of its intricacy, and because, in the second place, I run the risk of putting in danger the effectiveness of my general line of argument, what I now have to say is particularly difficult.

Infantile extremist sensationalism (as a by-product of self-seeking) is the curse of the pundit. What every artist should try to prevent is the car, in which is our civilized life, plunging over the side of the precipice—the exhibitionist extremist promoter driving the whole bag of tricks into a nihilistic nothingness or zero.

The Ability to See the Limit

Over thirty years ago I was teaching extremism, and I was myself an extreme artist. The extremist modes in European painting and sculpture of that time have not been exceeded, for the very good reason that there is no way of exceeding (developing a more spectacular extremism) Mondrian's geometric frames, Brancusi's eggs, or Kandinsky's atmospheric inventions or explosions. I have mentioned Henry Moore and Graham Sutherland as artists of the extreme whose adventures I do not look upon with a critical eye. Here is the great difficulty in such an anti-extremist argument as I am developing in this study. The trouble is, of course, that the extremism of Moore and Sutherland appears excessive to the majority of people; and my own work has offended, in the past, by its unorthodox character. The objection that will be made is that an extremist cannot be allowed to say, 'So far, but no farther!' It is quite arbitrary, fanciful, and irrational—so it must seem—this line beyond which there must be no advance.

Now the difficulty really is that no one not an artist can ever in fact *see* this line. He does not know enough about these matters to understand how, once you have accepted something described as 'extremism', there can ever be a *limit*. If a painter uses his thumb as a palette knife, and, jabbing it into various colours upon his palette, rubs them one after the other upon a blank canvas, and sends this 'picture' to the *Réalités Nouvelles* exhibition in Paris, that logically should be acceptable to anyone describable as an extremist. This is the conundrum which I have to tackle.

Now I must ask you to believe that I see the line beyond which the extreme is the nonsensical. But in any such discussion, those who are not painters will have to take a good deal on trust—simply because they cannot see what differentiates a highly logical piece of 'extremism' of Picasso's from an average work hung in the *Réalités Nouvelles* exhibitions. However, I hope you will continue with me, and much later in these pages I will make a final attempt to overcome this obstacle to comprehension.

'The Unknown Political Prisoner' and After

In England, the last example of militant extremism was the collection of works at the Tate Gallery, representing 'The Unknown Political Prisoner'. A touch of the old excitement was conjured up: first of all a prize was given, to the young sculptor, Reg Butler, of the most sensational kind, namely four thousand five hundred pounds. This small model of a proposed monument upon the white Cliffs of Dover appeared a very insignificant piece of eccentricity to those who had been reading in the papers, with amazement, of the vast sum it had gained for its creator. All the newspapers contained a photograph of this oddity. Then came the second sensation: a young Hungarian went to the Tate, and, seizing this little joke by its spine of wire, doubled it up and threw it on the floor. As a result of this demonstration the young Hungarian spent some time in gaol, lost his job, and at last the case was dismissed.

Because of these well-advertised events, Reg Butler became, for the public, a symbol of outrageous 'advancedness'. But this intellectual toy of his is not at all a novelty, since many thousands of similar things have been produced, over and over again, for the last thirty or forty years in every part of Europe and America.

Let me here make use of Reg Butler's name, then, as it will be familiar to most people. The interested spectator of these goings-on will no doubt enjoy a pleasurable expectation of *what next* will happen in this funny old game the artists keep on playing.

So, what next? Well, there is nothing much beyond this simple little stunt—that is the odd thing. The same thing, more or less, has served to focus the popular mind for a long time now. There is nothing new to be expected; we shall, I assume, see Reg Butlers and the fanatical sterilities of *Réalités Nouvelles* for a long time to come; for, as a matter of fact, the advances of the last forty years have about reached the limits of the visual. There is not much more that can be done in senseless progress.

In the end, of course, the pundits will be shamed out of stopping at Reg Butler. Someone will invent something or other which will *seem* a new departure. What ultimately must be expected is that a step will be taken outside or beyond nature. They will not be in a hurry to take this step—for it is a much better bet for these gentlemen to keep on marking time, as long as people will stand it, in the same spot more or less. For if they take Art over the edge, what will happen to *them*? But they are really so irresponsible, and probably have not thought out all this. So it is incumbent upon everybody to halt them here and now.

So there is no tomorrow, there is no *new* sensation to be expected. The rational limit has already been overstepped—there is nothing more to be anticipated. Indeed, what has been reached is hardening into a canon, behind which everything is described as bad.

All artists today, and art-critics, are familiar with what a painting, or a piece of sculpture, looks like when it has reached the *ne plus ultra* line. For thirty years, we all have become sickeningly familiar with these formulae. Even originality-in-extremeness is not encouraged: the new extremists must reproduce what is there already, what has been done many times before. You would think that that sickening feeling of which I have spoken would be felt by the newcomer, the young extremist, just as much as by everyone else. The curious thing is that he seems to think he is being wildly 'advanced' when he is reproducing, in reality, something done for the first time thirty or forty years ago. But there it is; there are certain set ways of doing things, it has all been laid down some time ago in the Anglo-Saxon countries. The young artist, when, at whatever point in his progress, he decides to go abstract, has a rigid and fixed number of directions he can take. All he can do is to pick such and such a well-trodden approach to zero, and, then, within that well-trodden approach to the Great Blank, he can indulge in a few minor and insignificant variations. Or, shall we say that he is like a performing white mouse entering a carefully defined and ingeniously worked out maze. No originality is possible any longer; what he paints or what he carves must look very much like thousands of other things we all have seen. The only original artist was he who pioneered in this elaborate game; who blazed the trail, marked out the paths to be taken, and reached the limit beyond which it was impossible to go. He was like the man who discovered the Pacific, 'silent upon a peak in Darien'. Well, there is only one Pacific. Once you have discovered the Pacific you can draw a map of this region, and show how other people can come and discover the Pacific too. After that, naturally, there is the Pacific to cross, its islands to be charted, the shores of Australia and of Asia reached;

and from there you just, stage by stage, come back to where you began, to the point from which you set out. All 'advancedness', in this kind of advancedness, is merely a repetition of this circumnavigation. The earth is round, and, in the technical 'advance' in the fine arts initiated in the second decade of this century, it is a question merely of going round and round. The young artist soon, now, reaches the 'peak in Darien'. Then, without having to be a very daring fellow, he crosses the Pacific; he reaches the Spice Islands and Asia; from there is a journey home that seems as old as the camel-route across Asia. To perform this journey the ingenious Calder has provided you with all the wire you will need, if you are travelling in the third dimension; Picasso and Braque, and hundreds of other initiators, have hammered away billions of models required by the Abstractist, from which you select if you are a painter. This is hard tack, or it may be thought of as pemmican, but anyway it is all the young 'adventurer' will need in his journey.

Now the painter 'travels light', as I have pointed out. The material he needs to be a painter costs him practically nothing. Theoretically his freedom should be very great. But as an 'advanced', Abstractist, painter or sculptor in our time, his *freedom* is merely theoretic, his originality nil. Everyone has been original before him. He is handed a guidebook, a set of rules, a lot of 'uplift'. He has to paint as he is told, he has to register his adherence to the laws of advance. What he eventually turns out must conform to what is by this time a well-tried formula.

Apart from the pundits, like Herbert Read, who provide books of 'advanced' theory, there are naturally, a great number of instructors in the art-schools (like the Central, the R.C.A., etc., in London, and similar places in all the large provincial cities) who can teach any student how to become an 'advanced' artist. These teachers can provide all the formulae of painting of the *Réalités Nouvelles* type, or of sculpture of the Reg Butler type; or, if 'mobiles' attract, it can be shown how this is done. If some kind of infantilism is what the student appears to be marked out for, encouragement and instruction are supplied. It is just the same as in the days of Frith, when students were given instruction, after they had gone through the preliminaries, in how to paint a 'Derby Day'. Thirty or forty years ago there were instructors in art-schools who would put a student on the road to produce a typical Van Gogh 'Sunflower'; but this is *vieux jeu*, literally, almost as much so as the 'Derby

Day', for Van Gogh was nowhere near the limit of technical 'advance'.

Near the limit of technical advance—the Twentieth Century front line.

The 'Progressive' Slave

The other day I was talking to one of those extremist painters whose work I greatly like. In the course of our conversation I was somewhat surprised to hear him speak as follows. 'It is strange,' he observed, 'but we have to struggle just as hard today to do something ... well, like painting a recognizable portrait ... as formerly we had for years to struggle to be allowed to do something "extremist" or whatever you like to call it. Today it is just the same thing the other way round. One's dealer raises his eyebrows, frowns upon a more or less straight portrait when one sends it in. It has become like a religious orthodoxy. Yet, when we began to depart from the traditional norm, it was not a departure that had anything religious about it—it was not a catholic doing something anti-catholic. It was just a desire to experiment in the medium one was using, no more than that, was it?'

I was delighted to learn that even the most successful extremist (of the rational kind) did not find it necessary to conceal the difficulty he encountered in defying the canon of advancedness. Under similar circumstances I am quite sure, of course, that Pablo Picasso did not have to ask permission of his dealer to paint a portrait, of a naturalistic kind. But then he had attained, long ago, to such a pinnacle of worldly success that to him all was permitted. To the rank and file extremist *nothing* is permitted. He is a slave of the great god Progress, who is a very jealous god indeed.

Lewis's literary criticism proceeded with a directness, and a disregard for orthodox gentility, that made him unacceptable as a contributor to such a magazine as *The Times Literary Supplement*, which then expected those who wrote for it not merely to be anonymous, but also to conform to something approaching a house-style. Eliot fitted naturally into such a requirement: but Lewis, who went straight for a perceived end, and offered opinions put in a manner always wholly individual and sometimes highly personal, caused many editors to fight shy for such reasons, quite apart from their possible dislike of the opinions expressed.

The 'analysis of the mind of James Joyce' in *Time and Western Man*, for example, was unacceptable both to Joyce's detractors and admirers: to the first because it regarded what they took to be a sometimes filthy and often unintelligible writer with admiration, to the latter because it regarded Joyce as innovative as a craftsman only, and otherwise a figure embalmed in the past. The piece ended the genuine friendship between the two, but still Joyce thought what Lewis wrote was the best hostile criticism *Ulysses* received. It is an odd kind of hostility, perhaps, that compares a writer favourably with Sterne and Stevenson. The extracts that follow comprise roughly a third of the piece. They suggest the way in which Lewis linked Joyce and other writers into his theories about the time-mind.

from TIME AND WESTERN MAN

An Analysis of the Mind of James Joyce

I cannot see that any work of Joyce—except *Ulysses*—is very significant. It was about six or seven years ago that I first became acquainted with his writing. The *Portrait of the Artist* seemed to me a rather cold and priggish book. It was well done, like the *Dubliners*, which I have just read; and that was all, that I could discover. *Chamber Music* would certainly not have secured its author a place 'among the english poets,'—it would hardly even have set the Liffey on fire for five minutes. No writing of his before *Ulysses* would have given him anything but an honourable position as the inevitable naturalist-french-influenced member of the romantic Irish Revival—a Maupassant of Dublin, but without the sinister force of Flaubert's disciple.

Ulysses was in a sense a different thing altogether. How far that is an effect of a merely technical order, resulting from stylistic complications and intensified display, with a *Dubliners* basis unchanged, or, further, a question of scale, and mechanical heaping up of detail, I should have only partly to decide here. But it places him—on that point every one is in agreement—very high in contemporary letters.

Its evident importance, its success, induced people to go outside the contemporary field for their analogies; and, to start with, it may be as well to remove from our path a few of the unnecessary names that time, in the first generous flush of praise, injudiciously imported. Ireland, of course, furnished the most obvious comparisons.

So, to start with, Joyce is not a homologue of Swift. That is a strange mistake. There is very little of the specific power of that terrible personage, that *terribilità*, in the amiable author of *Ulysses*. Another writer with whom he has been compared, and whom he is peculiarly unlike, is Flaubert. But to mention all the authors with whom Joyce has been matched would take an appreciable time. So I will rather attempt to find his true affinities. The choice would lie, to my mind, somewhere between Robert Louis Stevenson and Laurence Sterne, if you imagine those writers transplanted into a heavily-freudianized milieu, and subjected to all the influences resulting in the rich, confused ferment of *Ulysses*.

Contact with any of his writing must, to begin with, show that we are not in the presence of a tragic writer, of the description of Dostoievsky or of Flaubert. He is genial and comic; a humorous writer of the traditional English School—in temper, at his best, very like Sterne. But he has the technical itch of the 'sedulous ape'—the figure under which Stevenson (with peculiar modesty, it is true) revealed himself to his readers. The impression produced by his earlier books, merely as writing, is very like that of a page of Stevenson—not of Stevenson 'apeing,' but of the finished, a little too finished, article.

Ulysses, on the technical side, is an immense exercise in style, an orgy of 'apeishness,' decidedly 'sedulous.' It is an encyclopaedia of english literary technique, as well as a general-knowledge paper. The schoolmaster in Joyce is in great evidence throughout its pages.

Next, as to his position among the celebrated group of Irishmen contemporary with himself, or his immediate predecessors, that is now fairly well defined. What has distinguished all the famous irish literary figures of recent years, whether Wilde, Shaw or Yeats, has been the possession of what we call 'personality.' This really amounts to a vein of picturesqueness, an instinct for the value of the *person* in the picture, which dominates them, externally at all events. And they have probably always been led into making a freer use of this than would a Frenchman, for instance, of the same calibre, owing to the self-effacing, unassuming, over-plain habits of the english background, against which they have had to perform. Or it may have been that, as isolated adventurers—when they had passed from Ireland and descended into Piccadilly Circus, thenceforth watched by an Empire on which the sun never sets—they were as a matter of course mere *persons*, as contrasted with the new alien *crowds* they were amongst. This florid personal aplomb is, however, now expected of the Irishman by his english audience—although, owing to the political separation of the two countries, probably those times of genial interplay are passed.

Mr Joyce is by no means without the 'personal touch.' But in a sense he is not the 'personality' that Shaw or Yeats is, or that Wilde was. But that is in conformity with his rôle, which is a very different one from theirs. Joyce is the poet of the shabby-genteel, impoverished intellectualism of Dublin. His world is the small middle-class one, decorated with a little futile 'culture,' of the supper and dance-party in *The Dead*. Wilde, more brilliantly situated, was an extremely metropolitan personage, a man of the great social world, a great lion of the London drawing-room. Joyce is steeped in the sadness and the shabbiness of the pathetic gentility of the upper shopkeeping class, slumbering at the bottom of a neglected province;* never far, in its snobbishly circumscribed despair, from the pawn-shop and the 'pub.'

Shaw, again, escaped early from his provincial surroundings. Joyce resembles him in some striking particulars; but the more recent figure, this quiet, very positive, self-collected irish schoolmaster, with that well-known air of genteel decorum and *bienséance* of the irish middle-class, with his 'if you pleases' and 'no thank-yous,' his ceremonious Mister-this and Mister-that, is remote from what must have been the strapping, dashing George Bernard Shaw of the shavian heyday. He is also quite unlike the romantic, aristocratical, magic-loving William Butler Yeats.

Shaw is much more a world-figure; but Joyce and Yeats are the prose and poetry respectively of the Ireland that culminated in the

Rebellion. Yeats is the chivalrous embodiment of 'celtic' romance, more of St Brandon than of Ossian, with all the grand manners of a spiritual Past that cannot be obliterated, though it wear thin, and of a dispossessed and persecuted people. Joyce is the cold and stagnant reality at which that people had at last arrived in its civilized Reservation, with all the snobbish pathos of such a condition, the intense desire to keep-up-appearances at all costs, to be ladylike and gentlemanly, in spite of a beggared position—above which that yeatsian emanation floats.

But on the purely personal side, Joyce possesses a good deal of the intolerant arrogance of the dominie, veiled with an elaborate decency beneath the formal calm of the jesuit, left over as a handy property from his early years of catholic romance—of that irish variety that is so english that it seems stranger to a continental almost than its english protestant counterpart.

The Ireland that culminated in the Rebellion reached that event, however, in a very divided state. There was an artificial, pseudo-historical air about the Rebellion, as there was inevitably about the movement of 'celtic' revival; it seemed to be forced and vamped up long after its poignant occasion had passed. As elsewhere in Europe, the fanatical 'nationalist' consciousness invoked, seemed belated and unreal. Joyce was, I understand, against Sinn Fein. In his autobiographical books you obtain an unambiguous expression of his attitude in the matter. In the *Portrait of the Artist*, where the nationalist, Davin, is talking to him, Stephen (the author, of whom that is a self-portrait as a young man) says:—

> 'My ancestors threw off their language and took another. They allowed a handful of foreigners to subject them. Do you fancy I am going to pay in my own life and person debts they made? What for?'
>
> 'For our freedom,' said Davin.
>
> 'No honourable and sincere man,' said Stephen, 'has given up to you his life and his affections from the days of Tone to those of Parnell but you sold him to the enemy or failed him in need or reviled him and left him for another. And you invite me to be one of you. I'd see you damned first.'

A little later Stephen remarks: 'You talk to me of nationality, language, religion. I shall try to fly by those nets.' So from the start the answer of Joyce to the militant nationalist was plain enough. And he showed himself in that a very shrewd realist indeed, beset as Irishmen have been for so long with every romantic temptation, always being invited by this interested party or that, to jump back into 'history.' So Joyce is neither of the militant 'patriot' type, nor yet a historical romancer. In spite of that he is very 'irish.' He is ready enough, as a literary artist, to stand for Ireland, and has wrapped himself up in a gigantic cocoon of local colour in *Ulysses*.

It is at this point that we reach one of the fundamental questions of value brought out by his work. Although entertaining the most studied contempt for his compatriots—individually and in the mass—whom he did not regard at all as exceptionally brilliant and sympathetic creatures (in a green historical costume, with a fairy hovering near), but as average human cattle with an irish accent instead of a scotch or welsh, it will yet be insisted on that his irishness is an important feature of his talent; and he certainly also does exploit his irishness and theirs.

The appreciation of any author is, of course, largely composed of adventitious sentiment. For his vogue to last, or ever to be a serious one, he must have some unusual literary gift. With that he reaches a considerable renown. But then people proceed to admire him for something equally possessed by a quantity of other people, or for reasons that have nothing to do with, or which even contradict, his gifts. So Englishmen or Frenchmen who are inclined to virulent 'nationalism,' and disposed to sentiment where local colour is concerned, will admire Joyce for his alleged identity with what he detached himself from and even repudiated, when it took the militant, Sinn Fein form. And Joyce, like a shrewd sensible man, will no doubt encourage them. That, however, will not at all help us to be clear about this very confused issue. Nor should we be very certain, if we left the matter in that state, in our valuation of Joyce. We should find ourselves substituting orthodox political reactions to the idea of fanatical 'nationalism' (which it is quite evident holds little reality for Joyce) for direct reactions to what is in his work a considerable achievement of art . . .

Before turning to the more personal factors in the composition of *Ulysses*, I will briefly state what I have been approaching in the first phase of my analysis.

I regard *Ulysses* as a *time-book*; and by that I mean that it lays its emphasis upon, for choice manipulates, and in a doctrinaire manner, the self-conscious time-sense, that has now been erected into a universal philosophy. This it does beneath the spell of a similar creative impulse to that by which Proust worked. The classical unities of time and place are buried beneath its scale, however, and in this All-life-in-a-day scheme there is small place for them. Yet at the outset they are solemnly insisted on as a guiding principle to be fanatically observed. And certainly some barbarous version of the classical formula is at work throughout, like a conserted *daimon* attending the author, to keep him obsessionally faithful to the time-place, or space-time, programme.

The genteel-demotic, native subject-matter of Mr Joyce assists him to a great deal of intense, sad, insipid, local colour. An early life-experience that had removed him from the small middle-class milieu would also have removed him from his local colour, and to a less extent from his time-factor. To this he adds the legendary clatter and bustle of Donnybrook Fair. Beyond that he is not above stealing a few fairies from Mr Yeats, and then sending them in the company of Dr Freud to ride a broomstick on the Brocken. Adventures of that order, in the middle of the book, take us still further from the ideal of the Unities, and both Space and Time temporarily evaporate. But on the whole the reader is conscious that he is beneath the intensive dictatorship of Space-time—the god of Professor Alexander and such a great number of people, in fact, that we can almost be said to be treading on holy ground when we compose ourselves to read a work dedicated to that deity, either in philosophy or fiction.

That Joyce and Proust are both dedicated to Time is generally appreciated, of course; Joyce is often compared to Proust on that score. Both Proust and Joyce exhibit, it is said, the exasperated time-sense of the contemporary man of the industrial age; which is undeniable, if the outward form of their respective work is alone considered. The ardent recapitulation of a dead thing—though so recently dead, and not on its own merits a very significant one—and as much the 'local colour' as what may be called the *local time*, ally them. But having got so far, I should put in a qualification which would, I think, unexpectedly discriminate these two methods.

*

195

I will interject at this point a note on the subject of the temporal equivalent of 'local colour,' since I have had occasion to refer to it once or twice. I will not enter into the confusing discussion of which is space and which time in any given complex. I will suppose that there is some partly discrete quality which can come under the separate head of 'time,' and so for certain purposes be something else than the 'local colour.'

This psychological time, or duration, this mood that is as fixed as the matter accompanying it, is as romantic and picturesque as is 'local colour,' and usually as shallow a thing as that. Some realization of this is essential. *We can posit a time-district, as it were, just as much as we can a place with its individual physical properties.* And neither the local colour, nor the local time of the *time-district*, is what is recorded *sub specie aeternitatis*, it is unnecessary to say.

Both may, however, become obsessions, and are so, I believe, to-day. But that is merely—that is my argument—because people are in process of being locked into both places *and* times. (This can be illustrated, where place is concerned, in the way that Signor Mussolini is locking the Italians into Italy, and refusing them passports for abroad.)

We are now sufficiently prepared and can educe the heart of this obscure organism that so overshadows contemporary thought, by showing its analogies. That the time-fanaticism is in some way connected with the nationalisms and the regionalisms which are politically so much in evidence, and so intensively cultivated, seems certain—since 'time' is also to some extent a region, or it can be regarded in that light. We have spoken of a *time-district*, and that is exact. Professor Whitehead uses the significant phrase 'mental climate.' This is by no means a fanciful affiliation; for *time* and *place* are the closest neighbours, and what happens to one is likely to be shared by the other. And if that is so, the *time-mind* would be much the same as the geographic one, fanatically circumscribing this or that territorial unit with a superstitious exclusiveness, an aggressive nationalist romance. Has not time-romance, or a fierce partisanship on behalf of a *time*, a family likeness, at least, with similar partisanship on behalf of a *place*?

And then, too, the so much mocked and detested non-nationalist, universal mind (whose politics would be goëthean, we can say, to place them, and whose highest tolerance would approximate to that best seen in the classical chinese intelligence) would have to be reckoned with—once the *time-mind* had been isolated by a thorough analysis, and its essential antagonisms exposed. These two types of mind would be found confronted, eternally hostile to each other, or at least eternally different—for the hostility would be more noticeable on the side of the partisan, the 'time,' mind, the mind of fashion, than on the side of the other. This is all that I shall say on this very interesting point, for the moment.

The philosophy of the space-timeist is identical with the old, and as many people had hoped, exploded, bergsonian philosophy of *psychological time* (or *durée*, as he called it). It is essential to grasp this continuity between the earlier flux of Bergson, with its Time-god, and the einsteinian flux, with its god, Space-time. Alexander, and his pupil Whitehead, are the best-known exponents, of philosophers writing in English, of these doctrines. It will not require a very close scrutiny of *Space Time and Deity*, for instance, and then of some characteristic book of Bergson's, to assure yourself that you are dealing with minds of the same stamp.

Temperamentally—emotionally, that is, and emotion is as important in philosophy as in other things—the earlier bergsonian, such as Péguy, for instance, and the relativist or space-timeist, are identical. The best testimony of this is the enthusiastic reception given by Bergson, the old time-philosopher, to Einstein, the later space-timeist. He recognized his god, Duration, cast into the imposing material of a physical theory, improved and amalgamated with Space, in a more insidious unity than he had been able to give to his paramount philosophic principle. Similarly the attitude of Whitehead, Alexander and so forth, where Bergson is concerned, is noticeably one of a considered respect, very different from the atmosphere of disrepute into which Bergson had fallen prior to the triumph of Relativity Theory. The so-called 'Emergent' principle of Lloyd Morgan, adopted by Alexander and the rest, is our old friend 'Creative Evolution,' under another name, and with a few additional attributes. 'Emergent Evolution' can for all practical purposes be regarded as synonymous with 'Creative Evolution.'

So from, say, the birth of Bergson to the present day, one vast orthodoxy has been in process of maturing in the world of science and philosophy. The material had already collected into a considerable patrimony by the time Bergson was ready to give it a philosophic form. The Darwinian Theory and all the background of nineteenth-century materialistic thought was already behind it. Under the characteristic headings Duration and Relativity the nineteenth-century mechanistic belief has now assumed a final form. It is there for any one to study at his leisure, and to take or leave. It will assume, from time to time, many new shapes, but it will certainly not change its essential nature again till its doomsday; for I believe that in it we have reached one of the poles of the human intelligence, the negative, as it were. So it is deeply rooted, very ancient, and quite defined.

In this part of my essay I am not developing my purely philosophic argument more fully than is necessary for the purpose of the literary criticism. I leave my attitude in the 'time' discussion as an announcement of principle, merely. Students of the philosophies cited will be able at once to supply the outline of the position such an announcement involves. And the reader who is not conversant with those theories would not be much the wiser at the end of such brief analysis as I should be able to supply in this place. The plan I am following is to help the reader to an inductive understanding of the principle involved, in the course of this analysis of its literary and artistic expression. With Spengler the more technical region is reached. And after that the philosophical analysis is begun. I hope to have interested the reader sufficiently in the questions involved to take him with me into that.

The psychological history of the triumph of an idea is interesting to follow; and it is necessary to acquire some knowledge of those processes. To understand how ideas succeed you must first consider what that 'success' implies, especially with reference to this particular age. You would have to ask yourself who those men are who profess them, the manner in which they get advertised, the degree of orthodoxy imposed, and by what means, at the moment. Then, behind that professional and immediate ring of supporters, the mass of people who blindly receive them on faith—as helpless, confronted with the imposing machinery of their popularization, as new-born children—they, too, would have to be studied, and their reactions registered.

Some such analysis of the domination achieved by an idea and how it ceases to be an idea, and becomes an *ideology*, as Napoleon called it, an instrument of popular government, has to be undertaken before you can hope to be in a position to meet on equal terms, without superstition, such prevalent intellectual fashions. If you are of that great majority who ask nothing better than to have intellectual fashions provided for them—with little handbooks describing which way up the idea (if a 'difficult' one) should be worn, whether it should be worn with a flourish or a languish, with a simper or a pout, with fanatical intensity or an easy catholic grace—then you will have no use, it is needless to say, for such an arduous analytical discipline. It is only if you belong to that minority who care for ideas for their own sake, if you are philosophic in the truest sense, possessing a personal life that is not satisfied with the old-clothes shop, or its companion, the vast ready-made emporium, that this procedure will have any meaning for you.

The physical or philosophical theory in the ascendant at any moment is humbly and reverently picked up, in an abridged, and usually meaningless, form, by the majority of people. So it was with Darwin, so it is with Einstein. Apart from questions of expert qualification, few people are able to appreciate all that is involved in such theories. There is certainly never a question in their mind of 'doubting' it. It is not a thing to doubt, but one that is either easy or impossible to understand, as the case may be. To repudiate it would be a still wilder presumption. It has to be 'studied' in the few spare minutes that most people consider may be saved for such things from parties, golf, motoring and bridge, or the Russian Ballet. Then they will say in conversation, 'It appears that there is no such thing as time'; or 'Everything is relative, Einstein says. I always thought it was.' (Relativity seldom involves much more than that to people.) More often than not the professors, who adopt and expound whatever theory has just succeeded, examine it as little. It *amuses* them; professors, like other people, have their amusements—their work is theirs. It is uncomfortable to be unorthodox, life is short, science is long, much longer than art; that is sufficient.

When such a dominant theory is *applied* in literature or in art, then, certainly, even less does any one grasp the steps by which that theory has entered the mind of the author or artist; has either been welcomed at once as a friend and a brother, has taken up its abode there as a conqueror by main force, or else has seduced the sensitive little

199

intelligence from the outside, from beneath the prudent casement from which the peeping-mind inside has watched, fascinated, the big romantic notion swelling invitingly; or has, on the other hand, as a matter of traffic and mutual profit, come to terms with a possible assistant or colleague. In short, any of the hundred ways and degrees in which assent is arrived at, and an intellectual monopoly or hegemony consummated, is even more arcane to the majority than is the theory itself.

Bergson and his time-philosophy exactly corresponds to Proust, the abstract for the other's concrete. There is so far no outstanding exponent in literature or art of einsteinian physics, for necessarily there is a certain interval, as things are, between the idea and the representation. But such a figure will no doubt occur; and further theorists of this great school will be accompanied by yet further artists, applying its philosophy to life. Or perhaps, since now the general outline of the cult is settled, and the changes within it will be incidental, largely, they may crop up simultaneously. Indeed, Proust and Joyce are examples to hand of how already it does not matter very much to what phase of the one great movement the interpreter belongs.

Without all the uniform pervasive growth of the time-philosophy starting from the little seed planted by Bergson, discredited, and now spreading more vigorously than ever, there would be no *Ulysses*, or there would be no *A La Recherche du Temps Perdu*. There would be no 'time-composition' of Miss Stein; no fugues in words. In short, Mr Joyce is very strictly of the school of Bergson-Einstein, Stein-Proust. He is of the great time-school they represent. His book is a *time-book*, as I have said, in that sense. He has embraced the time-doctrine very completely. And it is as the critic of that doctrine and of that school that I have approached the analysis of his writings up to date. (I insert this last time-clause because there is no reason at all to suppose that he may not be influenced in turn by my criticism; and, indeed, I hope it may be so, for he would be a very valuable adherent.)

Yet that the time-sense is really exasperated in Joyce in the fashion that it is in Proust, Dada, Pound or Miss Stein, may be doubted. He has a very keen preoccupation with the Past, it is certain; he does lay things down side by side, carefully dated; and added to that, he has some rather loosely and romantically held notion of periodicity. But I believe that all these things amount to with him is this: as a careful, even meticulous, craftsman, with a long training of doctrinaire naturalism, the detail—the time-detail as much as anything else—assumes an exaggerated importance for him. And I am sure that he would be put to his trumps to say how he came by much of the time-machinery that he possesses. Until he was told, I dare say that he did not know he had it, even; for he is 'an instinctive,' like Pound, in that respect; there is not very much reflection going on at any time inside the head of Mr James Joyce. That is indeed the characteristic condition of *the craftsman*, pure and simple.

And that is what Joyce is above all things, essentially the craftsman. It is a thing more common, perhaps, in painting or the plastic arts than in literature. I do not mean by this that he works harder or more thoroughly than other people, but that he is not so much an inventive intelligence as an executant. He is certainly very 'shoppy', and professional to a fault, though in the midst of the amateurisms of the day it is a fault that can easily be forgiven.

What stimulates him is *ways of doing things*, and technical processes, and not *things to be done*. Between the various things to be done he shows a true craftsman's impartiality. He is become so much a writing-specialist that it matters very little to him *what* he writes, or what idea or world-view he expresses, so long as he is trying his hand at this manner and that, and displaying his enjoyable virtuosity. Strictly speaking, he has none at all, no special point of view, or none worth mentioning. It is such people that the creative intelligence fecundates and uses; and at present that intelligence is political, and its stimuli are masked ideologies. He is only a tool, an instrument, in short. That is why such a sensitive medium as Joyce, working in such a period, requires the attention of the independent critic.

So perhaps it is easy to see how, without much realizing what was happening, Joyce arrived where he did. We can regard it as a diathetic phenomenon partly—the craftsman is susceptible and unprotected. There are even slight, though not very grave, symptoms of disorder in his art. The painful preoccupation with the *exact* place of things in a room, for instance, could be mildly matched in his writing. The *things themselves* by which he is surrounded lose, for the hysterical subject, their importance, or even meaning. Their *position* absorbs all the attention of his mind. Some such uneasy pedantry, in a mild form, is likely to assail any conscientious craftsman—especially in an intensive 'space-time' atmosphere, surrounded by fanatical space-timeists. The poor craftsman has never been in such peril as to-day, for it is a frantic hornpipe indeed that his obedient legs are compelled to execute. But otherwise Joyce, with his highly-developed *physical* basis, is essentially sane.

The method that underlies *Ulysses* is known as the 'telling from the inside.' As that description denotes, it is psychological. Carried out in the particular manner used in *Ulysses*, it lands the reader inside an Aladdin's cave of incredible bric-à-brac in which a dense mass of dead stuff is collected, from 1901 toothpaste, a bar or two of Sweet Rosie O'Grady, to pre-nordic architecture. An immense *nature-morte is the result*. This ensues from the method of confining the reader in a circumscribed psychological space into which several encyclopaedias have been emptied. It results from the constipation induced in the movement of the narrative.

The amount of *stuff*—unorganized brute material—that the more active principle of drama has to wade through, under the circumstances, slows it down to the pace at which, inevitably, the sluggish tide of the author's bric-à-brac passes the observer, at the saluting post, or in this case, the reader. It is a suffocating, moeotic expanse of objects, all of them lifeless, the sewage of a Past twenty years old, all neatly arranged in a meticulous sequence. The newspaper in which Mr Bloom's bloater is wrapped up, say, must press on to the cold body of the fish, reversed, the account of the bicycle accident that was reported on the fated day chosen for this Odyssey; or that at least is the idea.

At the end of a long reading of *Ulysses* you feel that it is the very nightmare of the naturalistic method that you have been experiencing. Much as you may cherish the merely physical enthusiasm that expresses itself in this stupendous outpouring of *matter*, or *stuff*, you wish, on the spot, to be transported to some more abstract region for a time, where the dates of the various toothpastes, the brewery and laundry receipts, the growing pile of punched 'bus-tickets, the growing holes in the baby's socks and the darn that repairs them, assume less importance. It is your impulse perhaps quickly to get your mind where there is nothing but air and rock, however inhospitable and featureless, and a little timeless, too. You will have had a glut, for the moment (if you have really persevered), of *matter*, procured you by the turning on of all this river of what now is rubbish, but which was not *then*, by the obsessional application of the naturalistic method associated with the exacerbated time-sense. And the fact that you were not in the open air, but closed up inside somebody else's head, will not make things any better. It will have been your catharsis of the objective accumulations that obstinately collect in even the most active mind.

Now in the graphic and plastic arts that stage of fanatic naturalism long ago has been passed. All the machinery appropriate to its production has long since been discarded, luckily for the pure creative impulse of the artist. The nineteenth-century naturalism of that obsessional, fanatical order is what you find on the one hand in *Ulysses*. On the other, you have a great variety of recent influences enabling Mr Joyce to use it in the way that he did.

The effect of this rather fortunate confusion was highly stimulating to Joyce, who really got the maximum out of it, with an appetite that certainly will never be matched again for the actual *matter* revealed in his composition, or proved to have been lengthily secreted there. It is like a gigantic victorian quilt or antimacassar. Or it is the voluminous curtain that fell, belated (with the alarming momentum of a ton or two of personally organized rubbish), upon the victorian scene. So rich was its delivery, its pent-up outpouring so vehement, that it will remain, eternally cathartic, a monument like a record diarrhoea. No one who looks *at* it will ever want to look *behind* it. It is the sardonic catafalque of the victorian world.

Two opposite things were required for this result. Mr Joyce could never have performed this particular feat if he had not been, in his make-up, extremely immobile; and yet, in contradiction to that, very open to new technical influences. It is the *craftsman* in Joyce that is progressive; but the *man* has not moved since his early days in Dublin. He is on that side a 'young man' in some way embalmed. His technical adventures do not, apparently, stimulate him to think. On the contrary, what he thinks seems to be of a conventional and fixed order, as though perhaps not to embarrass the neighbouring evolution of his highly progressive and eclectic craftsmanship.

So he collected like a cistern in his youth the last stagnant pumpings of victorian anglo-irish life. This he held steadfastly intact for fifteen years or more—then when he was ripe, as it were, he discharged it, in a dense mass, to his eternal glory. That was *Ulysses*. Had the twenty-year-old Joyce of the *Dubliners* not remained almost miraculously intact, we should never have witnessed this peculiar spectacle.

That is, I believe, the true account of how this creative event occurred with Joyce; and, if that is so, it will be evident that we are in the presence of a very different phenomenon from Proust. Proust *returned* to the *temps perdu*. Joyce never left them. He discharged it as freshly as though the time he wrote about were still present, because it was *his* present. It rolled out with all the aplomb and vivacity of a contemporary experience, assisted in its slick discharge by the latest technical devices.

So though Joyce has written a time-book, he has done it, I believe, to some extent, by accident. Proust, on the contrary, was stimulated to all his efforts precisely by the thought of compassing a specifically time-creation—the *Recherche du Temps Perdu*. The unconscious artist has, in this case, the best of it, to my mind. Proust, on the other hand, romanticizes his Past, where Joyce (whose Present it is) does not.

To create new beauty, and to supply a new material, is the obvious affair of art of any kind to-day. But that is a statement that by itself would convey very little. Without stopping to unfold that now, I will summarize what I understand by its opposite. Its opposite is that that thrives upon the *time-philosophy* that it has invented for itself, or which has been imposed upon it or provided for it.

The inner meaning of the *time-philosophy*, from whatever standpoint you approach it, and however much you paste it over with confusing advertisements of 'life,' of 'organism,' is the doctrine of a mechanistic universe; periodic; timeless, or nothing but 'time,' whichever you prefer; and, above all, essentially *dead*. A certain *deadness*, a lack of nervous power, an aversion to anything suggesting animal vigour, characterizes all the art, as has already been pointed out, issuing from this philosophy. Or in the exact mixing in the space-timeist scheme of all the 'matter' and all the 'organism' together, you get to a sort of vegetable or vermiform *average*. It is very mechanical; and according to our human, aristocratic standards of highly-organized life, it is very dead.

The theoretic truth that the time-philosophy affirms is a mechanistic one. It is the conception of an aged intelligence, grown mechanical and living upon routine and memory, essentially; its tendency, in its characteristic working, is infallibly to transform the living into the machine, with a small, unascertained, but uninteresting margin of freedom. It is the fruit, of course, of the puritan mind, born in the nineteenth century upon the desolate principles promoted by the too-rapidly mechanized life of the European.

I will now turn to the scandalous element in *Ulysses*, its supposed obscenity. Actually it appears to me that the mind of Joyce is more chaste than most. Once you admit the licence that, at the start, Joyce set out to profit by, it is surprising how very little 'sex' matter there is in his pages. What is there is largely either freudian echoes (they had to enter into it), or else it is horse-play of a schoolboy or public-house order. The motif of the house-drain is once and for all put in its place, and not mentioned again. It is the fault of the reader if that page or two dealing with it assume, in retrospect, proportions it has not, as a fact, in Joyce's pages. That passage can be regarded in the light of the reply of Antigonus to the poet Hermodorus, when the latter had described him as the son of the Sun.

I will next take up in turn a few further items of importance, expiscating them one by one. Joyce is not a moralist, but he has a great relish, on the other hand, for politics. Indeed, Lady Bolingbroke's remark about Pope, that he 'played the politician about cabbages and turnips' (or as somebody else remarked, 'he hardly drank tea without a stratagem'), could be applied to the author of *Ulysses*—the mere name suggests a romantic predilection for guile.

He could claim another affinity with Pope—namely, that although a witty writer, he is, as far as his private and personal legend is concerned, a man of one story. 'One apothegm only stands upon record,' Johnson writes of Pope; it was directed at Patrick. Joyce has one story to his credit, and it is at the expense of Yeats. As it is the general custom, even in the briefest account of Joyce, to tell this story, lest I should be regarded as imperfectly documented, I will give it here. When Joyce was about twenty years old he was very hard up, we are told, and he decided to go to Yeats and see if that gentleman would do anything to help him. He seems to have foreboded the result, and provided himself with a plan of action in the event of a rebuff. The appointed time arrived.

As he entered the room, sure enough he read on the face of Mr Yeats the determination *not* to help him. Thereupon he bore down on Yeats, bade him good morning, and immediately inquired how old he was. On learning the extent of Yeats's seniority, with a start of shocked surprise, he mournfully shook his head, exclaimed, 'I fear I have come too late! I can do nothing to help you!' and, turning on his heel, left the apartment, the tables neatly turned.

A similarly unacceptable candour perceived that the tone of the narrator in Hemingway's early work is that of an animal speaking, and then identified the animal as an ox. One can understand Hemingway's fury when he read the piece, yet the image as it is developed, and combined with discussion of the 'neutralised vowel', gives a unique insight into the nature of Hemingway's writing. The piece comes from *Men Without Art* (1934), which includes also an essay on William Faulkner.

from MEN WITHOUT ART

Ernest Hemingway: The 'Dumb Ox'

Ernest Hemingway is a very considerable artist in prose-fiction. Besides this, or with this, his work possesses a penetrating quality, like an animal speaking. Compared often with Hemingway, William Faulkner is an excellent, big-strong, novelist: but a conscious artist he cannot be said to be. Artists are made, not born: but he is considerably older, I believe, than Hemingway, so it is not that. But my motive for discussing these two novelists has not been to arrive at estimates of that sort.

A quality in the work of the author of *Men Without Women* suggests that we are in the presence of a writer who is not merely a conspicuous chessman in the big-business book-game of the moment, but something much finer than that. Let me attempt to isolate that quality for you, in such a way as not to damage it too much: for having set out to demonstrate the political significance of this artist's work, I shall, in the course of that demonstration, resort to a dissection of it—not the best way, I am afraid, to bring out the beauties of the finished product. This dissection is, however, necessary for my purpose here. 'I have a weakness for Ernest Hemingway,' as the egregious Miss Stein says:[1] it is not agreeable to me to pry into his craft, but there is no help for it if I am to reach certain important conclusions.

But *political significance!* That is surely the last thing one would expect to find in such books as *In Our Time, The Sun Also Rises, Men Without Women,* or *A Farewell to Arms.* And indeed it is difficult to imagine a writer whose mind is more entirely closed to politics than is Hemingway's. I do not suppose he has ever heard of the Five-Year Plan, though I dare say he knows that artists pay no income tax in Mexico, and is quite likely to be following closely the agitation of the Mexican matadors to get themselves recognized as 'artists' so that they may pay no income tax. I expect he has heard of Hitler, but thinks of him mainly, if he is acquainted with the story, as the Boche who went down into a cellar with another Boche and captured thirty Frogs and came back with an Iron Cross. He probably knows that his friend Pound writes a good many letters every week to American papers on the subject of Social Credit, but I am sure Pound has never succeeded in making him read a line of *Credit-Power and Democracy.* He is interested in the sports of death, in the sad things that happen to those engaged in the sports of love—in sand-sharks and in Wilson-spoons—in war, but *not* in the things that cause war, or the people who profit by it, or in the ultimate human destinies involved in it. He lives, or affects to live, *submerged.* He is in the multitudinous ranks of *those to whom things happen*—terrible things of course, and of course stoically borne. He has never heard, or affects never to have heard, that there is another and superior element, inhabited by a type of unnatural men which preys upon that of the submerged type. Or perhaps it is not quite a submerged mankind to which he belongs, or affects to belong, but to something of the sort described in one of Faulkner's war stories: 'But after twelve years,' Faulkner writes, 'I think of us as bugs in the surface of the water, isolant and aimless and unflagging. Not on the

---

[1] *The Autobiography of Alice B. Toklas.*

surface; in it, within that line of demarcation not air and not water, sometimes submerged, sometimes not.'[2] (What a stupid and unpleasant word 'isolant' is! Hemingway would be incapable of using such a word.) But—twelve, fifteen years afterwards—to be *submerged*, most of the time, is Hemingway's idea. It is a little bit of an *art pur* notion, but it is, I think, extremely effective, in his case. Faulkner is much less preoccupied with art for its own sake, and although he has obtained his best successes by submerging himself again (in an intoxicating and hysterical fluid) he does not like being submerged quite as well as Hemingway, and dives rather because he is compelled to dive by public opinion, I imagine, than because he feels at home in the stupid medium of the sub-world, the *bêtise* of the herd. Hemingway has really taken up his quarters there, and has mastered the medium entirely, so that he is of it and yet not of it in a very satisfactory way.

Another manner of looking at it would be to say that Ernest Hemingway is the Noble Savage of Rousseau, but a white version, the simple American man. That is at all events the rôle that he has chosen, and he plays it with an imperturbable art and grace beyond praise.

It is not perhaps necessary to say that Hemingway's art is an art of the surface—and, as I look at it, none the worse for that. It is almost purely an art of action, and of very violent action, which is another qualification. Faulkner's is that too: but violence with Hemingway is deadly matter-of-fact (as if there were only violent action and nothing else in the world): whereas with Faulkner it is an excited crescendo of psychological working-up of a sluggish and not ungentle universe, where there *might* be something else than high-explosive—if it were given a Chinaman's chance, which it is not. The latter is a far less artistic purveyor of violence. He does it well: but as to the manner, he does it in a way that any fool could do it. Hemingway, on the other hand, serves it up like the master of this form of art that he is, immeasurably more effective than Faulkner—good as he is; or than say the Irish novelist O'Flaherty—who is a *raffiné* too, or rather a two-gun man; Hemingway really banishes melodrama (except for his absurd escapes, on a Hollywood pattern, in *A Farewell to Arms*).

*

[2] *Ad Astra*. William Faulkner.

To find a parallel to *In Our Time* or *A Farewell to Arms* you have to go to *Colomba* or to *Chronique du règne de Charles ix*: and in one sense Prosper Merimée supplies the historical key to these two ex-soldiers—married, in their literary craft, to a theatre of action *à l'outrance*. The scenes at the siege of La Rochelle in the *Chronique du règne de Charles ix* for instance: in the burning of the mill when the ensign is roasted in the window, that is the Hemingway subject-matter to perfection—a man melted in his armour like a shell-fish in its shell—melted lobster in its red armour.

> S'ils tentaient de sauter par les fenêtres, ils tombaient dans les flammes, ou bien étaient reçus sur la pointe des piques ... Un enseigne, revêtu d'une armure complète, essaya de sauter comme les autres par une fenêtre étroite. Sa cuirasse se terminait, suivant une mode alors assez commune, par une espèce de jupon en fer qui couvrait les cuisses et le ventre, et s'élargissait comme le haut d'un entonnoir, de manière à permettre de marcher facilement. La fenêtre n'était pas assez large pour laisser passer cette partie de son armure, et l'enseigne, dans son trouble, s'y était précipité avec tant de violence, qu'il se trouva avoir la plus grande partie du corps en dehors sans pouvoir remuer, et pris comme dans un étau. Cependant les flammes montaient jusqu'à lui, échauffaient son armure, et l'y brûlaient lentement comme dans une fournaise ou dans ce fameux taureau d'airain inventé par Phalaris.[3]

Compare this with the following:

> We were in a garden at Mons. Young Buckley came in with his patrol from across the river. The first German I saw climbed up over the garden wall. We waited till he got one leg over and then potted him. He had so much equipment on and looked awfully surprised and fell down into the garden. Then three more came over further down the wall. We shot them. They all came just like that.[4]

'In no century would Prosper Merimée have been a theologian or metaphysician,' and if that is true of Merimée, it is at least equally true of his American prototype. But their 'formulas' sound rather the same,

[3] *Chronique du règne de Charles ix*. Merimée.
[4] *In Our Time*. Hemingway.

indifferent in politics . . . all the while he is feeding all his scholarly curiosity, his imagination, the very eye, with the, to him ever delightful, relieving, reassuring spectacle, of those straightforward forces in human nature, which are also matters of fact. There is the formula of Merimée! the enthusiastic amateur of rude, crude, naked force in men and women wherever it could be found . . . there are no half-lights . . . Sylla, the false Demetrius, Carmen, Colomba, that impassioned self within himself, have no atmosphere. Painfully distinct in outline, inevitable to sight, unrelieved, there they stand, like solitary mountain forms on some hard, perfectly transparent day. What Merimée gets around his singularly sculpturesque creations is neither more nor less than empty space.[5]

I have quoted the whole of this passage because it gives you 'the formula,' equally for the author of *Carmen* and of *The Sun Also Rises*—namely *the enthusiastic amateur of rude, crude, naked force in men and women*: but it also brings out very well, subsequently, the nature of the radical and extremely significant *difference* existing between these two men, of differing nations and epochs—sharing so singularly a taste for physical violence and for fine writing, but nothing else. Between them there is this deep gulf fixed: that gifted he of today is 'the man that things are done to'—even the 'I' in *The Sun Also Rises* allows his Jew puppet to knock him about and 'put him to sleep' with a crash on the jaw, and this first person singular covers a very aimless, will-less person, to say the least of it: whereas that *he* of the world of *Carmen* (so much admired by Nietzsche for its bright Latin violence and directness—*la gaya scienza*) or of Corsican vendetta, he was in love with *will*, as much as with violence: he did not celebrate in his stories a spirit that suffered bodily injury and mental disaster with the stoicism of an athletic clown in a particularly brutal circus—or of oxen (however robust) beneath a crushing yoke: *he*, the inventor of Colomba, belonged to a race of men for whom action meant *their* acting, with all the weight and momentum of the whole of their being: *he* of post-Napoleonic France celebrated intense spiritual energy and purpose, using physical violence as a mere means to that only half-animal ideal. *Sylla, Demetrius, Colomba, even de Mergy,* summon to our mind a world bursting with purpose—even if always upon the personal and very animal plane, and with no more universal

5 *Miscellaneous Studies*. Walter Pater.

ends: while Hemingway's books, on the other hand, scarcely contain a figure who is not in some way futile, clown-like, passive, and above all *purposeless*. His world of men and women (*in violent action*, certainly) is completely empty of will. His puppets are leaves, *very violently* blown hither and thither; drugged or at least deeply intoxicated phantoms of a sort of matter-of-fact shell-shock.

In *A Farewell to Arms* the hero is a young American who has come over to Europe for the fun of the thing, as an alternative to baseball, to take part in the Sport of Kings. It has not occurred to him that it is no longer the sport of kings, but the turning-point in the history of the earth at which he is assisting, when men must either cease thinking like children and abandon such sports, or else lose their freedom for ever, much more effectively than any mere *king* could ever cause them to lose it. For him, it remains 'war' in the old-fashioned semi-sporting sense. Throughout this ghastly event, he proves himself a thoroughgoing sport, makes several hairbreadth, Fenimore Cooper-like, escapes, but never from first to last betrays a spark of intelligence. Indeed, his physical stoicism, admirable as it is, is as nothing to his really heroic imperviousness to thought. This 'war'—Gallipoli, Passchendaele, Caporetto—is just another 'scrap.' The Anglo-Saxon American—the 'Doughboy'—and the Anglo-Saxon Tommy—join hands, in fact, outrival each other in a stolid determination absolutely to ignore, come what may, what all this is about. Whoever may be in the secrets of destiny—may indeed be destiny itself—*they* are not nor ever will be. They are an integral part of that world *to whom things happen*: they are not those who cause or connive at the happenings, and that is perfectly clear.

> *Pack up your troubles in your old kit bag,*
> *Smile boys, that's the style*

and *keep smiling*, what's more, from ear to ear, *a should–I–worry?* 'good sport' smile, as do the Hollywood Stars when they are being photographed, as did the poor Bairnsfather 'Tommy'—the 'muddied oaf at the goal'—of all oafishness!

I hope this does not seem irrelevant to you: it is not, let me reassure you, but very much the contrary. The roots of all these books are in the War of 1914–1918, as much those of Faulkner as those of Hemingway: it would be ridiculous of course to say that either

211

of these two highly intelligent ex-soldiers shared the 'oafish' mentality altogether: but the war-years were a democratic, a *levelling*, school, and both come from a pretty thoroughly 'levelled' nation, where personality is the thing least liked. The rigid organization of the communal life as revealed in *Middletown*, for instance (or such a phenomenon as N.R.A.) is akin to the military state. So *will*, as expressed in the expansion of the individual, is not a thing we should expect to find illustrated by a deliberately typical American writer.

Those foci of passionate personal energy which we find in Merimée, we should look for in vain in the pages of Hemingway or Faulkner: in place of Don José or of Colomba we get a pack of drugged or intoxicated marionettes. These differences are exceedingly important. But I shall be dealing with that more carefully in my next chapter.

So any attempt to identify 'the formula' for Prosper Merimée with that of Ernest Hemingway would break down. You are led at once to a realization of the critical difference between these two universes of discourse, both employing nothing but physical terms; of how an appetite for the extremity of violence exists in both, but in the one case it is personal ambition, family pride, romantic love that are at stake, and their satisfaction is violently sought and undertaken, whereas in the other case purposeless violence, for the sake of the 'kick', is pursued and recorded, and the 'thinking subject' is to regard himself as nothing more significant than a ripple beneath the breeze upon a pond.

If we come down to the manner, specifically to the style, in which these sensational impressions are conveyed, again most interesting discoveries await us: for, especially with Mr Hemingway, the story is told in the tone, and with the vocabulary, of the persons described. The rhythm is the anonymous folk-rhythm of the urban proletariat. Mr Hemingway is, self-consciously, a folk-prose-poet in the way that Robert Burns was a folk-poet. But what is curious about this is that the modified *Beach-la-mar* in which he writes is, more or less, the speech that is proposed for everybody in the future—it is a volapuk which probably will be ours tomorrow. For if the chief executive of the United States greets the Roman Catholic democratic leader (Al Smith) with the exclamation 'Hallo old potato!' today, the English political leaders will be doing so the day after tomorrow. And the Anglo-Saxon *Beach-la-mar* of the future will not be quite the same thing as Chaucer or Dante, contrasted with the learned tongue. For the latter was the speech of a race rather than of a class, whereas our 'vulgar tongue' will really be *vulgar*.

But in the case of Hemingway the folk-business is very seriously complicated by a really surprising fact. He has suffered an overmastering influence, which cuts his work off from any other, except that of his mistress (for his master has been a *mistress*!). So much is this the case, that their destinies (his and that of the person who so strangely hypnotized him with her repeating habits and her *faux-naif* prattle) are for ever interlocked. His receptivity was so abnormally pronounced (even as a craftsman, this capacity for being *the person that things are done to* rather than the person who naturally initiates what is to be done to others, was so marked) and the affinity thus disclosed was found so powerful! I don't like speaking about this, for it is such a first-class complication, and yet it is in a way so irrelevant to the spirit which informs his work and must have informed it had he never made this apparently overwhelming 'contact.' But there it is: if you ask yourself how you would be able to tell a page of Hemingway, if it were unexpectedly placed before you, you would be compelled to answer, *Because it would be like Miss Stein!* And if you were asked how you would know it was not by Miss Stein, you would say, *Because it would probably be about prize-fighting, war, or the bull-ring, and Miss Stein does not write about war, boxing or bull-fighting!*

It is very uncomfortable in real life when people become so captivated with somebody else's tricks that they become a sort of caricature or echo of the other: and it is no less embarrassing in books, at least when one entertains any respect for the victim of the fascination. But let us take a passage or two and get this over—it is very unpleasant. Let us take Krebs—the 'he' in this passage is Krebs, a returned soldier in a Hemingway story:

When he was in town their appeal to him was not very strong. He did not like them when he saw them in the Greek's ice-cream parlor. He did not want them themselves really. They were too complicated. There was something else. Vaguely he wanted a girl but he did not want to have to work to get her. He would have liked to have a girl but he did not want to have to spend a long time getting her. He did not want to get into the

213

intrigue and the politics. He did not want to have to do any courting. He did not want to tell any more lies. It wasn't worth it.

He did not want any consequences. He did not want any consequences ever again. He wanted to live along without consequences. Besides he did not really need a girl. The army had taught him that. It was all right to pose as though you had to have a girl. Nearly everybody did that. But it wasn't true. You did not need a girl. That was the funny thing. First a fellow boasted how girls mean nothing to him, that he never thought of them, that they could not touch him. Then a fellow boasted that he could not get along without girls, that he had to have them all the time, that he could not go to sleep without them.

That was all a lie. It was all a lie both ways. You did not need a girl unless you thought about them. He learned that in the army. Then sooner or later you always got one. When you were really ripe for a girl you always got one. You did not have to think about it. Sooner or later it would come. He had learned that in the army.

Now he would have liked a girl if she had come to him and not wanted to talk. But here at home it was all too complicated. He knew he could never get through it all again. It was not worth the trouble. That was the thing about French girls and German girls. There was not all this talking. You couldn't talk much and you did not need to talk. It was simple and you were friends. He thought about France and then he began to think about Germany. On the whole he liked Germany better. He did not want to leave Germany. He did not want to come home. Still, he had come home. He sat on the front porch.

He liked the girls that were walking along the other side of the street. He liked the look of them much better than the French girls or the German girls. But the world they were in was not the world he was in. He would like to have one of them. But it was not worth it. They were such a nice pattern. He liked the pattern. It was exciting. But he would not go through all the talking. He did not want one badly enough. He liked to look at them all, though. It was not worth it.[6]

So much for Krebs: now open Miss Stein and 'meet' Melanctha.

Rose was lazy but not dirty, and Sam was careful but not fussy, and then there was Melanctha . . . When Rose's baby was coming to be born,

---

[6] *In Our Time*. Ernest Hemingway.

Rose came to stay in the house where Melanctha Herbert lived just then
... Rose went there to stay, so that she might have the doctor from the
hospital ... Melanctha Herbert had not made her life all simple like Rose
Johnson. Melanctha had not found it easy with herself to make her wants
and what she had, agree.

Melanctha Herbert was always losing what she had in wanting all the
things she saw. Melanctha was always being left when she was not leaving
others.

Melanctha Herbert always loved too hard and much too often. She
was always full with mystery and subtle movements ... etc., etc., etc.[7]

Or here is a typical bit from *Composition as Explanation*:

There is singularly nothing that makes a difference a difference in
beginning and in the middle and in ending except that each generation
has something different at which they are all looking. By this I mean so
simply that anybody knows it that composition is the difference which
makes each and all of them then different from other generations and
this is what makes everything different otherwise they are all alike and
everybody knows it because everybody says it.[8]

There is no possibility, I am afraid, of slurring over this. It is just
a thing that you have to accept as an unfortunate handicap in an artist
who is in some respects above praise. Sometimes it is less pronounced,
there are occasions when it is *almost* absent—Krebs, for instance, is a
full-blooded example of Hemingway steining away for all he is worth.
But it is never quite absent.

How much does it matter? If we blot out Gertrude Stein, and
suppose she does not exist, does this part of Hemingway's equipment
help or not? We must answer *Yes* I think. It does seem to help a good
deal: many of his best effects are obtained by means of it. It is so much
a part of his craft, indeed, that it is difficult now to imagine Hemingway
without this mannerism. He has never taken it over into a gibbering and
baboonish stage as has Miss Stein. He has kept it as a valuable oddity,
even if a flagrantly borrowed one—ever present it is true, but one to

[7] *Three Lives*. Gertrude Stein.
[8] *Composition as Explanation*. Gertrude Stein.

which we can easily get used and come to like even as a delightfully clumsy engine of innocence. I don't mind it very much.

To say that, near to communism as we all are, it cannot matter, and is indeed praiseworthy, for a celebrated artist to take over, lock, stock and barrel from another artist the very thing for which he is mainly known, seems to me to be going too far in the denial of the person, or the individual—especially as in a case of this sort, the trick is after all, in the first instance, a *personal* trick. Such a practice must result, if universally indulged in, in hybrid forms or monstrosities.

And my main criticism, indeed, of the *steining* of Hemingway is that it does impose upon him an ethos—*the Stein ethos*, as it might be called. With Stein's bag of tricks he also takes over a *Weltanschauung*, which may not at all be his, and does in fact seem to contradict his major personal quality. This infantile, dull-witted, dreamy stutter compels whoever uses it to conform to the infantile, dull-witted type. He passes over into the category of *those to whom things are done*, from that of those who execute—if the latter is indeed where he originally belonged. One might even go so far as to say that this brilliant Jewish lady had made a *clown* of him by teaching Ernest Hemingway her baby-talk! So it is a pity. And it is very difficult to know where Hemingway proper begins and Stein leaves off as an artist. It is an uncomfortable situation for the critic, especially for one who 'has a weakness' for the male member of this strange spiritual partnership, and very much prefers him to the female.

Hemingway's two principal books, *The Sun Also Rises* (for English publication called *Fiesta*) and *A Farewell to Arms*, are delivered in the first person singular. What that involves may not be at once apparent to those who have not given much attention to literary composition. But it is not at all difficult to explain. Suppose you, Raymond Robinson, sit down to write a romance; subject-matter, the War. You get your 'I' started off, say just before the outbreak of war, and then there is the outbreak, and then 'I flew to the nearest recruiting station and joined the army' you write. Then the 'I' goes off to the Western Front (or the Italian Front) and you will find yourself writing 'I seized the Boche by the throat with one hand and shot him in the stomach with the other,' or whatever it is you imagine your 'I' as doing. But this 'I', the reader will learn, does not bear the name on the title page, namely Raymond Robinson. He is called Geoffrey Jones. The reader will think, 'that is only a thin disguise. It is Robinson's personal experience all right!'

Now this difficulty (if it be a difficulty) is very much enhanced if (for some reason) Geoffrey Jones is *always* doing exactly the things that Raymond Robinson is known to have done. If Raymond Robinson fought gallantly at Caporetto, for instance, then Geoffrey Jones—with the choice of the whole earth at war to choose from—is at Caporetto too. If Raymond Robinson takes to the sport of bull-fighting, sure enough Geoffrey Jones—the 'I' of the novel—is there in the bull-ring too, as the night follows day. This, in fine, has been the case with Hemingway and *his* First-person-singular.

Evidently, in this situation—possessing a First-person-singular that invariably copies you in this flattering way—something must be done about it. The *First-person-singular* has to be endowed so palpably with qualities that could by no stretch of the imagination belong to its author that no confusion is possible. Upon this principle the 'I' of *The Sun Also Rises* is described as sexually impotent, which is a complete alibi, of course, for Hemingway.

But there is more than this. The sort of First-person-singular that Hemingway invariably invokes is a dull-witted, bovine, monosyllabic simpleton. This lethargic and stuttering dummy he conducts, or pushes from behind, through all the scenes that interest him. This burlesque First-person-singular behaves in them like a moronesque version of his brilliant author. He *Steins* up and down the world, with the big lustreless ruminatory orbs of a Picasso doll-woman (of the semi-classic type Picasso patented, with enormous hands and feet). It is, in short, the very dummy that is required for the literary mannerism of Miss Stein! It is the incarnation of the Stein-stutter—the male incarnation, it is understood.

But this constipated, baffled, 'frustrated'—yes, deeply and Freudianly 'frustrated'—this wooden-headed, leaden-witted, heavy-footed, loutish and oafish marionette—peering dully out into the surrounding universe like a great big bloated five-year-old—pointing at this and pointing at that—uttering simply 'CAT!'—'HAT!'—'FOOD!'—'SWEETIE!'—is, as a companion, infectious. His author has perhaps not been quite immune. Seen for ever through his nursery spectacles, the values

217

of life accommodate themselves, even in the mind of his author, to the limitations and peculiar requirements of this highly idiosyncratic puppet.

So the political aspects of Hemingway's work (if, as I started by saying, one can employ such a word as *political* in connection with a thing that is so divorced from reality as a super-innocent, queerly-sensitive, village-idiot of a few words and fewer ideas) have to be sought, if anywhere, in the personality of this *First-person-singular*, imposed upon him largely by the Stein-manner.

———

We can return to the folk-prose problem now and face all the questions that the 'done gones' and 'sorta gonnas' present. Mr H.L. Mencken in his well-known, extremely competent and exhaustive treatise, *The American Language* (a classic in this field of research, first published fifteen years ago) affirmed that the American dialect had not yet come to the stage where it could be said to have acquired charm for 'the purists.' If used (at that time) in narrative literature it still possessed only the status of a disagreeable and socially-inferior jargon, like the cockney occurring in a Dickens novel—or as it is still mostly used in William Faulkner's novels, never outside of inverted commas; the novelist, having invoked it to convey the manner of speech of his rustic or provincial puppets, steps smartly away and resumes the narrative in the language of Macaulay or Horace Walpole, more or less.

'In so far as it is apprehended at all,' Mencken wrote in 1920, 'it is only in the sense that Irish-English was apprehended a generation ago—that is, as something uncouth and comic. But that is the way that new dialects always come in—through a drum-fire of cackles. Given the poet, there may suddenly come a day when our *theirns* and *would 'a hads* will take on the barbaric stateliness of the peasant locution of old Maurya in "Riders to the Sea." '9

The reason that the dialect of the Aran Islands, or that used by Robert Burns, was so different from cockney or from the English educated speech was because it was a mixture of English and another language,

9 *The American Language.*

Gaelic or lowland Scotch, and with the intermixture of foreign words went a literal translation of foreign idioms and the distortions arrived at by a tongue accustomed to another language. It was 'broken-English,' in other words, not 'low-English,' or slum-English, as is cockney.

Americans are today un-English in blood—whatever names they may bear: and in view of this it is surprising how intact the English language remains in the United States. But the *Beach-la-mar*, as he calls it, to which Mencken is referring above, is as it were the cockney of America. It has this great advantage over cockney, that it is fed with a great variety of immigrant words. It is, however, fundamentally *a class-jargon*; not a jargon resulting from difference of race, and consequently of speech. It is the *patois* of the 'poor white,' the negro, or the uneducated immigrant. It is not the language spoken by Mrs Alice Roosevelt Longworth, for instance, or by Ernest Hemingway for that matter. But it is very *American*. And it is a *patois*, a fairly good rendering of which any American is competent to give. And you have read above the affectionate way Mencken refers to *our* 'theirns' and 'would 'a hads.'

English as spoken in America is more vigorous and expressive than Oxford English, I think. It is easy to mistake a native from the wilds of Dorsetshire for an American, I have found: and were 'educated' English used upon a good strong reverberant Dorsetshire basis, for instance, it would be all to the good, it is my opinion. Raleigh, Drake, and the rest of them, must have talked rather like that.

But with cockney it is not at all the same thing. There you get a degradation of English—it is *proletariat*, city-slum English, like Dublin-slum English. That is in a different category altogether to the weighty, rapid, and expressive torrent of the best Dorsetshire talk; and, as I have said, the *best* American is in the same category as the Dorsetshire—or as non-slum Irish—a good, sound accent, too. But the question to be answered is whether the *Beach-la-mar* Mr Mencken has in mind is not too much the deteriorated pidgin tongue of the United States; and whether, if that is *affectionné* too much by the *literati*—as being the most *American* thing available, like a jazz—it is not going to be a vulgar corruption, which will vulgarize, as well as enrich, the tongue. So far it exists generally in inverted commas, as in Mr Faulkner's books. Is it to be let out or not? A question for Americans.

For fifty years dialect-American has tended, what with negro and

immigrant pressure, to simplify itself grammatically, and I suppose is
still doing so at this moment.

His (the immigrant's) linguistic habits and limitations have to be
reckoned with in dealing with him and the concessions thus made
necessary have a very ponderable influence upon the general speech.
Of much importance is the support given to the native tendency by the
foreigner's incapacity for employing (or even comprehending) syntax of
any complexity, or words not of the simplest. This is the tendency towards
succinctness and clarity, at whatever sacrifice of grace. One English
observer, Sidney Low, puts the chief blame for the general explosiveness
of American upon the immigrant, who must be communicated with in
the plainest words available, and is not socially worthy of the suavity of
circumlocution anyhow. In his turn the immigrant seizes upon these
plainest words as upon a sort of convenient Lingua Franca—his quick
adoption of *damn* as a universal adjective is traditional—and throws his
influence upon the side of the underlying speech habit when he gets on
in the vulgate. Many characteristic Americanisms of the sort to stagger
lexicographers—for example, *near-silk*—have come from Jews, whose
progress in business is a good deal faster than their progress in English.

While England was a uniquely powerful empire-state, ruled by
an aristocratic caste, its influence upon the speech as upon the
psychology of the American ex-colonies was overwhelming. But today
that ascendancy has almost entirely vanished. The aristocratic caste is
nothing but a shadow of itself, the cinema has brought the American
scene and the American dialect nightly into the heart of England, and
the 'Americanizing' process is far advanced. 'Done gones,' 'good guys'
and 'buddies' sprout upon the lips of cockney children as readily as
upon those to the manner born, of New York or Chicago: and there
is no politically-powerful literate class any longer now, in our British
'Banker's Olympus,' to confer prestige upon an exact and intelligent
selective speech. Americanization—which is also for England, at least,
proletarianization—is too far advanced to require underlining, even
for people who fail usually to recognize anything until it has been
in existence for a quarter of a century.

But if America has come to England, there has been no reciprocal
movement of England into the United States: indeed, with the new

American nationalism, England is deliberately kept out: and all the great influence that England exerted formally—merely by being there and speaking the same tongue and sharing the same fundamental political principles—that is today a thing of the past. So the situation is this, as far as our common language is concerned: the destiny of England and the United States of America is more than ever one. But it is now the American influence that is paramount. The tables have effectively been turned in that respect.

————

But there is a larger issue even than that local to the English-speaking nations. English is of all languages the simplest grammatically and the easiest to make into a *Beach-la-mar* or *pidgin* tongue. Whether this fact, combined with its 'extraordinary tendency to degenerate into slang of every kind,' is against it, is of some importance for the future—for it will have less and less grammar, obviously, and more and more cosmopolitan slang.—Mr Mencken is of opinion that a language cannot be too simple—he is all for *Beach-la-mar*. The path towards analysis and the elimination of inflection, has been trod by English so thoroughly that, in its American form, it should today win the race for a universal volapuk. Indeed, as Mr Mencken says, 'the foreigner essaying it, indeed, finds his chief difficulty, not in mastering its forms, but in grasping its lack of form. He doesn't have to learn a new and complex grammar; what he has to do is to forget grammar. Once he has done so, the rest is a mere matter of acquiring a vocabulary.'

There is, it is true, the difficulty of the vowel sounds: but that is easily settled. Standard English possesses nineteen distinct vowel sounds: no other living European tongue except Portuguese, so Mr Mencken says, possesses so many. Modern Greek, for instance, can only boast of five, we are told. 'The (American) immigrant, facing all these vowels, finds some of them quite impossible: the Russian Jew, for example, cannot manage *ur*. As a result, he tends to employ a neutralized vowel in the situations which present difficulties, and this neutralized vowel, supported by the slip-shod speech-habits of the native proletariat, makes steady progress.'

That that 'neutralized vowel' has made great progress in America no one would deny who has been there; and, starting in the natural language-difficulties of the Central European immigrant, the above-mentioned 'neutralized vowel' will make its way over here in due course, who can doubt it? These vowels must be watched. *Watch your vowels* should be our next national slogan! The fatal grammatical easiness of English is responsible, however, for such problems as these, as much as the growing impressionability of the English nation, and the proletarianization, rather than the reverse, of the American.

As long ago as 1910 an English traveller, Mr Alexander Thompson, in a book called *Japan for a Week*, expresses himself as follows:

> It was only on reaching Italy that I began fully to realize this wonderful thing, that for nearly six weeks, on a German ship, in a journey of nearly ten thousand miles, we had heard little of any language but English!
>
> It is an amazing thing when one thinks of it.
>
> In Japan most of the tradespeople spoke English. At Shanghai, at Hong-Kong, at Singapore, at Penang, at Colombo, at Suez, at Port Said—all the way home to the Italian ports, the language of all the ship's traffic, the language of such discourse as the passengers held with natives, most of the language on board ship itself, was English.
>
> The German captain of our ship spoke English more often than German. All his officers spoke English.
>
> The Chinese man-o'-war's men who conveyed the Chinese prince on board at Shanghai, received commands and exchanged commands with our German sailors in English. The Chinese mandarins in their conversations with the ships' officers invariably spoke English. They use the same ideographs in writing as the Japanese, but to talk to our Japanese passengers they had to speak English. Nay, coming as they did from various provinces of the Empire, where the language greatly differs, they found it most convenient in conversation among themselves to speak English.

If you place side by side the unfortunate impressionability of Hemingway, which caused him to adopt integrally the half-wit simplicity of repetitive biblical diction patented by Miss Stein, and that other fact that Mr Hemingway, being an American nationalist by temperament, is inclined to gravitate stylistically towards the national underdog dialect, in the last resort to the kind of *Beach-la-mar* I have been discussing, you have the two principal factors in Hemingway as artist in prose-fiction, to make of what you can.

Take up any book of his, again, and open it at random: you will find a page of stuff that is, considered in isolation, valueless as writing. It is not written: it is lifted out of Nature and very artfully and adroitly tumbled out upon the page: it is the brute material of every-day proletarian speech and feeling. The *matière* is cheap and coarse: but not because it is proletarian speech merely, but because it is *the prose of reality*—the prose of the street-car or the provincial newspaper or the five and ten cent store. I have just opened *A Farewell to Arms* entirely at random, for instance, and this is what I find:

'If you had any foreign bodies in your legs they would set up an inflammation and you'd have fever.'

'All right,' I said. 'We'll see what comes out.'

She went out of the room and came back with the old nurse of the early morning. Together they made the bed with me in it. That was new to me and an admirable proceeding.

'Who is in charge here?'

'Miss Van Campen.'

'How many nurses are there?'

'Just us two.'

'Won't there be more?'

'Some more are coming.'

'When will they get here?'

'I don't know. You ask a great many questions for a sick boy.'

'I'm not sick,' I said, 'I'm wounded.'

They had finished making the bed and I lay with a clean, smooth sheet under me and another sheet over me. Mrs Walker went out and came back with a pyjama jacket. They put that on me and I felt very clean and dressed.

'You're awfully nice to me,' I said. The nurse called Miss Gage giggled. 'Could I have a drink of water?' I asked.

'Certainly. Then you can have breakfast.'

'I don't want breakfast. Can I have the shutters opened, please?'

The light had been dim in the room and when the shutters were opened it was bright sunlight, and I looked out on a balcony and beyond were the tiled roofs of houses and chimneys and the sky very blue.

'Don't you know when the other nurses are coming?'

'Why? Don't we take good care of you?'
'You're very nice.'
'Would you like to use the bedpan?'
'I might try.'
They helped me and held me up, but it was not any use. Afterward
I lay and looked out the open doors on to the balcony.
'When does the doctor come?'

It is not writing, if you like. When I read *A Farewell to Arms* doubtless
I read this page as I came to it, just as I should watch scenes unfolding
on the screen in the cinema, without pictorial criticism; and it, page
eighty-three, contributed its fraction to the general effect: and when I
had finished the book I thought it a very good book. By that I meant that
the cumulative effect was impressive, as *the events themselves* would be. Or
it is like reading a newspaper, day by day, about some matter of absorbing
interest—say the reports of a divorce, murder, or libel action. If you say
anyone could write it, you are mistaken there, because, to obtain that
smooth effect, of commonplace reality, there must be no sentimental or
other heightening, the number of words expended must be proportionate
to the importance and the length of the respective phases of the action,
and any false move or overstatement would at once stand out and tell
against it. If an inferior reporter to Hemingway took up the pen, that
fact would at once be detected by a person sensitive to reality.

It is an art, then, from this standpoint, like the cinema, or like those
'modernist' still-life pictures in which, in place of *painting* a match box
upon the canvas, a piece of actual match box is stuck on. A recent
example of this (I choose it because a good many people will have seen it)
is the cover design of the French periodical *Minotaure*, in which Picasso
has pasted and tacked various things together, sticking a line drawing of
the Minotaur in the middle. Hemingway's is a poster-art, in this sense:
or a *cinema in words*. The *steining* of the text of Hemingway is as it were
the hand-made part—if we are considering it as 'super-realist' design:
a manipulation of the photograph if we are regarding it as a film.

If you say that this is not the way that Dante wrote, that these are
not artistically permanent creations—or not permanent in the sense of
a verse of Bishop King, or a page of Gulliver, I agree. But it is what
we have got: there is actually *bad* and *good* of this kind; and I for my

part enjoy what I regard as the good, without worrying any more about it than that.

That a particular phase in the life of humanity is implicit in this art is certain. It is one of the first fruits of the *proletarianization* which, as a result of the amazing revolutions in the technique of industry, we are all undergoing, whether we like it or not. But this purely political, or sociological side to the question can be brought out, I believe, with great vividness by a quotation. Here, for instance, is a fragment of a story of a mutiny at sea:

I opened the door a little, about two inches, and saw there was a rope round the companion, which prevented the doors opening. Big Harry and Lips asked me what I wanted. I said I wanted to go down to the galley. Big Harry said: 'Plenty of time between this and eight o'clock; you stop down below.' I then went into the chief mate's room, which was the nearest to me. There was nobody there. I went to the second mate's room, he was not there. I went to the captain's pillow, it was standing up in his bed, and I found two revolvers loaded, one with six shots and one with four. I took possession of them and put them in my pockets. I then stood on the cabin table in the after cabin, and lifted the skylight up and tried to get out there. Renken was standing at the wheel, and he called out, 'Come aft, boys, the steward is coming out of the skylight.' I then closed the skylight and came down again. The after-skylight was close to the wheel, about 10 feet as near as I could guess. I could see him. The light used for the compass is in the skylight, and the wheel is in the back of it. The light is fastened to the skylight to light the compass, and the compass is just in front of the wheel. Before I could get the skylight closed I heard their steps coming aft, and I went down into the cabin and told the boy to light a fire. Shortly afterwards I heard five shots fired on deck . . . about a second afterwards the same as if somebody was running on deck. I could not judge which way they were running; the noise on the deck, and the vessel being in ballast, you could hear as well aft as forward. That was about twenty minutes after hearing the captain call out. I put the revolvers away in my locker. I then took it into my head to take the revolvers into my possession and chance it; if the men came down to me to do anything wrong, to save myself. I put them in my pockets, one on each side. About 5.30 Green, the boatswain, came down first, and French Peter, Big Harry, and all the other lot followed. The deck was left without anybody, and the wheel too, they came into the cabin; Trousillot was there as well. They

225

did not speak at first. The first thing they did was to rub me over. They could not feel anything. I had the two revolvers with me, but they did not feel them. French Peter and Big Harry felt me over. All the others were present. Green said, 'Well, steward, we have finished now.' I said, 'What the hell did you finish?' He said, 'We have finished captain, mate and second.' He said, 'We got our mind made up to go to Greece; if you like to save your own life you had better take charge of the ship and bring us to Greece. You bring us to Gibraltar, we will find Greece: you bring us there you will be all right, steward. We will take the boats when we get to Greece, and take the sails and everything into the boats, and sell them ashore and divide the money between ourselves. You will have your share, the same as anybody else; the charts and sextants, and all that belongs to the navigation, you can have. Me and my cousin, Johnny Moore, have got a rich uncle; he will buy everything. We will scuttle the ship. My uncle is a large owner there of some ships. We will see you right, that you will be master of one of those vessels.' I said, 'Well, men, come on deck and get them braces ready, and I hope you will agree and also obey my orders!' The other men said, 'All right, steward, very good, very good, steward, you do right.' That was all I could hear from them, from everybody. The conversation between me and Green was in English, and everybody standing round. He spoke to the other men in Greek. What he said I don't know. I said, 'Where are the bodies? Where is the captain?' Green said, 'Oh they are all right, they are overboard,' and all the men said the same . . .[10]

That is not by Hemingway, though it quite well might be. I should not be able to tell it was not by Hemingway if it were shown me as a fragment. But this is by him:

Across the bay they found the other boat beached. Uncle George was smoking a cigar in the dark. The young Indian pulled the boat way up the beach. Uncle George gave both the Indians cigars. They walked up from the beach through a meadow that was soaking wet with dew, following the young Indian who carried a lantern. Then they went into the woods and followed a trail that led to the logging road that ran back into the hills. It was much lighter on the logging road as the timber was cut away on both sides. The young Indian stopped and blew out his lantern and they all walked on along the road.

[10] *Forty Years at the Old Bailey*. F. Lamb.

They came around a bend and a dog came out barking. Ahead were the lights of the shanties where the Indian bark-peelers lived. More dogs rushed out at them. The two Indians sent them back to the shanties. In the shanty nearest the road there was a light in the window. An old woman stood in the doorway holding a lamp.

Inside on a wooden bunk lay a young Indian woman. She had been trying to have her baby for two days. All the old women in the camp had been helping her. The men had moved off up the road to sit in the dark and smoke out of range of the noise she made. She screamed just as Nick and the two Indians followed his father and Uncle George into the shanty. She lay in the lower bunk, very big under a quilt. Her head was turned to one side. In the upper bunk was her husband. He had cut his foot very badly with an axe three days before. He was smoking a pipe. The room smelled very bad. Nick's father ordered some water to be put on the stove, while it was heating he spoke to Nick. 'This lady is going to have a baby, Nick,' he said. 'I know,' said Nick. 'You don' know,' said his father. 'Listen to me. What she is going through is called being in labour. The baby wants to be born and she wants it to be born. All her muscles are trying to get the baby born. That is what is happening when she screams.' 'I see,' Nick said. Just then the woman cried out.[11]

The first of these two passages is from a book entitled *Forty Years at the Old Bailey*. It is the account of a mutiny and murder on the high seas, the trial occurring on May 3 and 4, 1876. It was evidence verbatim of one Constant von Hoydonck, a Belgian, twenty-five years of age, who joined the vessel *Lennie* at Antwerp, as chief steward, on October 22. This is a *Querschnitt*, a slice, of 'real life': and how close Hemingway is to such material as this can be seen by comparing it with the second passage out of *In Our Time*.

————

That, I think, should put you in possession of all that is essential for an understanding of the work of this very notable artist: an understanding I mean; I do not mean that, as a work of art, a book of his should be approached in this critical and anatomizing spirit. That

[11] *In Our Time*. Ernest Hemingway.

is another matter. Where the 'politics' come in I suppose by this time you will have gathered. This is the voice of the 'folk,' of the masses, who are the cannon-fodder, the cattle outside the slaughter-house, serenely chewing the cud—*of those to whom things are done*, in contrast to those who have executive will and intelligence. It is itself innocent of politics—one might almost add alas! That does not affect its quality as art. The expression of the soul of the dumb ox would have a penetrating beauty of its own, if it were uttered with genius—with bovine genius (and in the case of Hemingway that is what has happened): just as much as would the folk-song of the baboon, or of the 'Praying Mantis.' But where the politics crop up is that if we take this to be the typical art of a civilization—and there is no serious writer who stands higher in Anglo-Saxony today than does Ernest Hemingway—then we are by the same token saying something very definite about that civilization.

―――――――

It is in this book, more clearly and certainly than elsewhere, that Lewis defends the principles on which his satiric writing is based, asserts that it is not produced in the service of morality but of art, and allies himself with the great writers who worked from the outside, realistically like Flaubert or caricaturally like Dickens, against the majority twentieth-century view favouring the interpretation of personality via dreams, fantasy or psychology. This fitted very well beside his increasing concern as a visual artist with a stylised but still basically realistic rendering of external appearance.

from MEN WITHOUT ART

The Greatest Satire is Non-Moral

There is no man's 'shop' but must appear somewhat cynical to the outsider. To overhear two physicians conferring is enough to make the flesh of the bravest creep. That is classical. But it is the same with every profession. (Most pure business sounds to the outsider and non-business man like a confabulation of convicts of course, engaged in the preparation of some novel *coup de main*.) And the craft of the satirist must perforce retain a few of the more brutal fashions of thinking that are proper to his occupation. You know our Hogarth's face, in a nightcap?—it is like a bulldog, in a sense—the most brutal of animals, the *matador par excellence*.

There is, again, a whole world of difference between the satirist—so extended as to mean all artists not specifically beauty-doctors, as I have ordained here—and the 'realist.' Yet the 'materialism' of the matter of the grotesque is liable to shock. We shall be committed to an examination of all those controversial values pertaining to that naked world of the *Satyricon*, of *Volpone*, of the *Médecin malgré Lui*. We shall have to weigh the dictum of Taine:[1]

'Au plus bas degré sont les types que préfèrent la littérature réaliste et le théâtre comique, je veux dire les personnages bornés, plats, sots, égoïstes, faibles et communes . . .' against the opposite dictum of Flaubert:[2]

'Il n'y a ni beaux, ni vilains sujets . . . on pourrait presque établir comme axiome, en se posant au point de vue de l'art pur, qu'il n'y en a aucun, le style étant à lui tout seul une manière de voir les choses.'

And then *style* is of course a magician who can convert a ragged crone into an object of great beauty. It is *style* that checkmates subject-matter every time, and turns to naught the beauty-doctor laws of the metaphysician. But merely to decide, upon an aristocratic principle, which, in the view of Nietzsche, gave the *Mahomet* of Voltaire the palm over all subsequent and less 'classical' compositions, will scarcely satisfy a public of today. Flaubert stands accused of more than vulgarity: he is arraigned, by one of the masters of the catholic revival, for his turpitude in employing, in deliberate isolation, instincts that issued, certainly, in what he called 'style,' but which were intended for the service of a more elevated principle. 'La faute de Flaubert est grave, aussi. L'art substitué à Dieu, cela l'engage dans une voie . . . périlleuse.'[3]

---

[1] *L'art et la Morale*. Ferdinand Brunetière.

[2] Quoted by I.J. Bondy, *Classicisme de Ferdinand Brunetière*.

[3] *Trois grands hommes*. F. Mauriac.

It will be our duty to take into account the various motives which may decide a man to go and live among such vulgar and imbecile personages as satire, and comedy, require. In the case of Flaubert, to go no farther than he, 'style' was not the whole of the story. Like any Christian martyr he went and established himself in the centre of the bourgeois body—he regarded himself as possessing 'a message' of sorts—if only that of a plumber. And he dies at his post, struck down by the bourgeois, while at his unsavoury work, there is no dispute at least on that head. Hear Mauriac, his accuser: 'puisqu'il ne pouvait plus se soustraire à l'étude du Prudhomme moderne, eh bien, il prendrait le taureau par les cornes; cette énorme bêtise bourgeoise deviendrait le sujet de son livre, il l'incarnerait, ce serait son chef-d'oeuvre . . . Le Bourgeois . . . s'installe à sa table, se couche dans son lit, remplit ses journées et ses nuits, et finit par le prendre à la gorge. Le Bourgeois a eu sa peau enfin; il a, à la lettre, assassiné Flaubert. L'alchemiste de Croisset est mort victime des expériences qu'il tentait sur la créature humaine: il éliminait l'âme du composé humain, pour obtenir de la bêtise à l'état pur: elle l'a asphyxié.'[4]

We shall be in these pages, as we are in real life, haunted by this BOURGEOIS of Flaubert. Like a pneumatic carnival personage, incessantly expanding as the result of the fierce puffing of the Marxist into his ideologic bladder, the Bourgeois of Flaubert has assumed portentous proportions.

We are informed by Albalat that Gautier and Flaubert when they met, upon the occasion of the latter's periodic visits to Paris, would sit down and discuss 'the bourgeois' for hours together. 'Flaubert detested the "bourgeois" in overalls as much as the "bourgeois" in plus fours. When Théophile Gautier and he addressed themselves, at one of their séances, to the declamatory abuse of the 'bourgeois,' they worked themselves up to a great pitch of lyrical rage, became as red as turkey-cocks and were obliged afterwards to change their linen (*ils . . . devenaient rouges comme des coqs et se voyaient forcés de changer de chemise*).'

They really took their 'bourgeois' seriously! And these two charming and intelligent men, thundering away at each other in the past (an echo of their voices may still be caught, on a quiet afternoon) opposed to the

---

[4] *L'art et la Morale*. Ferdinand Brunetière.

bourgeois—but what do you suppose? It sounds absurd, in our present dispensation, but it was *the artist* that these two Frenchmen were thinking about, and 'bourgeois' meant nothing really but the enemy of art. They were as simple as a couple of noisy peasants—in a sense: and *art* filled the whole of their minds and bodies. A passion for a concrete realization of all the mysterious energies with which they were wound up like clocks, possessed them night and day. These two French craftsmen, drenching their shirts with perspiration as they cursed for hours on end the wicked giant who was the great enemy of their craft, were far more mad than Blake, I think. And as to Blake's 'prolonged vindication of the cause of all the artists in the world,' they did a good deal of that, too, between them.

These will be the sort of subjects among which we shall be picking our way. We shall interrogate these great profane figures composed of 'pure art'—these *hommes-plumes* compact of *mots justes*—and see what messages they may have for our even more *be-bourgeoised* period: we shall not be prevented from speculating as to what is our antithesis—with 'bourgeois' where it was before, but bigger and weaker, but 'artist' somehow changed, and perhaps paired off with some other abstraction. For the politician—whose art is anything but the *mot juste*—has pushed away the artist and now stands where the latter once stood, keeping all to himself the 'burgess-gentleman.' But if we have to range far afield before we have done with the questions which, one after the other, we shall find this critical enterprise calls up, we will now start with satire pure and simple, and join issue at once with the moralist, who regards satire as belonging pre-eminently to his domain.

There is no prejudice so inveterate, in even the educated mind, as that which sees in satire a work of edification. Indeed, for the satirist to acquire the right to hold up to contempt a fellow-mortal, he is supposed, first, to arm himself with the insignia of a sheriff or special constable. No age, for many centuries, has been so lawless as ours—nothing to compare with Capone it is said, for instance, has ever been known in America. And perhaps for this reason an unnatural sensitiveness to law and order is noticeable in all of us: and in the field of the ethical judgement, as much as in that of the civil law, is this the case. Perhaps that is the reason why, in this defence of the art of satire,

I give the place of honour to the moral law, and settle accounts with that source of interference first.—As to the law of libel, the anomalies and injustices of that have often been canvassed: I do not propose here to add to that already considerable body of criticism. It is rather the subtler forms of interference, generally neglected, which I have in mind and am proposing to pass under review.

I am a satirist, I am afraid there is no use denying that. But I am not a moralist: and about that I make no bones either. And it is these two facts, taken together, which constitute my particular difficulty. It is contended, against the satirist, that since man is not autonomous—and who but will agree to that I hope?—he cannot arm himself with laughter and invective, and sally forth to satirical attacks upon his neighbour, without first acquiring the moral sanction of the community—with whose standards and canons of conduct he must be at one—and first advertising himself as a champion of some outraged Mrs Grundy. So, with Mrs Grundy on the one side, and Dr Bowdler on the other, and with a big crocodile tear in his eye (at the thought of the pain he may have to inflict), he sets himself in motion. That is the popular picture. The more sophisticated picture would today only differ from this in the nature of the preparations prescribed: a short prayer for absolution regarding the blood he was about to spill, or if the god had the features of Demos, an invocation to his bloody fist—a brief class-war-dance, with a 'more power to my elbow' incantation! And so forward to battle, the Geneva Bible in the breast-pocket. But, whatever else it may be, it must be represented as a salutary expedition, undertaken on behalf of something with an infallible title to the moral judgement-seat.

There is of course no question that satire of the highest order has been achieved in the name of the ethical will. Most satire, indeed, has got through upon the understanding that the satirist first and foremost was a moralist. And some of the best satirists have been that as well. But not all. So one of the things it is proposed to do in these pages is to consider the character, and the function of, non-ethical satire; and if possible to provide it with a standing, alongside the other arts and sciences, as a recognized philosophic and artistic human activity, not contingent upon judgements which are not those specifically of the artistic or philosophic mind.

232

———

'The frantic rage which Dryden's satire provoked in his opponents' has been attributed, by Professor Saintsbury, to a *coolness* always to be discovered at the centre of his scorn. Further, Dryden dispensed with the protective moralistic machinery of the classical satire. It was, in short, not because his opponents were *naughty* that Dryden objected to them, but because they were *dull*. They had sinned against the Reason, rather than against the Mosaic Law. This it was that aroused the really 'frantic rage'! For all those satirized by Juvenal, or smarting beneath the scourges of most other satirists, of the classical or modern age, have been able at a pinch to snigger and remark that 'Yes, they *knew* that they were very wicked!' and to make, even, of such satire an advertisement.

But if you remove from satire its moralism, then it has no advertisement value whatever for the victim—then it is doubly deadly, and then also the satirist is doubly hated by those picked out for attack. And society also, the implicit ally of the moralist, is in a sense offended (though the way society takes it depends upon the society—ours luckily does not stand upon its moral dignity very much).

It could perhaps be asserted, even, that the greatest satire *cannot* be moralistic at all: if for no other reason, because no mind of the first order, expressing itself in art, has ever itself been taken in, nor consented to take in others, by the crude injunctions of any purely moral code. This does not mean that the mind in question was wanting in that consciousness of itself as a rational subject, which is never absent in an intellect of such an order: but that its abstract theory, as well as its concrete practice, of moral judgements, would differ from the common run, and that their introduction would merely confuse the issue. The artistic impulse is a more primitive one than the ethical: so much is this the case—so little is it a mere dialect of the rational language in which our human laws are formulated, but, on the contrary, an entirely independent tongue—that it is necessary for the artist to change his skin, almost, in passing from one department into the other. You cannot with the same instruments compass a work of edification and a work of beauty—and satire may be 'beautiful,' rather in the way that mathematics claims to be that—with a rational handsomeness peculiar to it; and even such a tub-thumper as Bunyan, being an artist, is there as witness to that fact, as has often been pointed out. With the person predestined to an artistic vocation, cheerfulness, or moods of a yet more anomalous order, *will* keep breaking in: so it is better, perhaps, to admit them at the start.

But how can satire stand without the moral sanction? you may ask. For satire can only exist *in contrast* to something else—it is a shadow, and an ugly shadow at that, of some perfection. And it is so disagreeable, and so painful (at least in the austere sense in which we appear to be defining it here) that no one would pursue it *for its own sake*, or take up the occupation of satirist unless compelled to do so, out of indignation at the spectacle of the neglect of beauty and virtue. That is I think the sort of objection that, at this point, we should expect to have to meet.

Provisionally I will reply as follows: it is my belief that 'satire' *for its own sake*—as much as anything else for its own sake—is possible: and that even the most virtuous and well-proportioned of men is only a shadow, after all, of some perfection; a shadow of an imperfect, and hence an 'ugly,' sort. And as to *laughter*, if you allow it in one place you must, I think, allow it in another. Laughter—humour and wit—has a function in relation to our tender consciousness; a function similar to that of art. It is the preserver much more than the destroyer. And, in a sense, *everyone* should be laughed at or else *no one* should be laughed at. It seems that ultimately that is the alternative.

When Addison introduced the word 'genius,' to take the place of the word used up to that time, 'wit,' he did us all a disservice. Wit as a generic term for all those possessed of an excellent judgement, would tend (apart from the advantages resulting from its less pretentious sound) to marshal the gifted upon the *laughing* side of the world. But that little change of a popular monosyllable made all the difference, and today *the laugh* is not wholly respectable: it requires to be explained, if not excused.

But satire is a special sort of laughter: *the laugh* alone possesses great powers of magnification. But *the laugh* that magnified Falstaff till he grew to be a giant like Pantagruel, is not the laugh of the satirist, which threw up the Maids of Honour in Brobdingnag. Now, no one resents the size of Falstaff: he is a routine figure of fun; the jolly toper. But everyone resents the scale of the Maids of Honour, and resents the sounds of the cataracts heard by Gulliver when they made use of their *pots de chambre*.

But I will produce the Maids of Honour, so that our sense of what we are discussing should become first hand.

> The Maids of Honour often invited Glumdalclitch to their apartments, and desired she should bring me along with her, on purpose to have the pleasure of seeing and touching me. They would often strip me naked from top to toe and lay me at full length in their bosoms: wherewith I was much disgusted: because, to say the truth, a very offensive smell came from their skins: which I do not mention or intend to the disadvantage of those excellent ladies, for whom I have all manner of respect . . . That which gave me most uneasiness among those Maids of Honour, when my nurse carried me to visit them, was to see them use me without any manner of ceremony, like a creature who had no sort of consequence. For they would strip themselves to the skin, and put on their smocks in my presence, while I was placed on their toilet directly before their naked bodies, which, I am sure, to me was very far from being a tempting sight, or from giving me any other emotions than those of horror and disgust. Their skins appeared so coarse and uneven, so variously coloured, when I saw them near, with a mole here and there as broad as a trencher, and hairs hanging from it thicker than packthreads, to say nothing further concerning the rest of their persons. Neither did they at all scruple, while I was by, to discharge what they had drunk, to the quantity of at least two hogsheads, in a vessel that held three tuns.

These are very painful passages. There is no question here of the mere he-man vulgarity of the egregious Scottish surgeon, Smollett. It is much more uncomfortable than that, not alone for the nice-minded but without exception for all the spokesmen of Mr Everybody.

In this painful effect of true satire we might expect to find the main avenue of attack of the moralist—he might say that it was *ill-natured* instead of *good-natured*, as is mere burlesque. But it is not to that that we must look today, when we are taking our measures of defence, as being the spot likely to draw the fire of the ethical batteries.

———

The painful nature of satire was recognized by Hazlitt, but promptly misunderstood; for he was looking for something in satire which under no circumstances belongs there, and which in consequence he could not find.

'Bare-faced impudence, an idiot imbecility, are his dramatic commonplaces,' he writes of Ben Jonson. So, although one would have thought that Ben Jonson had acquitted himself to admiration of what is after all, in the narrowest sense, the satirist's job, the good Hazlitt finds fault with him for that very reason—because, in fact, Hazlitt did not at all like satire.

The very reasons Hazlitt finds to attack Ben Jonson, do, it seems to me, exactly describe a master of that kind of art: and actually, what Hazlitt says could be applied, with more aptness, to other writers than to Ben Jonson—writers, to my mind, even more important than the author of *Volpone*. This point is one of such significance for an understanding of satire in general, that I will quote the entire passage.

> Shakespeare's characters are men; Ben Jonson's are more like machines, governed by mere routine, or by the convenience of the poet, whose property they are. In reading the one, we are let into the minds of his characters, we see the play of their thoughts, how their humours flow and work ... His humour (so to speak) bubbles, sparkles, and finds its way in all directions, like a natural spring. In Ben Jonson it is, as it were, confined in a leaden cistern, where it stagnates and corrupts; or directed only through certain artificial pipes and conduits to answer a given purpose ... Sheer ignorance, bare-faced impudence, or idiot imbecility, are his dramatic commonplaces—things that provoke pity or disgust, instead of laughter.[5]

But why should not idiot imbecility provoke laughter? Obviously the answer is: Because, being found in a human being, it is 'letting down' the species, and so to laugh at it would be unethical and *inhuman*. Physical deformity, again, is often comic. Many dwarfs are highly grotesque (superbly grotesque, one may say without offence in the case of dwarfs), and they even relish the sensation of their funniness. But most people only laugh covertly at such spectacles, or sternly repress a smile. For, they would say, these are 'things' which should 'provoke pity

[5] *The English Comic Writers*. Hazlitt.

or disgust, instead of laughter.' Such is the Anglo-Saxon point of view.

But the dago is different. Dwarfs, in Spain, are the object of constant mirth, on the part of their 'normal' fellow-citizens. Everyone pokes fun at them, there is no hypocrisy, as with us, and the dwarf gets on very well indeed. He is treated as a pet animal, and enjoys himself very much. Also, since he has a great deal of practice, from morning till night, he often ends by being a first-class clown. In short, neither disgust nor pity is experienced by these dagos where their dwarfs are concerned. They feel perhaps that God has made them a present of these hideous oddities to be their sport: and the dwarf feels that too, and is quite puffed-up with his own importance and proud of his god-sent job.

And, after all, pulling long faces at the dwarf, and surrounding him with an atmosphere of inhuman pity, is bad for the dwarf. It is better to explode with laughter at the sight of him—better for all concerned. So far so good: but what of the shell-shocked man, for instance? He is often very funny, and it is very difficult not to laugh. But that is like laughing at the contortions of a dying man, and it would be too brutal a society that made a habit of laughing at its shell-shocked persons—especially as it would be to the society of the laughers to which ultimately the responsibility for these disfigurements would have to be brought home. Therefore there is no society that does not refrain from guffawing at the antics, however 'screamingly funny,' of its shell-shocked men and war-idiots, and its poison-gas morons, and its mutilated battle-wrecks.

But here is also a principle, of use in the analysis of the comic. *Perfect laughter*, if there could be such a thing, would be inhuman. And it would select as the objects of its mirth as much the antics dependent upon pathologic maladjustments, injury, or disease, as the antics of clumsy and imperfectly functioning healthy people. At this point it is perhaps desirable to note that in general human beings display no delicacy about spiritual or mental shortcomings in their neighbours, but only physical. To be a fool with a robust body can be no more pleasant for the person in question than being an intelligent dwarf: yet no one scruples to laugh at the former, but parades a genteel sensitiveness regarding the latter. Infinitely more pain is inflicted by laughter provoked by some non-physical cause than by that provoked by the physical. So do not let us take too much for granted that we can put our finger blindfold upon *the supreme 'cad'*.

Our deepest laughter is not, however, inhuman laughter. And yet it is non-personal and non-moral. And it enters fields which are commonly regarded as the preserve of more 'serious' forms of reaction. There is no reason at all why we should not burst out laughing at a foetus, for instance. We should after all only be laughing *at ourselves*!—at ourselves early in our mortal career.

Returning to Hazlitt's misunderstanding; in Swift, in Dryden, in Pope, it is not the 'natural,' 'bubbling' laughter of Shakespearean comedy that you should expect to find, any more than you would look for a jovial heartiness in a surgeon at work, or, if you like (to take a romantic illustration), in an executioner. It would decidedly be out of place. *Laughter* is the medium employed, certainly, but there is laughter and laughter. That of true satire is as it were *tragic* laughter. It is not a genial guffaw nor the titillations provoked by a harmless entertainer. It is tragic, if a thing *can* be 'tragic' without pity and terror, and it seems to me it can.

But when Hazlitt speaks of the characters 'like machines, governed by mere routine,' there, I think, he gives himself entirely away. For what else is a character in satire but that? Is it not just because they are such *machines, governed by routine*—or creatures that stagnate, as it were 'in a leaden cistern'—that the satirist, in the first instance, has considered them suitable for satire? He who wants a jolly, carefree, bubbling, world chockfull of 'charm,' must not address himself to the satirist! The wind that blows through satire is as bitter as that that predominates in the pages of *Timon* or *King Lear*. Indeed, the former *is* a satire. And *Hamlet*, for instance, is very much that too—a central satire—developing now into comedy, now into tragedy.

Laughter is again an anti-toxin of the first order. As a matter of fact *no* man (as I have hinted above)—any more than the shell-shocked man—should be laughed at. It is unfair, therefore it is 'caddish,' to laugh at *anybody*: we all, as much as the shell-shocked man, really could cry *cad*, or have cad cried for us, at an outburst of mirth at our expense. And this does not only apply to the obviously defective. It is unnecessary to enumerate the tragic handicaps that our human conditions involve—the glaring mechanical imperfections, the nervous tics, the prodigality of objectless movement—the, to other creatures,

238

offensive smells, disagreeable moistures—the involuntary grimace, the lurch, roll, trot or stagger which we call our *walk*—it is only a matter of degree between us and the victim of locomotor-ataxy or St Vitus's dance.

By making a great deal of noise ourselves we at least drown the alarming noise made by our neighbours. And the noise that, above all others, has been bestowed on us for this purpose is the bark which we describe as our *laugh*. I approve of a *barking man* myself——I find that I have less occasion, with his likes, to anticipate a really serious *bite*. So laughter is *per se* a healthy clatter—that is one of the first things to realize about it.

An illustration of this principle, in a parallel order of feeling, is furnished by Henry James, where he is discussing the virtue in a novelist of hard work—and the clatter and bustle which, as it were, accompanies it. Put *laughter* for *hard work*, and you will see what I mean, I think. These are the words of that great puppet-manufacturer:

> It is, as you say, because I 'grind out' my men and women that I endure them. It is because I create them by the sweat of my brow that I venture to look them in the face. My *work* is my salvation. If this great army of puppets came forth at my simple bidding, then indeed I should die of their senseless clamour.

The survey or analysis of the situation in the arts *circa* 1934 ends with a pessimistic view of the likely future.

from MEN WITHOUT ART

Conclusion

Regarded as great herds of performing animals (the *behaviourist* view)—small, mischievous, physically insignificant and mentally extremely prone to endless imitation, very susceptible to hypnosis—as individuals and in the aggregate—regarded in that manner our *tricks*—and our 'fine arts' are only part of our repertoire of tricks, not necessarily our *finest* tricks, even—are indeed too unimportant a matter to detain us for so much as the twinkling of an eye. A good dinner, accompanied by as good wine as we can get hold of; a pleasant spin in the fresh air in as satisfactory a petrol wagon as we can afford; a nice digestive round of golf; a flirtation accompanied by the rhythmical movements prompted by a nigger drum, purging us of the secretions of sex—a nice detective volume, which purges us pleasantly of the secretions proper to us in our capacity of 'killers' and hunting-dogs (our lynching, arsenic-administering, and throat-cutting and policemanesque proclivities all rolled into one); all these things are far more *important* than anything that can be described as 'art'—art, that is, in any *highbrow* sense (to use the clownish democratic jargon to supply the requisite gutter-picture, of what we wish to describe)—the noblest intellectual exercises of The Animal, Man—exercises which to the vivid and vulgar folk-eye of the Tom Thumb of the Bowery slum, which has none of the purity and beauty of the peasant-vision—are symbolized by *a high forehead*, the sign of a 'brainy' chap.

It is regarding the *values* attaching to these tricks that we are liable to differ: for some of us attribute no significance to them at all. But all that I am arguing here is that they are *only* tricks, in the first place (we may consider the fine arts as the very fine manners of the mind) and, in the second place, that if they possess no value whatever, then *à plus forte raison*, life possesses absolutely no value either. In other words, I am taking their values for granted in this essay, I am not proceeding to their proof.

What should be said, then, it seems to me, first and last, about art (whether of the eye, ear, hand or what not) is that it is a pure game—a game, in its different forms, directly arising out of our functions of sight, hearing and so forth, and our functions as trained social animals, as political animals, of course, and as religious animals. And further, as I see it, there is no 'progressive' principle at work in life. This would 'class' the arts at once—to call them 'a game'—if it were not that life itself, the whole of the 'peculiar situation' in which we find ourselves, should also be considered purely as a game—a game in the sense that no value can attach to it *for itself*, but only in so far as it is well-played or badly-played. Art in this respect is in the same class as ritual, as civilized behaviour, and all ceremonial forms and observances—a discipline, a symbolic discipline.

It is at this point that we make contact with the moralist-at-large, having referred to *good* play and to *bad* play. With his humanist metre-stick our lay moralist (assenting, very grudgingly, to the above definition—for 'game' is a word that suggests something altogether too trivial and light-hearted to him) would approach these judgements—of 'good' and of 'bad' play. 'Very well!' he would perhaps exclaim, 'have it that way if you must. Call a good action a good piece of *playing* if you like. But the *good* in the good piece of acting is my province, anyway!' And it is, of course, just there that one is compelled to discourage him, very firmly indeed. For his idea of a *good play*—to narrow down for the moment this 'well-played' game in question to a theatrical performance—would always be a play of edification, which exhibited some ethical principle at work, triumphing in the face of considerable odds: just as the pure politician's idea of a 'good play' would be a play throwing into prominence a party-principle—*his* party's in fact.

In a word, the moralist's, or the politician's 'good,' is not universal enough, but is too deeply embrued respectively with the pragmatical values of the mere animal, Man, or the values of the parish-pump.

In conclusion, if then our arts are of no value, except as pretty ornaments to an otherwise futile life—of bread-and-butter and as far as possible beer-and-skittles, upon a dogmatically animal plane—then this and all other discussions are futile too. However this may be, the valuing of our arts is bound up with the valuing of our life, and vice versa. All I have done here has been, starting from the assumption that a non-material system of values attaches to the exercises of the artist, to denounce the various interferences, by the agency of which, at present, his activities are impaired. That has been the extent of what I have here proposed. And I do not think that, within this framework, I can usefully add anything to what I have already said, and so will leave the matter in your hands, hoping that at least I may have directed your attention to a question of great moment—namely, whether the society of the immediate future should be composed, for the first time in civilized history, of *Men without art*.

———————————

Almost twenty years later, in *The Writer and the Absolute*, Lewis considered the writers who had emerged after the War: Orwell, whom he thought the only good English writer of a decade or more, Sartre, Malraux and Camus. It was, typically, the way their social attitudes affected their literary output, and in particular the tendency towards nihilism he discovered in their work, that chiefly concerned Lewis. The idea of freedom as an absolute fascinated him even though he called himself a pluralist, and so did the absolutist attractions of Communism. In *Men Without Art* he had been careful to emphasise respect for 'many of the dogmas of Russian Communism' while expressing contempt for its Western spokesmen, and in the following analysis of existentialism it is a Communist critic he praises.

from THE WRITER AND THE ABSOLUTE

Twentieth Century Nihilism

In some places in Europe the writer's is an anxious and shackled freedom. In order to remain 'free'—in order to be something he wishes to be—a man will say a thousand things he does not wish to say, mutilate his thought, adulterate his doctrine, compel his will to wear a uniform imposed upon him *against* his will, cause the characters in his books (if a novelist) to behave in a manner that turns them into other characters—to associate with people they would never speak to if allowed to follow their own sweet will.—It has been my argument that to surrender his will to that one of the contemporary machines for compressing souls into given shapes which would leave him most of his original self would be a man's best policy; the machine whose standard shapes were the nearest to the native shape of his own soul.

To secure the evidence necessary to prove that these are queer times for the writer, it may be said that I might have picked a more attractive witness. That there is such silly aggressiveness in Sartre goes without saying. 'I have suppressed God the Father' (an often-quoted saying of his) is not the sort of levity that attracts one to him, or would incline anyone to take him seriously. He is much more polite to Marx than he is to God, because he regards the Marxists as much more formidable enemies than the believers in God. He has picked Marx's doctrine to pieces: yet he has not so far asserted that Marx has been 'suppressed' by him. The value of Sartre as a philosopher, as literary artist, or as controversialist, is not however the issue. He has a momentary importance, he is quite a substantial enough person to qualify as a witness. As a pluralist—the opposite of an absolutist—I should prefer a various world. Therefore I am for liberty: I should defend the right of far more disagreeable people than Sartre to write what they liked and to be heard, so long as our society continues in theory to secure to the individual freedom of speech, freedom of worship (or of no worship) and so on.

Of Sartre's critics the most effective are the Communists. Of these Henri Lefebvre is the best example, and a highly intelligent man. Lefebvre sees very clearly what a flirt Sartre is, but his reason for being that he does not seem to see.

> This dialectic brings M. Sartre [he writes] singularly close to the *materialist dialectic*: brings him near to it only. Upon the theoretic plane, as upon the political, he flirts with the (Marxist) solution of problems: he brushes it as closely as his anxiety not to compromise himself will allow—not, in fact, ever to bind himself. He gets as close (to marxism) as possible with the idea of supplanting it.

As you will observe, M. Lefebvre has a different explanation from my own: he believes that Sartre's pushing himself as far to the left as possible—short of communism—was done with the ambition of *supplanting* the Communists. I am sure this is a mistake. Sartre's affectation of more radical principles than he in fact holds is amply accounted for by the prestige and the popularity of the Left—as a protective and precautionary step, and because of great pressure leftwards when he was younger, and of his infatuation for Malraux. The

243

only way he could have escaped these pressures and infatuations was to move into the ranks of Rome. But there was no question of so tough a little rationalist doing that. Today Trotsky and anarcho-syndicalism offer him a respectable radical alternative to communism, or 'Stalinism'. Perhaps at last a solution has been found.

Now I will pass on, however, to my next subject. Its connexion with the problems of freedom will be less obvious at first sight. M. Lefebvre will effect the transition for me, in a passage where all of Western thought is assailed.

> For a whole series of philosophers, for more than a century [he writes] in fact, since Kierkegaard and Schopenhauer—there has been a secret, a revelation, a mystery, which would unveil itself in a magical illumination. The secret of the universe is going to be delivered up to us in an instant—in a flash. This saving instant is going to install us in the absolute. Only the secret is not going to reveal itself by means of a *thought*—the object of which would be beyond, and outside, what we *immediately* experience. No, it is here and now, hic et nunc. It awaits us, it lays siege to us, it haunts us. Present, and enveloped in the present, we are however obliged to tear it out, and to bring it out into the light of day—rending and shattering ourselves in the process.

This is excellently expressed. Formerly ultimate reality was 'beyond and outside what we immediately experience'. The origin of the term 'existential' is to be looked for in this *immediacy*—and also *concreteness*. The hypothesis of an absolute somewhere else than in existence (as posited in classical metaphysics) is rejected by the Existentialist. For the *reason* is substituted *intuition*. The absolute, implicated with our temporal existence, is to be contacted by ultra-rational, intuitive agencies. All ultimate cognitive possibilities are removed from their traditional seat in the human reason—that characteristic endowment of man—and transferred to those means of apprehension we share with the lizard and the bee. As a knower, even the big toe or the penis has priority over the mind. The eggs and bacon we have for breakfast—that rush to cut our nails on Saturday because if we do it on Sunday the devil will be after us all the week—becomes the stuff of the *Ding-an-Sich*.

As in so much modern thinking, then, so in existentialism, the human reason is discredited, and takes its place beside the liver and the glands of internal secretion (among which the so-called 'fighting-glands' are by no means the least important). Man is no longer an essentially thinking animal. Rather he is a willing and wishing animal: so—and above all—an *acting* animal: one step ahead of himself always, existing in the fruit of his acts. The activism of Sartre assumes the strangest forms in his novels. The hero of *L'Age de Raison*, for instance, looks upon his friend Daniel with new respect and reflects how *satisfied* he must feel, because Daniel has asked Marcelle to marry him. To buy a newspaper, or to cross the street, is after all *something*: but to ask your friend's discarded mistress to marry you! *That* unquestionably is *action*. *That* must make you feel good!—To murder somebody gives you somewhat the same satisfactory feeling, in the novels of Malraux. The heroes of Sartre are nothing like so tough as those of Malraux: indeed, almost any simple little action, like asking a man for a light in the street, impresses them. If a hero of Sartre met one of Malraux's tough homicidal heroes he would almost pass out with admiration.

Then, for the Existentialist, man is solely a creature of flesh and blood (an 'existence')! And only if all the flesh and blood goes with him can he go in search of the Absolute. Even Kierkegaard's 'leap' never took him outside the walls of his body. At most it was the leap of a flea, never beyond the electric field of the palpitating integument.—Man is a reasoning animal *on the side*: to think is, as it were, his hobby. His feeling is the big thing about him—it takes him farther than his thought. Such intuitional thinking (to which grouping existentialism belongs, merging the absolute in Time) affects a break with all traditional metaphysics, and of course with Christian traditional thinking. Remote as Marxist materialism is from the latter, nevertheless the Catholic and the Marxist unite to denounce the nihilism of the Existentialist. (The nihilistic conclusions of this teaching I will speak of shortly.)

> Here Marxist humanism protests [asserts M. Lefebvre] against the *dehumanization* of the Existentialist. For, as anyone can see, the human reason is a capital ingredient in our concept 'Man'. And that concept withers beneath our eyes if its rational advertisement and prestige are removed from it and the intellect becomes a little clockwork plaything—highly unreliable—in place of the living breath of what otherwise would be a mere machine.

Thus we find ourselves, not entirely unexpectedly, upon the side of the Marxists, in this particular issue.

Let us now contrast the humanist objections to existentialism of M. Lefebvre, with the words of an American follower of existentialism, Mr William Barrett. Having pointed out that existentialism is not an isolated system of thought, but merely a new expression of a widespread movement, eminent exponents of which have been Bergson, Whitehead, James, and Dewey: having remarked that 'Dewey had insisted on an existential context of thought', this American adherent announces:

> What we are present at is no longer a matter of schools, or isolated figures extracting explicit nuggets of influence from one another, but the whole Western mind—Europe and America—bending before a new climate of opinion; as the biologist portrays a whole species, scattered in space and without contact, moving along the same paths of adaption before a new geological upheaval.

Mr Barrett must I feel have formerly learnt to philosophize at Harvard with Professor Whitehead. The latter sage is very prominent in this pamphlet. I am taken back, as a result of the *Existenz* philosophy, to *Time and Western Man*. The cast of 'time-philosophers'—as they were there described—is almost *au grand complet* in the pages of Mr Barrett. The key-word of this new school was published about the same date as my *Time* book: its title is *Sein und Zeit*—Being and Time. *Zeit* is of its essence as it is of one and all of these thinkers.

I recall that eighteen years ago, when I grouped all these thinkers together, in a solid company, with the concept 'time' as a quite unifying principle,[1] and stated what you have just seen Mr Barrett stating, that 'the whole Western mind' was 'moving along the same paths', it was objected that I had arbitrarily associated them. When I described them all as suffering from the effects of the same poison, I found few to agree with me except the Catholics. The intellectuals of the 'thirties were without exception hostile to such a judgement. They felt themselves

---

[1] Heidegger was not amongst them: though had I known of him then, he would have been one of my most valuable exhibits.

quite rightly, *solidaire* with this philosophy: they were an integral part of that 'Western mind' which was 'moving along the same paths'. This involved an unusual degree of isolation for me. Yet today I am very far from being the only person who rejects existentialism as nihilistic and a symptom not of our health and sanity, but of the reverse. I even, at last, am almost upon the side of the majority.

I have spoken of the nihilism of the existential thinkers. Very briefly let me explain my use of that expression. As one or two of the critics of this system have shown, it is the *bracketing* that has in fact led to the situation we find. A man, having delivered up his soul, not to the Devil but to the tree outside his window—to his coal scuttle and 'bedroom suite' and to all the objects he can lay his eyes on, then suddenly cuts himself off from all this, from the external world. This comes about as a result of the Husserlian device called 'bracketing'. But he finds himself (suddenly, also) in an empty house—a void, a *nothing*. For this man—this philosopher—had beforehand scrupulously emptied, purified, the consciousness or ego (which is the *house* of which I speak, of which this wretched man is the inmate) of everything. When he inherited it he found that ancestors during thousands of years had accumulated in it all that a man needs for life. All kinds of quite invaluable gadgets. His vanity is such that he had cleared this out entirely—disinfected it of all tell-tale odour of 'essence', reduced the Reason to the status of a despised drudge. So—having cut himself off from the phenomenal world outside—in this empty shell our Existentialist flings himself on the floor and contemplates this echoless vacuity. Hence all the accompaniments of existential thought—'Angst' or 'Anguish', 'Dereliction', 'Loneliness', and 'Despair'. This is the despondent vocabulary of the most recent of these cults, with which everyone who has read a little about it will be familiar.

Or again: man has uncovered his nothingness, naturally enough, in identifying himself *absolutely* with his chairs and tables, his Ford car and his tabby-cat, producing an 'essence' in this act of union—or semi-union, for what I have spoken of figuratively as the 'empty house' still remains, and is still called a 'consciousness'. 'Existence precedes essence!' So says Sartre, after Heidegger. And when the Existentialist boils down (figuratively) his chairs and tables, his Ford car, etc., and values them, the result is not far from Zero for the philosophic mind.—It does not help matters at all to assert that man *creates* himself as he goes along (though there are some people stupid enough I suppose to feel rather puffed up at the thought of self-creation): nor is it really an advantage that man is always a few jumps ahead of himself—and in fact is not only largely *nothing* ('permeated with nothingness') but *nowhere*, too.

Upon reflection, and after the momentary elation of feeling that he is battling *his* way into *his* future—like an American marine in a tropical jungle infested with Japs; or 'creating' himself, as an artist 'creates'—the more modest and sensible man recognizes that he is not after all a work of art—that the *initial* creation was far beyond his powers or that of any man: that as to his *future* (for all his self-creation and following the precepts of action-at-any-price) all that can happen is that the Ford car may increase in size and (with luck) he may do rather more than keep-up-with-the-Joneses.

No help comes either, in the Existentialist picture, from the starring of the magical word, *liberty*. Of course I suppose people will get the usual kick at the mere sight of it. Then we are assured by Sartre that owing to the final disappearance of God our liberty is *absolute*! At this the entire audience waves its hat or claps its hands. But this natural enthusiasm is turned abruptly into something much less buoyant when it is learnt that this liberty weighs us down immediately with tremendous *responsibilities*. We now have to take all God's worries on our shoulders—now that we are become 'men like gods'. It is at this point that the Anxiety and Despondency begin, ending in utter despair.

But let us hear Sartre.

> Man is free, [he says][2] man is Freedom. If, on the other hand, God does not exist we do not find prescribed for us values or directions legitimizing our conduct. Thus we have neither . . . justifications nor excuses. We are alone—without excuses. This I shall express by saying that man is condemned to be free. Condemned, because he has not created himself: free, because once he is thrown into the world, he is responsible for everything he does.

[2] *L'Existentialisme est un humanisme.* J.P. Sartre.

This is a typical Sartre argument. For why should a creature who not only has had no hand in his own creation, but has not been consulted as to whether he wished to exist or not, be 'responsible for everything he does'? This does not follow at all. On the contrary, if his life were a difficult and unpleasant one and his behaviour became very violent and disorderly, although he might be shot like a mad dog it would not be *just* to do so. The fault would not be his, since he had not asked to live, or had any choice in the matter.

Then 'man is condemned to be free'. By whom or what is man condemned? And why call it freedom? It is a most misleading word for such a condition as is subsequently described (which description I shall shortly be outlining).—As to God not existing: since many people believe that He does exist, in announcing his non-existence Sartre might have offered a few reasons for his own disbelief.

Why trouble for that matter to mention God at all? Why not ignore what he regards as this Christian superstition altogether? There is no novelty in a declaration of God's non-existence—it is a disbelief that is as old as the hills.—The answer to this very natural question is that God plays a major part in existentialist philosophy. (It is a part of it that bores Sartre considerably, but there it is.) There are excellent reasons why he has to mention God.

Existentialism could not exist without the Christian background: to put it another way, it could not exist without Soren Kierkegaard, who is responsible for its atmosphere of crisis and despair—whereas Husserl supplied it with its vitalist framework. It is surely one of the oddest mass-borrowings in the history of ideas—this removal intact of a group of expressions belonging to a mystic experience that had no relation to the system into which they were introduced.[3]

That the possession of this element in his existential vocabulary is an embarrassment to Sartre is most evident. With characteristic hard-boiled bustle he tackles the problem in the book from which I quote above. He has been talking about his responsibilities.

'Ceci nous permet de comprendre ce que recouvrent des mots un

---

[3] I refer throughout to the systems of Heidegger and Sartre, though there are of course Christian Existentialists, such as Jaspers.

peu grandiloquent comme angoisse, délaissement, désespoir. Comme vous allez voir, c'est extrêmement simple.'

I have left this in French that you may catch better the tone of this voice—exact, official, aggresssively matter-of-fact. For these 'somewhat grandiloquent' words are *not* 'extremely simple' to explain away, in an offhand manner. M. Pierre Boutang, for instance, shows this very well as that concerns the Existentialist word 'anguish'.

> On this point [he writes],[4] Sartre is much less coherent than Marx, who rejects once and for all in his 'German Ideology' the conception of creation along with *all* problems of origin. If there is no creation there is no non-creation either and the idea of an anguish founded upon the non-creation of man by himself is another example of theological nostalgia. The idea of *dereliction* again can in no fashion be dissociated from its religious significance. Who then can feel himself *abandoned* without having been abandoned by somebody? Who laments his solitude, without having harboured an invincible idea of communion?

But let me return to the text of Sartre, where we shall be able to observe him at work gelding, explaining away the mystical jargon of Kierkegaard. I translate:

> First of all, what is to be understood by the word *angoisse* ? The Existentialist declares without beating about the bush that man is anguish. Here is what that signifies: the man who engages himself and who is quite clear that he is not only that which he chooses to be, but also a legislator choosing at the same time as himself the whole of humanity, can scarcely escape a sense of his total and profound responsibility.

[The reader who was expecting to see a little of the 'grandiloquence' removed from this doctrine will be distinctly surprised at this. So Man (every one of us) is a *legislator* (grander and grander!) for the whole of humanity!]

> Certainly [Sartre goes on] many people feel no anxiety. But what we say is that they hide from themselves (*se masquent*) their anguish—that they fly from it. Certainly there are many people who believe that in

[4] *Sartre, est-il un possédé?*

their actions they engage themselves, and when one says to them: 'But supposing *everybody* acted like that?' they shrug their shoulders.

You perceive however that we are now in the midst of a homily. A great moralist we have here: then is not 'existentialism a humanism'? This factitious curtain-lecture continues for some time: the 'anguish', however, is accounted for by the staggering responsibility: 'The Existentialist believes that man, without any support, without any help, is condemned, at every instant, to invent man.' Only a coward or a 'quietist' would sigh and murmur, 'What a pity it is you have suppressed God the Father, M. Sartre! He would have done all this "creating" and "inventing" for me. You are causing me a great deal of quite gratuitous "anguish"!'—'The doctrine which I offer you is the exact opposite of quietism. There is no reality except in *action!*' When Sartre speaks of 'action' it might be Teddy Roosevelt, or Mussolini, speaking.

'Despair' he polishes off much more smartly than 'Anguish'. 'As to "despair", that expression has an extremely simple meaning.' It turns upon the relation of the two French words *espoir* and *désespoir*—hope and despair. 'Désespoir' in the language of existentialism is simply 'agir sans espoir'. When the grandiloquent word 'despair' is used all that is meant is *act*—create yourself !—but don't hope too much. Sit down and *despair* is the last thing it means: with Sartre you would be doing that just as little as you would be doing it with the 'Bull Moose'!—*Délaissement* (abandonment) he says rather crossly, 'implies that we ourselves choose our being. It goes with the Anguish.'

To express our boredom at having to do for ourselves something that formerly was done for us, is it necessary to employ a word so charged with emotion?—we certainly should ask if we did not know how it got into Sartre's books. Is it necessary to make use of a word so weighted with misery as 'despair' to describe the man of action's justifiable scepticism regarding his actions redounding very much to his credit or furthering the interests of humanity? And it would indeed be childish hypocrisy were we intended to take him quite seriously, and believe that Sartre was weighed down with anguish at every moment of his life at the thought of the fearful responsibility of being Sartre; of how the 'inventing' by him (in the absence of God) or a *bad* Sartre would darken the outlook for the whole of mankind!

La rigueur philosophique is not to be expected of Sartre. The elaborate requirements of his publicity, his sense of a semi-official responsibility preclude that. I entirely agree with M. Henri Lefebvre that what is honest and rigorous in French atheistic existentialism is to be found in the pages of Albert Camus and Benjamin Fondane. In both cases the irrational—the Absurd—is an openly venerated principle. The unrelenting pursuit of this principle leads Fondane back to Primitive Man, and even farther. 'Biological being', I quote from Lefebvre, ' "is" metaphysic and absolute. In an hallucination à la Rimbaud the slug "is" an angel, and the mole, blind and virginal, represents existence before original sin.'

Lefebvre quotes: ' "There is only one means of getting rid of abstraction—it is the qualitative leap into the absurd." ' Fondane and Camus speak exactly the same language: their view of life is almost identical; a very much sterner one than that of Sartre. But 'what absurd'? asks Lefebvre: 'That of the negro (covered with his painted mask, abandoning himself to the fury of his ritualistic dance): that of the Christian, or that of Caligula?' That is a question to which many people would like an answer today beside M. Lefebvre. I gave the answer, over and over again, in a group of books dealing with precisely these questions. For of course a state of mind does not have to be called 'existential' (though eventually it has acquired this name) to reveal all these characteristics, more or less developed according to circumstances. Lefebvre for instance quotes van der Zeew as saying that 'primitive mentality is distinguished from the mentality of modern man by the fact that with primitive man the subject and the object are separated by a very much smaller interval—primitive life is much more direct (*moins réfléchie*), it is existential'. That the young child or primitive man effects with difficulty the separation of subject and object is a commonplace, but the above quotation is a better key perhaps to existentialism than a score of treatises.

Those a little familiar with movements in the various arts during the past forty years will have no difficulty in relating to the existentialist philosophers the infantilism of Klee, for instance, or the superbly effective adaptation to the European scene of the primitive vision (African, Mexican, Pacific Islands) of l'école de Paris, or the more literary primitivism of Gauguin, or the sculpture of Brancusi, Archipenko, etc. All this is of a piece: as Mr Barrett truly remarks, 'the whole Western mind—European and American—bending before a new climate of opinion'. It is a more violent and sultry climate than Europeans have known at any time in their history. It is an historic climate, it could be said—historic and political. As the European consciousness has expanded to take in the entire earth, with all its historic cultures, the climate of opinion has naturally become very different. A wind from Asia has blown down into Europe, and one up from Africa. The cool good sense and politeness surviving from the XVIIIth Century until quite recently has got to look like Dresden figures in a Saharan sandstorm. But the European thinks like a European: therein resides the tragedy. Culturally the expansion into universalism has been too rapid. The logical vessel has split wide open.—Let us agree that many undesirable things have rushed in, through the breach in the rationalist defences.

No work I know of is more beautifully suited to make dazzlingly clear the inner meaning of existentialism than *L'Etranger*, by Albert Camus. To the 'Dumb Ox' of whom I wrote must now be added the 'Surd'. In little Monsieur Mersault you not only get the irrationality of the 'Surd', and the dull speechlessness of the 'Dumb', but the 'Blindness' which I discussed you will recall *à propos* of Sartre's 'cyclone literature' (the deliberate myopia of the man who would not care to show History undressed). But I am beginning to encroach upon my next chapter. Let me in ending this one ask how it comes about that M. Lefebvre, the French Communist, and myself, reveal such strange identity of outlook: why our responses to these phenomena appear so nearly to agree. The reason has nothing whatever to do with the doctrine of communism—we certainly should not see eye to eye if it were a question of that. It has been helpful, of course, M. Lefebvre being so much more intelligent than one has any right to expect of one engaged in Marxist polemic; but it is not that either.

The explanation is to be found in the fact that the Stalinist thinks in terms now of the metropolitan mother-state. But were I legislating culturally for a new and powerful society, like the Russian, I should not recommend a diet of Gide's thievish schoolboys, of Malraux's homosexual homicidal romantics, of Heidegger's 'despair' and 'anguish', of Camus's moronic little sleepwalking killers, of Klee's infantile pastiches, of Picasso's more obscene masks. Obviously I should regard them as hysterical, artificial, socially destructive. But that is political. I have always myself, since I am an artist, been of two minds. When in the late 'twenties and 'thirties I attacked the type of thinking of which Heidegger is, as I have observed, so fine a specimen, it was because I was momentarily dismayed at the prospect of the imminent collapse of the culture of the West, and with it the reduction (as a result of repeated major wars) to political helplessness and helotry of all the Western nations, to which collapse this type of thinking was a contributory cause. The arts that derived from or reflected that philosophy were included in my attack.

For precisely the same reason M. Henri Lefebvre denounces those philosophies and those arts—except that in his case it is, as a good Party man, the Soviet Socialist Republics that he is concerned to protect from contamination (or that branch of them established on French soil); whereas in my case it is Western society I had uniquely in mind. I still automatically engage in the defence of a phantom. Then it happens—and needless to say this has its weight—I am not attracted to those types of thought—I refer to the chronologic school—and they run contrary to certain of my beliefs. But politics alone, at this moment, as we stand at the deathbed of a civilization that is after all ours, is more than a sufficient explanation.

There are other things that belong here—complications I fear. The agencies of decomposition (the philosophies and the arts) served the interests of communism of course: *originally*, in view of this, the 'fellow-traveller' defended them, violently denouncing anyone who criticized them. Another thing to be considered is that since today we are all precariously existing in the ruins of the Western nations, there would be no sense (if there ever was any) in defending this extinct life, this shell. Consequently what I have said in this chapter about the latest of the temporal absolutisms is an expression of what I believe, and in order to keep the intellectual record straight.

The parallel between the Europe of the 'twenties and 'thirties, and the Athens of antiquity after the Spartan Wars, is in some ways so remarkable and instructive that I will, I hope, be forgiven for providing this chapter with a sort of historic footnote.

Let me first quote an eminent authority in which the bare facts of

Plato's position are made plain. (The Communists do not require to prove that they are not their militant opposites.) What was the Fascist régime—in XXth Century language—followed years of democratic excesses in Athens; and Plato, invited to participate, refused.

> Socrates had made the close acquaintance of Plato's uncle Charmides in the year 431 B.C. and was even then familiar with Critias ... Plato tells us that at the time of the oligarchical usurpation of 404-3 ... he was urged by relatives who were among the (oligarchical) revolutionaries—no doubt Critias and Charmides—to enter public life under their auspices. But Plato first wanted to see what their policy would be.
>
> He was horrified to find that they soon showed signs of lawless violence, and finally disgusted when they attempted to make his 'elderly friend Socrates', the best man of his time, an accomplice in the illegal arrest and execution of a fellow-citizen whose property they intended to confiscate.—The leaders of the restored democracy did worse, for they actually put Socrates to death on an absurd charge of impiety. This Plato says put an end to his own political aspirations.[5]

As you see, the 'lawless violence' of these militant reactionaries repelled Plato once and for all: and had he been born in the XXth Century there is no reason to believe that Fascist violence would have pleased him any better than Communist violence. It is the dilemma of the 'intellectual', in whatever age he finds himself: for power is won by violence, and theories of the State have to cut their way over the bodies of men to power.—Unless we are to say that every person who is not a Communist (or its equivalent) is a Fascist, Plato was not the latter, but he was by birth an aristocrat, and he felt and professed the greatest dislike for Democracy. He admitted that Democracy is exceedingly agreeable. 'Is not this a way of life which for the moment is supremely delightful?' But according to him it was altogether too delightful for human beings, and with Aristotle he insisted it could not continue for long, despotism invariably supervening.

[5] A.E. Taylor.

Here, as throughout his adult life, Lewis is finally in favour of man as a thinking and reasoning animal, rather than as a figure permanently primed for automatic action executed in the service of feeling. Could it be said that he did not always follow such a precept in his own life? No doubt: but it is the hallmark of his work.

PART THREE

IMAGINATIVE WRITING

Lewis as prophet, Lewis as social and literary critic, are all very well it may be said, but it is by his imaginative work that a man who pulls round his shoulders the mantle of the artist must be remembered. True enough, and true too that Lewis is in this respect a special case. His approach was inveterately intellectual, all his novels contain characters who express ideas, and few British or American readers care for fictions that tax the mind rather than feed the emotions. There are plenty of attitudes but not many ideas in Dickens, Henry James, George Eliot, Edith Wharton. There *are* ideas—about the nature and proper ordering of society among other things—in Kingsley Amis, Saul Bellow, Evelyn Waugh, but in their most successful works the ideas are subordinate to the doings and human requirements of the characters.

It has to be granted to hostile critics that for the most part Lewis's fictions are not like that: the characters behave in accordance with the ideas they exemplify in their creator's mind; they are much more like people in Ben Jonson than in Shakespeare, they exist in a determinist universe and not in one that permits them free will. There are many memorable characters in the fictions, but they are seen from the outside by a writer who deliberately stands back from them, and is rarely personally involved in their fates. But to say this is only to call Lewis an artist in the mould of Jonson, Swift and Voltaire. To label his characters inadequate because they are not the creations of all-too-human naturalism to which popular novelists have accustomed us would be as absurd as to condemn *Candide* as one-dimensional, or complain that Jonson should have persuaded us to sympathise with the gulls rooked by Volpone. It is true also that Lewis cannot offer us the perfection of form attained by *The Great Gatsby* or the

259

subtleties of *The Ambassadors*, but his virtues as a fiction writer are unique. He is the intellectual novelist *par excellence* of the twentieth century. His finest work offers a continual sparkle of ideas, parables about the use and abuse of power, and constant interest in the relationship between the individual and society, the one and the many. His work is not all of a piece. In the writing of fiction, as in visual art, his attitude moved with the years, so that the nature of the fictions changed too.

The unequal struggle of the one and the many, the conflict between intellect and will: that is the basic subject of *The Enemy of the Stars*, the play published in *Blast 1* and then reissued much revised in 1932. As a play it is unactable, even though it has once been staged, but in some respects it anticipates the approach of Joyce in the Walpurgis Nacht scenes of *Ulysses*, and the stage directions and settings (in one scene 'up-ended egg-boxes, casks, rubble, chevaux-de-frise, collections of clay-loam and brick-dust', succeeded in the next by a hut entrance like a mine shaft) may well have influenced Beckett. Through the almost impenetrable density of Lewis's early prose the two principal characters emerge: Arghol the gladiator who has come to do battle with an ideologic phantom, namely, 'Humanity', and the goatish but moronic Hanp, 'hideous and stupid . . . the masculine, the rough stuff of the fecund horde of man'. Arghol is beaten up, but refuses to take revenge on those who beat him, answers Hanp's urging to reciprocal violence ('you are big enough—you could knock the spunk out of him inside a minute! Smash his great ugly jaw for him, I know I would!') with painful logic. Yet *Hanp is part of Arghol*, and Arghol acknowledges that he has tried to make Hanp a second, inferior self, a self who will fetch and carry for his lower nature, 'a yapping Poodle-parasite, a sort of mechanical bow-wow'. At the end of the play the infuriated Hanp kills Arghol and then destroys himself. 'He sinks like the plummet in the imagery of his murdered master.'

To the revised version of this indigestible but remarkable play Lewis added a coda in the form of notes called 'The Physics of the Not-Self'. The play is intended, he says, 'to show the human mind in its traditional role of the enemy of life, as an oddity outside the machine'. The machine therefore works to destroy it, and a series of contrasts is drawn between the insensate will and the intellect, which however great its apparent egoism contains at its core something impersonal and essentially truthful, the 'not-self' which 'betrays at every moment its transient human associate'. The will takes its revenge upon the intellect, as Hanp in the end upon Arghol or ordinary humanity on those extraordinary beings whom they should nourish. The play contains the germ of the ideas developed fully in *The Art of Being Ruled* and *Time and Western Man*, although in a comparatively rudimentary form. The contrast between will and idea, body and brain, recurs again and again: for instance, in the brief notes called 'Inferior Religions' which form a kind of comment to the stories about fairly primitive people collected in *The Wild Body*:

> The Wild Body, I have said, triumphs in its laughter. What is the Wild Body?
>
> The Wild Body, as understood here, is that small, primitive, literally antediluvian vessel in which we set out on our adventures. Or regarded as a brain, it is rather a winged magic horse, that transports us hither and thither, sometimes rushing as in the chinese cosmogonies, up and down the outer reaches of space.

Bestre, in the story printed here, shows the wild body in action, and exemplifies also one aspect of Lewis's writing. It is sometimes said of fiction writers that they are 'painting in words', a casually used phrase which generally means nothing more than that the novelist has attempted a bit of 'fine writing'. In Lewis the phrase is meaningful and particular. We see Bestre through his appearance, and this appearance is much more like a description of a painting (as in the paragraph beginning 'His very large eyeballs') than like the customary literary view of a character. And more than this, what Bestre does (his 'campaigns') merges with what he is, so that he appears less a person than a force of nature.

The story exists in three versions, the first published in 1909. The one used here is the third, the story as it appeared in *The Wild Body*.

from THE WILD BODY

Bestre

As I walked along the quay at Kermanac, there was a pretty footfall in my rear. Turning my head, I found an athletic frenchwoman, of the bourgeois class, looking at me.

The crocket-like floral postiches on the ridges of her head-gear looked crisped down in a threatening way: her nodular pink veil was an apoplectic gristle round her stormy brow; steam came out of her lips upon the harsh white atmosphere. Her eyes were dark, and the contiguous colour of her cheeks of a redness quasi-venetian, with something like the feminine colouring of battle. This was surely a feline battle-mask, then; but in such a pacific and slumbrous spot I thought it an anomalous ornament.

My dented *bidon* of a hat—cantankerous beard—hungarian boots, the soles like the rind of a thin melon slice, the uppers in stark calcinous segments; my cassock-like blue broadcloth coat (why was I like this?— the habits of needy travel grew this composite shell), this uncouthness might have raised in her the question of defiance and offence. I glided swiftly along on my centipedal boots, dragging my eye upon the rough walls of the houses to my right like a listless cane. Low houses faced the small vasey port. It was there I saw Bestre.

This is how I became aware of Bestre.

The detritus of some weeks' hurried experience was being dealt with in my mind, on this crystalline, extremely cold walk through Kermanac to Braspartz, and was being established in orderly heaps. At work in my untidy hive, I was alone: the atmosphere of the workshop dammed me in. That I moved forward was no more strange than if a carpenter's shop or chemist's laboratory, installed in a boat, should move forward on the tide of a stream. Now, what seemed to happen was that, as I bent over my work, an odiously grinning face peered in at my window. The impression of an intrusion was so strong, that I did not even realize at first that it was I who was the intruder. That the window was not my window, and that the face was not peering in but out: that, in fact, it was I myself who was guilty of peering into somebody else's window: this was hidden from me in the first moment of consciousness about the odious brown person of Bestre. It is a wonder that the curse did not at once fall from me on this detestable inquisitive head. What I did do was to pull up in my automatic progress, and, instead of passing on, to continue to stare in at Bestre's kitchen window, and scowl at Bestre's sienna-coloured gourd of a head.

Bestre in his turn was nonplussed. He knew that some one was looking in at his kitchen window, all right: he had expected some one to do so, some one who in fact had contracted the habit of doing that. But he had mistaken my steps for this other person's; and the appearance of my face was in a measure as disturbing to him as his had been to me. My information on these points afterwards became complete. With a flexibile imbrication reminiscent of a shutter-lipped ape, a bud of tongue still showing, he shot the latch of his upper lip down in front of the nether one, and depressed the interior extremities of his eyebrows sharply from their quizzing perch—only this monkey-on-a-stick mechanical pull—down the face's centre. At the same time, his arms still folded like bulky lizards, blue tattoo on brown ground, upon the escarpment of his vesicular middle, not a hair or muscle moving, he made a quick, slight motion to me with one hand to get out of the picture without speaking—to efface myself. It was the suggestion of a theatrical sportsman. I was in the line of fire. I moved on: a couple of steps did it. That lady was twenty yards distant: but nowhere was there anything in sight evidently related to Bestre's gestures. 'Pension de Famille?' What prices?—and how charmingly placed! I remarked the vine: the building, of one storey, was exceedingly long, it took some time to pass along it. I reached the principal door. I concluded this entrance was really disused, although more imposing. So emerging on the quay once more, and turning along the front of the house, I again discovered myself in contact with Bestre. He was facing towards me, and down the quay, immobile as before, and the attitude so much a replica as to make it seem a plagiarism of his kitchen piece. Only now his head was on one side, a verminous grin had dispersed the equally unpleasant entity of his shut mouth. The new facial arrangement and angle for the head imposed on what seemed his stock pose for the body, must mean: 'Am I not rather smart? Not just a little bit smart? Don't you think? A little, you will concede? You did not expect that, did you? That was a nasty jar for you, was it not? Ha! my lapin, that was unexpected, that is plain! Did you think you would find Bestre asleep? He is always awake! He watched you being born, and has watched you ever since. Don't be too sure that he did not play some part in planting the little seed from which you grew into such a big, fine (many withering exclamation marks) boy (or girl). He will be in at your finish too. But he is in no hurry about that. He is never in a hurry! He bides his time. Meanwhile he laughs at you. He finds you a little funny. That's right! Yes! I am still looking!'

His very large eyeballs, the small saffron ocellation in their centre, the tiny spot through which light entered the obese wilderness of his body; his bronzed bovine arms, swollen handles for a variety of indolent little ingenuities; his inflated digestive case, lent their combined expressiveness to say these things; with every tart and biting condiment that eye-fluid, flaunting of fatness (the well-filled), the insult of the comic, implications of indecency, could provide. Every variety of bottom-tapping resounded from his dumb bulk. His tongue stuck out, his lips eructated with the incredible indecorum that appears to be the monopoly of liquids, his brown arms were for the moment genitals, snakes in one massive twist beneath his mamillary slabs, gently riding on a pancreatic swell, each hair on his oil-bearing skin contributing its message of porcine affront.

Taken fairly in the chest by this magnetic attack, I wavered. Turning the house corner it was like confronting a hard meaty gust. But I perceived that the central gyroduct passed a few feet clear of me. Turning my back, arching it a little, perhaps, I was just in time to receive on the boko a parting volley from the female figure of the obscure encounter, before she disappeared behind a rock which brought Kermanac to a close on this side of the port. She was evidently replying to Bestre. It was the rash grating philippic of a battered cat, limping into safety. At the moment that she vanished behind the boulder, Bestre must have vanished too, for a moment later the quay was empty. On reaching the door into which he had sunk, plump and slick as into a stage trap, there he was inside—this grease-bred old mammifer—his tufted vertex charging about the plank ceiling—generally ricochetting like a dripping sturgeon in a boat's bottom—arms warm brown, ju-jitsu of his guts, tan canvas shoes and trousers rippling in ribbed planes as he darted about—with a filthy snicker for the scuttling female, and a stark cock of the eye for an unknown figure miles to his right: he filled this short tunnel with clever parabolas and vortices, little neat stutterings of triumph, goggle-eyed hypnotisms, in retrospect, for his hearers.

'T'as vu? T'as vu? Je l'ai fichu c'es' qu'elle n'attendait pas! Ah, la rosse! Qu'elle aille raconter ça à son crapule de mari. Si, si, s'il vient ici, tu sais—'

His head nodded up and down in batches of blood-curdling

affirmations; his hand, pudgy hieratic disc, tapped the air gently, then sawed tenderly up and down.

Bestre, on catching sight of me, hailed me as a witness. 'Tiens! Ce monsieur peut vous le dire: il était là. Il m'a vu là-dedans qui l'attendait!'

I bore witness to the subtleties of his warlike ambush. I told his sister and two boarders that I had seldom been privy to such a rich encounter. They squinted at me, and at each other, dragging their eyes off with slow tosses of the head. I took a room in this house immediately—the stage-box in fact, just above the kitchen. For a week I was perpetually entertained.

Before attempting to discover the significance of Bestre's proceedings when I clattered into the silken zone of his hostilities, I settled down in his house; watched him idly from both my windows—from that looking on to the back—(cleaning his gun in the yard, killing chickens, examining the peas), from the front one—rather shyly sucking up to a fisherman upon the quay. I went into his kitchen and his shed and watched him. I realized as little as he did that I was patting and prodding a subject of these stories. There was no intention in these stoppages on my zigzag course across Western France of taking a human species, as an entomologist would take a Distoma or a Narbonne Lycosa, to study. Later, at the time of my spanish adventure (which was separated by two years from Bestre), I had grown more professional. Also, I had become more conscious of myself and of my powers of personally provoking a series of typhoons in tea-cups. But with my Bretons I was very new to my resources, and was living in a mild and early millennium of mirth. It was at the end of a few months' roaming in the country that I saw I had been a good deal in contact with a tribe, some more and some less generic. And it is only now that it has seemed to me an amusing labour to gather some of these individuals in retrospect and group them under their function, to which all in some diverting way were attached.

So my stoppage at Kermanac, for example, was because Bestre was a little excitement. I had never seen brown flesh put to those uses. And the situation of his boarding-house would allow of unlimited pococurantism, idling and eating, sunning myself in one of my windows, with Berkeley or Cudworth in my hand, and a staring eye that lost itself in reveries that suddenly took on flesh and acted some obstinate little part or other, the phases of whose dramatic life I would follow stealthily from window to window, a book still in my hand, shaking with the most innocent laughter. I was never for a minute unoccupied. Fête followed fête, fêtes of the mind. Then, as well, the small cliffs of the scurfy little port, its desertion and queer train of life, reached a system of very early dreams I had considered effaced. But all the same, although not self-conscious, I went laughing after Bestre, tapping him, setting traps for the game that he decidedly contained for my curiosity. So it was almost as though Fabre could have established himself within the masonries of the bee, and lived on its honey, while investigating for the human species: or stretched himself on a bed of raphia and pebbles at the bottom of the Lycosa's pit, and lived on flies and locusts. I lay on Bestre's billowy beds, drank his ambrosial cider, fished from his boat; he brought me birds and beasts that he had chased and killed. It was an idyllic life of the calmest adventure. We were the best of friends: he thought I slapped him because contact with his fat gladdened me, and to establish contact with the feminine vein in his brown-coated ducts and muscles. Also he was Bestre, and it must be nice to pat and buffet him as it would be to do that with a dreadful lion.

He offered himself, sometimes wincing coquettishly, occasionally rolling his eyes a little, as the lion might do to remind you of your natural dread, and heighten the luxurious privilege.

Bestre's boarding-house is only open from June to October: the winter months he passes in hunting and trapping. He is a stranger to Kermanac, a Boulonnais, and at constant feud with the natives. For some generations his family have been strangers where they lived; and he carries on his face the mark of an origin even more distant than Picardy. His great-grandfather came into France from the Peninsula, with the armies of Napoleon. Possibly his alertness, combativeness and timidity are the result of these exilings and difficult adjustments to new surroundings, working in his blood, and in his own history.

He is a large, tall man, corpulent and ox-like: you can see by his movements that the slow aggrandisement of his stomach has hardly been noticed by him. It is still compact with the rest of his body, and he is as nimble as a flea. It has been for him like the peculations of a minister, enriching himself under the nose of the caliph; Bestre's kingly indifference can be accounted for by the many delights and benefits procured through this subtle misappropriation of the general resources of the body. Sunburnt, with large yellow-white moustache, little eyes protruding with the cute strenuosity already noticed, when he meets any one for the first time his mouth stops open, a cigarette end adhering to the lower lip. He will assume an expression of expectancy and repressed amusement, like a man accustomed to nonplussing: the expression the company wears in those games of divination when they have made the choice of an object, and he whose task it is to guess its nature is called in, and commences the cross-examination. Bestre is jocose; he will beset you with mocking thoughts as the blindfold man is danced round in a game of blind man's buff. He may have regarded my taps as a myopic clutch at his illusive person. He gazes at a new acquaintance as though this poor man, without guessing it, were entering a world of astonishing things! A would-be boarder arrives and asks him if he has a room with two beds. Bestre fixes him steadily for twenty seconds with an amused yellow eye. Without uttering a word, he then leads the way to a neighbouring door, lets the visitor pass into the room, stands watching him with the expression of a conjurer who has just drawn a curtain aside and revealed to the stupefied audience a horse and cart, or a life-size portrait of the Shah of Persia, where a moment ago there was nothing.

Suppose the following thing happened. A madman, who believes himself a hen, escapes from Charenton, and gets, somehow or other, as far as Finisterre. He turns up at Kermanac, knocks at Bestre's door and asks him with a perfect stereotyped courtesy for a large, airy room, with a comfortable perch to roost on, and a little straw in the corner where he might sit. Bestre a few days before has been visited by the very idea of arranging such a room: all is ready. He conducts his demented client to it. Now his manner with his everyday client would be thoroughly appropriate under these circumstances. They are carefully suited to a very weak-minded and whimsical visitor indeed.

Bestre has another group of tricks, pertaining directly to the commerce of his hospitable trade. When a customer is confessing in the fullest way his paraesthesias, allowing this new host an engaging glimpse of his nastiest propriums and kinks, Bestre behaves, with unconscious logic, as though a secret of the most disreputable nature were being imparted to him. Were, in fact, the requirements of a vice being enumerated, he could not display more plainly the qualms caused by his rôle of accessory. He will lower his voice, whisper in the client's ear; before doing so glance over his shoulder apprehensively two or three times, and push his guest roughly into the darkest corner of the passage or kitchen. It is his perfect understanding—is he not the only man who does, at once, forestall your eager whim: there is something of the fortune-teller in him—that produces the air of mystery. For his information is not always of the nicest, is it? He must know more about you than I daresay you would like many people to know. And Bestre will in his turn mention certain little delicacies that he, Bestre, will see that you have, and that the other guests will not share with you. So there you are committed at the start to a subtle collusion. But Bestre means it. Every one he sees for the first time he is thrilled about, until they have got used to him. He would give you anything while he is still strange to you. But you see the interest die down in his eyes, at the end of twenty-four hours, whether you have assimilated him or not. He only gives you about a day for your meal. He then assumes that you have finished him, and he feels chilled by your scheduled disillusion. A fresh face and an enemy he depends on for that 'new' feeling—or what can we call this firework that he sends up for the stranger, that he enjoys so much himself—or this rare bottle he can only open when hospitality compels—his own blood?

I had arrived at the master-moment of one of Bestre's campaigns. These were long and bitter affairs. But they consisted almost entirely of dumb show. The few words that passed were generally misleading. A vast deal of talking went on in the different camps. But a dead and pulverizing silence reigned on the field of battle, with few exceptions.

It was a matter of who could be most silent and move least: it was a stark stand-up fight between one personality and another, unaided by adventitious muscle or tongue. It was more like phases of a combat or courtship in the insect-world. The Eye was really Bestre's weapon: the ammunition with which he loaded it was drawn from all the most skunk-like provender, the most ugly mucins, fungoid glands, of his physique. Excrement as well as sputum would be shot from this luminous hole, with the same certainty in its unsavoury appulsion. Every resource of metonymy, bloody mind transfusion or irony were also his. What he selected as an arm in his duels, then, was the Eye.

As he was always the offended party, he considered that he had this choice. I traced the predilection for this weapon and method to a very fiery source—to the land of his ancestry—Spain. How had the knife dropped out of his outfit? Who can tell? But he retained the *mirada* whole and entire enough to please any one, all the more active for the absence of the dagger. I pretend that Bestre behaved as he did directly because his sweet forebears had to rely so much on the furious languishing and jolly conversational properties of their eyes to secure their ends at all. The spanish beauty imprisoned behind her casement can only roll her eyes at her lover in the street below. The result of these and similar Eastern restraints develops the eye almost out of recognition. Bestre in his kitchen, behind his casement, was unconsciously employing this gift from his semi-arabian past. And it is not even the unsupported female side of Bestre. For the lover in the street as well must keep his eye in constant training to bear out the furibond jugular drops, the mettlesome stamping, of the guitar. And all the haughty chevaleresque habits of this bellicose race have substituted the eye for the mouth in a hundred ways. The Grandee's eye is terrible, and at his best is he not speechless with pride? Eyes, eyes: for defiance, for shrivelling subordinates, for courtesy, for love. A 'spanish eye' might be used as we say, 'Toledo blade.' There, anyway, is my argument; I place on the one side Bestre's eye; on the other I isolate the iberian eye. Bestre's grandfather, we know, was a Castilian. To show how he was beholden to this extraction, and again how the blood clung to him, Bestre was in no way grasping. It went so far that he was noticeably careless about money. This, in France, could not be accounted for in any other way.

Bestre's quarrels turned up as regularly as work for a good shoemaker or dentist. Antagonism after antagonism flashed forth: became more acute through several weeks: detonated in the dumb pyrotechnic I have described; then wore itself out with its very exhausting and exacting violence.—At the passing of an enemy Bestre will pull up his blind with a snap. There he is, with his insult stewing lusciously in his yellow sweat. The eyes fix on the enemy, on his weakest spot, and do their work. He has the anatomical instinct of the hymenopter for his prey's most morbid spot; for an old wound; for a lurking vanity. He goes into the other's eye, seeks it, and strikes. On a physical blemish he turns a scornful and careless rain like a garden hose. If the deep vanity is on the wearer's back, or in his walk or gaze, he sluices it with an abundance you would not expect his small eyes to be capable of delivering.

But the *mise en scène* for his successes is always the same. Bestre is *discovered* somewhere, behind a blind, in a doorway, beside a rock, when least expected. He regards the material world as so many ambushes for his body.

Then the key principle of his strategy is provocation. The enemy must be exasperated to the point at which it is difficult for him to keep his hands off his aggressor. The desire to administer the blow is as painful as a blow received. That the blow should be taken back into the enemy's own bosom, and that he should be stifled by his own oath—*that* Bestre regards as so many blows, and so much abuse, of *his*, Bestre's, although he has never so much as taken his hands out of his pockets, or opened his mouth.

I learnt a great deal from Bestre. He is one of my masters. When the moment came for me to discover myself—a thing I believe few people have done so thoroughly, so early in life and so quickly—I recognized more and more the beauty of Bestre. I was only prevented from turning my eye upon myself even at that primitive period of speculative adolescence by that one-sidedness that only the most daring tamper with.

The immediate quay-side neighbours of Bestre afford him a constant war-food. I have seen him slipping out in the evening and depositing refuse in front of his neighbour's house. I have seen a woman screeching at him in pidgin french from a window of the débit two doors off, while he pared his nails a yard from his own front door. This was to show his endurance. The subtle notoriety, too, of his person is dear to him. But local functionaries and fishermen are not his only fare. During summer, time hangs heavy with the visitor from Paris. When the first ennui comes upon him, he wanders about desperately, and his eye in due course falls on Bestre.

It depends how busy Bestre is at the moment. But often enough he will take on the visitor at once in his canine way. The visitor shivers, opens his eyes, bristles at the quizzing pursuit of Bestre's oeillade; the remainder of his holiday flies in a round of singular plots, passionate conversations and prodigious encounters with this born broiler.

Now, a well-known painter and his family, who rented a house in the neighbourhood, were, it seemed, particularly responsive to Bestre. I could not—arrived, with some perseverance, at the bottom of it—find any cause for his quarrel. The most insignificant pretext was absent. The pretentious peppery Paris Salon artist, and this Boulogne-bred Breton inhabited the same village, and they grew larger and larger in each other's eyes at a certain moment, in this armorican wilderness. As Bestre swelled and swelled for the painter, he was seen to be the possessor of some insult incarnate, that was an intolerable factor in the life of so lonely a place. War was inevitable. Bestre saw himself growing and growing, with the glee of battle in his heart, and the flicker of budding affront in his little eye. He did nothing to arrest this alarming aggrandizement. Pretexts could have been found: but they were dispensed with, by mutual consent. This is how I reconstructed the obscure and early phases of that history. What is certain, is that there had been much eye-play on the quay between Monsieur Rivière and Monsieur Bestre. And the scene that I had taken part in was the culmination of a rather humiliating phase in the annals of Bestre's campaigns.

The distinguished painter's wife, I learnt, had contracted the habit of passing Bestre's kitchen window of a morning when Mademoiselle Marie was alone there—gazing glassily in, but never looking at Mademoiselle Marie. This had such a depressing effect on Bestre's old sister, that it reduced her vitality considerably, and in the end brought on diarrhoea. Why did Bestre permit the war to be brought into his own camp with such impunity? The only reason that I could discover for this was, that the attacks were of very irregular timing. He had been out fishing in one or two cases, employed in his garden or elsewhere. But on the penultimate occasion Madame Rivière had practically finished off the last surviving female of Bestre's notable stock. As usual, the wife of the parisian Salon master had looked into the kitchen; but this time she had looked *at* Mademoiselle Marie, and in such a way as practically to curl her up on the floor. Bestre's sister had none of her brother's ferocity, and in every way departed considerably from his type, except in a mild and sentimental imitation of his colouring. The distinguished painter's wife, on the other hand, had a touch of Bestre about her. Bestre did not have it all his own way. Because of this, recognizing the redoubtable and Bestre-like quality of his enemy, he had resorted no doubt to such extreme measures as I suspect him of employing. She had chosen her own ground—his kitchen. That was a vast mistake. On that ground, I am satisfied, Bestre was invincible. It was even surprising that there any trump should have been lavished.

On that morning when I drifted into the picture what happened to induce such a disarray in his opponent? What superlative shaft, with deadly aim, did he direct against her vitals? She would take only a few seconds to pass the kitchen window. He had brought her down with a stupendous rush. In principle, as I have said, Bestre sacrifices the claims any individual portion of his anatomy might have to independent expressiveness to a tyrannical appropriation of all this varied battery of bestial significance by his *eye*. The eye was his chosen weapon. Had he any theory, however, that certain occasions warranted, or required, the auxiliary offices of some unit of the otherwise subordinated mass? Can the sex of his assailant give us a clue? I am convinced in my own mind that another agent was called in on this occasion. I am certain that he struck the death-blow with another engine than his eye. I believe that the most savage and obnoxious means of affront were employed to cope with the distinguished painter's wife. His rejoinder would perhaps be of that unanswerable description, that it would be stamped on the spot, for an adversary, as an authentic last word. No further appeal to arms of that sort would be rational: it must have been right up against litigation and physical assault.

Monsieur Rivière, with his painting-pack and campstool, came along the quay shortly afterwards, going in the same direction as his wife. Bestre was at his door; and he came in later, and let us know how he had behaved.

'I wasn't such a fool as to insult him: there were witnesses; let him do that. But if I come upon him in one of those lanes at the back there, you know ... I was standing at my door; he came along and looked at my house and scanned my windows' (this is equivalent in Bestre-warfare to a bombardment). 'As he passed I did not move. I thought to myself, "Hurry home, old fellow, and ask Madame what she has seen during her little walk!" *I looked him in the white of the eyes.* He thought I'd lower mine; he doesn't know me. And, after all, what is he, though he's got the Riband of the Legion of Honour? I don't carry my decorations on my coat! I have mine marked on my body. Did I ever show you what I've got here? No; I'm going to show you.' He had shown all this before, but my presence encouraged a repetition of former successes. So while he was speaking he jumped up quickly, undid his shirt, bared his chest and stomach, and pointed to something beneath his arm. Then, rapidly rolling up his sleeves, he pointed to a cicatrice rather like a vaccination mark, but larger. While showing his scars he slaps his body, with a sort of sneering rattle or chuckle between his words, his eyes protruding more than usual. His customary wooden expression is disintegrated: this compound of a constant foreboded reflection of the expression of astonishment your face will acquire when you learn of his wisdom, valour, or wit: the slightest shade of sneering triumph, and a touch of calm relish at your wonder. Or he seems teaching you by his staring grimace the amazement you should feel: and his grimace gathers force and blooms as the full sense of what you are witnessing, hearing, bursts upon you, while your gaping face conforms more and more to Bestre's prefiguring mask.

As to his battles, Bestre is profoundly unaware of what strange category he has got himself into. The principles of his strategy are possibly the possession of his libido, but most certainly not that of the bulky and surface citizen, Bestre. On the contrary, he considers himself on the verge of a death struggle at any moment when in the presence of one of his enemies.

Like all people who spend their lives talking about their deeds, he presents a very particular aspect in the moment of action. When discovered in the thick of one of his dumb battles, he has the air of a fine company promoter, concerned, trying to corrupt some sombre fact into shielding for an hour his unwieldy fiction, until some fresh wangle can retrieve it. Or he will display a great empirical expertness in reality, without being altogether at home in it.

Bestre in the moment of action feels as though he were already talking. His action has the exaggerated character of his speech, only oddly curbed by the exigencies of reality. In his moments of most violent action he retains something of his dumb passivity. He never seems quite entering into reality, but observing it. He is looking at the reality with a professional eye, so to speak: with a professional liar's.

I have noticed that the more cramped and meagre his action has been, the more exuberant his account of the affair is afterwards. The more restrictions reality has put on him, the more unbridled is his gusto as historian of his deeds, immediately afterwards. Then he has the common impulse to avenge that self that has been perishing under the famine and knout of a bad reality, by glorifying and surfeiting it on its return to the imagination.

━━━━━━

All the dichotomies coalesce in *Tarr*, published in 1918 but begun much earlier. The story's action takes place in the art world of Paris. The eponymous central character, who voices many of his author's views, is the artist, the superior would-be detached figure still subject to the sexual and other demands of clownish humanity. The other important figure, Otto Kreisler, is frantic action incarnate, an embodiment of sensation driven by the need for violence. And Kreisler is not merely action, but specifically *German* action incarnate. The image of Kreisler may have been developed over the years so that he suggested a destructive Teutonic will to power. Tarr and Kreisler: art and life, thought and action. Tarr does relatively little in the book, except move from one love affair to another. Love affairs are life, and hence an inferior substitute for art, but it is made clear that Tarr like Arghol is part of the 'life' he deprecates. Tarr, even, is linked with Kreisler, who rapes Tarr's girl Bertha, kills a Pole named Soltyk in a duel, runs away, and eventually hangs himself after arrest by the police. Kreisler, it is suggested, is what Tarr might have become if he had not been an artist. Much of this potentially tragic material is presented as comedy. Moral lessons are avoided, indeed specifically disclaimed.

Many years afterwards Lewis said in a letter that the writer of *Tarr* had been an extremist. 'I wanted at the same time for it to be a novel, and to do a piece of writing worthy of the hand of the abstractist innovator . . . It was my object to eliminate anything less essential than a noun or a verb. Prepositions, pronouns, articles—the small fry—as far as might be, I would abolish. Of course I was unable to do this, but for the purposes of the *novel* I produced a somewhat jagged prose.' *Tarr* was greeted on publication as a remarkable work, but the jaggedness of the prose undoubtedly limited the number of readers. In the revised version of 1928 a good many of the rough edges have been smoothed, the small fry reinstated, the narrative made to flow more easily, although at the cost of some dilution in its extraordinary power. The latter version is without doubt easier to read, and I have used it in this chapter which finds Kreisler at a dance. Kreisler is hard up, his dress shirt or 'frac' is in pawn, he has made love to Bertha but feels an overwhelming passion for the stylish, intelligent Anastasya. All this makes him behave more outrageously than usual, and the result is one of the great comic scenes in modern literature.

from TARR

Tarr, Part III, Chapter 2

One certain thing (amongst many uncertainties) about the english club, the Bonnington Club, was that it could not be said as yet to have found itself quite. Its central room (and that was almost all there was of it) reminded you of a Public Swimming Bath when it was used as a Ball-room, and when used as a studio, you thought of a Concert Hall. But it had cost a good deal to build. It made a cheerful show, with pink, red and pale blue paper chains and Chinese Lanterns, one week, for some festivity, and the next, sparely robed in dark red curtains, would settle its walls gravely to receive some houseless quartet. In this manner it paid its way. Some phlegmatic divinity seemed to have brought it into existence—'Found a club, found a club!' it had reiterated in the depths of certain minds probably with sleepy tenacity.—Someone sighed, got up and went round to another individual of the same sort, and said perhaps a club had better be founded. The second assented and subscribed something, to get rid of the other. In the course of time, a young french architect had been entrusted with the job. A club. Yes. What sort of a club? The architect could not find out. Something to be used for drawing-classes, social functions, a reading-room, he knew the sort of thing! He saw he was on the wrong tack. He went away and made his arrangements accordingly. He had produced a design of an impressive and to all appearance finished house: it was a sincerely ironic masterpiece, but with a perfect gravity, and even stateliness of appearance. It was the most non-committing façade, the most absolutely unfinal interior, the most tentative set of doors, ever seen: a monster of reservations.

Not only had the building been put to every conceivable use itself, but it dragged the Club with it. The members of the Bonnington Club changed and metamorphosed themselves with *its* changes. They became athletic or sedentary according to the shifts and exigencies of this building's existence. They turned out in dress clothes or gymnasium get-ups as its destiny prompted, to back it up: one month they would have to prove that it *was* a gymnasium, the next that it *was* a drawing-school, so they stippled and vaulted, played table-tennis and listened to debates.

The inviting of the german contingent was a business move: they might be enticed into membership and would in any event spread the fame of the Club, getting and subsequently giving some conception of the resources of the club-house building. The hall had been very prettily arranged: the adjoining rooms were hung with the drawings and paintings of the club members.

Kreisler, ever since the occurrence on the Boulevard, had felt a reckless irresponsibility, which he did not care to conceal. His assurance even came to smack of braggadocio.

With his abashed english hostess he carried on a strange conversation full of indirect references to that 'stately edifice in the Rue de Rennes' of which he had spoken to Bertha. 'That stately edifice in the Rue de Rennes—but of course you don't know it—!'

With smiling german ceremoniousness, with heavy circumlocutions, he bent down to her nervously smiling face, and poured into her startled ear symbols and images of pawn-shops, usury, three gold balls, 'pious mountains,' 'Smokkin' or 'Frac' complets, which he seemed a little to confuse, overwhelmed her with a serious terminology, all in a dialect calculated to bewilder the most acute philologist.

'Yes it *is* interesting,' she said with strained conviction.

'Isn't it?' Kreisler replied. A comparative estimate of the facilities for the disposing of a watch in Germany and France had been the subject of his last remarks.

'I'm going to introduce you, Herr Kreisler, to a friend of mine—Mrs Bevelage.'

She wanted to give the german guests a particularly cordial reception. Kreisler did not seem, superficially, a great acquisition to any club, but he was with the others. As a means of concluding this very painful interview—he was getting nearer every minute to the word that he yet solemnly forbade himself the use of—she led him up to a self-possessed exemplar of mid-victorian lovely womanhood, whose attitude suggested that she might even yet stoop to Folly if the occasion arose. Mrs Bevelage could listen to all this, and would be able to cope with a certain disquieting element she recognized in this young German.

He saw the motive of her move: and, looking with ostentatious regret at a long-legged flapper seated next to them, cast a reproachful glance at his hostess.

Left alone with the widow, he surveyed her prosperous, velvet and cuirassed form.

'Get thee to a nunnery!' he said dejectedly.

'I beg your pardon?'

'Yes. You have omitted "My Lord"!'

Mrs Bevelage looked pleased and puzzled. Possibly he was a count or baron, being german.

'Do you know that stingy but magnificent edifice—.'

'Yes—?'

'That sumptuous home of precarious "Fracs," situated Rue de Rennes—?'

'I'm afraid I don't quite understand—.' The widow had not got used to his composite tongue. She liked Kreisler, however.

The music burst forth, and the club members leapt to their feet to affirm with fire their festive intentions.

'Shall we dance?' he said, getting up quickly.

He clasped her firmly in the small of the back and they got ponderously in motion, he stamping a little bit, as though he mistook the waltz for a more primitive music.

He took her twice, with ever-increasing velocity, round the large hall, and at the third round, at breakneck speed, spun with her in the direction of the front door. The impetus was so great that she, although seeing her peril, could not act sufficiently as a brake on her impetuous companion to avert the disaster. Another moment and they would have been in the street, amongst the traffic, a disturbing meteor, whizzing out of sight, had not they met the alarmed resistance of a considerable british family entering the front door as Kreisler bore down upon it. It was one of those large featureless human groups built up by a frigid and melancholy pair, uncannily fecund, during an interminable intercourse. They received this violent couple in their midst. The rush took Kreisler and his partner half-way through, and there they stood embedded and unconscious for many seconds. The british family then, with great dignity, disgorged them, and moved on.

The widow had come somewhat under the sudden fascination of Kreisler's mood: she was really his woman, the goods, had he known it: she felt deliciously rapt in the midst of a simoom—she had not two connected thoughts. All her worldly Victorian grace and good management of her fat had vanished: her face had become coarsened in those few breathless minutes. But she buzzed back again into the dance, and began a second mad, but this time merely circular, career.

Kreisler took care to provide his actions with some plausible air of purpose: thus: he was abominably short-sighted; he had mistaken the front door for one leading into the third room, merely! His burden, not in the best condition, was becoming more and more puffed and heavier-footed at every step. When satisfied with this part of his work, he led Mrs Bevelage into a sort of improvised conservatory and talked about pawn-shops for ten minutes or so—in a mixture of french english and german. He then reconducted her, more dead than alive, to her seat, where he left her with great sweeps of his tall figure.

He had during this incident regained his former impassivity. He stalked away now to the conservatory once more, which he regarded as a suitable headquarters.

Bertha had soon been called on to dance vigorously, without much intermission. In the convolutions of the dance, however, she matured a bold and new plan. She whirled and trotted with a preoccupied air.

Would Tarr hear of all this? Now it was done she was alarmed. Also the Liepmann, the van Bencke's attitude towards the Kreisler kissing was a prospect that cowed her as she got used to it. Undoubtedly she must secure herself. The plan she hit on offered a 'noble' rôle that she would, in any circumstances, have found irresistible.

Her scheme was plain and clever: she would simply 'tell the truth.' This is how the account would go.

'She had recognized something distracting in Kreisler's life, in short the presence of crisis. *On an impulse*, she had offered him her sympathy. He had taken up her offer immediately but in the brutal manner already seen. (One against him: two for her!) Such lurid sympathy he claimed. She was sorry for him still, but he was very brutal.'

So she jogged out her strategies with theatrically abstracted face and rolling eyes.

At this point of her story she would hint, by an ambiguous hesitation, that she, in truth, had been ready even for this sacrifice: had made it, if her hearers wished! She would imply rather that from modesty—not wanting to appear *too* 'noble'—she refrained from telling them the whole truth.

For such a confession it is true she had many precedents. Only a week ago Fräulein van Bencke herself, inflating her stout handsome person, had told them that while in Berlin she had allowed a young painter to 'kiss' her: she believed 'that the caresses of a pure woman would be helpful to him at that juncture of his life.' But this had not been, it was to be supposed, in the middle of the street: no one had ever seen, or ever would see, the young painter in question, or the kiss.

Busy with these plans, Bertha had not much time to notice Kreisler's further deportment. She came across him occasionally, and keyed her solid face into an intimate flush and such mask as results from any sickly physical straining. '*Poor* Mensch! Poor luckless Mensch!' was the idea.

Soltyk surprised one anglo-saxon partner after another with his wonderful english—unnecessarily like the real thing. He exhibited no signs of pleasure (except as much as was testified to by his action, merely) at this sort of astonishment.

Only twice did Kreisler observe him with Anastasya. On those occasions he could not, on the strength of what he saw, pin him down as a rival. Yet he was thirsting for conventional figures. His melancholy could only be satisfied by *active* things, unlike itself. Soltyk's self-possession, his ready social accomplishment, depressed Kreisler: for it was not in his nature to respect those qualities, yet he felt they were what he had always lacked. The Russian was, more distantly, an attribute of Vokt. How it would satisfy him to dig his fingers into that flesh, and tear it like thick cloth! He Otto Kreisler was 'for it': he was down and out (revolutionary motif): he was being assisted off the stage by this and by that. Why did he not *shout*? He longed to act: the rusty machine had a thirst for action.

Soltyk liked his soul to be marked with little delicate wounds and wistfulnesses: he enjoyed an understanding, a little melancholy, with a woman: they would just divine in each other possibilities of passion, that was yet too 'lasse' and sad to rise to the winding of Love's horns that were heard, nevertheless, in a décor Versaillesque and polonais. They were people who looked forward as others look back: they would say farewell to the future as most men gaze upon the past. At the most they played the slight dawning and disappearing of passion, cutting, fastidiously, all the rest of the piece. So he was often found with women. But for Anastasya, Soltyk was one of her many impresarios, who helped her on to and off the scene of Life. He bored her completely, they had something equivalent to pleasant business relations: she had recognized at once his merits as an impresario. There could not therefore have been less material for passion: even Kreisler was nonplussed. He was surrounded by unresponsive shapes.

Conventional figures of drama lacked: Kreisler had in fact got into the wrong company. But he conformed for the sake of the Invisible Audience haunting life: he emulated the matter-of-factness and aplomb that impressed him in the others: so far indeed was he successful in this that the Audience took some time to notice him—the vein of scandal running through an otherwise dull performance.

In the conservatory he dug himself in by a cleverly arranged breastwork of chairs. From thence he issued forth on various errands. All his errands showed the gusto of the logic of his personality: he might indeed have been enjoying himself. He invented outrage that was natural to him, and enjoyed slightly the licence and scope of his indifference.

At the first sortie he observed a rather congested, flushed and spectacled young woman, her features set in a spasm of duty. It was a hungry sex in charge of a flustered automaton. Having picked her for a partner, he gained her confidence by his scrupulous german politeness. But he soon got to work. While marking time in a crush, he disengaged his hand and appeared to wish to alter the lie of her bosom, very apologetically and holding her tight with the other hand.

'Excuse me! it's awkward—. More to the left—so! Clumsy things and some women are so proud of them! (No: I'm sure you're not!) No. Allow me. Let it hang to the left!' The young lady, very red, and snorting almost in his face, escaped brusquely from his clutch and fled towards her nearest friends.

Several young women, and notably a flapper, radiant with heavy inexperience and loaded with bristling bronze curls, he lured into the conservatory. They all came out with scarlet faces: but that did not prevent others from following him in.

For the first hour he paid no attention to Anastasya: he prosecuted his antics as though he had forgotten all about her. He knew she was there and left her alone, even in thought; he hid coquettishly behind his solemn laughter-in-action, the pleasant veil of his hysteria, Anastasya was no longer of the least importance: he had realized that she had been all along a mere survival of days when such individuals mattered. Now he was *en pleine abstraction*—a very stormy and concrete nothingness.

At length he became generally noticed in the room, although there were a great many people present. The last flapper had screamed and had escaped at the gallop. He had even been observed for a moment, an uncouth faun, in pursuit, in the flowery mouth of the conservatory. Fräulein Liepmann hesitated now. She thought at length that he was insane. In speaking to him and getting him removed if necessary, a scandalous scene was almost certain to occur.

Again the tall, and in spite of the studied dishevelment, still preternaturally 'correct,' satyric form appeared upon the threshold of the conservatory.—An expectant tremor invaded several backs. But on this occasion he just stalked round on a tour of inspection, as though to see that all was going along as it should. Heavily and significantly he stared at those young ladies who had been his partners, when he came across them: one he abruptly stopped in front of and gazed at severely. She did not denounce him but blushed and even tittered. He left this exhibition of cynicism in disgust, and returned to his conservatory.

In his deck chair, his head stretched back, glasses horizontal and facing the ceiling, he considered the graceless Hamlet that he was.

'Go to a nunnery, Widow!'

He should have been saying that to his Ophelia. He hiccuped. Why did he not *go to her?*—contact was the essential thing: his thoughts returned to Anastasya. He must bare her soul. If he could insult her enough she would be bare-souled. There would be the naked *weibliche*

Seele. Then he would spit on it. Soltyk however offered a conventional target for violence: Soltyk was evading him with his indifference. Soltyk! What should be done with Soltyk? Why (a prolonged and stormily rising 'why'), there was no difficulty about *that*. He got up from his chair, and walked deliberately and quickly into the central room gazing fiercely to right and left. But Soltyk was nowhere to be seen.

The dancers were circling rapidly past with athletic elation, talking in the way people do when they are working. Their intelligences floated and flew above the waves of these graceful exercises, but with frequent drenchings, as it were. Each new pair of dancers seemed coming straight for him: their voices were loud, a hole was cut out of the general noise, as it were opening a passage into it. The two or three instruments behind the screen of palms produced the necessary measures to keep this throng of people careering, like the spoon stirring in a saucepan: it stirred and stirred and they jerked and huddled insipidly round and round, in sluggish currents with small eddies here and there.

Kreisler was drawn up short at the first door and had to flatten himself against the wall for a moment. He was just advancing again to work his way round to the next exit when he caught sight of Anastasya dancing with (he supposed) some Englishman. He stopped, paralysed by her appearance: the part she had played in present events gave her a great prestige in his image-life: when in the flesh she burst into his dream she still was able to disturb everything for a moment. Now he stood like somebody surprised in a questionable act. The next moment he was furious at this interference. She and her partner stood in his way: he took her partner roughly by the arm, pushing him against her, hustling him, fixing him with his eye. He passed beyond them then, through the passage he had made. The young man handled in this manner, shy and unprompt, stared after Kreisler with a 'What the devil!'—People are seldom rude in England. Kreisler, without apology, but as if waiting for more vigorous expostulation, was also looking back, while he stepped slowly along the wall towards the door beyond—the one leading to the refreshment room.

Anastasya freed herself at once from her partner, and pale and frowning (but as though waiting) was looking after Kreisler curiously. She would have liked him to stop. He had done something strange and was as suddenly going away. That was unsatisfactory. They looked at each other without getting any farther, he showed no sign of stopping: she continued to stare. She burst out laughing. They had clashed (like people in the dance). The *contact* had been brought about. He was still as surprised at his action as she was. Anastasya felt too, in what way this had been *contact*: she felt his hand on her arm as though it had been she he had seized. Something difficult to understand and which should have been alarming, the sensation of the first tugs of the maelstrom he was producing and conducting all by himself which required her for its heart she had experienced: and then laughed, necessarily; once one was in that atmosphere, like laughing gas with its gusty tickling, it could not be helped.

Now this rough figure of comic mystery disappeared in the doorway, incapable of explaining anything. She shivered nervously as she grasped her partner's arm again, at this merely physical contact. 'What's the matter with that chap?'—her partner asked, conscious of the lameness of this question. Elsewhere Kreisler was now a subject of conversation. 'Herr Kreisler is behaving very strangely. Do you think he's been drinking?' Fräulein Liepmann asked Eckhart.

Eckhart was a little drunk himself: he took a very decided view of Kreisler's case.

'Comme toute la Pologne! as drunk as the whole of Poland!' he affirmed. He only gave it as an opinion, with no sign of particular indignation: he was beaming with greedy generosity at his Great Amoureuse.

'Ah! here he comes again!' said Fräulein Liepmann at the door.

So Kreisler disappeared in the doorway after the 'contact'; he passed through the refreshment room. In a small chamber beyond he sat down by an open window.

When Anastasya had laughed Kreisler's inner life had for a moment been violently disturbed. He could not respond, or retaliate, the door being in front of him he vanished, as Mephistopheles might sink with suddenness into the floor at the receipt of some affront, to some sulphurous regions beneath, in a second—come to a stop alone, upright—stick his fingers in his mouth nearly biting them in two, his eyes staring: so stand stock-still, breathless and haggard for some minutes: then shoot up again, head foremost, in some other direction, like some darting and skulking fish, to the face of the earth. Kreisler sat on staring in front of him, quite forgetful where he was and how long he had sat there, in the midst of a hot riot of thoughts.

Suddenly he sat up and looked about him like a man who has been asleep for whom work is waiting; with certain hesitation he rose and again made for the door. Glancing reflectively and solemnly about he perceived the widow talking to a little reddish Englishman. He bore down upon them with courtly chicken-like undulations.

'May I take the widow away for a little?' he asked her companion.

(He always addressed her as 'Widow': all he said to her began with a solemn 'Widow!' occasionally alternating with '*Derelict!*' All uttered in a jumbled tongue, it lost most of its significance.)

On being addressed the small Briton gave the britannic equivalent of a jump—a sudden moving of his body and shuffling of his feet, still looking at the floor, where he had cast his eyes as Kreisler approached.

'What? I—.'

'Widow! permit me—' Kreisler said and encircled her with a heavy arm.

Manipulating her with a leisurely gusto, he circled into the dance.

The band was playing the 'Merry Widow' waltz.

'*Merry* Widow!' he said smilingly to his partner. 'Yes!' shaking his head at her roguishly: '*merry* Widow!'

The music fumbled in a confused mass of memory, all it managed to bring to light was a small cheap photograph, taken at a Bauern Ball, with a flat german student's cap. He saw this solemn lad with pity, this early Otto. Their hostess also was dancing: Kreisler remarked her with a wink of recognition. Dancing very slowly, mournfully even, he and his partner bumped into her each time as they passed: each time it was a deliberate collision. Thud went the massive buffers of the two ladies. The widow felt the impact, but it was only at the third round that she perceived the method presiding at these bumps. She then realized that they were without fail about to collide with the other lady once more: the collision could not be avoided, but she shrank away, made herself as small as possible, bumped gently and apologized over her shoulder, with a smile and screwing up of the eyes, full of dumb worldly significance. At the fourth turn of the room, however, Kreisler having increased her speed sensibly, she was on her guard. In fact she had already suggested that she should be taken back to her seat. He pretended to be giving their hostess a wide berth this time; then suddenly and gently he swerved and bore down upon her. The widow frantically veered, took a false step, tripped over her dress of state, tearing it in several places, and fell to the ground. They caused a circular undulating commotion throughout the neighbouring dancers, like a stone falling in a pond.

Several people bent down to help Mrs Bevelage. Kreisler's assistance was angrily dispensed with, the widow was roused at last: she scrambled to her feet and limped to the nearest chair, followed by a group of sympathizers.

'Who is he?'

'He's drunk.'

'What happened?'

'He ought to be turned out!' people exclaimed who had witnessed the accident.

With great dignity Herr Otto Kreisler regained the conservatory. As he lay stretched in his chair Fräulein Liepmann, alone, appeared before him and said in a tight, breaking voice,

'I think Herr Kreisler you would do well now, as you have done nothing all evening but render yourself objectionable, to relieve us of your company.'

He sat up frowning.

'I don't understand you!'

'I suppose you're drunk. I hope so, for—.'

'You hope I'm drunk, Fräulein?' he asked in an astonished voice.

He reclined at full length again.

'A lady I was dancing with fell over,' he remarked 'owing entirely to her own clumsiness and intractability.—But perhaps she was drunk, I never thought of that. Of course that explains it.'

'So you're not going?'

'Certainly Fräulein—when you go! We'll go together.'

'Schurke!' Hurling hotly this epithet at him—her breath had risen many degrees in temperature at its passage, and her breast heaved in dashing it out (as though, in fact, the word 'Schurke' had been the living thing, and she were emptying her breast of it violently)—she left the room. His last exploit had been accomplished in a half-disillusioned condition. The evening had been a failure from his point of view. Everything had conspired to cheat him of the violent relief he required; his farcing proceeded because he could think of nothing else to do. Anastasya laughing had disorganized 'imaginary life' at a promising juncture. He told himself now without conviction that he *hated* her. 'Ich hasse dich! Ich hasse dich!' he hissed over to himself, enjoying the wind of the 'hasse' in his moustaches but otherwise not very impressed. His sensuality had been somewhat stirred: he wanted to *kiss* her now: he must get his mouth on hers he told himself juicily and fiercely; he must revel in the laugh, where it grew! She was a fatal woman: she was in fact evidently *the Devil*.

He began thinking about her with a slow moistening of the lips. 'I *shall possess* her!' he said to himself, seeing himself in the rôle of the berserker warrior, ravening and irresistible: the use of the word *shall* in that way was enough.

But this *infernal* dance! He was no longer romantically 'desperate,' but bored with his useless position there. His attention was now concentrated on a practical issue, that of the 'possession' of Anastasya though even that depended on a juicy vocabulary, hissed in the form of an incantation and he lost sight of it the moment he ceased deliberately to attend to it.

He was tired as though he had been dancing the whole evening. Getting up, he threw his cigarette away; he even dusted his coat a little with his hand. He then, not being able to get at the white patch on the shoulder, took it off and shook it. A large grey handkerchief was used to flick his boots with.

'So!' he grunted, smartly shooting on his coat.

The central room, when he got to it, appeared a different place: people were standing about and waiting for the next tune. He had become a practical man, surrounded by facts: but he was much more worried and tired than at the beginning of the evening.

To get away was his immediate thought. But he felt hungry: he made for the refreshment room. On the same side as the door, a couple of feet to the right, was a couch: the improvised trestle-bar with the refreshments ran the length of the opposite wall: the room was quiet and almost empty. Out of the tail of his eye, as he entered, he became conscious of something. He turned towards the couch: Soltyk and Anastasya were sitting there, and looking at him with the abrupt embarrassment people show when an absentee under discussion suddenly appears. He flushed and was about to turn back to the door. This humiliating full-stop beneath their eyes must be wiped out at once: he walked on steadily to the bar, with a truculent swagger.

A consciousness of his physique beset him: the outcast feeling returned in the presence of these toffs—class-inferiority-feeling beset him. He must be leisurely: he *was* leisurely. He thought when he stretched his hand out to take his cup of coffee that it would never reach it. He felt a crab dragged out of its hole, which was in this case perhaps the conservatory. *Inactive*, he was ridiculous: he had not reckoned on being watched. This was a fiasco: here he was posing nude for Anastasya and the Russian.

He munched sandwiches without the faintest sense of their taste. Suddenly conscious of an awkwardness in his legs, he changed his position: his arms were ludicrously disabled. The sensation of standing neck-deep in horrid filth beset him. The noise of the dancing began again and filled the room: this purified things somewhat.

But his anger kept rising. He stood there deliberately longer now: in fact on and on, almost in the same position. She should wait his pleasure till he liked to turn round, and—then. He allowed her laughter to accumulate on his back, like a coat of mud. In his illogical vision he felt her there behind him laughing and laughing interminably. Soltyk was sharing it of course. More and more *his* laughter became intolerable: the traditional solution again presented itself. Laugh! Laugh! He would stand there letting the debt grow, they might gorge themselves upon his back. The attendant behind the bar began observing him with severe curiosity: he had stood in almost the same position for five minutes and kept staring darkly past her, very red in the face.

Then suddenly a laugh burst out behind him—a blow, full of insult, in his ears: he nearly jumped off the ground: after his long immobility the jump was of the last drollery: fists clenched, his face emptied of every drop of colour, in the mere action he had almost knocked a man standing beside him off his feet. The laugh, for him, had risen with tropic suddenness, a simoom of intolerable offence: it had swept him from stem to stern, or whirled him completely round rather, in a second. A young english girl, already terrified at Kreisler's appearance, and a man, almost as much so, stood open-mouthed in front of him. As to Anastasya and Soltyk, they had entirely disappeared, long before in all probability.

To find that he had been struggling and perspiring in the grasp of a shadow, was a fresh offence merely. It counted against the absentees but even more it swelled the debt against a more terrible, abstract, antagonist. He had been again beating the air: this should have been a climax—of blows, hard words, definite things. But still there was *nothing*.

He smiled, rather hideously, at the two english people near him and walked away. All he wanted now was to get away from the English Club as soon as possible, this ill-fated Club.

While making towards the vestibule he was confronted again with Fräulein Liepmann.

'Herr Kreisler, I wish to speak to you' he heard her say.

'Go to the devil!' he answered in a muffled voice, without paying more attention. Her voice bawled suddenly in his ear:

'Besotted fool! if you don't go at once I'll get—.'

Turning on her like lightning, with exasperation perfectly meeting hers, his right hand threatening, quickly raised towards his left shoulder, he shouted with a crashing distinctness:

'Lass' mich doch, gemeine alte Sau!'

The hissing, thunderous explosion was the last thing in teutonic virulence: the muscles all seemed gathered up at his ears like reins, the flesh tightened and white round his mouth, everything contributed to the effect.

Fräulein Liepmann took several steps back: with equal quickness Kreisler turned away, rapped upon the counter, while the attendant looked for his hat; then passed out of the club. Fräulein Liepmann was left with the heavy, unforgettable word 'sow' deposited in her boiling spirit, that, boil as it might, would hardly reduce this word to tenderness or digestibility. *Sow*, common-old-sow—the words went on raging through her spirit like a herd of Gadarene Swine.

Lewis was indignant when V.S. Pritchett said to him that his fiction was very funny. *Funny*, he repeated derisively, and the word is not adequate, although I have not found a better one, especially for the comic scenes in *Tarr*. They have depths and subtleties that their writer perhaps did not intend, blending as Dostoevsky sometimes did rasping comedy with suggestions of human oppositions that far transcend the surface level of quarrels between artistic 'types'. Tarr's encounter with Anastasya late in the book embraces his view of Kreisler as a man who attempted 'to get out of Art back into Life', along with his own attitude to art as something requiring 'absence of soul, in the human and sentimental sense'. Yet this slanging match with Anastasya, enjoyable enough simply as an exchange of insults when Tarr realises that she is offering him not simple straightforward sex, but 'life'—that is, emotional involvement—implicitly explores also permanent differences in the male and female psyches. *Tarr* is a comic masterpiece, but one with tragic implications.

from TARR

Tarr, Part VII, Chapter 2

On August the tenth Tarr had an appointment with Anastasya at his studio in Montmartre. They had arranged to dine at a restaurant with a terrace upon the rue de l'Obelisk. It was their tenth meeting. Tarr had just come from his daily cure. He hurried back and found her lounging against the door, reading the newspaper.

'Ah there you are! You're late, Mr Tarr.'

'Have you been waiting long?'

'No. Fräulein Lunken I suppose—.'

'Yes. I couldn't get away.'

'Poor Bertha!'

'Poor Bertha!'

He let her in. The backwardness of his senses was causing him some anxiety: his intellect now stepped in, determined to do their business for them. He put his arm round her waist and planting his lips firmly upon hers, began kissing. Meanwhile he slipped a hand sideways beneath her coat, and pressed still tighter an athletic, sinuous hulk against him. The various bulging and retreating contacts of her body brought monotonous german reminders and the senses obediently awoke.

It was the first time he had kissed her: she showed no disinclination, but no return. Was Miss Vasek in the unfortunate position of an unawakened mass? He felt a twinge of anxiety. Had she not perhaps, though, so rationalized her intimate possessions that there was no precocious fancy left? Mature animal ardour must be set up perhaps: he had the sensation of embracing a tiger, who was not unsympathetic but rather surprised. Perhaps he had been too sudden or too slow—he had not the technique *des fauves, des grands fauves*: he ran his hand upwards along her body: all was statuesquely genuine. His hand took a more pensive course. She took his hand away.

'We haven't come to that yet,' she said.

'Haven't we?'

'I didn't think we had.'

Smiling at each other, they separated.

'Let us take your greatcoat off. You'll be hot in here.'

Her coat was all in florid redundancies of heavy cloth, like a Tintoretto mantle. Underneath she was wearing a very plain dark belted smock and skirt, like a working girl, which exaggerated the breadth and straightness of her shoulders. Not to sentimentalize it, she had open-work stockings on underneath, such as the genuine girl would have worn on her night-out, at two-and-eleven-three the pair.

'You look very well ' Tarr said.

'I put these on for you.'

Tarr had, while he was kissing her, recovered his sensual balance; his senses indeed had flared up in such a way that the reason had been offended and exercised some check at last. Hence a conflict: *they* were not going to have the credit—!

He became shy: he was ashamed of his sudden interest, which had been so long in coming, and hid it instinctively from her. He was committed to the rôle marked out by reason.

'I am very flattered ' Tarr said ' by your thoughtfulness.'

'I am on show Tarr.'

He sat smoking, his eyes upon the floor lest his sudden cupidity should be too apparent.

'Do you think we shall always be the audience?'

'Whatever do you mean by that—who are your *we*?'

'I meant the remark about "on show," menfolk of course being the audience.'

'I see what you mean: I should think the spectators' rôle was the one to be preferred but I can quite imagine the audience breaking up and the rôles being reversed. Meantime I'm the puppet.'

Fixing upon him a diabolical smile, set in a precocious frill of double chin and punctuated with prominent dimples she lay back in the chair. A most respectable bulk of hip occupied the space between the two arms of the chair, not enough completely to satisfy a Dago, but too much to please a dandy of the West. Tarr furtively noted this opulence and compared it with Bertha's. He confessed that it outdid his fiancée's.

'Yes I am even a peep-show for all peeping Toms and Dicks—you know when the Principal Boy turns round, you know the supreme moment of Pantomime?'

'When she is stern-on?'

'Well I'm like that too when I'm going away and not facing the audience, and tell me how you would like to be a show-girl anyway Tarr? You shake your head—a little girlishly—all the same I can see you're not the show-girl sort, but why should I? I have got these things here' she laid a hand upon the nearest breast to it 'as a stark high-brow I ask you, can you respect such objects upon a person, right on top of a person?'

'I don't mind them. I think they are nice.'

'Not as a high-brow, it's imposs; they class me, I am one of the Bertha-birds, all the small boobies know what I'm made for when I run to catch a bus. "Look at that milch-cow short of wind—here! wait till I catch you bending!" It's beastly.'

'What's it matter what they say? They are street-arabs merely.'

'They roam the gutters but they have eyes in their heads.'

'I am all for a breast or two.'

'No, you are laughing at me too—you are being a small boobie.'

'No' Tarr quavered: then he added at once: 'I am hallucinated.'

'That's what it is, you have hit the nail on the head, once I was like you and liked this—I might even learn to love it again' she muttered, casting her eyes into a distant recess.

'The Man dreams but what the Boy believed.'

'The Man dreams—what is that? What the Child believes to be real with his eyes open, the Man can only believe in—in his sleep and then not quite—I know, there was a time when I was a child of nature who took myself for granted from top to toe, I was mad then.'

'You make me mad now, in a way. Yes' he touched himself with the tips of his fingers: 'I am mad, that's correct: just a touch of passion and off you go again—you are a mad believer once more for the moment!'

'Have you just a touch of passion?'

'Just a touch.' He grinned passionately. 'Something is real.'

She sighed, and licked her lips.

'Aside from that' she said, and lifted up her breast a little way in the palm of her proud hand, 'what would you do under the circumstances Tarr—it's a handicap, there's no blinking the fact.'

'I should do nothing.'

'And there is nothing to do—*rien à faire!* it's all part of the beastly shop-window—I have to stick frills around them even, just as pork-merchants in their shop-fronts decorate the carcasses of their sucking-pigs.'

Tarr laughed as he pictured to himself the lattice-work of the silk receptacle, and as she threatened deliberately to pout, remarked:

'It is part of the reality is lady's underwear—what the child *believes* and the adult only dreams, though they both see it—when visited with a little passion which goes a long way I can believe and become quite genuinely mad, but I am with you if you object to those ravings which would then issue from my mouth being given out as reason, or even as beauty. It's not Beauty. It is Belief, if you like.'

'Of course it's not—we agree in the most marvellous way Tarr. These things, all things that are stamped feminine gender, is not a thing that bears cold print, unless it is to be read by madmen.'

'Of course not.'

'But as you say a little passion goes a long way and I can go anywhere and pass myself off as a most lovely creature. It's a fact.'

'Can you do that?'

'Why yes—I'll pass myself off on you if you're not careful.'

'Je ne demande pas mieux!' Tarr said indifferently, peering over at her as if through a gathering mist.

'I'm still here,' she answered. 'What are we going to do about it?'

'It's—it's not the *thing itself—*.'

'Why no. But it is no use, no woman should be intelligent, it's no use.'

But Tarr rejoined, with mock-indignation:

'Nor he-men for the matter of that, it's six one and half a dozen the other—have you ever considered what a man has to carry about with him too?'

'What.'

'It's just the same, I am a man, I trim my moustaches for instance as though this hole here were the better for a black frill of hair—is it?—it's as bad as your sacro-sanct dugs, my kisser's no better!'

'I don't think so: men have never sat down and become lace-makers to embellish their strange hairy beauties like us women. Their little pigs stay at home.'

'I think they are just as bad. They are terrible.'

'Oh no.'

Tarr decided to marry Anastasya after they had finished talking, for the sake of her little pigs, that went to market so beautifully.

'I think Tarr I know your opinion of women with intellects—how right you are, how right you are!'

'Not at all!'

'No, you are, I agree with you all along the line: it must madden you to hear me talking about this in such a matter-of-fact way—have I disgusted you, I expect so? Some things *should* be sacro-sanct!'

She crossed her legs. The cold grape-bloom mauve silk stockings ended in a dark slash each against her two snowy stallion thighs which they bisected, visible, one above the other, in naked expanses of tempting undercut, issuing from a dead-white foam of central lace worthy of the *Can-Can* exhibitionists of the tourist resorts of *Paris-by-night.*

Tarr grinned with brisk appreciation of the big full-fledged baby's coquetry pointing the swinish moral under the rose and mock-modestly belowstairs, and he blinked and blinked as if partly dazzled, his mohammedan eye did not refuse the conventional bait; his butcher-sensibility pressed his fancy into professional details, appraising this milky ox soon to be shambled in his slaughter-box, or upon his high divan.

'Sacro-sanct' she repeated heavily, letting fall upon him a slow and sultry eye, not without a Bovril-bathos in its human depths—like all conversational cattle, it hinted! Expelling his wistfulness, it looked him squarely in the whites, and she said passionately:

'It's usual and we should do as the Romans do—not that these are Romans!—we should observe a decent emotionality about these coarse mysteries—worship and appetite are one!—who said you could dispense with the veil?—it is impossible, try it!—there should be a blush of animal shame upon the joint of mutton—.'

'You will break my heart!'

She pursued impetuously—

'I don't need you to tell me—there should be no trifling with the objects of sexual appetite—they are sacro-sanct I have agreed, under the fanatical frown of the mosaic code—we are not pagans—you need not say it, I am already reminded!'

She recrossed the two massive dangling serpents of her legs—up above their thick white necks flashing as she changed them—up under her fore and aft serge apron.

'We intellectuals' she insisted 'talk far too much about things that simply will not bear talking of and looking into—a high-brow girl such as me must be sexually (oh that's very very american) an abomination: I am convinced that with me a man would become impotent within a month at the outside, I mean it.'

Sitting crouched like a stage Whittington cat upon his chair, with eyes devoutly riveted upon the exhibits of the demonstration as though he expected a Brocken ghost-mouse to hop out and were sitting at the cock to pounce when it did, Tarr grinned painfully, without removing his eyes from the neighbourhood of the supposed exit.

'A man's leg in Ladies' Hose is just as nice as a woman's leg' she remarked.

Tarr did not let go, unblinking he made haste to answer, motionless:

'Or just as dull, as you would have it; both are—outside the imagination that is—.'

The intensity of his painful stare deepened and his face flushed. She uncrossed her legs and brought them to attention, pushing her skirt down enquiringly.

'*Outside the imagination*—what is that? What do you consider the imagination is?'

Tarr flung himself back in his chair, took a cigarette from a yellow packet at his side, and lighted it with anxious fixity, the fixed look transferred from the mightier cylinders of meat to it, puny nothing of smoke.

'In the case of the sucking-pig' said Tarr, magisterially, flinging his flushed face up for air towards the ceiling 'it is the tongue. The thing seen is merely disgusting to the eye, but it is delightful to the tongue: therefore the eye passes beneath the spell of the palate, and it is not an image but a taste—much more abstract, in consequence—that it sees—if one can say that it sees. The body of the sucking-pig is blotted out.'

Anastasya sniffed.

'I think you forget that it is my breast from which we started this rambling argument. Also I would take leave to observe that it is not so easy to blot out a food-unit as you appear to think.'

'You sound like the Duchess in Alice.'

'Who on earth may that be—the Duchess of What?'

'Of Alice.'

'Oh. I was saying, it is by no means so easy—.'

'I'm with you, I'm with you, you lovely contraption! But nevertheless it is time I were gone!'

'He bursts into song!'

Tarr sprang up in his chair and delivered himself rather breathlessly as follows:

'Listen to my explanation, I would give all the world from the Baltic to the Rhine—*bis an den Rin*—Geliebte—darling—pig-girl! to embrace a sucking-pig if it possessed all the other attributes, of body and the rest, of the person I am now addressing, but I meant only that everything we *see*—you understand, this universe of distinct images—must be reinterpreted to tally with all the senses and beyond that with our minds: so that was my meaning, the eye alone sees nothing at all but conventional phantoms.'

Anastasya laughed shrilly and stretched up her arms above her head, looking down at the expansion of her breasts as she extended her torso to its limit.

'So long as we understand each other—that is everything!'

He stood up.

'I am hungry, let us go and discuss these matters over a rump steak' she said rising after him, shivering a little. 'How damp this place is! I am cold.'

He crossed the room to where his hat and coat were lying.

'What does the good Bertha say to your new workshop? Now there's a real woman for you! There's no mistake about *her!*'

'Yes good old Bertha's the right stuff: she's prime!'

'My dear, she must be the world's premier sucking-pig!'

'The *ne plus ultra!*'

'The *Ding an sich!*' in the driest and most prolonged american she sang and they turned laughing unkindly at a certain homely womanly form towards the burnished door of the new workshop, passing the easel upon which the greek athlete, attacked with religion, disintegrated before the eyes of a watching harpie.

As they descended the Boulevard Rochechouart Tarr stepped with an unmistakable male straddle: no bourgeoise this time! thought he to himself, but the perfect article! It rolled and swept beside him and more and more of its swagger got into his own gait until he was compelled to call a halt: he halted 'the face that launched a thousand ships'—a thousand transports crowded in her carriage and the impetuous rush of her advance—before a Charcuterie.

'Delicatessen!' he hissed significantly in her ear. In a protracted reverie they both directed their gaze upon a Frankfort sausage. They passed on, Tarr toning himself down as best he could but rehearsing to himself her perfections—no Grail-lady or any phantom of the celtic mind but perfect meat, horse-sense, accent of Minnesota, music of the Steppes, german *Weltweisheit, Wesengefühl* and what-not—a prodigious mate!

They entered an expensive trippers' restaurant and devoured the Menu with hungry eyes from top to bottom in an immediate scamper. They ordered oysters: they would be his first, he had never before dared to eat an oyster, because it was alive.

When he told her that it was his first oyster she was exultant.

'You perfect savage—your palate is as conservative as an ox's. Kiss me Tarr—you have never done that either properly.'

The use of his gentile name was a tremendous caress. She presented her salt wet eating lips, he kissed them properly with solemnity, adjusting his glasses afterwards.

'Why have you never eaten oysters?'

'The fact that they were alive has so far deterred me but I now see that I was wrong.'

'You are afraid of everything that is alive!' she assured him with a portentous nod.

'Until I find that it is really not to be feared on that score I believe that is true.'

'You have a marked prejudice in favour of what is dead?'

'But all human food is killed first and is dead—all except oysters' he objected.

'You have a down on life—it's no good!'

'I am an artist.'

'Yes I've heard that before!' she blustered gaily with a german conviviality that made him feel more than ever at home. 'But the artist has to hunt and kill his material so to speak just as primitive man had to do his own trapping butchering and cooking—it will not do to be squeamish if you are to become a great artist, Mister Tarr!'

Tarr looked the great artist every inch as he haughtily replied:

'Nevertheless there stands the fact that life is art's rival in all particulars. They are *de puntos* for ever and ever, you will see, if you observe closely.'

'That I do not see.'

'No because you mix them up in your own practice.'

'The woman, I suppose?'

Tarr gave her a hard dogmatic look and then asserted roundly, and probably finally:

'*As such*, and with such resources, you are the arch-enemy of any picture.'

Anastasya looked pleased, and looked a picture.

'Yes I see how I might be that. But let us have a definition here and there. What is art?—it sounds like Pompous Pilate!'

'Life with all the humbug of living taken out of it: will that do?'

'Very well: but what is life?'

'Everything that is not yet purified so that it is art.'

'No.'

'Very well: *Death* is the one attribute that is peculiar to life.'

'And to art as well.'

'Ah but it is impossible to *imagine* it in connection with art—that is if you understand art—that is the test for your understanding. Death is the *motif* of all reality: the purest thought is ignorant of that *motif.*'

'I ask you as a favour to define art for me, you have not. A picture is art if I am not mistaken, but a living person is life. We sitting here are life, if we were talking on a stage we should be art.'

'A picture, and also the actors on a stage, are pure life. Art is merely what the picture and the stage-scene represent, and what we now, or any living person as such, only, does *not*: that is why you could say that the true statue can be smashed, and yet not die.'

'Still.'

'This is the essential point to grasp: *Death* is the thing that differentiates art and life. Art is identical with the idea of permanence. Art is a continuity and not an individual spasm: but life is the idea of the person.'

Both their faces lost some of their colour, hers her white, his the strong, almost the 'high,' yellow. They flung themselves upon each other socratically, stowing away course after course.

'You say that the actors upon the stage are pure life, yet they represent something that *we* do not. But "all the world's a stage," isn't it?'

'It was an actor that said that. I say it's all an atelier—"all the world's a workshop" I should say. Consider the content of what we call art. A statue is art. It is a dead thing, a lump of stone or wood. Its lines and proportions are its soul. Anything living, quick and changing is bad art always; naked men and women are the worst art of all, because there are fewer semi-dead things about them. The shell of the tortoise, the plumage of a bird, makes these animals approach nearer to art. Soft, quivering and quick flesh is as far from art as it is possible for an object to be.'

'Art is merely *the dead*, then?'

'No, but deadness is the first condition of art. The armoured hide of the hippopotamus, the shell of the tortoise, feathers and machinery, you may put in one camp; naked pulsing and moving of the soft inside of life—along with elasticity of movement and consciousness—that goes in the opposite camp. Deadness is the first condition for art: the second is absence of soul, in the human and sentimental sense. With the statue its lines and masses are its soul, no restless inflammable ego is imagined for its interior: it has *no inside*: good art must have no inside: that is capital.'

'Then why should human beings be chiefly represented in art?'

'Because it is human beings that commission and buy the art.'

A mixed grill *Montebello* and two *Poulets grain* had disappeared; a *Soufflé Rothschild* was appearing through the hatchway of the lift and a *corbeille* of fruit, comprising figs, peaches, nectarines and oranges, was held in readiness, a prominent still-life, upon a dresser. Anastasya now stretched herself, clasping her hands in her lap. She smiled at Tarr. She had been driving hard inscrutable Art deeper and deeper into herself: she now drew it out and showed it to Tarr.

'Art is all you say—have it your way: also something else: we will stick a little flag up and come back another day. I wish intensely to hear about life.'

Tarr was staring, suspended, with a defunct smile, cut in half, at the still life. He turned his head slowly, with his mutilated smile, his glasses pitched forward somewhat.

He looked at her for some time in a steady, depressed way: his eye was grateful not to have to be gibing. Kindness—*bestial kindness*—would be an out-of-work thank God in this neighbourhood. The upper part of her head was massive and intelligent, the middle of her body was massive and exciting, there was no animalism-out-of-place in the shape of a weight of jaw—all the weight was in the head and hips. His steadfast ideas of the flower surrounded by dung were certainly challenged: but he brooded not yet convinced. Irritants were useful—he reached back doubtfully towards his bourgeoise: he was revolted as he recalled that mess, with this clean and solid object beneath his eyes, but he remained pensive. He preferred a cabin to a palace, and thought that a villa was better for him than either. The second bottle of champagne was finished; its legendary sparkle dampened his spirits.

'What do you make of Kreisler's proceedings? He was a queer fish!' she asked.

'Most.'

'Do you suppose he and Bertha got on very well?'

'Was Bertha his mistress? I can't say. That is not very interesting is it?'

'Not Bertha, of course, but Kreisler had his points.'

'You're very hard on Bertha.'

She put her tongue out at him as much as a small almond, and wrinkled up her nose.

'What were Kreisler's relations with you by the way?' he enquired.

'My relations with Kreisler consisted in a half-hour's conversation with him in a restaurant, no more: I spoke to him several times after that but only for a few minutes. He was very excited the last time we met. I have a theory that his duel was due to unrequited passion for me. Your Bertha, on the other hand, has a theory that it was due to unrequited passion for her. I merely wondered if you had any information that might confirm her case or mine.'

'No, I know nothing about it. I hold, myself, a quite different theory.'

'What is that? That he was in love with *you?*'

'My theory has not the charming simplicity of your theory or Bertha's. I don't believe that he was in love with anybody, I think that it was however a sex-tumult of sorts—.'

'What is that?'

'This is my theory. I believe that all the fuss he made was an attempt to get out of Art back into Life again. He was like a fish floundering about who had got into the wrong tank. *Back into sex* I think would describe where he wanted to get to: he was doing his best to get back into sex again out of a little puddle of art where he felt he was gradually expiring. He was an art-student without any talent you see, so the poor devil was leading a slovenly meaningless existence like thousands of others in the same case. He was very hard up, also. The sex-instinct of the average sensual man had become perverted into a false channel. Put it the other way round and say his art-instinct had been rooted out of sex, where it was useful, and naturally flourished, and had been exalted into a department by itself, where it bungled. The nearest the general run get to art is *Action*: sex is their form of art: the battle for existence is their picture. The moment they *think* or *dream* they develop an immense weight of cheap stagnating passion. Art, in the hands of the second-rate, is a curse, it is on a par with "freedom"—but we are not allowed to say *second-rate* are we' he grinned 'in the midst of a democracy! particularly such a "cultivated" one as this! But if you are forbidden to say *second-rate*, why then you must leave behind you all good sense—*nothing* can be discussed at all if you can't say *second-rate!*'

The drunkenness of Tarr had passed through the first despondent silence, and as his intelligence grew less firm in battle with the *Roederer* he began to bluster in a sheepish sing-song interlarding his spasms of argument with dumb *prosits*.

'Nobody's claim is individual—*issit!*' he hiccuped at his vis-à-vis, who now did nothing but eat. She shook her head, her mouth full.

'Nobody's!—an important type or original—as a pattern, *that* is the sanction of the first-ranker, am I right? The Many they are the eccentric—what do they matter? am I right or not?—they are "the individuals," yes. Individuals! Well! Prosit Anastasya, let us drink to their confusion! To hell with economy, in any shape or form, to hell with it! Long live Waste! Hoch!'

'I'll drink to that!' she exclaimed raising her glass. 'Here's to Waste. Hoch! Waste!'

'Of course! Curse curse the principle of Humanity, curse that principle! Mute inglorious Miltons are not mute for God in Heaven—they have the Silence!'

'Ah. The Silence, that's what they must have—Heaven is silent! How did you guess that?'

'Bless Waste—Heaven bless Waste! Hoch Waste!'

'Hoch!'

'Here's to Waste!' Tarr announced loudly to the two waiters in front of the table. 'Waste, *waste*; fling out into the streets: accept fools, compromise yourselves with the poor in spirit, it will all come in handy! Live like the lions in the forests, with fleas on your back. Above all, down with the *Efficient Chimpanzee!*'

Anastasya's eyes were bloodshot, Tarr patted her on the back.

'There are no lions in the forests!' she hiccuped, aiming blows at her chest. 'You're pulling my leg.'

They had finished the fruit and were sitting before coffee filters while the *sommelier* hunted for vodka. Tarr had grown extremely expansive in every way: he began slapping her thighs to emphasize his points, as Diderot was in the habit of doing with the Princesse de Clèves. After that he began kissing her when he had made a successful remark, to celebrate it. Their third bottle of wine had put art to flight; he lay back in his chair in prolonged bursts of laughter. She, in german fashion, clapped her hand over his mouth. He seized it with his teeth and made pale shell shapes in its brown fat.

301

In a Café opposite the restaurant, where they next went, they had more vodka. They caressed each other's hands now continually and even allowed themselves more intimate caresses: indifferent to the supercilious and bitter natives they became lost in lengthy kisses, their arms round each other's necks.

In a little cave of intoxicated affection, a conversation took place.

'Have you darling often?'

'What's that you say dear?' she asked with eager sleepy seriousness. The 'dear' reminded his dim spirit of accostings in the night-streets.

'Have you often, I mean are you a grande amoureuse—on the grand scale?'

'Why do you ask? are you curious?'

'Only out of sympathy, only out of sympathy!'

'I mustn't tell you, you'd despise me terribly.'

'I promise not to!'

'I know I shall regret it!'

'Never.'

'I shall, all men are the same.'

'Make an exception with me!'

'Oh I mustn't!'

'Mustn't you?'

'Well I'll tell you!'

'Darling! Don't if it hurts you!'

'Not at all. Well then—I know you'll hate me—well then, only one old Russian—oh yes and a Japanese, but that was a mistake.'

'Have you only, with one old Russian?'

'I knew you'd despise me, I should not have told you!'

'Only one old Russian!'

'There was the Japanese—but he was a mistake.'

'Of what nature? Are you quite sure?'

'Alas yes! He betrayed me upon the links in New England.'

'The cad!'

'He was a caddie—but he apologized, he was most polite: he assured me it was an accident and I believe it was an accident.'

'But how grim—I should have thought the colour line.'

'He explained how it was a complete misunderstanding. His politeness left nothing to be desired, he was a perfect gentleman!'

'Oh I am so glad!'

'You despise me now?'

'No women pals?'

'Nothing nothing nothing! I have told you except one old Russian!'

She began sobbing upon his shoulder, her face covered with a lace handkerchief. He kissed her through the handkerchief and struck her gently upon the back.

'Never mind' he muttered 'it's all over now. It's *all* over now!'

She put her mouth up to be kissed exclaiming brokenly:

'Say you don't despise me too terribly Tarr! I want *you* so much! I really do want you—so much, so much! *You* will make up for everything!'

A frown had gathered upon his flushed forehead.

'Shall I? Why should I? I'm not going to be made a convenience of !'

'I want you, I really do, enormously, I know you don't believe me! I feel most terribly, oh! back-to-nature-like—*do please* believe me!'

He thrust her rather brutally away on to her chair and himself lurched in the opposite direction, eyeing her askance.

'Why should I? I don't see that! One paltry—*one*—!'

'Tell me what you want!'

'I want a woman. What I want is a woman, you understand, I want a woman badly, that's all!'

'But I am one!'

'I agree, of sorts—very much of sorts!'

She whispered in his ear, hanging upon his neck.

'No no!' he answered: 'all that may be true but—.'

'It is.'

He sat frowning intently at the table.

'Don't be quarrelsome Tarr!'

For a moment she considered him then she pushed her glass away, lay back and remarked with rapid truculence.

'It's all right when you're talking about art but at present you are engaged in the preliminaries to love with a woman.'

'So you say.'

'This is something that can die! Ha! Ha! we're in life my Tarr: we represent *absolutely nothing* thank God!'

'I realize I'm in life, but I don't like being reminded of it in that way. It makes me feel as though I were in a "mauvais lieu." '

'My confession has been unavailing I observe.'

'To cut a long story short, you disgust me!'

'Give me a kiss you *efficient chimpanzee.*'

Tarr scowled at her but did not alter the half embrace in which they sat.

'You won't give me a kiss? Silly old *in*efficient chimpanzee!'

She sat back in her chair, and head down, looked through her eyelashes at him with arch menace.

'Garçon! garçon!' she called.

'Mademoiselle?' the waiter said, approaching slowly, with dignified scepticism.

'This gentleman, waiter, wants to be a lion with fleas on his back—at least so he says! At the same time he wants a woman if we are to believe him. I don't know if he expects the woman to catch his fleas or not, I haven't asked him: but he's a funny looking bird isn't he?'

The waiter withdrew with hauteur.

'What's the meaning of your latest tack you great he-man of a german art-tart?'

'What am I?'

'I called you german pastry on the large side, with the icing laid on with a shovel.'

'Oh, *tart* is it—?'

'Quite well made, well puffed out, with a great line of talk—.'

'And what, good God, shall we call the cow-faced specimen you spend the greater part of your days with—?'

'She, too, is german pastry, more homely than you though—.'

'Homely's the word!'

'But not quite so fly-blown and not above all, at least, *pretentious*—yes pre-ten—.'

'I see, and takes you more seriously than other people would be likely to: that's what all your "quatsch" about "woman" means. I guess you know that?'

She had recovered from the effect of the drinks. Sitting up stiffly she examined him as he spoke.

'I know you are a famous whore who becomes rather acid in her cups!—when you showed me your legs this evening I suppose I was meant—.'

'Assez! Assez!!' She struck the table with her fist and flashed her eyes picturesquely over him.

'Let's get to business.' He put his hat on and leant towards her. 'It's getting late. Twenty-five francs, I'm afraid, is all I can manage, you've cleaned me out with the meal.'

'Twenty-five francs for *what*? with you—it would be robbery! Twenty-five francs to be your audience while you drivel about art? Keep your money and buy Bertha an—*efficient chimpanzee*—she will need it poor bitch if she marries you!'

Her mouth uncurled, a thin red line, her eyes glaring and her hands in her overcoat pockets she walked out of the door of the Café.

Tarr ordered another drink.

'It's like a moral tale told on behalf of Bertha' he pondered. That was the temper of Paradise!

Much sobered, he sat in a grim sulk at the thought of the good time he had lost. For half an hour he plotted his revenge and satisfaction together. With a certain buffoonish lightness he went back to his studio with smug, thick secretive pleasure settling down upon his body's exquisite reproaches and burning retaliations.

———————

The Childermass is a work in three parts, of which the first appeared in 1928, while the second and third—called *The Human Age*—were written in the Fifties after Lewis had gone blind. The whole is a kind of philosophical fantasy set outside heaven and within the 'Magnetic City' or 'Third City', but the first part is much concerned with present-day politics and literature (that is, with the Twenties), the later ones with the relationship between God and humankind. A fourth part, 'The Trial of Man', was projected but not written.

The first volume covers ground most of which has been explored in *The Art of Being Ruled*, but the arguments here are put into dialogues of immense verve between the Punch-like Bailiff and his opponents. The most notable of these is Hyperides, who often voices identifiably Lewisian views, while the hunchbacked Bailiff is a kind of time philosopher, although Lewis evidently became so delighted by his monstrous creation that he is the most memorable figure in the book. The Bloomsburyish Pullman and his former school fag Satters wander through the work as spectators rather than participants, although they are candidates for entry into the Magnetic City, their fate to be decided by the Bailiff. This first volume was written perhaps with the intention of popularising the arguments of *The Art of Being Ruled* by a semi-fictional presentation. It contains some magnificent descriptive passages, like the opening view of the landscape outside the Magnetic City, and the physical appearance of a central character, Pullman.

from THE CHILDERMASS

The city lies in a plain, ornamented with mountains. These appear as a fringe of crystals to the heavenly north. One minute bronze cone has a black plume of smoke. Beyond the oasis-plain is the desert. The sand-devils perform up to its northern and southern borders. The alluvial bench has recently gained, in the celestial region, upon the wall of the dunes. The 'pulse of Asia' never ceases beating. But the outer aeolian element has been worsted locally by the element of the oasis.

The approach to the so-called Yang Gate is over a ridge of nummulitic limestone. From its red crest the city and its walls are seen as though in an isometric plan. Two miles across, a tract of mist and dust separates this ridge from the river. It is here that in a shimmering obscurity the emigrant mass is collected within sight of the walls of the magnetic city. To the accompaniment of innumerable lowing horns along the banks of the river, a chorus of mournful messages, the day breaks. At the dully sparkling margin, their feet in the hot waves, stand the watermen, signalling from shore to shore. An exhausted movement disturbs the night-camp stretching on either side of the highway—which when it reaches the abrupt sides of the ridge turns at right angles northward. Mules and oxen are being driven out on to the road: like the tiny scratches of a needle upon this drum, having the horizon as its perimeter, cries are carried to the neighbourhood of the river.

The western horizon behind the ridge, where the camp ends inland, but southward from the highroad, is a mist that seems to thunder. A heavy murmur resembling the rolling of ritualistic drums shakes the atmosphere. It is the outposts or investing belt of Beelzebub, threatening Heaven from that direction, but at a distance of a hundred leagues, composed of his resonant subjects. Occasionally upon a long-winded blast the frittered corpse of a mosquito may be borne. As it strikes the heavenly soil a small sanguine flame bursts up, and is consumed or rescued. A dark ganglion of the bodies of anopheles, mayflies, locusts, ephemerids, will sometimes be hurled down upon the road; a whiff of plague and splenic fever, the diabolic flame, and the nodal obscenity is gone.

With the gait of Cartophilus some homing solitary shadow is continually arriving in the restless dust of the turnpike, challenged at the tollgate thrown across it at the first milestone from the water-front. Like black drops falling into a cistern these slow but incessant forms feed the camp to overflowing. Where the highway terminates at the riverside is a ferry-station. Facing this on the metropolitan shore is, to the right, the citadel, rising plumb from the water, a crown of silver rock, as florets towers arranged around its summit.

At the ferry-station there is a frail figure planted on the discoloured stones facing the stream. Hatless, feet thrust into old leather slippers, the brown vamp prolonged up the instep by a japanned tongue of black, it might be a morning in the breezy popular summer, a visitor halted on the quay of the holiday-port, to watch the early-morning catch. Sandy-grey hair in dejected spandrils strays in rusty wisps: a thin rank moustache is pressed by the wind, bearing first from one direction then another, back against the small self-possessed mouth. Shoulders high and studious, the right arm hugs, as a paradoxical ally, a humble limb of nature, an oaken sapling Wicklow-bred. The suit of nondescript dark grey for ordinary day-wear, well-cut and a little shabby, is coquettishly tight and small, on the trunk and limbs of a child. Reaching up with a girlish hand to the stick cuddled under the miniature oxter, with the other hand the glasses are shaded against the light, as the eyes follow the flight of a wild duck along the city walls northward, the knee slightly flexed to allow the body to move gracefully from the slender hips.

The Apes of God, published in 1930, but—again—much of it written earlier, is probably the best-known of Lewis's fictions. The period between the World Wars was, he said later, 'a moronic inferno of insipidity and decay', and the *Apes* is a look into that inferno. The novel became notorious on its publication as a vast battue of Lewis's enemies like the Sitwells, and even some of his friends, all of them excoriated as the Apes of art. It is a satire conceived on the model of 'MacFlecknoe' or the *Dunciad*, with the victims allowed no redeeming traits of character or appearance. Their features are caught with astonishing accuracy, as can be seen by comparing a photograph of Osbert Sitwell with this description of Lord Osmund Finnian-Shaw:

> In colour Lord Osmund was a pale coral, with flaxen hair brushed tightly back, his blond pencilled pap rising straight from his sloping forehead: galb-like wings to his nostrils—the goat-like profile of Edward the Peacemaker. The lips were curved. They were thickly profiled as though belonging to a moslem portrait of a stark-lipped sultan. His eyes, vacillating and easily discomfited, slanted down to the heavy curved nose. Eyes, nose and lips contributed to one effect, so that they seemed one feature. It was the effect of the jouissant animal—the licking, eating, sniffing, fat-muzzled machine—dedicated to Wine, Womanry, and Free Verse-cum-soda-water.

Lewis made an effective reply to those who complained that his subjects were too trivial to warrant the vast attention paid to them, remarking truly that all objects of satire must seem trivial or despicable. The great limitation of the work is rather that the machine of destruction moves too slowly and achieves too little. The *Dunciad* is a long but readable poem, a satire with a thread of narrative running through it, but the *Apes* is not much more than a tour of Bloomsbury and its environs, conducted for the enlightenment of the blushing semi-moronic poet Dan Boleyn. The book has been called an expression of despair about the decay of the European vision of life. That may have been the intention, but the result seems too often almost purely parochial, in a way that must diminish its effectiveness.

Yet the *Apes* too has merits unique to its author. In it Lewis's genius for writing lifelike dialogue was for the first time perfected. He is the great master of dialogue as truly spoken, and the effects he achieved through oddities of phrasing and grammar are like those of no other modern novelist. In the excerpt that follows Julius Ratner, a minor ape, is in bed suffering from a cold, reluctant to get up. He is talking to his Cockney charlady.

from THE APES OF GOD

The Split-Man

After a prostrate spell of sudden inanition, too sluggish to want to come-to-life at all (habits of hibernation in the serpent-blood) Mr Ratner was ready. He brought to mind his cold. A low harsh rattle from the direction of his pillow surprised Mrs Lochore. Mr Ratner had had a slight temperature—apprehensive, she remembered her wages which were good with a twinge under the corn-plaster—she looked over towards the bed: apathetic but preoccupied, she bustled round the wash-hand stand. She saw him out of the corner of her eye moving his neck a little, circumspectly like a snake, and swallowing. The large rugged thyroid cartilage travelled up and down the front of his throat. She poured the discoloured water of the wash-hand basin into the service slop-pail.

'The cold's not gone has it Mr Ratner sir. It's a bitter wind this morning, you should be careful and see you don't get a worst one sir. These winds we're having is very treacherous.'

The papers said daily, pneumonia was very prevalent, and the wind was very treacherous. She read of all the deaths from colds.

'I know Mrs Lochore. But that's so dif-fi-cult' Joo whined with condescension.

He analysed as usual some seemingly selected three or two-syllable word.

'That's what you gentlemen always say you "can't stop in"—prevention's better than cure, if you didn't go out in this bitter wind Mr Ratner sir it'd be gone tomorrow' she whinnied back at the whining invalid and coughed, to lend point to her exordium.

309

'But I caant Mrs Lochore I wish I could!' Joo's plaintive rusty pipe exploded. 'I *caant* Mrs Lochore stop in!'

Oh shut up, she thought. Now *why* can't he for once the old char perforce must reflect, deny himself to those outside just for once! 'Oh I believe you could sir!' cried she in a loud tone.

'But I have to go and play TENNIS!' hissed Joo while he watched the rugged old bitch of the bull-dog-breed shake his pretext roughly—before dropping it to reply, as she quickly did—

'Play tennis Mr Ratner sir!'

'Tennis!' he nodded, his eyes alight. *Tayern-neece* was the way Jimmiejulius pronounced this last word of his piteous crescendo. And the disgust of the old bondwoman, anticipated, was reproduced in the prompter's voice.

Most mornings Jamesjulius put himself in a good morning mood with this familiar crone and this was the way it was done. At will he would press a few stops, from his recumbent position, in the rickety instrument, and caused it to play

God save our Gracious Naughty Mr Ratner sir! Amen!

'Play tennis!' char exclaimed again, but the dummy overdid well-nigh, in imitation of Ratner, the horror-struck part. To the rôle of deep humble reproof she was too much to-the-manner-born altogether. Too crude a volume of indignant servility escaped from Mrs Lochore. It gave the effect of fooling-the-fooler. The contrasted points of view showed up too stark. Julius frowned in his yellow-soap-sculptured sleep as he lay back and heard it. But the good woman knew it was up to her and was at a loss—she thought he had meant it was an unsuitable time of the year perhaps or he had no racket, or was tennis not his sport or too hot work or what?—for often they misunderstood each other and her *tennis* was not his *tayerniss*, nor his gods her gods. But they got on fine for all that and money spoke soft and sweet.

Reserve a court—Ratner made the note (speaking of tennis). His mind that hated all physical games, of ball bat foot or club, forgot he knew on purpose, he was never reminded. So he blocked in this memo, in bold black cursive script up in his cock-loft on top of everything else, where he could not neglect it.

'You'll go and run about and get hot and then you'll catch another cold before you know where you are Mr Ratner sir!'

'No I shaaant Mrs Lochore!' Joo wailed in teasing gritty growl, very pleased—very very Spoilt-boy at this, very Naughty-man.

'Well I hope you don't sir, I'm sure I do Mr Ratner!'

'Thank you ever so much Mrs Lochore, I won't run about too much!' He naughtily yapped.

'I shouldn't sir if I was you! You'll pardon me for sayin' so Mr Ratner, but you want to be careful in these treacherous winds.'

'Ah these treacherous winds!' he chanted in mockery.

Beneath the crafty swollen eyes of the salaried british bond-woman foster-mother, he cuddled his pillow openly. For two pins he would pluck a pis-en-lit in his bed, under the old grog-blossom nose of her he would. Becoming very siamese-kittenish Joo cooed, with the runculation of the matutinal catarrh.

'Mrs Lochore!'

'Sir?'

Mrs Lochore put down the pail, standing wiping heavy chapped domestic fists upon her canvas apron.

'Used you when you were young ever to feel you would like to go away by yourself, and escape from all the young men you knew, and . . .!'

Joo stalled, making a long expressive sigh but before it ended a cough came.

'*Never see them again!*' completing his sentence, he passionately wailed.

Mrs Lochore leered at Mr Ratner for a moment, and said:

'I wasn't so what you might call sought-after not as all that Mr Ratner sir!'

'I expect you were Mrs Lochore!' Joo retorted in swift sneering patronage, from the pillow.

'I daresay I had a young man or two like the rest' said Mrs Lochore. 'We're only young once Mr Ratner!' she said.

'Didn't you ever feel Mrs Lochore that you *hated* all your young men and wished you could never see them again!' Jimmie insinuated from the pillow.

'*All my young men*—listen to you Mr Ratner! I don't think I had scarcely so many as all that Mr Ratner sir! We wasn't not so fast, time

I was young, as what they are now you might say.'

'Do you think *we* are so dreadfully fast now Mrs Lochore!' blared Joo at her at this, raising himself an eager inch from the pillow to give her a better view of the *young idea*.

'I don't know sir' said she, who was unprepared: 'I don't think I ever thought much about it sir. I don't see why people shouldn't amuse themselves,' she sniffed with indifference.

'I wish I could go away and never come back!' boomed the tragic voice of Joo, in vibrant sotto voce, the martyr of the fastness of the New Age.

Mrs Lochore was put upon her mettle: she knew Mr Ratner sir had put her on her mettle. She knew what Mr Ratner was doing.

'If you goes on like that Mr Ratner' and she eyed him like a suicide boasting of his cowardly crime, 'I shall think you ought to see a doctor sir!'

But he sneered back, with criminal eye, a cruel encouragement. So she responded.

'What have you got to be miserable about my dear sir, I should say you was very lucky.'

'But I dooo Mrs Lochore—I want to leave all my present life!'

In 1933 Lewis surprised many people who thought of him purely as a prose writer with publication of the long poem *One-Way Song*, some of it written in the little-used fourteener, but more in couplets. The poem is an adjunct to Lewis's theories about the illusions nursed by those who cling to historical Time and to 'revolutionary' ideas of Progress. Such Time-bound Progress, the poem says, is really backward-looking, involved with sex ('Sex is of the same clay as Time'), and truly reactionary about what is happening in the world:

> Our tri-classed life-express carries oh far more
> Back-to-the-engine fares than those face-fore.
> Gazing at yesterdays, they squat back-first—
> Blindfolded into brand-new futures burst!

Some of this he had said more effectively in prose, but in this poem as elsewhere he strays from the central theme into exhilarating comic pyrotechnics of which the most brilliant is the opening 'Engine Fight-Talk', which finds Lewis as teacher instructing a class of Audenic poets in the proper attitude towards machinery:

> I said (and I always say these things with the same voice)
> 'Say it with locomotives! Mark well that animal puff!'
> Each man-jack of them marked it, every man-jack—all were
> boys.
> 'If you must, say it with locofocos! Radical Tammany stuff!
> Hot and heavy! As if you meant it! Don't stick at a rough
> house—real rough!'

The word 'radical' of course delights the class. And this opening section sees an almost lyrical evocation of past literary glories:

> I should like to have you tell me why Browne's urn
> Makes all the Past with firework colours burn—
> Why Taliesin steps in Peacock I should be very glad to learn,
> Or why the lungs of Guinevar swell with coarse breath again.
>
> I would give my passport to find out what whore
> Has come to live with Swinburne—I would fain
> Find out what page the sorcerer John Keats tore
> From the shut book—and how even Beckford came to wake
> A litter of earthquaking spooks to make the walls of Lisbon
> shake.
> Can you call up the consciousness that the sleepy Pater used
> To wake the Middleages—with what senses was it fused?
> For that matter explain to me how the pages of *Cathay*
> Came out of the time-bound Ezra into the light of common
> day!'

And the jokes continue when, in 'The Song of the Militant Romance', Lewis extols the old-fashioned fourteener:

> As to the trick of the prosody, the method of conveying
> the matter,
> Frankly I shall provoke the maximum of saxophone clatter.
> I shall not take 'limping' iambics, nor borrow from
> Archilochous

313

His 'light-horse gallop', nor drive us into a short distich
that would bog us.
I shall *not* go back to Skeltonics, nor listen to Doctor Guest.
I know with my bold Fourteener I have the measure that
suits us best.
I shall drive the matter along as I have driven it from the first,
My peristalsis is well-nigh perfect in burst upon well-timed
burst—
I shall drive my coach and four through the strictest of
hippical treatises.
I do not want to know too closely the number of beats it is.

In the following section, 'If So The Man You Are', Lewis parodies himself, but with seriousness tingeing the laughter. Was he the perfect guest, the perfect host? Does he really mean what he is saying? The section ends with a splendid flourish:

If so the man you are commissionaire,
If so the man *marchand de mégots* there,
If so the man you are, *oh merde alors*!
If so the man to bang each taxi-door,
If so the man bemedalled, a 'man's-man' too,
If so the man you are to *all* men true,
If so you are the servant-man, why then,
If so the man (a scarecrow among men)
If so the man you are, these words we waste,
If so the man by nature's hand disgraced.
If so the man you be for the back-seat,
If so the man out of the hand to eat,
A fetch-and-carry fellow to salute,
If so the man that's just above the brute.
If so the man like the majority of men,
If so the man that's envious of the pen,
If so the man you are of the other cheek,
If so the man that's venomous and sleek,
If so the man that's Everyman—these words,
If so a man, we throw to the dicky-birds!

The overflowing energy of this underrated poem gives pleasure from beginning to end, the argument often forgotten in admiration of the conjuring skill of the Enemy at play. Of the many fine couplets one stays particularly in the memory:

> These times require a tongue that naked goes
> Without more fuss than Dryden's or Defoe's.

Lewis's naked tongue moved often, as in this poem, from one target to another, so that in the end the whole is less than the sum of its parts. Yet as a display of gusting humour, and a casual skill in handling verse forms, the poem could hardly be bettered.

The Apes of God is a turning point in the fiction. It marks the abandonment of the modernist style, thick as clotted cream, that reached its peak in *Tarr* but can still be found in passages of the *Apes*, and a turn towards construction of complex but coherent plots. The three novels of the Thirties are all plotted with care, and the plots are basically thrillers. *Snooty Baronet* (1932) is about the attempt of a literary agent to arrange a fake kidnapping as part of a publicity stunt on behalf of an author. *The Revenge For Love*, published in 1937 during the Spanish Civil War but completed before it began, has for backbone a plot that deals with gun-running across the Spanish border, in which an artist and his girl friend become innocently involved. The central character in *The Vulgar Streak* (1941) is a man passing counterfeit money who is himself a counterfeit, a working-class figure passing as a leisured member of the English upper-class. All three books end in violence, the second in the death of the artist and his girl, the third in the counterfeiter's suicide. H.G. Wells called this last book a 'shocker', but Lewis said in a letter of reply that to produce a mere shocker was not his intention:

> I will tell you, in as few words as possible, what I *thought* I was doing. The time in which we live appears to me, qua period, to be a 'shocker'. Well, the rather shocking nature of the book was to my mind a faithful interpretation of an epoch where violence is everywhere. The hero in *Le Rouge et le Noir* lived his tragic life according to the Napoleonic code of conduct. The 'ruthless' way . . . In *Crime & Punishment* the hero follows in the footsteps of Julian Sorel (and of Napoleon). It seemed to me that the time had come to

add another book to this line: that the doctrine extracted by Mussolini from *Les Reflections sur la Violence* and from Nietzsche (who got his stuff fundamentally from Darwin)—it seemed to me that this doctrine taken over by Hitler, and influencing so many minds in Europe, might be made to do its fell work in the soul of a character in fiction, once again.

These then are all books *against* violence in its form of mindless meaningless action—and it should be remembered that one of Lewis's reasons for supporting the idea of world government was that it would make nationalist wars obsolete. Yet there is a contradiction in the Thirties novels, present but much less obvious in the satirical and allegorical fictions, in that this opponent of violence is also fascinated by it. The scenes of violence, when they come, are very vivid: and indeed the novels' effectiveness is based on the duality by which the writer is both emotionally involved with the actions he describes and also able to stand back and comment on them.

The three books are not all equally successful. The ambitious, even magnificent, conception of *The Vulgar Streak*—the exposure of the counterfeiter set against the background of a Europe doomed to war and ruin—needed a richer tapestry and a fuller view of the central character than Lewis was able to give it, yet this is a failure more interesting than many minor writers' successes. *Snooty Baronet* contains wonderful comic scenes, and although less than fully satisfactory as a novel, is a book that seems to have influenced other writers. Certainly the Samuel Butler manner adopted by Snooty when visiting his girl friend Val has echoes in the faces pulled by Lucky Jim Dixon and in some scenes of Angus Wilson's *No Laughing Matter*, to look no further. The book also provides a brilliant and compelling example of the author's view that men are really machines pretending to be human. Snooty, an observer of crowd behaviour, is himself something like an automaton, with a silver plate in his head, and a wooden leg which he unscrews before making love. In the chapter 'The Hatter's Automaton', he sees a crowd staring into a hatter's shop-window. What follows, as Snooty becomes identified with the Automaton, is reminiscent of the mirror-image scene in the Marx Brothers' *Duck Soup*, with the addition that rich philosophical comedy is made out of it. Humph, mentioned in the extract, is the narrator's agent.

from SNOOTY BARONET

The Hatter's Automaton

What the people were looking at was a puppet. It was a Hatter's show-window and the Hatter by means of this ceremonious mannikin was advertising a new straw hat. This little gentleman had been created for that purpose. He belonged to the personnel of the Hatter.

I approached, as I have said, and I placed my hat upon my head (it may have seemed as a retort) at the moment the puppet removed his, with a roguish civility darting his eye at me as a new-comer—just as I thrust my way in amongst his spellbound admirers.

The puppet was a good size. I have called him 'a little gentleman' but his head at all events was at least of average human scale, I am not sure it was not over. He was not 'little.' He was a sturdy well-kept puppet. He was fashionably-dressed, in a somewhat loud, I thought, summer-suiting. But in England, he might have argued, where the summer is such as it is, the *summer-suit* has to be a bit on the *loud* side, and over-summery if anything.

His character interested me at once. It is absurd to say these things (if you insist upon calling them *things*) have no character. Those that are made to-day are, like characters in books, often much more real than live people. Next I observed his movements.

He removed his hat with a well-timed flourish, brought it down in a suitable parabola, twisted it about once or twice, to show off its beauties to us—all this time his face working about in the most expressive dumb show—except that it was not dumb show either, for his lips were in constant movement—he was evidently speaking, in a rather mincing way, not loud, but with his lips, and reinforcing his words, with a consummate salesmanship, by a half-closing, seductive veiling, of his eyes. He slowly winked or blinked once or twice. Then suddenly he opened his eyes wide, in a blank but not uncivil stare, as he ceased his salesman's patter, and stuck his hat down jauntily upon his head. Bowing from the waist once more in our direction, he carried to his eye a monocle, and, turning swiftly, looked up into the ceiling of the shop, then slowly he turned back his head, and scrutinized the door upon his right, smiling slightly to himself.—Then once more he removed his hat, with the well-timed flourish, bowing from the waist and smiling at us, he swept it down—turned it hither and thither, delivering, in well-chosen words, his little lecture—moving his eyes from one to the other of us, seeking to read the effect of his words upon our faces—then straightening himself out, put on his hat again at a somewhat rakish angle in his particular, a little dandyish, manner: raised his eyebrows, to admit of the insertion of the monocle, parted his lips to show a well-kept set of teeth—his smile spoke volumes as to his feelings at his position in the window—his nose was wrinkled slightly as he smiled, and I could swear that his eyes lightened as he looked down for a moment in our direction.

But what struck me most was the enormous *chin* of this creature. It dominated all his appearance. It alone was non-mobile and lifeless. For the rest, the springs that actuated his lips, nose and cheeks were excellently thought out. It was impossible as one watched him not to feel that he was in some real sense *alive*. At certain moments of course the imperfections of the apparatus would betray him. But is not this the case, for the matter of that, with the best of us?—At other times, as I say, he really deceived us—or at least he deceived me. I stood looking in the deepest astonishment at him. And the illusion certainly had communicated itself to the other people who were there.

I know well enough how I look—no one can tell me anything about that. I have made a careful study of myself. (Externally I am perhaps not unlike Sir Walter Scott or Stendhal—I mean that, as to my cast of countenance, I am no oil-painting.) But *of all things*, I know *to perfection* that heavy puzzled look that comes into my face apropos of anything almost! When I am uncertain about something—when for instance my brain has some difficulty in establishing contact with something outside it. That's the time to catch the look I mention! I must look as like an utter simpleton as a man can well be, in the face. If you saw me you would take me for a nobody, a great big puzzled dunce.

But, I have said it, I have literally to drill holes in this sheep's-head of mine before it can get an at all difficult notion, or sometimes any at all, into it properly. In all but purely mechanical things, of an external order (that is my strong suit) I am a profoundly dense person, I cannot help it. Mine is anything but a quick mind.—This may be why I am a *behaviorist.* If there is such a thing as a 'soul,' I at all events have never been able to catch it on the hop. (But I doubt it.) Again, a notion goes *so far* in with me and not an inch farther. That is what is oddest of all. It seems to stick in the surface shell. It remains embedded in the bone, quite hard and fast. Nothing will budge it. I have often tried but never been able to.

I understand only too well the meaning of the american 'bonehead.' Someone—a bonehead I guess!—asked me once upon a time what 'bonehead' meant, or how the expression had arisen, and abused the Americans for being *obscure* in their slang. Mine was certainly a dud answer—I had never thought about it—I had just said 'bonehead' for 'stupid' I guess, like any other expression. But the american chap who first used it may have been a bonehead (and so thought of it) but he was no fool. It was a good word. That chap meant *a head like mine*—just opaque and solid skull, or it feels like that if you happen to own one, as I do.

Ideas come out of the blue, fiercely to get us, like wasps, or like a bacillus or a weevil dropped on a cork. I can feel one *strike* me. Then I feel it get stuck, quite plainly—the thing can make no headway at all. This is my difficulty as a research-worker. Yet ideas like me, if one may say that—I am 'susceptible to ideas.' But I keep them stuck on the outside of me. They will not penetrate, it's no use.—I tell you all this to account for that painful baffled mask I have got. That in its turn affects people's behavior to me, as you can guess. They look at my frowning and puzzled stare and they act accordingly. That is only natural. And I act back—that's only good sense too. That's 'Behavior.'

As for the puppet, he went through his evolutions over and over again—each cycle was quite elaborate. I watched him with a painful amazement, attempting to penetrate what he meant, by being what he was. I had replaced my hat—I again removed it, as it happened it was just as he was taking off his. The fellow who was standing at my elbow had been watching me in the plate-glass window I think—I suppose I had pushed him. He had I suppose remarked that I was *partly* mechanical myself. My leg had not escaped his attention in short as it seemed to me, and now something about my manner appeared to amuse him. I became conscious of this. He was looking *at me*, instead of at the puppet. Of course this must have been because of my expression. I was not surprised of course, nor do I mind such creatures examining me as if I were of another clay. That is all in the day's work—the day's *field-work*.

That dull and baffled look you would see if you came face to face with me—heaven avert the omen, you would find it a strange encounter! If I could come out of this paper at you, you would find me a manner of man such as you did not expect I think, you would burst your eyes in your effort to fix me, if I rose from the floor at your feet—terribly *real*, with a whiff of stale tobacco, rough, crippled, with my staring startled difficultly-focussed glances and corn-lemon hair—that tense-as-well-as-dense expression, which when it lifts leaves an empty face behind it—for me to grin with and yawn with. But in the ordinary commerce of life I am always a little astonished if not startled—often I am absolutely amazed. So this Hatter's puppet was large, and in addition to this chin he possessed another characteristic belonging to Captain Carter. Namely, he was all trunk with practically no legs. This was of course in the case of the automaton done in order to give him more solidity and poise, essential in a puppet—also, to make him more startlingly grotesque. But was not that also perhaps the reason for Humph's appearance? It was highly probable, I was constrained to admit.

I had begun smiling to myself as I thought of Humph. And then the puppet turned to me, bowed from the waist, and, raising his hat, smiled in the most formal and agreeable way possible. The fellow was playacting—and what I resented in this comedy was the fact that I knew (or thought I knew) that he was not *real*. There was something abstruse and unfathomable in this automaton. Beside me a new arrival smiled back at the bowing Hatter's doll. I turned towards him in alarm. Was not perhaps this fellow who had come up beside me a puppet too? I could not swear that he was not! I turned my eyes away from him, back to the smiling phantom in the window, with intense uneasiness. For I thought to myself as I caught sight of him in the glass, smiling away in response to our mechanical friend, *certainly he is a puppet too!* Of course he was, but dogging that was the brother-thought, *but equally so am I!*—And so I was (a very thoughtful and important puppet—wandering in this sinister thoroughfare, in search of an american Club-sandwich—a place in my breadbasket, scooped out in wind, the size of a small melon like a plaster mould).

Now next why exactly had this light-hearted new-comer, standing beside me, been so ready to smile up? The good man would not smile if an acquaintance raised his hat to himself and his wife as they were taking their sunday walk in their suburb. That would seem perfectly natural to him, quite solemnly he would return the salute. To me *nothing* seemed natural. Often I have smiled upon occasions of that sort. Every day I was smiling hard at such common or garden things. Everything that passed as natural with him, looked exceedingly odd to me. The most customary things in the world struck me continually as particularly ludicrous. *How* ludicrous—or how normal on the other hand—would depend upon how I was feeling at the moment.

I shifted uneasily up and down upon my real leg and my false leg—I had become almost as much a fixture before the Hatter's window as the puppet inside it. The puppet had begun to notice me. His chin grew larger and larger. And the Hatter himself came out to have a look at me on two occasions as I remarked.

There were six of us now. I regarded with a dark astonishment our uneasy superiority, insecure as everything else about us—we outside (wrapped in our thoughts, disturbed in the secret places of our consciousness) with someone there so profoundly of our kind exhibited for our amusement within the show-window. We stood in a contemplative group without on the pavement (rather an absurd collection), the puppet he stood within. He was on show, but we were not.

There was something *absolute* in this distinction, recognized by everybody there excepting myself. I alone did not see it. What essentially was the difference however? The situation was exactly the same, was it not, as that of the animals in their cages at the Zoo. The other animals (who catch them and keep them there) walking about outside the cages, gazing at them talking and laughing at them—that was us over against the puppet. How surprisingly small is the difference between a mandrill and a man! Certainly—but still slenderer was the difference between this stiffly-bowing so-called automaton, and my literary agent, for example.

Obviously the mandrill was a far more complex machine than was this Hatter's automaton, and men were still more complex than the mandrill. But this automaton *looked*, was dressed and behaved itself, far more like a man than did a mandrill. And that word *looked*, that was for me *everything*.

What was Humph, for instance, more than an appearance? For me he was a fixed apparition. I believed that this creature before me possessed intestines of sawdust. But I knew no more of Humph's intestines (except by hearsay and unwarrantable assumption) than I did of this chap's in the window.

While I watched this creature, who was so like a man, I was in spite of myself beneath the spell of his reality. I could have spoken to him as if he had been one of us outside on the pavement. He was *one of us*, as much as the people at my side, about whom I *knew* no more than I knew of him, indeed rather less.

Was I certain, for instance, that Humph still existed, now that I no longer had him beneath my eyes? No I was not. That would be indeed an absurd assumption. It was far *more* absurd to suppose him still moving about, and behaving as I expected him to behave, now that I was no longer there, than to suppose him blotted out or dropped out of existence. (When I next saw him he would tell me all the things he had done in my absence of course, but I should know that that was all the merest bluff, or that *quite likely* it was the merest bluff.)

But while Humph was beneath my eyes—how was that really so different? There was just what I *saw* there, with my eyes, nothing else. And often he seemed to creak, did he not, or to weaken, or slightly wobble, like a dummy suddenly out of its depth—a machine attempting something for which it was not quite fitted. (Constantly there was this sensation of *strain*, was there not?)

There is of course nothing metaphysical or mysterious about these matters. The contrary in fact. So please do not allow yourself to be rebuffed by such a topic, because you believe it to be 'over your head' or anything of that sort. The world that we imagine—that that we call the world of common sense—existing in independence of our senses, is a far odder one, about that there is no question at all, than that world to which we feel ourself constrained to deny reality, what we can neither see, smell, touch nor hear!

Now of course my coming across this particularly vivid dummy did not teach me to reflect after that fashion. Such modes of thinking were habitual with me. It was the teaching of 'Behavior,' and this had become so much a part of myself that I could with difficulty imagine the time when I saw the world with other eyes—when, in the grip of a complex inherited technique, I shut out illusion, and saw what I did not see, and heard what I did not hear! This little fellow in the shop window I was as much at home with as a keeper at the Zoo is at home with one of the imprisoned creatures delivered into his care.—It was not that at all.

I have told you that when I get ideas into my head, they only go *a certain distance*. But this is true I think of all of us. You are familiar I am sure with how some reasoning impresses you, to a *greater* or to a *less* extent. Far as it may go in, it could always go *farther*, and get a more convincing hold. Sometimes after remaining stationary for years, it will suddenly move a little deeper in. Do you know that sensation? When some idea with which you are perfectly familiar becomes charged all of a sudden with a far greater reality than before, or takes on other and more intensely coloured aspects?

This was what happened with me now. The inner meaning of 'Behavior,' as a notion, *got in motion* within my consciousness, stimulated I can only suppose by all the circumstances of my pact with Val and Humph. It went in deeper, that is to say. It penetrated into my consciousness *deeper* than it had ever done before. But another thing that had happened was very curious. 'Behavior' had as it were turned round upon me as well. As the man at my side observed me putting on my hat, I was for the first time placed in the position *of the dummy!* I saw all round Behavior as it were—for the first time. I knew that *I* was not always existing, either: in fact that I was a fitful appearance. That I was apt to *go out* at any moment, and turn up again, in some other place—like a light turned on by accident, or a figure upon a cinematographic screen.—And must I confess it? I was very slightly alarmed. I saw that I had to *compete* with these other creatures bursting up all over the imaginary landscape, and struggling against me to be *real*—like a passionate battle for necessary air, in a confined place. And as a result of all this I said to myself that, in my absurd conceit, I was giving Humph far too much rope. To hang himself—that was the idea. But would he not hang *me*, perhaps?

I turned away from the Hatter's window a dense scowl settling upon my face. As I looked up I saw, in great letters, posted across the façade of a Picture-theatre, the words—

THE MAN-MADE MONSTER

Beneath this, in smaller letters, was the word Frankenstein.—Was this an accident? Had I not said, as I emerged from the Adelphi, 'I will in the end become their Frankenstein?' And I looked back at the Hatter's window as if to extract an answer from the being inside. All chin, he was smiling sardonically at me, as he bowed from the waist and raised his hat with a well-trained civility. I raised my hat, with a certain sweep, bowed slightly, and—my stomach echoing with report after report, thundering for the Club-sandwich—I continued on my way to the Luncheon-bar. I had a double whisky as soon as I reached it. Immediately I thought of Lily, and in the light of all that had just occurred I understood why it was I so greatly preferred her, and I made out a telegram then and there. That night I insisted we should be together.

———

The masterpiece of this decade is *The Revenge For Love*. Here all Lewis's gifts come together, with the addition of a sympathy for the human puppets destroyed by the forces of the 'epoch when violence is everywhere' present in his work for the first, although not the last time. In *Rude Assignment* he said too pessimistically that the novel would remain out of print in his lifetime (it was reprinted in 1952, again in 1982 and is now available from Penguin), adding the hope that one day 'people will take it up and read it as a *novel*—not glare at it with an eye inflamed by politics'. But *The Revenge For Love* is a political novel, one of the three or four great political novels of the century. It reveals the deceits and savagery of Communist practice (distinct from the theory, for which Lewis retained respect) as much as does *Darkness At Noon*, although Lewis's intentions were very different from Koestler's. The gallery of gulls, who deceive other people as well as being fooled themselves, ranges from upper-class Gillian to the working-class professional agitator Percy Hardcaster. The full-length portrait of Percy is all the more convincing because he is not seen as utterly contemptible, but as a man who feels genuine indignation about injustice, providing such feeling does not run counter to the Party line.

But these exploiters are themselves puppets, along with the innocent painter Victor Stamp and his girl Margot, in the hands of the realistic villains

324

whose object is simply to make money out of art and politics, Sean O'Hara, Abershaw and Freddy Salmon. In the following scene Victor, a dud artist, a man of integrity but desperate for money, has been persuaded to become part of a 'factory' producing fake Van Goghs.

from THE REVENGE FOR LOVE

from Chapter 2, Part VI

In the fake-masterpiece factory at Shepherd's Bush, Stamp sat his workstool easily, with a limber grace—erect in the saddle. A frowning eye was fixed upon his image in the glass. He was disguised in the fur cap of a Canadian trapper. A heavy white bandage, descending under the chin, covered his right ear. He was supposed to be Van Gogh. He was engaged in the manufacture of a Van Gogh 'self-portrait.'

Stamp's face did not exactly lend itself to this device. The face of the imitator was high-cheekboned, certainly, and that was as it should be. But it was far too swarthy; cooked, as it had been, in the Pacific sun. Its tan would have been better suited for the faking of the self-portrait of a brown-skinned Venetian than for counterfeiting this sentimental pink rat from the hysterical North. Still, Stamp could distort himself, he found, after a fashion. That the man was a beastly blond could not be helped, could it? So allowing for the bleak albino look of the Dutchman's face, Stamp had decided to use his own face in a looking-glass as best he could. And now he sat scowling into this looking-glass as nearly as possible as Van G. had sat scowling into *his* looking-glass.

Stamp had come heartily to dislike these red-rimmed ferret-eyes that watched him from a dozen examples—photogravures, half-tones, and photographs—pinned-up for reference. His own big calmly hostile eyes surveyed with disgust this affected prison-crop (as he considered it). He had never liked him much as a painter. And as a man—now that he had been compelled to climb into his skin for the purposes of this portrait—he liked him even less.

In consultation with Tristy, Stamp had got his palette about right. The Van Gogh palette was a gay palette, of pure colours. A child's-paintbox palette it would look like to the layman. The complementary colours, of course, must be kept at arm's length from each other. *Red* and *green*, being 'complementaries,' must never meet, much less mix—to conform to the practice of this purist.

For a number of weeks now Stamp had been at work on these counterfeit pictures. He had formulas, by this time, for everything. The pupils of the eyes, for instance, in a typical Van Gogh, were painted—it was Tristy had pointed this out—as a nest of concentric wedges of greens, reds, blues and yellows, with their apex inwards. He had got the trick of that. And he had mastered the bald look of the pale eyebrows, which marked the base of the bony swellings. Then more wedges stuck on end, a miniature hedge of them, for the tissue of the lips. He could do a Van Gogh self-mouth pretty well by this time. And he had got the collarless neck, like a halter. An old pilot-jacket had been obtained for him by his employer, which, in combination with a seaman's shirt, produced the weighty yoke that was required.

Why Stamp had a bandage on his ear was because, when they first talked the matter over, they had decided to do a *bandaged* portrait of the mad master. That would make identification easier. Half the likeness was there, ready-made, once you had the famous bandage over the famous ear. Everyone seeing the familiar square woodenness of these gauche likenesses, and then the famous bandage, would say 'Van Gogh!' as soon as ever they clapped eyes on it. 'Look,' they would cry, 'where he has cut off his ear!'

Here is the story of the ear. All artists have heard the story of Van Gogh's ear—Stamp had read his letters too. But Vincent Van Gogh lost his ear somewhat as follows. Vincent Van Gogh was a Dutchman, as his name would suggest. He was the mystic and naturalist painter: he was a great friend of Paul Gauguin, the exotic faker of South Sea scenes (who pretended to be a half-caste to account for this Pacific sensibility). Van Gogh was very jealous of his friend's astonishing skill as an oil-painter; for he admired skilfulness very much. And as his intellect clouded, as it did about that time, this jealousy of the skilful French painter made him quite dangerous at last.

He and Paul Gauguin were in the South of France together, and they occupied the same bedroom—since they were neither of them rich, though the latter had started as a stockbroker. And at last one night Gauguin was woken up by hearing his room mate—this Dutchman of the unquiet mind and abhorrence of his clumsy fist—prowling about in the dark without good cause. He called out to him, and immediately the other scuttled back to his bed. But later on he was again woken up, and he found Van Gogh in a crouching position, not a yard away from him, with his eyes fixed upon his face.

. 'What is it, Vincent?' he shouted out angrily, as he did not move. 'Go back to your bed, Vincent!' And Vincent obeyed him at once and returned to his bed without speaking. A third time however he was disturbed. And on this occasion he saw Vincent approaching with an open razor. He drove him off with a few massive French curses. But this was enough for Monsieur Paul Gauguin, and next morning he changed his hotel. A few days later he received a small postal packet, and discovered inside, carefully wrapped up, a human ear. It was a present from his friend. For Vincent had cut it off and sent it to him as a little surprise. He was a simple man, and now was become a little over-simple maybe. And it occurred to him, thinking the matter over, that having intended to cut his friend's ear off, and driven him away, by advertising too crudely the intention, the least he could do was to mutilate himself, and sort of give his friend his revenge, but without his being put to the trouble of *taking* it!

But this made Paul Gauguin think, as he looked at the ear lying in the palm of his hand, that he had been wise in a way to move when he did, from the bedroom where he had slept with the unbalanced impressionist, struggling so dourly with his medium. And I think we must agree that beyond question he had shown his good judgment.

The place that had been selected by Freddie Salmon for his factory of counterfeiting pictures was a large studio in the yard of a private house converted into flats, within sight of the White City. It was entered *via* the front hall.

Tristy was established in the opposite corner to Stamp. He, like Stamp, was busy increasing the number of pictures by Van Gogh in the world. At present he was engaged in solemnly faking, with the utmost dignity, a largish picture, which was a cunning variation upon a well-known Provençal sunset: the idea being that Van Gogh painted two sunsets instead of one, and that this was the best, although it had never been heard of before.

Tristram conferred a peculiar respectability upon the whole proceedings: his mere presence made faking almost an august occupation. He lifted it upon a plane where Public Spirit reigned supreme, in a disinterested lustre—as, obviously from the very highest motives, he applied himself to deceive the public as to the authorship of this remarkable masterpiece, whose very existence had up till then been unsuspected.

Salmon had several experts in his pocket who could be relied on, the moment the piece was completed, to cover it with their authority in the market. Indeed, it was destined for the collection of a specific American, who already had absorbed half a dozen spurious canvases signed 'Vincent,' which would almost certainly be joined by Tristy's little contraption. Three thousand bucks was as good as added to Salmon's bank balance, for what he planned he planned well, and generally was found to execute. It was a pretty foxy collector who slipped through Salmon's fingers, once that gentleman had marked him down for a deal.

Stamp's self-portrait was another matter. If Stamp was not a dud—and Salmon was not entirely satisfied that Stamp was the goods, for he had made a mess of one self-portrait, which had to be thrown upon the market for what it was worth, without an expensive O.K. from a world-famous 'expert,' and take its chance in the sale-room—if Stamp earned his four quid a week and had the stuff in him to pull it off— this wounded hero of the art-racket (the romance of the missing ear playing its lucrative part) should represent a really worth-while profit.

Salmon had all the dope ready. This self-portrait was a little surprise of Vincent's for his brother, the Amsterdam dealer, that was the idea. But, as usual, the cantankerous Vincent was dissatisfied with his work. That was why it had been left at one of his favourite brothels, to discharge a food-debt. And Salmon was so exercised about this little nest-egg that it was all he could do to leave Stamp alone, and not paint the picture for him, or at least interfere, at every step.

For Salmon had his doubts about Stamp, and he had not concealed them from Stamp either—he could not, for he felt too strongly on the subject. He wished he had put somebody else on this job now. And between Stamp and himself no love was lost, by and large, and he knew it. And a quite good West-End dinner he had given Stamp, with wine *ad lib*, if not of the best, made no difference. It made no difference at all. He could not get Stamp to like him and regard him as a jolly good sort. So he chafed continually as he recognized that Stamp's heart was not in his work.

Without Stamp's perhaps being conscious of it Salmon knew that Stamp might as likely as not play him up. He knew that Stamp's limitations as an artist were not the only drawbacks an employer had to reckon with. The man was a surly mule, no doubt with a kick ready, too, for his benefactor. (For Salmon was of course a benefactor in all this, as, seeing what his sufferings were, most people would agree.) This human mule, as vicious as they make 'em, might quite well bitch the picture just out of cussedness! One could never establish with any exactitude, in dealing with such a *crétin*, where incompetence left off and cussedness began. Ah, these idiot-roughnecks that one was compelled to employ for one's sins! hissed to himself the unhappy Freddie Salmon; and young Isaac Wohl, who turned out with exemplary neatness forgery after forgery almost for the love of the thing, in the respectable shadow of Tristram, sympathized with poor Freddie on the quiet—everything about Isaac was on the quiet, for he was a quietist (who worked quietly, walked quietly, and thought quietly, even).

What differences there were in the human material! This deft young Jew, now, was a perfect, reliable machine—for turning out Marie Laurencins, be it understood. Marie Laurencin herself could not have told the difference between one of *his* and one of *her* Marie Laurencins. And what a comfort, too, on the personal side! There was no damned nonsense about *him*, none. He did not mind whether he did a Marie Laurencin or an Isaac Wohl—unless it might be that it amused him slightly more, intellectually (or, if you like, it bored him less) to be somebody else than to 'be himself,' and he relished sleight-of-hand for its own sake.

But Isaac could only be used on certain stuff. Here was the ever-recurring difficulty in this business. Isaac Wohl was a better artist than Stamp, yes. But he was not man enough, as it were, to be put on to the big rough stuff of a Van Gogh portrait. This Salmon understood quite well.

You had to pick a roughneck for that work. You had to pick him big—yes, even physically sizeable. But, at the end of it all, was Stamp *artist* enough? For you had to pick an *artist*, somehow, too! Here was the major problem in employing this type of labour. Among the heavyweights there were so few who could be trusted even to understudy the 'giants.' And it was in the 'giant' class—and especially in their figure-work—that the big money lay. An agonizing problem for a poor business man!

Van Gogh, in effigy, got up from his work-stool, stretched with a mighty abandon, and, with a slow buttock-waggle, swaggered over to where Tristy was at work.

Tristy was in the thick of the sunset. He gave a smile to Stamp, and went on with his painting. The sunset piece was a great rain of opaque particles of light—each particle dipped in a bath of a reddish, or brazen, solution. Gnarled figures of peasants, with the striations of tree trunks, gathered in the foreground like hobos in a hailstorm. But this hailstorm was the sunset. And the hailstones were the opaque particles showering down from the conflagration of the romantic solar disk, about to set, like a bloated firework.

There was a big clumsy cartwheel system, ordering the distribution of the particles. The nave of the cartwheel was the body of the crimson sun. The usual woolwork effect proper to Van Gogh obsessed everything that was terra firma—the rocks, the olives, the farms, the churches. There was a small town half submerged in the welter of incendiary particles.

More mannered than any Van Gogh, except for his pictures after he got into the asylum, it was a most successful specimen of the forger's art. Tristy had turned out a commercial article of a high order—quite in the diamond-pendant class. He had earned his fortnight's keep. Stamp considered the result in silence, as Tristy peppered a corner with a minor vortex of atoms.

'Why don't you put in a dog, to account for that little disturbance there, Trist?' he asked at last.

Tristy laughed.

'There are no dogs in the South of France,' he said.

'That doesn't matter. Put in a jackal.'

'There are no jackals in Van Gogh's pictures,' Mr Phipps told him demurely.

'Then let this be "the Van Gogh with the jackal," ' Stamp insisted.

Tristy shook his head. He refused to have anything to do with a jackal. 'No, that would be risky. I don't think Freddie would like it.'

'To hell with Freddie!' Stamp exclaimed with robust conviction.

Isaac Wohl looked up from his Marie Laurencin and smiled. He had a sly appetite for massive disrespect, when he encountered it. Such outbursts on the part of the stupid side of creation should be encouraged. Stagnation could not occur where such breezy expressiveness obtained. So he flashed out a quiet smile, a discreet salute for rebellion, and quietly returned to his *bleuâtre* and pallid *Jeune fille en fleur*.

Victor Stamp sat down, and took out of Van Gogh's pocket a packet of cigarettes.

'Have you finished the right eye?' asked Tristy. He picked up a large magnifying glass, and approached it to a photo-gravure of a late Van Gogh, which was pinned upon a drawing-board, resting against the back of a chair. 'These late things of his always fall away to the left,' he said. 'His right hand must have been losing its priority.'

'How do you mean, Trist?'

'Like a man would always hold up a falling wall with his *right* hand, I mean. A right-handed man.' Tristy looked round at him, and then away again.

'He may have been a left-handed man,' said Stamp.

'No. In his self-portraits it's his right hand he's using.'

'You're right,' said Stamp.

'Have you finished the right eye?' Tristy asked once more, dreamily but deliberately, as he mixed colour on his palette with a clean brush.

'Yes,' Stamp said.

And as he said *yes*, a little sullenly, the door of the studio opened, admitting a nervous burst of jocular voices, an aroma of cigars, and the elegant person of Freddie Salmon followed by Abershaw, towering behind him with a broad sardonic grin.

Freddie Salmon had a really enormous false bottom to his face. The face proper obviously terminated a short distance below the line of the lower lip: and what was palpably a bogus jaw had been superadded, for some not very evident purpose, by inscrutable nature; unless, of course, he had grown it himself, in the progress of his mortal career, for ends which, again, were none too clear. It caused him to have a somewhat stupid look, however, at times. And he may of course have desired to look stupid. And it perhaps imparted, observed from immediately in front, a somewhat *soft* appearance to the face. It was not impossible that he may have desired to appear 'soft.' But it was so patently *postiche* that it could only have deceived a very inattentive man.

'Hallo, Tristy—how is the sunset? All set?' he called out heartily as he came in, swinging a lunch edition of the *Evening Standard* in his hand.

'When a sunset is *all set*,' in a gigantic purr Abershaw put it to his hearty pal, 'what remains should be a *nocturne*, shouldn't it?'

It was four o'clock. These two impresarios were dressed like twins in city suits that exactly matched, of braided black, with striped whipcord trousers—the black wings and the white wings of their neckties and collars discovering the spacious laundry, beneath the neckline, of an immaculate chest, which passed down out of sight—if not out of mind—behind the perfectly jiggered panels of the double-breasted waistcoats.

They had lunched well at their club, the Sackville, in Grosvenor Street, or rather the drinks and cigars had been upon a prosperous scale, even if Ye Olde English Clubbe had lived up to the traditions stipulated by ye members (determined at all costs to be of *la vieille roche* or nothing) and provided a stolid British brisket succeeded by a bald apple tart and custard. There these two immaculate macaronis, in this White's *de nos jours*, had met other gentlemen like themselves—agents, publishers, touts, critics (both of art and of letters), shilling-a-liners, experts, museum-officials and moneylenders. And they had become loudly, if mildly, intoxicated, exchanging tips and gratulatory jokes and messages, and cocky topdog gibes—re such matters as the spot price of American 'mystery' best-sellers, or the heavy backwardation on forward pieces of the early Umbrian school.

How could they, therefore, as they entered the dirty workshop together, avoid appearing like two Olympian personages a little, visiting some unsavoury underdog sweat-shop—paradoxically and amusingly enough belonging to one of them, run as a profitable joke as a society lady may run a steam-laundry—and they were at no pains at all to tone themselves down, that was not their way, or to affect *not* to be flushed with insolence and liqueur-brandies.

Stamp eyed this brace of prancing sharpshooters, who had burst in so blandly, with aloof disfavour. Abershaw snapped him a naughty wink above his wholetime grin, and Stamp nodded back with lazy condescension. They came up and stood behind Tristy, inspecting the sunset. Salmon looked at Abershaw.

'It's the best Van Gogh I've seen,' said Abershaw, playing the outsider. 'Most impressive—I can't believe he didn't do it himself! How much?'

'Ask Van Gogh!' Salmon answered, looking at Tristy.

Abershaw turned to Victor Stamp—who, *for him*, was the master, he would have it understood.

'I admire your picture very much, Mr Gogh. May I acquire it? I should like to. What will you part with it for?'

'I'm not Van Gogh, sir!' Stamp answered with a surly smile. 'You've made a mistake.'

'You look remarkably like him, sir!' Abershaw insisted, in an energetic Johnsonian boom, fixing upon the other's fancy dress an eye big with doubt and sturdy conviction.

But Stamp began divesting himself of his disguise: he pulled off his trapper's fur-bonnet and removed the dressing from his operatic ear.

'I don't know what I've got this stuff on for,' he said, with distaste, as he did so.

Freddie looked greatly alarmed.

'You haven't finished, have you, Vic?' he clamoured suddenly, expostulation, or not far from it, dramatically tinging his voice—turning towards the self-portrait, his chin seeming to swell inordinately with dumb protest.

'Yes, that's finished,' said Stamp. 'That's finished, Freddie. How do you like it?'

And the tone could leave no doubt in anyone's mind as to his consciousness of Freddie's secret feelings about the portrait, nor his degree of concern regarding the feelings of Freddie.

The scene ends with Victor rebelling against his paymasters in disgust and self-disgust, refusing to add to the picture, and giving up picture-faking. In time Abershaw takes his revenge. Victor and Margot, along with Percy Hardcaster, are persuaded to run a cargo of guns into Spain. They are mere decoys, however, for the real gun-running which is carried out elsewhere. The concealed 'guns' in the truck Victor is driving turn out to be bricks, Victor and Margot die, and Percy finds himself where he was when the book began, in a Spanish prison. This is the last chapter.

from THE REVENGE FOR LOVE

from Chapter 8, Part VII

Percy Hardcaster knew his place. No illusions with regard to abstract justice troubled the upright cynicism of his outlook. He 'played the game.' As ever, with an incorruptible mind, he remained a true 'sportsman.' To *himself*, at least, he never pretended that he was hardly used. He accepted, for his political opinions, the status of a game—a game, of course, of life and death. He would have been more the 'happy warrior' certainly, in the class-battle, if he had been possessed of a more dishonest mind. But fresh hardships only seemed to have the effect of seasoning his vision. His integrity stiffened after each fresh buffet of fate. He looked out more bleakly upon life, seeing it steadily, seeing it whole, and computing his handicap to a millimetre. There was even a certain crisp logic about finding himself back in a Spanish prison which appealed to him—it was so grim that it had a logical fitness. Yes, in his way, and all allowance made for the backslidings of the spirit, he was glad to be back in prison! Was it not in the last analysis his proper place? It was what the trench was for the Tommy.

But these considerations did not prevent Mr Hardcaster from lifting up his voice in protest after protest, floridly delivered, with all the pomp of moral indignation. *And* as he fixed his flashing eye upon the limb of the law, the passing turnkey, he did not disguise the presence of the tongue in his cheek. All must, with him, be transacted upon a basis of impeccable veracity. It was never a question of what society *should* do to you, but of what society *could* do to you. 'You can't keep me here!' was what in effect he said. 'By all rights I *should* be here. But you just can't do it! Let me out!'

He was not let out. But he was not surprised. For he was only half-fooling when he insisted that they *could* not.

So in spite of protests he still was the occupant of an insanitary, overcrowded cell. His health suffered. After a week he was still there in the company of a half-dozen insignificant criminals and vagrants. He was not popular with his fellow-prisoners. This was partly on account of his undisguised attempts to separate himself from them at all costs, and his loud complaints at finding himself among them, as if he had been of a finer clay. Also his face was of such patently honest cast, so pink, so soap-conscious, that, although harmless enough perhaps, it was not exactly a thing to live with, for a sensitive cutpurse.

But they talked among themselves, and more than anything else his politics upset them. To start with, they were a self-righteous type of politics, full of a disagreeable rectitude they did not relish. But there was another thing. Since his politics were reputed to be so remarkably unconservative, how was it, they asked themselves, that he was left where he was? They felt that he ought, according to all precedent, and if their experience as old jail-birds went for anything—they would certainly have expected him to be lodged in the most luxurious cell in the prison. And they concluded that he must have done something unnecessarily ungentlemanly to find himself thrust in among the likes of them. So at last they cut him. And one pushed his wooden leg out of the way, informing him that he did not own the cell and that he took up too much room. Only an old crone who was a professional beggar was even passably civil to him. This was because, hearing he was English, she thought he must have some money on him somewhere. So part of the time she kept her hand in by holding out her well-worn palm in his direction, and whining loudly for alms. Once he gave her a piece of chocolate, and she immediately spat at him.

Percy's satisfaction at being back in prison was confined of course to his calmer moments, or such times as he was really put on his mettle. He was subject to acute depression for the greater part of the day. He did not see life steadily from morning till night. That would be too much to expect, though he got better as things came to look blacker, as they did very soon. For before long he realized that in responsible quarters—probably Madrid—people were hardening their hearts.

Of course, no pains would be spared to bring pressure to bear in the highest quarters, to have him immediately released. A suitable apology, it would be suggested, should accompany his release. But he was downcast, there was no denying it. He did not exaggerate the influence possessed by the government of His Britannic Majesty. Its legations and consulates, where it was a question of a notorious Communist, cut less ice every day. All this had been gone into again and again. The Spanish republican authorities *would* argue that after all it was impossible that the King of England could be so anxious as he *seemed* to befriend persons of no social standing, except at Moscow, who were, all said and done, his most implacable enemies. The Comintern had decreed him the same fate as for his cousin the Tsar. It was absurd that he should wish to protect its agents!

It was merely national pride, they argued, on the part of these haughty British officials, that was what it was; and when it came down to brass tacks they would not be so offended as all that if these ruffians were not given up. It had been proved over and over again that this was the way they argued. You could not cure them of it. They were hopelessly ill-informed. That vague entity, that all-powerful, *de facto* ruler of Great Britain, which went by the name of the 'Left Wing,' meant nothing to these Spanish boobies. They confused it with the Parliamentary Labour Party, probably! To their backward, provincial intelligence, these unteachable, stiff-necked romantics had no idea at all with whom they had to deal. The world they lived in—the real world, in contrast to the legal world—was to them a closed book.

But Percy, on his side, had no inclination to make the same mistake. He was in a Spanish prison: and these unintelligent, pigheaded *politicos* also were *facts*. Facts had to be faced all round. And this time, he knew, with a Civil Guard killed outright, that the outlook was unpromising. When would he have an opportunity, even, of stating his case? He would be lucky if his case came for trial within the twelvemonth. So Percy's spirits could not but be low. And when he allowed himself to reflect upon the manner of his arrest, and what had led up to it, he sat frowning stolidly at the wall, as downcast as he had ever been in his life. For this man of truth was not in the habit of sparing himself. Indeed, he somewhat enjoyed exercising his incorruptible intellect upon the dissection of Percy Hardcaster. He was like a painter fond of self-portraiture: and his self-portraits were not chocolate-boxes! He hit hard when he hit Percy.

Mateu was right! He told himself that Mateu had been not far wrong about him. Perhaps after all he did somewhat suffer from a weakness that was very common. Women after all were perhaps his weak spot! It looked uncommonly like it. For why had he followed Margot as he had?

Upon the seventh day the turnkey put his head in at the door, fixed his eye fishily upon Percy, then brought his body inside and straddled truculently in front of the seated prisoner. Percy took no notice at all. The turnkey dragged a greasy copy of the morning paper out of his side-pocket, thrust it under Percy's nose, and pointed in savage dumbshow at something it contained. His forefinger stalked backwards and forwards upon a heavily leaded headline, standing here and there for emphasis upon some particularly juicy capital. Then shouting in his prisoner's ear, as if being short of one leg caused one to be hard of hearing, he exclaimed:

'*Muertos! Muertos! Los dos!* Both! The women too! Both of them. Dead!'

Taking the newspaper from the man's hand with the deliberation of offended dignity (professionally assumed, in the natural course of things) and spreading it out carefully—throwing in a slight shake, as if to expel any lice which, seeing where it came from, might be expected to be quartered in it—Percy allowed his eyes to travel over it. They made their way in one condescending non-stop descent the length of the column to which his attention had been so rudely drawn. What his eye took in only deepened his detachment—it seemed even to freeze his face. He also took on a much more offended expression than before.

TWO OF THE GANG. CONTRABANDISTAS. DEAD.
A POSTMAN. PRECIPICE

What nonsense was this, which had been put before him? demanded the poker-face of this proud professional.

337

In the three seconds—no more—he allowed himself, Hardcaster saw that the bodies of one Victor Stamp and of a woman known as Margot had been found. They were at the foot of a precipice. A French postman found them—proceeding to a mountain village. Assumption: the pair had walked over the edge of the precipice. Probably in a storm. There had been a storm. High passes blocked with snow. Car found in Spain. Shepherd. Bricks. Abandoned. Letter in pocket of corpse. From Stamp's associate. Dangerous agitator—under lock and key. The notorious Hardcaster.

Percy Hardcaster sniffed. He returned the newspaper to the turnkey. His lack of interest was manifest even in the attitude of his artificial limb.

'Thank you,' he said. 'Thanks!'

'Well?' exclaimed the turnkey. 'Well?'

'Your papers as usual are full of lies,' Percy rejoined, stifling a yawn out of politeness to himself.

'You have seen enough? Don't you want the paper?' The turnkey held the newspaper invitingly in his hand, glaring indignantly at his prisoner.

'It is your paper, isn't it?' Percy asked him.

'Yes. Mine.'

'If you will give me back the money you took from me, I would then buy a newspaper of my own.'

'You can have this one!'

'No, thanks. Not one of your lying ones!'

The turnkey thrust the newspaper back into his pocket with a disappointed snarl and had turned to leave the cell when Percy Hardcaster suddenly clamoured, so that the official jumped as if he had been struck and wheeled about upon this alarming megaphone of a man.

'When am I to be moved from this putrid and evil-smelling room where I am kept boxed up with verminous pickpockets?'

An outburst of disapproving oaths broke from the pickpockets.

'Why do I not receive a visit from my consul?' bellowed Percy above the uproar. 'Am I to have no tobacco? I demand to see the governor of the prison!'

But the turnkey had left the cell and slammed the door behind him before Percy had terminated his customary speech. A heavy silence fell. The pickpockets glared at Percy and Percy at the pickpockets.

Swollen with an affected speechlessness, Percy proceeded to give a sculpturesque impersonation of THE INJURED PARTY. His cell-mates watched him surreptitiously, with an admiration it was out of their power to withhold. Heavily clamped upon his brick-red countenance, held in position by every muscle that responded to Righteous Wrath, was a mask which entirely succeeded the workaday face. It was the mask of THE INJURED PARTY (model for militant agents in distress). Obedient to the best technique of party-training, he sustained it for a considerable time.

But meanwhile a strained and hollow voice, part of a sham-culture outfit, but tender and halting, as if dismayed at the sound of its own bitter words, was talking in his ears, in a reproachful singsong. It was denouncing him out of the past, where alone now it was able to articulate; it was singling him out as a man who led people into mortal danger, people who were dear beyond expression to the possessor of the passionate, the artificial, the unreal, yet penetrating, voice, and crying to him now to give back, she implored him, the young man, Absolom, whose life he had had in his keeping, and who had somehow, unaccountably, been lost, out of the world and out of Time! He saw a precipice. And the eyes in the mask of THE INJURED PARTY dilated in a spasm of astonished self-pity. And down the front of the mask rolled a sudden tear, which fell upon the dirty floor of the prison.

———————

The Wyndham Lewis who returned to England after World War II was not the 'extremist' author of *Tarr*, nor even the politically concerned writer of *The Revenge For Love*. He had hopes for a short time that in the hands of a Labour Government 'all necessary measures of nationalisation will be carried through, and exploitation of the people . . . be made impossible', but these soon faded as he saw the realities of Crippsian austerity. In 1949 his sight began to fail, and in 1951 his five years of reviewing current art for *The Listener* ended. He announced the reason for it in the moving piece that follows.

The Sea-Mists of the Winter

It became evident quite early that it was going to be a deplorable winter. The cold was unvarying, it had purpose, it seemed. Usually in a London winter it forgets to be cold half the time; it strays back to autumn or wanders dreamily forward to spring, after a brief attempt at winter toughness, perhaps, squeezing out a few flakes of snow. But *this* winter though it experienced its usual difficulty of producing anything but a contemptible snowfall there has been an un-British quality, an unseemly continuity.

Speaking for myself, what struck me most was the veil of moisture like a sea-mist which never left my part of the town. I remember first remarking this just before Christmas. I said to Scott, my journalist-newsagent-friend, that these perpetual mists must slow him down in the morning; he drives up to business in his car, from his home in the outer suburbs. He did not seem to mind a light sea-mist for he shook his head absent-mindedly. Another time I was talking to him over the magazine counter of the shop and indicating the street outside, with its transparent film of blue-grey. I protested, 'Another mist!' He looked out and said, a little sharply, 'There is no mist.' I did not argue, I suppose that he meant it was not up to the specification of what *he* called 'a mist'.

But you may have seen through my innocent device. The truth is that there was *no* mist. The mist was in my eyes: there was no sea-mist in nature. In spite of conditions which, one would have supposed, would have made it quite clear what these atmospheric opacities were, it took me a considerable time to understand. It was not, you see, like this that I had imagined my sight would finally fade out. 'You have been going blind for a long time,' said the neuro-surgeon. And I had imagined that I should go on going blind for a long time yet: just gradually losing the power of vision. I had never visualized mentally, a sea-mist.

In such cases as mine there always arrives a time when normal existence becomes impossible, and you have to turn towards the consultant who has made a speciality of your kind of misfortune. When I started my second portrait of T.S. Eliot, which now hangs in Magdalene College, Cambridge, in the early summer of 'forty-nine', I had to draw up very closely to the sitter to see exactly how the hair sprouted out of the forehead, and how the curl of the nostril wound up into the dark interior of the nose. There was no question of my not succeeding, my sight was still adequate. But I had to move too close to the forms I was studying. Some months later, when I started a portrait of Stella Newton, I had to draw still closer and even then I could not quite see. So I had to have my eyes examined again. This was the turning-point, the date, December 1949. What, in brief, is my problem, is that the optic nerves, at their chiasma, or crossing, are pressed upon by something with the pleasing name of cranial pharyngeoma. It is therefore a more implacable order of misfortune than if I had a jolly little cataract. There has been a great acceleration of failure of vision during the last seven months or so. Of course I was told that I should first lose my 'central vision', which would mean that I should no longer be able to read or write. Already I was obliged to read with a magnifying glass. Then I found I could no longer read the names of streets, see the numbers on houses, or see what stations I was passing through on the railway. About that time everything except banner headlines was invisible: then I found I could no longer read the letters inside the finger-holes of a telephone-dial. At present, if I wish to dial a number, I count the holes with my fingertips until I reach the opening where I know the letter I have to locate is situated. Thus seven is P.R.S. five is J.K.L. I know what letters the holes near the beginning and end of the half-circle contain, and what the figures are as well.

As to typing, it is some time ago now that I ceased to see distinctly the letters on the keys. I still write a certain amount with a pen or pencil, but I write blind. However much I write on it the page before me is still an unsullied white: and sometimes the lines I have written distressingly amalgamate. The two books on which I am at present working, one a novel, the other an art book, will proceed quite smoothly, but the method of their production will be changed. A dictaphone, or 'recorder' as the Americans call it, will supersede the pen or the typewriter, at least as far as the first stages of composition are concerned. Many American writers I am informed employ the recorder, although possessing ordinary visual powers.

As to the sea-mist, that is now too pretty a name for it. Five or six weeks ago I still went to my newsagent to have a talk with

Scott and make some purchases. He of course would move about as a fresh customer would come in and demand attention. At any given time I found it extremely difficult to decide whether he was there before me or not, for he would come back and stand silently near me, and often it was only because of the tobacco he was smoking, and a slight movement in the mist before me, or at my side, that I knew that he had returned. Recently he has told me that he realized that half the time I did not know he was there. I went to other shops as well, as long as it was possible: but when for me the butcher became nothing but a white apron, and the skinned back of a bullock protruding, as it hung, seemed to me a fleshly housewife, I ceased to be a shopper. Now I take my exercise arm-in-arm with some pleasant companion, and it's surprising how easily one can thread one's way in and out of the shadowy pedestrians, very slightly steered by another but sharp-eyed person.

Sometimes I am still at large solo, though increasingly rarely. I may go out, for instance, and some twenty yards away look for a taxicab. In these cases I will stand upon the edge of the pavement, calling imperiously 'Are you *free?*' to owner-drivers, who probably observe me coldly from behind their steering wheels as if I were the Yonghi-Bongi-Bo. I signal small vans, I peer hopefully at baby-trucks. At length I get a response. It *is* a taxi! But I assure you that it is one thing to hail a taxi-cab, another to get into it. This is quite extraordinarily difficult. I try to force my way in beside the indignant driver. He or I will open the door. But as I see everything so indistinctly I attempt to effect a passage through the wood of the door itself, in Alice Through the Looking Glass fashion, rather than take advantage of the gaping hole in the side of the taxi produced by the opening of the door. It is with a sigh of relief that I at last find my way in, after vainly assaulting the stationary vehicle in two or three places. This I realize must be extremely difficult to understand for a person with rude eyesight and piercing vision. It is also difficult for the acquaintance who comes up, as I am staring through the slabs of dark grey at darker slabs, which I hope may be taxis, who addresses me with familiar cordiality. For he is just another slab of nondescript grey, at which I stare, inquiring a little unceremoniously, 'Who are you?'

When visited by friends, which will be usually in the evening, in a room lit by electric light properly shaded (for I have not removed these obstacles to sight, belonging to an era out of which I am passing) I see them after a fashion, but fragmentarily, obliquely, and spasmodically. I can see no one immediately in front of me. But I sit and talk to them without embarrassment, of course, just as if I could see them. It is rather like telephone conversation, where the voice is the main thing. But an awareness of the bodily presence is always there, and as one turns one's head hither and thither, glimpses constantly recur, delivering to one's fading eyesight a piece of old so-and-so's waistcoat or bald head, or dear Janet's protruding nose. These token odds and ends of personality are really just as good as seeing them whole, and their voices have an added significance.

The failure of sight which is already so advanced, will of course become worse from week to week until in the end I shall only be able to see the external world through little patches in the midst of a blacked out tissue. On the other hand, instead of little patches, the last stage may be the absolute black-out. Pushed into an unlighted room, the door banged and locked for ever, I shall then have to light a lamp of aggressive voltage in my mind to keep at bay the night.

New as I am to the land of blind-man's-buff I can only register the novel sensations, and not deny myself the enjoyment of this curious experience. It amuses me to collide with a walking belly; I quite enjoy being treated as a lay-figure, seized by the elbows and heaved up in the air as I approach a kerb, or flung into a car. I relish the absurdity of gossiping with somebody the other side of the partition. And everyone is at the other side of the partition. I am not allowed to see them. I am like a prisoner condemned to invisibility, although permitted an unrestricted number of visitors. Or I have been condemned to be a blind-folded delinquent, but not otherwise interfered with. And meanwhile I gaze backward over the centuries at my fellow condamnés. Homer heads the list, but there are surprisingly few. I see John Milton sitting with his three daughters (the origin of this image, is to my shame, it seems to me, a Royal Academy picture), the fearful blow at his still youthful pride distorting his face with its frustrations. He is beginning his great incantation: 'Of Man's first Disobedience and the Fruit of that Forbidden Tree', while one of the women sits, her quill-pen poised ready to transcribe the poetry. Well, Milton had his daughters, I have my dictaphone.

This short story of mine has the drawback of having its tragedy to some extent sublimated. Also, we have no ending. Were I a dentist, or an attorney I should probably be weighing the respective advantages of the sleek luminol, or the noisy revolver. For there is no such thing as a blind dentist, or a blind lawyer. But as a writer, I merely change from pen to dictaphone. If you ask, 'And as an *artist*, what about that?' I should perhaps answer, 'Ah, sir, as to the artist in England, I have often thought that it would solve a great many problems if English painters were born blind.'

And finally, which is the main reason for this unseemly autobiographical outburst, my articles on contemporary art exhibitions necessarily end, for I can no longer see a picture.

———————

It was typical of this particular face Lewis presented to the world that he should regard his blindness as partly comic. To one of the many readers who wrote after reading the article he replied: 'I am so glad I succeed in making you laugh in unison with me. For it is of course idiotically funny suddenly to be deprived of one's main prop, the EYE.'

So his career as a visual artist was over: and loss of sight changed his writing also, perhaps more than he foresaw or understood. In spite of that fine phrase about Milton's daughters he found the dictaphone uncongenial, and wrote on sheets of paper with wire stretched across to guide his pen, sheets that he dropped to the floor after writing a few lines, so that he sat surrounded by a pile of papers that had to be sorted, typed, and read back to him. The blindness affected his style. In the most important of his last works, *Self Condemned* and the two volumes of *The Human Age*, the Vorticist eye that had fixed the physical appearance of men and women unerringly was closed. The surface of these books, their manner of saying things, is generally smooth and uncomplicated, much nearer to that of a straightforward narrative by John Updike or Graham Greene than the fully-sighted Lewis would have envisaged.

When René, the protagonist of *Self Condemned*, says goodbye to his sister Helen on his departure from England, 'He put his arm around her waist, and tears came into his eyes.' The level surface of such writing encouraged readers who had been disconcerted or dismayed by the form, as well as the message, of earlier fictions. *Self Condemned* is, as its author said, the story of a perfectionist who abandons his job as professor of history at an English university and goes to Canada in pursuit of—what, exactly? That we never learn, but René's profound dissatisfaction with the world, the humans who inhabit it and the futile, self-deceptive nature of their activities is made clear. René's immolation of himself and his long-suffering wife Hester in a dismal Toronto hotel is, in a way, a futile gesture towards saintliness, one punished by the wretched lives they lead there, and in the end by Hester's suicide. A defeated René returns to academic life, 'and the Faculty had no idea that it was a glacial shell of a man who had come to live among them, mainly because they were themselves unfilled with anything more than a little academic stuffing'.

The novel's course follows closely Lewis's own life in Canada. The book's Hotel Blundell is the Hotel Tudor, Momaco is Toronto, some of the other places and characters were drawn from life, and the fire described in the book was an actual fire that destroyed much of the Hotel Tudor. Yet the power of the work exists outside such actualities, as the miseries endured by the Lewises are transformed through an account of the difficulties René experiences in making an honourable living into a pessimistic statement about the human condition, and the inevitable defeat of René's perfectionism. The intensity of this novel leaves it standing alone among Lewis's work. It is a book in which the detachment and impersonality of the satirist (impersonal even when most personally offensive) have been abandoned. No individual passage can give the work's full cumulative flavour, but 'Twenty-five Feet by Twelve', the chapter describing the room where René and Hester live, gets near to it.

from SELF CONDEMNED

Twenty-five Feet by Twelve

The Room, in the Hotel Blundell, was twenty-five feet by twelve about. It was no cell. It was lit by six windows: three composed a bay, in which well-lit area they spent most of their time—René sat at one side of the bay, writing upon his knee on a large scribbling pad. Hester sat at the other side, reading or knitting or sleeping.

For the first year she had sat upon a piece of monumental hotel-junk, a bluish sofa. But it secreted bed-bugs, the summer heat disclosed, as it caused one occasionally to walk upon one of its dirty velvet arms.

Once the identity of the bug had been established, and before it moved from the velvet structure on to the human body, René acted. Overcoming loud protests from the management, who insisted that the bugs were innocent tree-insects, the sofa was expelled. Next Hester sat on a large blue velvet armchair. It was closely related to the sofa, but no bugs had shown up. Lastly, they were furnished with a fairly new and bugless settee.

It was René's habit to place an upended suitcase upon a high chair and drape it with a blanket. He stood this between his wife and himself, so blotting her out while he wrote or read. He could still see, over the crest of this stockade, a movement of soft ash-gold English hair, among which moved sometimes a scratching crimson fingernail. This minimum of privacy, this substitute for a booklined study, was all he had for three years and three months—to date it from the sailing of the *Empress of Labrador* from Southampton.

In summer René lowered the centre blind to shut out the glare. At present it was December, and another glare, that of the Canadian snow, filled the room with its chilly radiation. There was a small stack of books upon a chair to the left of him; he wrote in silence, hour after hour, dropping each page, as it was completed, into a deep, wooden tray on the floor at his side.

They never left this Room, these two people, except to shop at the corner of the block. They were as isolated as are the men of the police-posts on Coronation Gulf or Baffin Bay. They were surrounded by a coldness as great as that of the ice-pack; but this was a human pack upon the edge of which they lived. They had practically no social contacts whatever. They were hermits in this horrid place. They were pioneers in this kind of cold, in this new sort of human refrigeration; and no equivalent of a central heat system had, of course, as yet been developed for the human nature in question. They just took it, year after year, and like backwoodsmen (however unwilling) they had become hardened to the icy atmosphere. They had grown used to communicating only with themselves; to being friendless, in an inhuman void.

The room, as mentioned above, was twenty-five feet by twelve about, but six of these, out of the length, you have to deduct for bathroom and kitchenette. Those figures still in no way express the size, because it was immense. Two human beings had been almost forcibly bottled up in it for a thousand years.

In the Rip van Winkle existence of René and Hester—of suspended existence so that they might as well have been asleep—a thousand years is the same as one tick of the clock. It was a dense, interminable, painful vibration, this great whirring, agelong, thunderous *Tick*. Bloat therefore the minutes into years, express its months as geological periods, in order to arrive at the correct chronology of this too-long-lived-in unit of space, this one dully aching throb of time.

A prison has a smell, as distinct as that of a hospital with its reek of ether. Incarceration has its gases, those of a place where people are battened down and locked up, year after year. There is a wrong sort of hotel; one dedicated to the care of guests who have been deprived of their freedom, and have been kidnapped into solitude and forced inertia.—The Hotel Blundell was the wrong sort of hotel. It was just a hotel, it was not a prison, but for the Hardings, husband and wife, it stank of exile and penury and confinement.

Their never-ending disappointments, in the battle to get work—wild efforts to liberate themselves, ghastly repulses—had made of this hotel room no more personal than a railway carriage, something as personal as a suit of clothes. As time passed, it had become a museum of misery. There were drawers packed with letters, each of which once had represented a towering hope of escape. Each effort had resulted in their being thrown back with a bang into this futility.

Number 27A, the number of the apartment (for apartment was the correct term for it), was consequently a miniature shadow, anchored upon another plane, of the great reality, which they had willy nilly built up about them in their loneliness. They must vegetate, violent and morose—sometimes blissfully drunken, sometimes with no money for drink—within these four walls, in this identical daily scene—from breakfast until the time came to tear down the Murphy bed, to pant and sweat in the night temperatures kicked up by the radiators—until the war's-end or the world's-end was it? Until they had died or had become different people and the world that they had left had changed its identity too, or died as they had died. This was the great curse of exile—reinforced by the rigours of the times—as experienced upon such harsh terms as had fallen to their lot.

Then they hid things from each other; as when one morning she saw a report of the suicide of Stefan Zweig, refugee novelist. He and his wife had killed themselves in their apartment at Rio.—To begin life again, was Zweig's reported explanation, once the war was ended, would demand a greater effort than he felt he would be capable of making; he preferred to die and the wife who had shared with him the bitter pangs of exile accompanied him, with that austere and robust fidelity of the jewish woman to her mate.

But as she stared and brooded over this ugly news-item, during a laconic breakfast—the sun with a great display of geniality glittering over the frosty backyards—Hester recalled how earlier in the week she had praised electricity as against gas, for fixing food and as a heating agent. René had given his gothic headpiece a rebutting shake. The substitution of electricity for gas, he had objected, removed from those who were tired of life one of the only not-too-brutal modes of making one's exit from it: one available to anybody, costing nothing, requiring no specialist technique. A foolproof key to the *néant*. Just turn on the tap and lie down.—So she stopped herself from exclaiming about this tragedy, remarking instead that the egg ration in England was at present one a month.

But this roused him to controversy. 'I'd rather have that one egg and be in England . . .'

'Oh yes—you'd probably find it was a bad one when you got it!' she told him. There was no chance of their getting back to England; she discouraged regrets.

'All right, all right! I'd rather have that one rotten egg . . .'

She gave in with a big sigh, no longer denying her nostalgia. 'I too, René!—I'd give all the eggs in Momaco for half an hour in London!'

However, ten minutes later her husband came across the Zweig report. He exclaimed 'ha!' as he glanced through it and then he passed it over to her.

For the class of things they hid from each other was not identical. René did not picture Hester with her head in a gas oven. His Hester was strongly prejudiced against death. What *he* concealed from her was rather newspaper announcements of appointments to academic posts, even of a quite minor order. He hurriedly shuffled out of sight anything with a hint in it of horridness towards himself: such as when a local columnist referred to the presence among us 'of a certain historian for whom history ended at the Repeal of the Corn Laws'.

'Zweig,' said René, tapping the paper with his finger, 'put down his act to his own incompetence, and to the future not the present.'

'So I noticed.' Her anger broke up into her face, giving her suddenly the mask of a tricoteuse. 'I would like to rub their damned noses in that sort of thing,' she exclaimed.

'Where's the use? It's human nature.'

'It's like *animals*! . . . Human nature!'

They took up their respective rôles at once. He became austerely watchful that no missile should get past which he regarded as irrational, and therefore unlikely to find its mark and kill its man. Thus it was no use calling people 'animals'. Just as well say they had hair in their crutches and armpits, and discharged the waste products of their nutritive system. 'We are animals,' René shrugged. 'Besides, he was just bored probably. I expect it was that.'

Hester shook her head. 'Don't you believe it! How about Toller. How about . . .'

'That's right enough . . . It's pretty bloody for a german-speaking and german-writing man.'

'Pretty awful,' Hester retorted, 'for any temporarily displaced person. Among people who pay lip-service to "culture" as they call it—to the objects of this war, but . . .'

'Oh well,' he interrupted her, 'the devil takes the hindmost everywhere. Hitler had kicked him down to the bottom of the class. So the devil got him. You can't expect a lot of Portuguese mulattos . . .'

'Nor Canadians for that matter!'

René laughed. 'Ah, he had never had the misfortune to encounter them . . . !'

But René was wrong. The real backgrounds of this act of despair were

349

made apparent—with, as René put it, 'a lousy naïveté'—by the literary editor of the *Momaco Gazette-Herald*. Zweig *had*, it seemed, encountered these dwellers of the far-north, for he had spent some time in Momaco, obviously in search of a refuge, of not too inhospitable a spot to weather the storm in.

But individuals of world renown, the starry few, are only welcome in such parts as unreal and glittering apparitions, upon a lecture platform. To 'stick around' is not well received.—In his obituary notice the literary authority of the *Momaco Gazette-Herald* recalled, upon a lachrymose note, how this most distinguished novelist, during his sojourn in Momaco, *offered me his friendship*. He was sorry now he had not responded.

René burst out laughing as he reached this climax of the obituary.

'Means poor old Zweig tried to get some reviewing to do in their beastly paper. But that would be too big a name ... overshadow the other contributors. So ...'

'So!'

'But a pretty fellow. He might have left out that bit about how he'd snubbed him and how kind of regretful and contrite he was ... kind of half feeling he'd done the poor chap in. What a rat!'

In such moments as this they changed rôles. Hester became sweetly reasonable.

'My dear René,' she mildly protested, 'you take this little bush-tick too much to task. He was only *advertising* himself, to his little circle of bush-bookworms. If a newspaperman can't advertise himself ... !'

So they conversed, these two inmates of this lethal chamber. Its depths were dark. Looked into from without—by a contemplative bird established upon the maple bough about a foot from the middle window—the Hardings would have seemed (as they moved about their circumscribed tasks, or rested sluggishly upon the bottom as it were) provided with an aquatic medium, lit where it grew dark by milky bulbs. So they must have appeared to the visiting squirrel, applying his large expressive eye to the pane, to discover if his presence had been noted by the two odd fish in the dark interior, who fed him peanuts, when they had the jack. Of the six windows, three, half the year, resembled very closely the plateglass sides of a tank in an aquarium. The green twilight that pervaded the lair of the Hardings was composed of the coloration from the wall of leaves of the summer maple, abetted by the acrid green veil of the mosquito netting. Green blinds latticed with use further contributed to this effect of water, thickening the bloomy cavity.

In the winter a dark pallor, or the blue glare of the snow, replaced the green. For weeks the windows would be a calloused sheet of ice, in places a half-inch thick. That was the only way the window ever got a cleaning. The Hardings had to go over them with a sponge, plunged in hot water, in order to see at all, and some of the callouses, of the density of icicles, required more than one kettle of boiling water. Immediately a new coat of ice would form, but the dirt of a twelvemonth poured down with the dissolving ice. The smoke of thirty thousand cigarettes, and a hundred fish, roasts, or 'offal', rolled down upon the window-sills. Of course the film of factory smoke from the chimneys of Momaco upon the outside surface of the window never departed.

'This is not real,' René insisted one day, as he sat looking towards the daylight from an inner seat, sniffing the rancid smoke from the grill. 'It isn't poverty. That is the worst of it.'

'No?'

'I am rich—in a city where people die every day from under-nourishment. Idle—and rich.'

Hester, her face flushed from the sub-tropical kitchenette, shook her head. She felt sick from the smoke.

'The pukka-poor would laugh at us,' he told her.

'The rich would laugh at us too . . . they do.'

'Those top-booted blackcoated Jews out of the Ghetto in Cracow, who have a look in their eyes, you or I shall never have.'

'Not?'

'Their lips are pale with blood that has never been thickened with anything that would keep in decent gloss the coat of a well-cared-for dog.—And their lips are etched with the extraordinary bitterness of their sense of that fact. They have tasted every injustice. They live ten in a room. *We* cannot fill this room properly. There are only two of us.'

'I consider it full,' she answered.

He stared round, as if looking for somebody.

'No. This is a joke,' he said. He got up. 'The fat from our food

351

collects in the bottom of the oven. If we scraped it out and ate it on our bread, that would be hard times—though in hard times there would be no fat in the bottom of the oven.'

'These are hard times,' she told him. 'Different from the poverty of a rag-picker, but in some ways worse.'

The Hardings were exiles, not from Poland, or France or Germany, but from Great Britain. They were not romantic political exiles but economic exiles—exiles by accident, frozen in their tracks, as it were, by the magic of total war, and the unavoidable restrictions upon travel that entailed, and the iron laws dividing dollar currency from sterling currency, and so cutting English nationals in Canada off economically from their own country.

As an 'involuntary squatter' in the Dominion of Canada René described himself, if he wrote to a friend in England. Locked up in this dollar country as solidly as if he were in Sing Sing—no farthing reaching him from England—he and his wife had been marooned. In Tahiti, a Swedish best-seller, the papers had reported, was an even worse case. He had no money at all and lived by what he could beg or catch in the sea. In Massachusetts, an American friend had written them, 'an English millionaire' was marooned. He scarcely had enough money for a pack of cigarettes. So this ex-professor was one of quite a lot.

But as an 'involuntary squatter' René had chosen to squat far too near to the University of Momaco. There are hard and fast rules about squatting in new countries, of which he had not been aware. It is not a good thing if you are a potential professor to squat too near to the institution where actual professors function. That is regarded as a little threatening. That is not well received.

So for the Hardings exile was complicated by other matters, which was what made it so peculiarly bad. Their isolation was now complete. People in Momaco were even tired of gossiping about them. They had at last really forgotten Professor Harding was there. But René had not forgotten *them*. As he sat crouched in his corner of the bay window, behind his palisade, he would sometimes take up a notebook, marked Momaco, and make a little note for future use.

'I remembered something just now, Hester,' he might remark to his invisible wife.

'What was it, darling?' For she knew by the tone of his voice that it was something she would be glad to hear.

'I thought, "Oh, God. Oh, Montreal." '

'Yes?'

'What exclamation could Butler have found to apostrophize Momaco!'

Hester gave vent to a cat-like rumble of feline anger. She had long ago given up trying to find words for what she felt about Momaco.

This prison had been theirs for more than three full years. When René read reports in the newspapers about Daladier, Blum and the other French politicians in their place of confinement in France (Daladier described as tirelessly reading all the papers he could get and never speaking, Blum writing, Guy La Chambre complaining all day about the food, or so their Vichy captors had it) he decided that the all-important difference that he, René, *could*, if he possessed the necessary money, take a ticket to Chicago or for that matter to Mexico City, did certainly count for a lot. It was a big advantage. But he had not even got the money to buy a ticket for a spot thirty miles up the line and spend the day at a lake. He could get the money to just buy enough good food and a car-fare to go downtown once a week. The city limits were his limits and Hester's.

For a period of four months Hester had not gone out at all because she had no shoes to wear. All the shopping had to be done by him; and when the meat famine had come in Momaco, he had to go as far as the downtown market. This took up half the day, while she sat at home, at the mercy of her miserable fancies, counting the hours of this senseless captivity.

At last Hester could buy a pair of shoes. A New York friend had unexpectedly sent a present of thirty dollars. She cried a little. It was like a cripple recovering the use of her legs!

Through always conversing only with each other, their voices sounded strange to them when they were visited once in a way. Their 'company' voices were like the voices of two strangers. So if they had a couple of visitors—as once had occurred—it was like having four people *as well as* themselves in the Room. It was quite a party.

And the Room: that became something else. For anyone from the outside to come into that, was like someone walking into one's mind—if one's mind had been a room and could be entered through a door and sat down in. René found he disliked their Room being entered by other people. The less people had come into it, until practically nobody came—the more they suffered in it boxed up there in interminable lonely idleness—the more he felt that if he must see people he preferred to see them upon neutral ground. That they should see where he and his wife had been so unspeakably miserable he looked upon as an affront. If he had lost his reason he would probably have burnt down the hotel, so that no one should ever come in and boast, 'This is where we shut up the dumbbell René Harding.'

If this was a prison, and it was, the three bay windows twelve feet above the soil-level had a better outlook than most jails. It could not be an authentic prison, anyway, because of a coil of heavy rope hung at the side of one window—a precaution decreed by the city fire headquarters. No prison has a coil of rope invitingly attached by one of its ends to the wall at the side of a window. That would be an odd kind of prison—as this one was.

Momaco, the city in which the Hotel Blundell was situated, was one of the greatest Canadian cities. It was a big, predominantly anglo-saxon city, though the french-canadian population, if anything, exceeded the english-canadian, the two together around half a million souls. It swelled and shrank like a river: it swelled in boom years, when the mines of nickel and gold were booming. It shrank if the mine interests weakened. But it was always a big place: it had got so big it couldn't shrink as much as the economic fluctuations decreed. Now the war was swelling it to bursting: it was swollen like a great tick with the young blood of farming areas, as the war factories mushroomed up. The experts predicted a catastrophic deflation, when Canada passed back out of total war into total peace. But Momaco could never become a ghost city, like Cobalt or Kirkland Lake, unless the Province became a ghost. This bush metropolis had the appearance of an English midland city, which had gone in for a few skyscrapers. Its business quarter, in spite of a dozen of these monsters, was mean. It even succeeded very successfully in concealing them; as if having committed itself to a skyscraper, it resented its size.

Momaco was so ugly, and so devoid of all character as of any trace of charm, that it was disagreeable to walk about in. It was as if the elegance and charm of Montreal had been attributed to the seductions of the Fiend by the puritan founders of Momaco: as if they had said to themselves that at least in Momaco the god-fearing citizen, going about his lawful occasions, should do so without the danger of being seduced by way of his senses.

Had this city not been, with so rare a consistency, ugly and dull, the Hardings might have been less cooped up. Being friendless, there was no temptation to leave their neighbourhood, and be depressed by the squalid monotony. Accordingly the rows of backyards, twelve feet beneath their windows, constituted their unchanging horizon. The walls of the penitentiary were the houses enclosing the backyards. Their room was cell 27A. But they were blessed with an amusing and loquacious warder, in the person of the maid.

How much land does a man require? The landowner Count Tolstoi asked that. It is one of the massive fundamental questions. His answer was six feet by two, the space demanded by a man's body when he is dead.—Alive twenty-five feet by twelve is all right, with the dusty trough of half a dozen backyards thrown in, and a dusty company of maples—in which pursuing their beautiful lives robins and jays, starlings and doves abound: not to mention the eternal passerine chorus, or the small black Canadian squirrel who vaults on to the windowsill.

The Hardings even had two favourite pigeons, who always came together. They named them Brown and Philips, after the two well-known picture dealers of Leicester Square.—But Brown and Philips vanished, in spite of the great reliance these two birds had come to place on the Hardings' bounty. And their promenade—or sports-ground where they played bread-polo—on the flat roof of the kitchen quarters, tacked on to the next house, lost much of its glamour.

There was one occasion when an escaped budgerigar turned up to the amazement of all the birds present at the time upon Brown and Philips' sports-ground. 'Poor beast,' muttered René. 'Look at it . . . It has no pride—it's a lovebird, it wants love.' A group of sparrows was repulsing its frantic advances. So gaudy a novelty in the way of a bird was not, it was plain, to their taste. 'That's not love,' Hester advised him. 'It's his big heart, only . . . How matey he is!' she exclaimed, as he knocked one of the sparrows off a ledge, and engaged the next in what René decided was in fact only energetic conversation. 'He is a darling!' Hester insisted. 'He does look so funny among all those sparrows, the wonderful little lost ball of fire!' But a captor came up a ladder, tiptoed across the roof and caught him in his hand. 'Back to the cage, buddy!' said René. 'To die in captivity.' At that moment Philips alighted heavily upon the neighbouring roof, decorously arranging his lavender wings, and Brown dropped beside him, with an eye cocked towards the intruder carrying off the escaped prisoner.

The Hardings' Room was not by itself. It was one of a family of over one hundred apartments, as they were one of a family of people called 'guests', comprising one of the six apartment-hotels of Momaco. The bathroom, lavatory, and kitchenette made of it a complete living-quarters. You need never move out of it, if you did not want to, or did not have to go to work. By telephone—the instrument was on your writing table—you could order all your food from the groceteria, the dirty backyard of which you could see from the bay window. During the meat famine it was even possible to observe the carcasses of beef or lamb being carried in at the side of the door, rush to the telephone and secure a small hunk before they sold out.

In the flank of the Hotel, on its south side, was a drinking saloon. To placate the Methodists a saloon or a beer-parlour was called a 'Beverage-room' all over Canada. It did not pacify the Methodists, who would never be satisfied until Momaco was a hundred per cent bootleg city: and in the war they saw their opportunity.—A dirty and generally drunken waiter would bring you beer, or, if he knew you weren't a dick, bootleg Rye or Scotch. If you were a 'wine-hound' you could have what in Canada is laughingly called wine.

Should you find it undesirable to move far from the front door and expose yourself to the saddening and depressing sensations produced by the streets and alleys of Momaco, you were obviously well-placed to stand a siege. For the Hardings it was a siege. Their resistance was an epic of human endurance, and some day, René felt sure, would make Momaco famous.

The sense of the passage of time depended largely upon the recurrence of Sunday. You got lost in the week itself.—Monday was very distinct. You knew when the week *began*. Mondaymorningishness was an unmistakable something that entered the room as Bess came in at 10.30 with her sheaf of towels and sheets. She was swollen with a sense of accumulated wrongs—during the week-end all the insults of the week had had time to mobilize and organize inside her, in her lonely room, and on Monday morning she discharged these humours as she passed from room to room.

Tuesday and Wednesday were sometimes a little difficult to identify. Thursday and Friday had a way of getting mixed up: and Thursday and Wednesday were a no man's land in the centre of the week: it didn't really matter which it was, and they were usually indistinguishable.

Friday has this advantage over Thursday, that it is unlucky. You can't cut your nails. You can't start on a journey: if you are one of those people who are lucky enough to be leaving Momaco, you have to restrain your impatience until Saturday. Something unpleasant is pretty sure to happen on Friday anyway (especially in Momaco) that reminds you what day it is you are passing through.

Saturday has a very definite function of its own among the days of the week. It is easy to identify—it is the last day as Monday is the first. Shopping is a more urgent matter, because of Sunday. It is your last chance until Monday to buy what you want. And as to Sunday, no one can mistake *that*. From the Gulf of Mexico to Hudson's Bay everyone is in bed until noon, so it is only half a day. But it is the day of days, because you know you have lived a week more, and with luck, or ill-luck, will soon be treading another week—towards another Sunday.

The radio roars all day on Sunday. It vibrates with the tremulous thunder of the organ. From a million pulpits sing-song voices assure us that war is a holy thing. It is a day of verbal bloodletting, of exhortations to homicide and quivering organpipes. It is at once—cooped up in an hotel Room with a radio—an uncommonly noisy day, and a very blank one. It is a vacuum, full of a fierce and sanctimonious voice, hollow with bogus emotion, calling for blood, and another one, sweet and tender, promising love to the brave. *Why* you should be stridently homicidal on Sunday is so obviously because Christ would desire it, for when He talked about the 'other cheek' He was only fooling, and He likes a good old christian war just as much as any other Christian.

There is *no* voice telling people that this is a very great revolution rather than the stupid war every booby thinks it is—because it will afford all the nations an authentic *chance* (whether they take it or not, which is up to them) of escape from the unmentionable chaos which brought it about, that a more intelligent society *may* be in the making. One in which the men of creative capacity, instead of wasting ninety per cent of their lives wrestling with the obstructive inertia of the majority, will be freed for their creative tasks.—Instead of such voices as that, which would be far too real a thing to be tolerated on the highly respectable ether, there is just the old fustian. A loud voice saying nothing: the nihilistic screech of the pep-doctor—the platitudinous drone of the reverend gentleman in the god-business, assuring us that Jesus was a kind of Elite Guard, and God a sort of Super-Thor, and that we are headed for a Valhalla of mediocrity.

So Sunday is a good day to anchor your timetable to. It is a day that is a vacuum in more senses than one, because it is quite impossible to get any news on Sunday, or to find out what is going on. *Nothing* apparently is going on, in a world where nothing is more important than something, and nobody than somebody. A war is going on somewhere no doubt—our lovely boys are dying somewhere up in the ether waves, piloting their ships, hounded by Zeros in unequal fight, because some fool or knave prevented them having anything but 'too little and too late'. But the children are not supposed to be disturbed on Sunday. We are the children—so all the news becomes emptily rosy.

But about seven o'clock Eastern war-time Jack Benny brings far more than comic-relief. He brings a great gust of reality and heaven-sent respite from Godliness—and from verbal thunder of bulletins telling of battles that probably were never fought (or not that way). A salvo of wisecracks dispels the fog. We are back upon the earth again with Jack and Rochester, among things that matter to men, and things that are good for human consumption. Once more we are among things just as real as this war is—if we were ever allowed to know about it, or treat it as a real thing, rather than a dummy.

So the week wings by: really it is from Sunday to Sunday. From, and towards, that great blank empty End of every week. As the poet so justly sang in his melancholy youth:

> *From the Intense Inane to the Inane Intense*
> *My soul took flight upon the wings of sense.*
> *But very soon my soul flew back again*
> *From the Inane Intense to the Intense Inane.*

Sunday in Momaco, from x a.m. war-time to x p.m. war-time, was the

Intense Inane, to which the soul flew back as to rest, after its flight across the other six days of the week, so replete with a meaningless intensity.

But the Hardings, placed as they were, were painfully reminded of another unit beside the week, namely the year. It was borne in upon them that there are fifty-two weeks in the year. Just as the week has a shape of sorts, so had for them the year. Christmas is to the year what Sunday is to the week.

But a year is a higher organism than a week. Its shape is more distinct. By looking out of the window you can see more or less where you have got in your weary road across the year, from Christmas to Christmas. Whereas it is no use looking out of the window to see what day of the week it is (always excepting Sunday).

As year succeeds year, marooned in Momaco, you become very conscious of the seasons, as if you were engaged in husbandry instead of being engaged in wasting your life—day by day, week by week, and year by year. Actually you can *see* the seasons, as these two people did, and watch them revolve with a painful slowness, if you have a window, and if that window is not of milled glass, as they are in the rooms where Japanese confine their political prisoners.

Not to be able to see out, thought René, must be truly fearful, when he read the interview with the American correspondent who had been exchanged for one of their nationals, after four months of solitary confinement: this man had told his interviewer that the first thing he noticed after his release—noticed with a thrill of delight—was that *doors had handles.*

René sighed. He looked over at the handle of his door. There was the handle—that delicious handle, signifying *freedom.* He sighed again. For *à quoi bon?* What was the use of having a handle to a door, if in fact there was nowhere to go outside the room? If anywhere you could go outside was worse than stopping where you were? What was the use of living in a free country, as a free man, where doors had handles and windows had no bars, if that freedom was of no use to you—was freedom with a bar sinister, freedom with a great big catch in it somewhere? From the big bay window where the Hardings sat all day long and in the summer all the evening, the seasons made themselves visible in the backyards of Momaco. They waited for the so-called Squaws' Winter which in Canada precedes the Indian Summer—for the feeble snowfall which has to take place before the false lovely gentle summertime of the Indian can come in and make believe for a week perhaps. After that in Momaco there was no fooling. The first blizzard hit them soon afterwards.

The backyards became a strange submerged version of themselves; with a deep soft icing of the Angel-cake variety all seemed phantasy of a sudden, its relation to what was underneath beautifully pathologic. Every branch or twig had on a furry coat of snow that swelled it out as a kitten's hair puffs out its miniature limbs. Festoons and lianas of this souffléish substance of weightless young snow made a super Christmas card of what had a short while before been a piece of drab and brutal impressionism.

Icicles six feet long, and as thick as a man's arm, hung from the eaves and gutters. The heat of the hot-water pipes could some days scarcely be felt. Yet they knew that in fact they were giving forth a heat comparable to that of a Central American jungle. Below zero temperatures started when the cold came down from Hudson's Bay and higher, and the Polar Sea walked right through the walls of the hotel as if it had been a radio wave and went clean through your bones. At 50 below zero, in a place by no means perfectly dry, like Momaco, with a sizable river running through the middle of it, it was as impossible to keep it out as radium, in the imperfectly-heated apartment of the Blundell. It walked through your heart, it dissolved your kidney, it flashed down your marrow and made an icicle of your coccyx.

If in Momaco there was never any temptation to make use of your privilege of a free man, and stroll out upon the streets beyond the door of the Hotel, there was the need for exercise, and with eyes shut the Hardings would occasionally walk round the block. But when it got really cold there was something that competed even with Momaco itself to keep you indoors; if summer or autumn you were never tempted to remember 'that you had a doorhandle', even less in the winter did you desire to insist upon your quota of prisoners' exercise.

From the Hotel up to the main road was a matter of three blocks. To walk it when the wind was from the north or east, and when there was a wind, in this sub-zero weather, was a feat for anyone who was a stranger to such things. Your face would be wet with tears which would freeze upon the face, or the wind would catch the tears as they came over the rim of the eyelid and dash them on to your shoulder. Your

360

ears would become cauliflower ears, and the drums would set up an ache, which would not leave you for some time. Your lips would crack. It was very severe indeed. But this was only when there was a wind. If the wind falls the glass does not fall, but you do not feel it much any longer, even at 30 below. In sunny weather, with no wind, 5 or 10 below is just pleasantly fresh. It is the wind that does it.

Bad as is the wind, in the periods of great cold, there is something even more disagreeable. That is the ice. It is very difficult not to slip: and people in Momaco often, walking too confidently along the street, break a leg or an arm. In general the Momaconians of the more prosperous—and as they believe more civilized—kind like to think that Momaco's winter is a marked but not excessive falling away from civilized standards of warmth. So they often dress improperly in the winter.

All shop messengers or errand boys have ear flaps of fur after October, and could not go their rounds without them. They are as sure-footed as goats, but they are beaten by the ice. Then splinters of ice have a function, and one pierced a boy's eye and blinded him outside the Blundell Hotel. So the ice is abnormally bad, whereas the snow forms an engagingly soft material to tread on. The snow is beautiful to look at and to walk on: but at Momaco, and of course farther north, it gets worse, there is a little too much of it. It goes on for too long, and it is the eyes that are probably the worst sufferers.

Blindness is very prevalent. You meet blind people everywhere, tapping along the edges of the sidewalks with their sticks. The number of people in Momaco who wear smoked glasses is surprisingly great. They get so used to wearing them in the winter, against the dazzle of the snow, that they are also very apt to wear them in the summer, against the dazzle of the sun. They become conscious of violent light in general. And the light is for some reason very violent. In the morning it seems to bang you in the face, as it glares in at the window. Canada is no land for those with delicate eyes.

There is perhaps something more than the ice, the glaring snow, and the pulverizing zero wind. That is the mud. René and his wife found, during the foul period of mud, such small sorties as in the summer they permitted themselves, impracticable. The telephone had to be resorted to. There is no spring in Momaco. There is a period of winds—milder than the winter ones, but very fierce and quite cold, which is said to come in March but which really comes in April. Everything arrives a month later than it is supposed to do. May is very violent, too. Off and on there is a great deal of wind in Momaco; not so much as in Chicago or Buffalo, where ropes along the sidewalks have to be provided for pedestrians at times, but still it is far windier than anywhere in Europe, except as you approach the Sahara. Unlike an ocean-wind, it is charged with no pep. It is a violent annoyance: you are being pushed around by an element you do not respect. When it finds its highest expression is in the tornadoes of the central United States. But Canada east of the Rockies is part of that unstable system.

Suddenly in Momaco you get summer. The leaves all come out overnight. Agriculturally, between frost and frost, it is a summer of a hundred days. After that the cattle go back to the barns, and often the cereal farmer locks up his farm and goes south to California.

The summer is in two parts. There is the summer and then a super-summer. The latter is a heatwave, which is hotter than the Red Sea—only in Momaco you cannot console yourself with the thought that, being 'east of Suez' there 'ain't no Ten Commandments'. There are Ten Commandments in Momaco, as in no other city in the world. It is the city of the Ten Commandments, all of which are so violently broken that they can never be forgotten, as they can be in a place where no one pays any particular attention to them.

The Indian must have been a gentleman, to have a beautiful moderate summer of his own in November—in protest perhaps at the indecent explosion of silly heat seven months earlier. This sort of Yahoo Summer—in contrast to the Indian Summer—has no rationale. For why should it occur in a country so typically northern as is 'My Lady of the Snows'?

So in the hotel Room the seasons revolve and have a sad repercussion. They deepen the solitude, like the ticking of a great ominous clock. They are of the nature of a clock, as much as is a sundial.

The face of each new section brought a new despair to the two people in the Room. If the leaves appeared on the trees again it was not a matter of rejoicing—it spelt another section of one's life wasted in corrosive idleness. If the leaves turned russet and yellow and fell off the trees, that was another disagreeable pang. It meant more months had been consumed, with nothing to show for it; months of so-called life in which nothing had been done except wait for the mail, which always brought discouraging news, or listen to the radio, which droned on in its senseless ritual, or write something which might never see the light.

So the seasons were a curse. They were less anonymous than the days of the week—for Monday did not snow, or Thursday make itself known by its great heats, or Friday announce itself by shedding its leaves. Really, if it were not for Sunday, one could more or less feel one was always living on the same day. The seasons kept reminding you of the stupid plodding feet of Time.

───────

No works of Lewis's divide his admirers more than *Monstre Gai* and *Malign Fiesta*, published together in 1955 along with the first part of *The Childermass* as *The Human Age*. Lewis himself hoped that he would be remembered by these works, and he has found critics to agree with him. Eliot saw a deeper seriousness here than in anything else Lewis had written, and Hugh Kenner thought that here he was 'challenging, without swank or irrelevance, comparison with Swift and Milton', and implied that the challenge was survived. To the other side are those who felt disappointment, even boredom: Geoffrey Grigson was unable to finish the books, I pulled through them only with an effort. The division is essentially between those, like Grigson and myself, who valued the scorching critic of society, and the artist who said 'I am for the Great Without, for the method of *external* approach—for the wisdom of the eye, rather than that of the ear', and those who looked in his work for deep visionary truths, and believed that in these books they had found them.

Monstre Gai and *Malign Fiesta* owe little to the outer world the writer could no longer see, much to thoughts about the relationship between Man and the God whose existence remains unconsidered in the earlier works. The texture of the writing, whether descriptive or conversational, is what the earlier Lewis might have called commonplace. When Pullman sees a woman deliberately thrown by the Lord Sammael for beasts to tear and devour he feels an 'unsurpassable' horror, experiences a 'tremendous' silence and a 'violent conflict in his psyche'. When, earlier, he spurns a male

seducer in the womanless Third City, he says: 'My imagination is defective
. . . Apart from the question of certain outstanding anatomical details, you
have not the necessary lovely husky voice.' Such facetiousness would not
have been tolerated by the author of *Tarr* or *The Revenge For Love*.

For the books' admirers the compensations rest in the grandeur of
the conception, and the sense of a man striving to reach some final
truths about the conflict between man as a social animal and as a creature
potentially divine. 'In the last book of all', Lewis wrote to Hugh Kenner
(this 'last book' being the unwritten *Trial of Man*) 'the hero, Pullman, is
at last in Divine Society. He favours the Divine. I favour the Divine.' It is
certainly likely that the unwritten concluding volume would have embodied
a positive attitude towards religious belief, a realisation of the perfectionism
towards which René Harding aspired. But *The Trial of Man* was not written,
and what we have is an outsize piece of something resembling supernatural
science fiction with a moral flavour in which Pullman, hardly recognisable
as the figure met long ago in *The Childermass*, passes in the company of the
Bailiff from Third City to Matapolis.

This is another name for Hell which is, the Bailiff assures Pullman, a
quiet little place filled with very serious people. They meet the Bailiff's
mother, who tells them that her husband was the Supervisor of Dis. And
what is Dis, Pullman asks? 'It is where people are punished for their sins.'
There are glancing references to both the restrictions of post-war Britain
and the German concentration camps. It is the latter that come to mind
when Pullman is told by the Bailiff's mother that her husband would treat
a woman who talked too much by telling a surgeon to cut her tongue in
strips, shorten it, and if necessary cut it out altogether. 'Mr Pullman, that
was not said in order to frighten me. It was a pleasantry.'

One of the most powerful scenes is that in which Sammael, otherwise
the Devil, gives Pullman a tour of Dis in a car.

from THE HUMAN AGE

Infernal Preliminary

Pullman was coming out of his bedroom. 'If I am to be presentable tomorrow morning,' he announced, 'I must have a fresh packet of razor blades. I must go down and see Mark at once.' He stood still. 'What is that?'

There was the sound, in the street without, of a loud horn. Three insistent blasts were heard.

'I will go down and find out, Pulley.' Thereupon, with hideous fracas, Satters began hurling himself down the stairs; Pullman took his hat, and followed him at a leisurely pace. Meawhile the three blasts were repeated. Then Satters' voice roared up from below.

'Pulley, it's a great big car, it's very swish, Pulley. It's about to drive off; shall I stop it? No, it isn't. Here comes a bloke.'

As Pullman arrived in the hall, Satters had just received, from a uniformed man, a large sealed letter, which he now passed on, and Pullman lost no time in opening it.

'Would you like a short ride in the country? Sending car to fetch you. If otherwise engaged, please tell chauffeur.—Just shake your head. Yrs sincerely, Sammael.'

Satters need have no alarm, Pullman told him: he would be away for an hour or so at most. Then he went down rapidly, and entered the waiting car. There was no one in the car except a chauffeur who, without any recognition, put the automobile in movement as soon as he was seated. It was as if Pullman's posterior, in pressing the cushion of the seat, automatically started the machine.

The majestic vehicle moved along to the road upon which Mark and he had watched the procession of Sinners, turned to the right, and ran along it for several miles. They then reached a place with a great deal of movement—the place of punishment. There was a mountain at one side. The car drew up at the entrance to a large building across the road. Several men were waiting; two of them ran back into the door, and shortly appeared leading a woman, protesting. They pushed her inside the car, and chained her wrists to an iron ring. They then sprang back, for they heard a quick step. The lord Sammael entered the car, and Pullman removed his hat.

'Good morning,' said Sammael, as he sat down. The door clicked. A figure mounted beside the chauffeur, and the car moved away. 'I am afraid, Pullman, that this is a rather unsavoury fellow-passenger for you, but it is a little job I sometimes take on, for a certain reason.'

A groan came from the woman. 'Where are you taking me, sir?' she asked in French. 'Why am I chained up like this? I wish for an immediate explanation! You understand, sir!'

The woman could speak no language but French, it appeared; when they conversed in English she listened querulously, but there was no evidence that she understood anything.

'To travel in the company of this woman is extremely disagreeable. I must have these people transported in another car; I don't see why I should use mine.'

He leaned towards the woman and said sharply, 'Listen, Madame. If, *chemin faisant*, you force your personality upon our attention, you will be silenced. I do not enjoy the sound of your voice.'

'And how about me? Do you suppose I enjoy *yours*? Do you suppose your personality is agreeable to *me*?'

The lord Sammael tapped upon the window behind the chauffeur, and the car came to a halt. The man sitting beside the chauffeur sprang out, and the door opened where the woman lay. Pullman saw a hypodermic syringe in the man's hand. An indignant scream came from the woman. The man was brutally excavating the lower female garments.

'Listen, listen . . . what is this! You allow yourself to . . . !'

A section of bottom was laid bare, then was obscured by coarse hands. This was followed by a shriek of pain as the needle was plunged into her flesh.

'This is abominable! What a way to treat a woman . . . It is unheard of . . . It is ignoble!' But the voice weakened, and the next minute she fell in a heap on the floor, her arms in the air, her wrists still attached to the ring. The car proceeded on its way.

'Her voice is redolent of the unreal life lived by the French bourgeoisie,' said Sammael. 'But she is now happily asleep. Let us have a look at the landscape,' said he, turning his attention to the

366

wild scene without. 'There'—he pointed through the window beside Pullman—'is the beginning of the country where we used to operate, four or five hundred years ago.'

Pullman saw a valley of volcanic rock opening up, of the utmost savagery. There was no building of any kind, or any cultivation. Matapolis was a walled city on this side, and the inhabitants never ventured outside the walls.

'It was down into this valley that we used to drive the Sinners. It bore no resemblance to Dante's literary composition. Plenty of bonfires were kindled for the wicked, but the fires were not so concentrated as they are today.'

Pullman saw, in his mind's eye, the mediaeval scene. There was a long stream of miserable sinners, some of them beating their breasts, some praying. Their costumes came out of the museums where Pullman had studied them, or out of albums of costumes, or old history books. Coloured designs of the Canterbury Pilgrims mingled with the rest, hooded apprentices and shaven monks, and women like Christmas trees. It was a rushing multitude of mediaeval nobodies, with staring eyes and chattering teeth, urged on by demons with pricking pitchforks, dressed in red, with reddened faces, jumping and screaming at the heels of the condemned.

A ragged cliff stood behind this torrent of the damned, among its rocks were contorted nudes, both white and red, to identify them either as miserable sinners, or members of the infernal staff. At the extremity of the cliff a Sinner attempted to save himself by fighting off a demon, who kept slashing him with a butcher's knife. But another naked figure was writhing through the air, halfway down to the leaping flames below. In the valley flames were being kindled everywhere by dozens of horned and tailed supers. These busy performers jumped up and down, grimacing upwards at those about to be tossed down from the rocks, by their costume and their gestures complying as far as possible with horror stories originating in mundane monasteries.

The debunking by Sammael of those distant days had painted in his vivid imagination a period piece, Hell in full swing; but great as his desire was to please the growling creature at his side, Pullman could not help wishing he could observe this scene at an off moment, and watch the staff sitting about and chatting, spinning yarns and rolling on the rocks with laughter.

Nevertheless, he accepted entirely the scornful rejection of the traditional picture. It never occurred to him to doubt the historic arch-demon with whom he was visiting the legendary landscape.

As the car took them a little farther along, they passed the mouth of a ravine.

'Down there,' Sammael told him with a gentle grimace, 'was our famous "lake of blood". The blood, of course, was some earth we found, which we mixed with water, and red paint, to improve the rocks which protruded from it here and there.—We really did make our valley a rather unpleasant place.'

As he gazed out of the window, Pullman thought that it still would repel the sensitive.

Soon they emerged into wider perspectives. There were ravines on ravines, brick-red cliffs, and mountains which rose much higher in the distance.

'Wait a little, and it will become uncommonly fierce-looking.'

'It is already quite uncivilized enough—to satisfy the Hollywood producer,' Pullman said.

'We reach something beyond the powers of Hollywood before very long.'

Pullman uttered an 'Aha!', and Sammael smiled—a civilized smile. Pullman was asked to report on his adventures, if he had any.

Briefly he recounted their attempt to view the city, the police sergeant's challenge, the gathering of a crowd, the appearance of the Major. Sammael was very interested.

'The little rats! They will not allow a man—two men—to walk around the streets. It is not zeal. They do not care whether a person is a Sinner or the reverse. They are merely thirsty for blood—they are greedy for excitement. They have no more principles than a minor bird of prey.'

He asked the name of the Major, and when Pullman named him, he exclaimed, 'Oh, Staffo—of the Fifth Regiment! A wonderfully good officer! You were indeed lucky to come across him. I shall write him a note. But Mark, on his own, is quite able to extricate you from such an embarrassing situation. The Sergeant who stopped you belonged to the

Punishment Service I expect. Mark could put him in his place quite easily. They are of use to me in a Punishment Cell; they do my dirty work. But Mark is a match for ten of them.'

Pullman made no comment, except to say that Mark was a splendid fellow, and that he was very happy in this hotel which the lord Sammael had been so kind as to put at their disposal. Upon this, Sammael told him that he believed he was on the track of a job for him and his young friend—nothing very much, but it would do for a start. Pullman was profoundly relieved; for to be living the life of a gentleman of independent means *here* was impracticable, and anyway it would involve never going outside one's front door—living as if one were a member of some proscribed community.

The sort of whimpering noise a dog makes in its sleep came from the floor, and the woman also faintly burped. But there was no other sign of life. Sammael looked out of the window, stretching his neck to see as far as possible ahead.

'She will have to wake up soon. Perhaps ten minutes.'

Suddenly the woman was betrayed into a nasty flatulence. Though muffled, it was quite loud.

'Disgusting bitch!' almost hissed Sammael. 'That I should have to transport this cattle about!'

'Could not one of the Punishment Staff do the job?' Pullman ventured to ask.

Sammael shook his head. 'No,' he answered. 'This one is *pretty.*' The disgust and distaste with which he uttered this word profoundly impressed his listener: the mad puritan did not attempt to conceal the extent of his bias. 'The difficulty is that almost whoever you might send would fornicate with her on the way. It is not even certain that finally he would do what he had been told to do: He might hide her, he might find some way of keeping her for himself. The only safe procedure seems to be, in the case of attractive females, for me or some responsible person to take them. I strongly object to having to do this. But so long as one takes any part in these disgusting proceedings one likes to see them properly carried out.' He turned towards Pullman. 'I am long past taking any interest in this wholesale punishment. It is an efficient service in most ways. I maintain an excellent "Hell"—which is my function. It is only when Sex raises its ugly head that the proper carrying out of the service

369

has to be watched. And that, as I see it, is the most important part of it.'

He said this, without heat, coldly, and one might say indolently.

The footman opened a small window, and said something, looking away. Sammael uttered two words in reply, the car stopped, and the footman moved quickly around. Once more the hypodermic syringe was in evidence. On this occasion he rolled up the woman's sleeve, and his syringe entered the flesh easily.

He returned to his seat beside the chauffeur, and the car started moving again. The figure of the woman remained inert for some minutes, then her eyes opened, and fixed themselves upon Sammael.

'Ah there you are!' she said listlessly. 'In a word, you are the Devil—just the Devil!' she said. She crossed herself. Sammael turned away. 'Answer me—where are you taking me to? Terrible man, I am to be offered to the wild animals, is not that true, is not that where you are taking me? Spirit of the Pit! Evil One! How hatefully ugly you are, like everyone who breathes corruption as you do, horrible man. Are you not ashamed of being so vile, man who works in something which is a thousand times dirtier than the sewers! Crapulous individual, who lies in the dung of the world because you know of nothing softer or sweeter-smelling! You believe that you are a handsome man—que vous avez la tête belle—don't you, fungus? Yours is a beast's head, and not a man's. You are an animal—not one of the high animals, but a most ill-favoured monster. Ugh! Your face is not human as you believe it to be—not human as is this person's here, for instance.'

She pointed at Pullman, who smiled superciliously, glancing at Sammael.

She now began addressing Pullman. 'As for you, sir, you have that little smile of yours because you are afraid. Yes, yes. You are afraid of this terrible monster who takes human form but is none the less terrifying for that. But you are intelligent, you see what is underneath. You see the terrifying monster—you are not deceived by the face like that of a man. Ah yes, like myself, you are human, you have *reason* to tremble—what else could you do but smile scornfully to order! You do not want to be in my shoes, you poor little fellow. The implacable *merde* you divine, the merciless excrement which serves him for blood!'

The woman crossed herself, to write finis to her diatribe.

'Woman!' said sternly the lord Sammael. 'It would be far more logical if you crossed yourself lower down, over your sex.'

The car slowly drew up, and there was a wild stampede outside, and a goatish grimace of ineffable self-satisfied lubricity—a kind of quiet, conceited, knowing subtlety always seen in profile, covered with silken hair, appeared for a flash at the window beside which Sammael sat, and violently vanished. This was a very different place to meet these beasts than in a well-guarded Piazza in Third City. Pullman was suddenly overwhelmed with horror, as he thought of the fate of the woman at his feet, who crouched there apparently in prayer.

'She is not actually thrown to those animals, is she?' he exclaimed in spite of himself. 'It is just to scare her, is it not?'

'The best way to answer that question is like this,' said Sammael, seizing the cowering woman, he flung her over to his side of the car. 'Pitié! Pitié!' she screamed.

'Autant de pitié, Madame,' Sammael answered sternly, 'que vous avez montré à Gabriel.'

He flung the door open, getting bitten in the hand by one of the ravening beasts. There burst into the car the fearful stench, there was a scarlet flash of sexual monstrosity, the whining and snorting of a score of faces—the beasts leaping on one another's backs, so that several appeared to be about to spring on to the roof of the car.—Scores of sinewy arms terminating in claws shot into the car, and snatched the woman out of it.

There was her body, shoulder-high, for the fraction of a second, in the midst of the stinking pack—the sickening odour increasing in intensity. Just for that fractional speck of time a dozen claws could be seen defiling her person. The most terrible scream Pullman had ever heard filled aurally that speck of time. The car gathered speed, the door was violently closed, and that was that. The silence was tremendous and Pullman was alone—more alone than he had ever been with anyone in his life—with the lord Sammael.

Sammael sat, spitting blood into a white handkerchief, after sucking the gash in his hand.

Pullman was trembling: the suddenness of the dénouement, and the shocking momentary vision of ferocity had deeply shaken him. The woman's denunciation of Sammael immediately before the climax had affected him in a way he had to be very careful not to reveal. His sympathy for the woman grew and subterraneously developed; and when he *saw* (with unexpected suddenness) the unsurpassable horror of her punishment he started trembling as in response to horror, because of the violent conflict in his psyche. He was on the verge of an outburst. The woman, praying and crossing herself, was doing what he ought to have been doing. She was defying the superhuman strength of the infernal power. The same situation began to develop as the conflict in Third City when the time came when he ought to have severed his connection with that *monstre gai*. Here it was a new kind of monster—and there was no alternative in a shorter or longer time, except death.—He felt, if he played along with this monster until the end, that then a third and last monster ought to make his appearance; and with him there would be no choice (such as Mark or some 'job'), but there could be in *that* situation, No.3, nothing but immediate death, identical with that suffered by the woman, but roaring and stinking. He would be a different kind of monster again. He would look at you, and you would die. His heart would be blacker than Satan, his magic more deadly than Medusa.

So he was in an evil dream, he was stunned and he trembled. He asked, his voice shaken, 'Is the bite in your hand . . . ?'

'Yes, it is,' Sammael answered smoothly. 'Very. But I am going to the Clinic and they will perfectly bathe me in penicillin.' He looked up softly from the gash made by the animal, and smiled, as it were mockingly, at the pale and trembling figure in the other corner of the car. 'You are shocked, Pullman, because of the horrible fate allotted to the woman. Had you perused the dossier as I did, did you know how callous she was when alive, how she broke the heart of her young husband Gabriel, and, it was believed, infected her third husband with the King's Evil, you would feel differently. She was as bad a woman as you could find anywhere. You saw her crossing herself and supplicating God. Well, it would have been no use her appealing to any judge, competent to try her. The Pope has several times refused her absolution.'

'I see, I see,' said Pullman.

The lord Sammael looked up quizzically, a cold smile in the depth of his eyes.

Pullman saw the smile, and said (with an answering smile):

'Yes. I *see*. I *see*. I have a way of speaking adapted for commune with the unintelligent. Of men, ninety per cent are that. I am the one per cent who is (for a man) intelligent. You must, sir, be indulgent—first, because I am only a man: and in the second place, because I have always lived with men, poorer in intellect than myself.'

Sammael again smiled, but in the warmer surface of his eye.

'I am aware that you forget that you are speaking to the Devil. Treat me always as a man: I shall like that best.'

Pullman was looking out of the window at his side, more than formerly he had done, and noticed a number of bones on the verge or near it. Some were even in the road.

'There are many bones,' he said, as he looked out.

'Quite a few,' Sammael replied, glancing negligently out of the window, his accent dry and Satanaelic.

'All female ossatures?' Pullman quietly surmised.

'I suppose so. As you may have realized, the beasts soon kill the women, they are so violent. As they fornicate, they *eat*. They bite mouthfuls out of them, regardless of the fact that, with the human, death is found a very short distance beneath the surface.'

Pullman kept his eyes lowered: he thought of the woman, there at his feet, not hours, but minutes ago, and it was all he could do not to vomit. He fought the threatened emission as hard as any young man at his first drinking party, but for an extremely different motive. He discouraged the vomit sternly. He *must not* be sick.

'About a year ago,' Sammael told him easily, 'we got a lot of bad daughters of Eve at once. There is an extremely large cave, twenty miles farther inland. We took a batch of about a hundred there. We lighted it with electricity, and rounded up about two hundred of the animals. We had plenty of troops at hand, with machine-guns trained upon the entrance of the cave. I did not go myself, but my secretary was there and he gave me a vivid description—it was so vivid that I felt I could hear and smell as he was telling me every detail of the ferocious scene. The towering cavern was malodorous to a degree, and the characteristic stench of these filthy animals was intensified during the orgasm. When the women were first released among them, the noise was horrifying. To cite the screams of terror of the women in no way conveys the vocal tempest which broke loose. Voices of every calibre and every kind split and rent the air in this maddening uproar.

'Some of the voices obviously believed it was possible to save

373

themselves if only they made noise enough, which is the teaching of the earth. Other women had, it was obvious, a truer appreciation of their position; they wept, some loudly, some quietly. Some roared like bulls or crazy cows, or snarled in preparation to do combat with the animals. Some were so intensely terrified that they were actually demented. The animals, so disgustingly numerous, could be heard mainly as a kind of universal whinny, and later, eating and guzzling sounds.'

'How fearful,' Pullman said.

'I have a recording of it, a number of discs. If you like, I will let you hear it.'

'I wish you would,' Pullman said firmly.

———

It is nonsense, Pullman says later, to compare Sammael with Cesare Borgia, because Cesare knew he was destroying human beings, whereas Sammael (like the leading Nazis, we may think) is not personally cruel. 'It is only cruel if you realise that the people you are injuring or destroying have feelings', and Sammael makes no such recognition. In a sentence much quoted Pullman goes on: 'God *values* man: that is the important thing to remember.'

Such is the ultimate message of a book in which God has replaced the intellect as a final good. The conclusion is bound to be uncongenial to those who remember that earlier praise of 'the life of the intelligence' as something of which the 'disciplines are less arbitrary and less *political* than those of religion'. But perhaps it is fitting that the Great Outsider, whose jokes and satires so greatly angered his enemies, should find no agreement after his death among his friends.

LIST OF WORKS

Those marked + are of particular importance. Books not quoted or discussed in the selection are very briefly described here.

1917 *The Ideal Giant.*
Contains 'The Code of a Herdsman', the story 'Cantleman's Spring Mate', and a playlet.

+ 1918 *Tarr*

1919 *Harold Gilman*
A brief appreciation of Gilman's art.

+ *The Caliph's Design*

+ 1926 *The Art of Being Ruled*

+ 1927 *The Lion and the Fox*
Time and Western Man
The Wild Body

1928 *The Childermass*, Section 1

1929 *Paleface*

+ 1930 *The Apes of God*

1931 *Hitler*
The Diabolical Principle and The Dithyrambic Spectator
The first part of the book is an attack on the magazine *transition*, the second strongly critical of current anthropological views about the primitive origins of art.

1932 *The Doom of Youth*
Book-length pamphlet attacking the 'cult of youth', the text supported by many extracts from the current press. Suppressed in Britain because of threatened libel actions.
Filibusters in Barbary
Lively travel book about a trip to Morocco. Withdrawn

in Britain because of libel suit. Reissued in 1983 with some additional material, as *Journey Into Barbary*, edited by C. J. Fox.

Enemy of the Stars

Considerably revised version of the play which first appeared in *Blast*.

Snooty Baronet

1933   *The Old Gang and the New Gang*

Short book restating some of the points about power and politics made in *The Art of Being Ruled*.

One-Way Song

+   1934   *Men Without Art*

1936   *The Roaring Queen*

Overdone but enjoyable satirical novel caricaturing several celebrated figures, including Arnold Bennett and Virginia Woolf. Withdrawn before publication for fear of libel, eventually published in 1973.

Left Wings Over Europe

1937   *Count Your Dead: They Are Alive*

+   *The Revenge For Love*

+   *Blasting and Bombardiering*

1938   *The Mysterious Mr Bull*

A little brother of *The Art of Being Ruled*, chiefly about John Bull as a political animal, notable in its admiration for the Jews, elaborated in

1939   *The Jews: Are They Human?*

Wyndham Lewis the Artist: From Blast to Burlington House

Selection from writings on art. Includes *The Caliph's Design*.

The Hitler Cult

1940   *America, I Presume*

Lightweight, mostly light-hearted sketches of the USA.

1941   *Anglosaxony: A League That Works*

Short, feeble propaganda piece, stressing the virtues of British democracy—a contradiction of much written in the Twenties.

The Vulgar Streak

+   1948   *America and Cosmic Man*

1950   *Rude Assignment*

Second of the autobiographical volumes. Includes defensive

apologies for some past political stances.

1951　*Rotting Hill*

　　Uneven, but often impressively powerful, view of post-war Britain through semi-factual tales.

+　1952　*The Writer and the Absolute*

+　1954　*Self Condemned*

+　　　　*The Demon of Progress in the Arts*

　　Important as a final statement on the nature and development of art in Lewis's time.

+　1955　*The Human Age: Monstre Gai and Malign Fiesta*

　1956　*The Red Priest*

　　Minor, misanthropic novel about a priest who becomes celebrated when he compares the Sermon on the Mount to Russian Communism.

+　1963　*The Letters of Wyndham Lewis*

+　1969　*Wyndham Lewis on Art*, edited by Walter Michel and C. J. Fox.

　　Collected writings on Art, excluding *The Demon of Progress*. Shows Lewis's generosity to younger British artists in his *Listener* articles.

　1973　*Unlucky For Pringle*, edited by C. J. Fox and Robert Chapman

　　Uncollected stories, most of them early.

　　Wyndham Lewis: Fictions and Satires, edited by Robert Chapman

　　Interesting critical readings of the fiction, particularly good on the attempt to blend fiction and philosophy.

　1976　*Enemy Salvoes*, edited by C. J. Fox

　　Brief, well-chosen extracts from a number of books.

　1977　*Mrs Dukes' Million*

　　Written in 1908 or earlier and called by the author 'a miserable potboiler'. Nevertheless contains the seeds of much in the later fiction.

　1979　*Collected Poems and Plays*, edited by Alan Munton

　　One-Way Song and both versions of *The Enemy of the Stars* in a single volume.

　1985　*Pound/Lewis* edited by Timothy Materer

　　Letters between Pound and Lewis. Contains material not included in the selected *Letters*.

FURTHER READING

BIOGRAPHY

The Enemy by Jeffrey Meyers (1980) is the only serious biographical study. It is thorough, comprehensive and well-balanced, although at times heavy-handed in its approach.

LITERARY CRITICISM

Hugh Gordon Porteus's *Wyndham Lewis: A Discursive Exposition* (1932) is a pioneer work, particularly interesting in its view of Lewis as a visionary, not merely or mainly satiric, artist. *Wyndham Lewis* by Hugh Kenner (1954) and *Wyndham Lewis* by William H. Pritchard (1968) are the two best general introductions to the work. The first contains brilliant aperçus, as in the analysis of the early writing to show that Lewis was almost constantly concerned with genius and its ape, the second is admirably discriminating and rational throughout, respectful of Lewis the artist, much less so of Lewis the seer. D.G. Bridson's *The Filibuster* (1972) is a sound and comprehensive study of the political ideas. Fredric Jameson's *Fables of Aggression* (1979) has as sub-title 'the Modernist as Fascist', but that is misleadingly crude. This is a brilliant study, written basically from a Marxist viewpoint, and thus illuminating particular aspects of the work in a way no other critic has done. Nor is it hostile in the way the sub-title suggests. Jameson appreciates that Lewis was 'the most European and least insular of all the great contemporary British writers'. *Wyndham Lewis: A Revaluation*, edited by Jeffrey Meyers, contains eighteen essays, with pieces of particular interest on *Tarr* ('a Nietzschean novel') and *The Apes of God*. Timothy Materer's *Wyndham Lewis, The Novelist* (1976) is the only book devoted wholly to the fiction.

There are other interesting essays, some uncollected, by Hugh Kenner, Walter Allen and John Holloway. Special numbers of *Shenandoah* (1953), *Agenda* (1970) and *Canadian Literature* (1971) are given to Lewis's work.

ART CRITICISM

Wyndham Lewis, Paintings and Drawings by Walter Michel (1971) is a comprehensive view of the visual artist, which contains more than 700 illustrations. *Vorticism and Abstract Art in the First Machine Age* by Richard Cork (2 vols, 1976) contains much well-informed but often grudging criticism of Lewis, and some colour plates not found in Michel.